< C H P Cant ☞ W9-ADB-930

<< Lines Addressed to a NC >>

BYRON AND
GREEK LOVE

BYRON AND GREEK LOVE

HOMOPHOBIA IN
19th-CENTURY ENGLAND

Louis Crompton

University of California Press
Berkeley
Los Angeles

College-Reserves

PR
4392
·H56
C7
1985
c.1

University of California Press
Berkeley and Los Angeles, California

University of California Press, Ltd.
London, England

© 1985 by
The Regents of the University of California

Printed in the United States of America
1   2   3   4   5   6   7   8   9

Library of Congress Cataloging in Publication Data

Crompton, Louis, 1925–
  Byron and Greek love.

  Bibliography: p.
  Includes index.
    1. Byron, George Gordon Byron, Baron, 1788–1824.
2. Homosexuality, Male, in literature.   3. Homosexuality,
Male—Great Britain—History—19th century.   4. Sex in
literature.   5. Poets, English—19th century—Biography.
I. Title.
PR4392.H56C7   1985   821'.7   84-16463
ISBN 0-520-05172-6

For Luis Diaz-Perdomo

Contents

Acknowledgments and Permissions

I am much indebted to Mrs. J. Percival and the staff of the D. M. S. Watson Library for providing me with xeroxes and microfilms of Jeremy Bentham's manuscripts on the subject of homosexuality in the possession of University College, London, and for answering inquiries. I owe a special debt to my friend and former colleague Professor Frank Rice, of the Department of English of the University of Nebraska, for devoting many months to helping decipher hundreds of pages of Bentham's difficult hand. I regret only that he did not live to see the final results of his labors. I have also been aided in this task of transcription by David Seward, to whom I would also like to express my thanks. Throughout this lengthy project I have been encouraged by the warm support of my friend Dr. Arthur Warner of Princeton.

I wish to thank Peter W. Graham for replying to inquiries about the correspondence of John Cam Hobhouse and Jerome McGann, John Murray, and Doris Langley Moore for taking time to respond generously to my questions about Byron documents. The latter has also kindly granted permission to quote extensively from her two studies, *The Late Lord Byron: Posthumous Dramas* and *Lord Byron: Accounts Rendered*. However, Mrs. Moore has not read the manuscript of the present study, and her generosity should not be interpreted as an endorsement of its conclusions. It is her view that "Byron was telling the perfect truth when he said his heart always alighted on the nearest perch, and when there were women about (which was not the case, for instance, in a Cambridge college) the perch was likely to be feminine." Insofar as this implies that

ix

Byron was a bisexual in whom the heterosexual element predominated, I certainly agree. However, it seems to me that the heterosexual-homosexual balance in Byron's make-up shifted from time to time, and I have tried to analyze and—to the extent that such mysteries can be accounted for—give some suggestions as to why the homosexual side of his nature came to the fore at certain moments of his life.

Kathryn McGinnis and the staff of the Interlibrary Loan Service at the University of Nebraska, Scott Stebelman, Humanities Librarian, and Eva Sartori of the Humanities–Social Sciences Division of Love Library have all rendered valuable assistance in tracking down rare books and periodicals. Valdis Leinieks, Thomas Winter, and Thomas Rinkevich of the Department of Classics have patiently borne with queries and cheerfully responded to them. Hugh Luke of the Department of English has kindly made available to me his collection of Byroniana and rare early nineteenth-century books and pamphlets.

Above all, I am grateful to Cid Donnelly-Nixon for the patience, accuracy, and perspicuity she has brought to the typing of my manuscript and for exercising something like divination in deciphering its much scribbled-over pages.

Permission has been granted by copyright holders to quote from the following works: Duke University Press— James A. Notopoulos, *The Platonism of Shelley: A Study of Platonism and the Poetic Mind*, 1949; the Estate of Malcolm Elwin—*Lord Byron's Wife*, 1962, and *Lord Byron's Family*, 1975; John Murray—*Byron's Letters and Journals*, 12 vols., ed. Leslie A. Marchand, 1973–1982; Oxford University Press— Lord Byron, *The Complete Poetical Works*, vols. 1–3, ed. Jerome J. McGann, 1980–1981. In quoting from eighteenth- and nineteenth-century sources, I have regularly retained the writer's idiosyncratic spelling, punctuation, capitalization, and use of italics. However, for the sake of clarity and ease of comprehension, I have sometimes substituted periods in Byron's letters when he himself has used commas to separate sentences.

I have been assisted in the writing of this study by a Faculty Development Fellowship from the Department of English of the University of Nebraska.

Part of the epilogue to this book appeared, in slightly different form, in the *Journal of Homosexuality* 8 (Spring-Summer 1983) and in *Literary Visions of Homosexuality*, ed. Stuart Kellogg (New York: Haworth Press, 1983).

List of Abbreviations

The following works are referred to in the notes by abbreviations:

BB   Leslie A. Marchand. *Byron: A Biography*. 3 vols. New York: Alfred A. Knopf, 1957.

BLJ   *Byron's Letters and Journals*. Edited by Leslie A. Marchand. 12 vols. Cambridge: Harvard University Press, 1973–1982.

CPW   Lord Byron. *The Complete Poetical Works*. Edited by Jerome J. McGann. Vols. 1–3. Oxford: Clarendon Press, 1980–1981.

LBAR   Doris Langley Moore. *Lord Byron: Accounts Rendered*. London: John Murray, 1974.

LJL   Thomas Moore. *Letters and Journals of Lord Byron with Notices of His Life*. 2 vols. London: John Murray, 1830.

LLB   Doris Langley Moore. *The Late Lord Byron: Posthumous Dramas*. Rev. ed. New York: Harper & Row, 1977.

Introduction

This book is the offshoot of a wider scheme, rashly entertained, to write a history of attitudes toward homosexuality in Western civilization. Originally my plan called for an essay of fifty or sixty pages on Byron that would combine biographical, historical, literary, legal, and religious themes, as an experiment in interdisciplinary gay studies. What first drew me to the early nineteenth century was not, in fact, Byron, but the discovery of an unprecedented number of executions of homosexuals in England in the statistical reports of his day. In the centuries between the Inquisition and Hitler this suggested a persecution of perhaps unparalleled duration and intensity and raised the question of its social origins. Why should England, of all countries, with its reputation as a pioneer in civic freedom, have experienced so ugly an episode?

But statistical tables, though telling, need humanizing. Few victims of earlier homophobic witch hunts have left records of their lives. We do not know what it was like to face the agents of Justinian and Theodora, of Torquemada, or of the Dutch courts in 1730. Friends and relatives, including parents and children, were more likely to disown the victims than to collect memorials in such cases. Would it be possible to find someone who would reflect the pressures of this social terror in his personal life? It would have to be a man since lesbians in England (unlike their sisters in Europe) were not criminals under the law.

William Beckford was one possible choice, but his early ostracism removed him from English society too completely. It was the discovery of G. Wilson Knight's *Lord*

Byron's Marriage (1957) that suggested an alternative; Knight's study showed in detail how, at certain periods of his short career, Byron's deepest emotions were stirred by love for his own sex. The problem was whether it could be established beyond a doubt that these feelings were unequivocally homosexual and whether there was evidence that Byron's writings reflected Regency anxieties. Fortunately, the meticulously detailed biographical studies of Leslie Marchand and Doris Langley Moore that appeared shortly after Knight's book placed the first matter beyond a doubt though they showed little or no awareness of the background of persecution.

What swung the balance finally in favor of this undertaking was a chance discovery. Browsing through the legal section of the main library of Indiana University in Bloomington on a weekend when the Kinsey Institute was closed, I stumbled on C. K. Ogden's 1931 edition of Jeremy Bentham's *Theory of Legislation* with its appendix entitled "Bentham on Sex." Had Bentham ever been interested in the law and homosexuality? Ogden's prefatory note, written in the typically veiled style of the day, revealed that he had. The abstruse excerpts from Bentham that Ogden had transcribed showed a keen, even passionate, interest in the subject. An appeal to the D. M. S. Watson Library at University College, London, eventually produced over five hundred manuscript pages, all, except for Ogden's short extracts, unpublished, composed over a period of more than fifty years. They were remarkably far-ranging in their perspectives, analyzing the subject from a legal, moral, psychological, anthropological, and even a literary point of view. What was more remarkable was that Bentham, in an age of acute prejudice, looked at the social phenomenon of homophobia from a position that had more in common with the late twentieth century than with his own era.

The effort to touch on all this in a short essay inevitably proved a ludicrous failure. Step by step, the project grew into a book. To set the stage for and explain the frenzy of the Regency persecutions, it was necessary to look at eighteenth-century opinion in England. A reading of poets and novelists, theologians, journal writers, and historians, along with newspapers, political speeches, reports of religious societies, and popular pamphlets, helped explain what in the history of the time produced so hostile a milieu, whose decades of greatest animosity coincided almost exactly with Byron's lifetime. The result was the first chapter of this study, which serves as a prelude to the story of Byron's own pederastic involvements. Bentham's first writings on homosexuality are contemporaneous with the careers of Gibbon and Burke; his subsequent (and even more voluminous) notes belong to the age of Byron and Shelley and are discussed after the account of Byron's marriage and exile. Shelley's own essay on Greek homosexuality, until recently almost totally ignored, seemed also worth exploring not only because Shelley was Byron's friend and contemporary but also because the essay reveals the contrary views of a very different liberal. Shelley's death preceded by a few days two sensational national scandals: the arrest of the Bishop of Clogher on a homosexual charge and the suicide of Lord Castlereagh, who had been blackmailed and threatened with exposure. Chronologically, these episodes form a prelude to Byron's last journey to Greece.

My chapters on Byron are overwhelmingly indebted to three predecessors. Knight, in *Lord Byron's Marriage*, identified significant passages by and about Byron that still remain central to any discussion of this side of his life. Like all other recent writers on Byron, I have pillaged Leslie Marchand's three-volume biography, which also appeared in 1957 and confirmed Knight's conjectures (on this theme at least) and added much crucial new evidence. Constrained by the prejudices of others whose cooperation he was dependent on, Marchand obviously did not feel free to be overly explicit. He addresses the subject directly only once, in a significant note. As a result, his treatment of

Byron's bisexuality, though extremely perceptive, is so subtle and so interwoven with other matter that even highly sophisticated readers have failed to grasp the significance of his discoveries and comments. Marchand's work has since been supplemented by two important specialized studies by Doris Langley Moore. Both *The Late Lord Byron* (first published in 1961) and *Lord Byron: Accounts Rendered* (1974) include important new materials that help us understand how Byron's close associates regarded his homosexuality. Moore has summarized her views in an essay titled "Byron's Sexual Ambivalence," appended to her second book; though brief, it is sympathetic and generally just in its conclusions. I have come to disagree with her findings on only a few points. My final chapter steals another idea from her by examining the writings of Byron's critics and biographers to see how they treated this highly controversial matter in the books and essays that have appeared since his death.

Until well into the twentieth century the record shows much deliberate suppression and obfuscation. In part, this sprang from the taboo against any discussion of homosexuality in England. The "discursive explosion" Michel Foucault purports to have discovered in eighteenth- and nineteenth-century French sexology did not cross the channel. Nowhere did English Francophobia find more impassioned expression than in attitudes toward sex. English jurists congratulated themselves that no counterpart to the forensic studies in French existed in their language, and the courts ordered the first English scientific text on homosexuality destroyed shortly after its appearance in 1898. The earliest important account of Byron's bisexuality suffered a similar fate; circulating only as an underground pamphlet by an anonymous poet, *Don Leon* (1866) was also suppressed when the Fortune Press published it in the 1930s.

In attempting to reconstruct and understand the past, gay studies face two specific critical problems—the identification of documents and their interpretation. Homophobia has made both of these tasks difficult. Many literary texts have not survived. Sappho's poems, for example, were ordered destroyed by the Bishop of Constantinople in the fourth century. It was probably not just the vagaries of time that decreed that the well-documented plays by Aeschylus, Sophocles, and Euripides on the theme of Greek love should disappear. Byron himself was persuaded by his friend John Cam Hobhouse to destroy his early Cambridge journals, probably the most revealing of all his autobiographical writings on this subject. It is likely that fears of possible revelations about homosexuality were among the concerns that moved his friend after Byron's death to insist on the burning of Byron's memoirs. Hobhouse certainly destroyed manuscript poems on the subject. Thomas Moore published extracts from the surviving journals in his biography of Byron in 1830, but only after deleting passages touching on this topic, replacing them with asterisks, and destroying the originals. Some letters were similarly expurgated. Others have survived despite excisions so that we can now see what was cut out. Leslie Marchand's superb new edition includes much candid correspondence formerly omitted and deciphers the code by which Byron communicated his homosexual adventures to Hobhouse in England.

Literature from earlier ages on homosexual themes has not always been destroyed. Bowdlerization has been an alternative strategy for editors. Translators of Greek and Latin poetry have, until recently, often juggled genders to disguise the homoerotic nature of the originals. In Byron's day Persian poetry underwent a similar metamorphosis. Michelangelo's poems were revised by his great-nephew to remove references to his love for Tommaso Cavalieri. The first editor of Shakespeare's sonnets changed some male pronouns to female and scrambled their order, blurring the distinction between poems addressed to the young man and those written to the dark lady: this explains why the controversy over their possible homosexual implications did not surface until so late as 1780, a few years before Byron was born. It is not surprising that Byron removed passages about the homosexuality of some of his famous contemporaries from the draft of the first canto of *Childe Harold* or that he felt he had to pretend that a series of poems he wrote celebrating a male love affair was addressed to a woman.

When we turn to interpretation, the central issue confronting gay studies may be called "the friendship problem." If a novel, poem, or essay describes or expresses ardent feelings for a member of the same sex, when are we to interpret these as homosexual and when are we to regard them merely as reflections of what is usually called romantic friendship? We may be genuinely perplexed by Shakespeare's sonnets, by Montaigne's account of his love for Etienne de La Boëtie, or by Mary Wollstonecraft's novels, Melville's stories, and Emily Dickinson's poems. In Byron's day there was a popular cult of romantic friendship to which Byron as a boy had wholeheartedly responded. Many of his early poems were certainly inspired by it. But he also went beyond this by falling in love with boys and (at least during part of his early life) by becoming a homosexual lover in the physical sense. The second chapter of this study discusses these problems from a historical and cross-cultural point of view.

Accorded an honored place in Greek, Latin, Islamic, and Far Eastern literature, love poems addressed by males to other males have generally been taboo in postclassical Western civilization. Andreas Capellanus undoubtedly described the norm of his culture when he laid down the rule that love could exist only between persons of the opposite sex, all else being "unnatural," and eighteenth-century England was, if anything, even more certain that poems addressed to youths were impious and immoral.

In the light of this tradition, interpreters have often refused to find a homosexual meaning in poetry unless conclusive biographical evidence has been forthcoming, and this, for obvious reasons, has often been the most incomplete part of the personal record. Yet in Byron's case the miracle is how much has now come to light. If Hobhouse presided over the burning of Byron's memoirs, he nevertheless preserved crucial correspondence and poems. Marchand has published a very revealing note from Byron to their common friend, Charles Skinner Matthews. Though this book, as far as Byron is concerned, relies almost entirely on published documents, it does present for the first time the text of two remarkable letters in which Matthews replied to Byron; these show how their Cambridge circle looked at their shared pederastic interests and the fears with which they observed the hostility of English society. For other clues, Marchand's new edition of the letters has proved invaluable. In preparing his biography, Marchand did not have access to the Lovelace papers, which contain Lady Byron's memoranda. Doris Langley Moore's *Late Lord Byron* includes very important excerpts from the latter source. Malcolm Elwin's *Lord Byron's Wife* (1962), which quotes extensively from these papers, has also yielded much new information though Elwin himself tends to downplay the issue of homosexuality and often, one feels, fails to see the significance of all he quotes. Jerome McGann's comprehensive new edition of the poetry (the first since the turn of the century) has been consulted and has provided useful information on the genesis of problematic poems.

One novelty of my approach is that I have tried to shape this deluge of new material into a narrative. Knight's book, though it discusses Byron's homosexuality at length, does not present a connected story, with the result that it is easily intelligible only to specialists. Anyone trying to follow the theme of Byron's bisexuality through Marchand has to disentangle his oblique hints from an overwhelming mass of other materials. Moore's new discoveries are scattered, except in her brief essay. Though the story of Byron's life has been told many times, I have tried to provide at least minimal background information in order that this book be accessible and meaningful to the nonspecialist. Not surprisingly, a century of repression of the truth has inevitably produced its own reaction: Harold Bloom in his Oxford anthology of *Romantic Poetry and Prose* (1973) calls Byron "basically homosexual." But this is a mistake in the other direction. Byron's heterosexual impulses were fully as real as his homosexual ones and, if we take his life as a whole, more persistent and significant though (apart from his incest with his sister) less dramatically threatening. Since Byron was not exclusively homosexual even in the period this book focuses on, namely, the years 1807 to 1816, I have interwoven a brief account of his heterosexual affairs and of his disastrous marriage. After 1816 his homosexual side seems to vanish until his last days at Missolonghi when his early feelings revived in full force in his love for the youthful Lukas Chalandrutsanos.

Does Byron's bisexuality explain the psychology of the so-called Byronic hero? When we consider the extreme animus felt toward homosexuals in Byron's England, with its hangings, pilloryings, ostracism, and exiles, this is a tempting theory. English homophobia in itself seems more than enough to explain the gloom, alienation, wounded pride, and guilt embodied in the literary archetype that in many ways reflected Byron's own personality. At first such an interpretation seemed strongly appealing. But on consideration I have come to regard this as a powerfully aggravating influence rather than the unique explanation of "Byronism." Byron's intense sense of guilt had many sources and seems almost to have formed the essence of his identity. For Byron, to be was to be guilty, a condition rendered all the more painful by the fact that he could not accept the conventional idea of religious atonement. But English contempt for unorthodox sexual dispositions must have dramatically exacerbated an already painful condition. Byron himself hinted that his bisexuality was an important key to his poetic personality.

In treating homosexuality in a historical context, whether the subject is biography or social history, a serious dilemma inevitably faces any writer. This is the dilemma of vocabulary. The problem is especially acute when the writer seeks to address two different audiences—in this case a general audience and America's newly self-aware gay community, whose vocabularies differ. "It is by the power of names, of signs originally arbitrary and insignificant, that the course of imagination has in great measure been guided."[1] So Bentham wrote of the language used by his contemporaries to refer to homosexuality. The language problem, as we may call it, is one that inevitably obtrudes in the following pages. The language of Byron's era was uniformly hostile, often violently so, where homosexuality was concerned. This rhetoric of abuse was remarkably pervasive—it is to be found in Tobias Smollett's diatribes, in the venomous piety of Hester Thrale, in Gibbon's moralistic analyses, and even in Burke's eloquent appeal for reform. Byron himself uses it, as when he remarked in a note to *Childe Harold* that "the death of Antinous was as heroic as his life was infamous."[2] Even Bentham employs the conventional pejorative language of the day in his early notes and in his one essay on the subject. It was not until late in life that he reacted against this vituperative style and tried to coin a new vocabulary free from its negative implications.

One reason I have been unusually liberal with quotations is to let the reader experience the language of Byron's contemporaries and thus realize their mind-set at first hand. This may help historians to become more aware of

1. Bentham manuscripts, University College, London; Code Penal, April 25, 1814, box 74a, folio 175. For a description of these manuscripts, see the appendix.
2. *CPW*, 2:190.

the elaborate circumlocutions by which Georgian England spoke of homosexuality and to feel more assurance in deciphering obscure references. There are also other reasons for this amplitude of quotation. The passages from Bentham's unpublished notes are, by and large, otherwise inaccessible. So too (comparatively speaking) are many of the newspapers and pamphlets I draw on. In the case of Byron's descriptions of his own experiences, the motivation was different. We are all understandably skeptical in reading interpretations of purported references to homosexuality in older literature, letters, and journals. We often wonder if a commentator is reading more into a passage than the actual words will bear, or, on the other hand, whether he or she is missing important implications. Consequently, I have tried to be generous in quoting essential passages at length. There is, of course, an incidental dividend. Byron's prose has a racy liveliness unmatched in epistolatory literature and a surer style than many of his poems.

But if the language of Byron's age poses difficulties through its bias or indirectness, the language in which the modern critic analyzes the subject raises other issues. In essence this is because of our position on a linguistic watershed. America's gay community (like those of other English-speaking countries) speaks and writes of gay rights, gay pride, gay consciousness, and gay history; these terms still seem strange to others principally because the point of view they signify is so novel. The worlds of journalism and politics are rapidly assimilating this new vocabulary. Academic bodies traditionally move more slowly though most scholarly disciplines with nationally organized associations now have gay caucuses, and the Modern Language Association has formally recognized a Division of Gay Studies in Language and Literature. My aim, as a gay scholar, has not been simply to revive forgotten history but to reperceive it and Byron's career in the light of this developing consciousness. This aim has naturally forced some hard decisions. Frequently, I felt the adjective *gay* to be too startlingly anachronistic in this context, though the word I do use—*homosexual*—would have sounded quite as strange to Byron or his contemporaries. I have consequently used the term *gay* sparingly, usually restricting it to ideas that could not be expressed otherwise—"gay consciousness," for instance.

But if *homosexual* and *gay* are both words that would have puzzled Byron's contemporaries, the expression *Greek love*—which I have used in the title of this work—would have been intelligible to them and would have carried resonant historical and literary associations. From moral prejudice, scholars in England had made an effort to keep a knowledge of the ancient Greeks' approval of male homosexuality from men and women who could not read the relevant documents in their original language. But to anyone as intimately familiar with the classics as Byron was, the phrase would have brought immediately to mind such poetic or historical traditions as the legends of Ganymede and Hyacinth, the exploits of Aristogiton and Harmodius, and the story of Antinous. Indeed, Byron himself refers to all of these in his writings. He was, if anything, even more familiar with the classical tradition of male love as it was reflected in the Latin of Catullus, Horace, Virgil and Petronius. Byron was to translate or quote homoerotic passages from all these writers, in moods that varied from the heroic to the playful. In his Cambridge circle, "Horatian" became a code word for "bisexual." But Italy in the early nineteenth century did not offer the classical freedom which the Turkish conquest had restored to Greece in sexual, if not in political, matters. There, as the *Don Leon* poet put it, no "erotic statutes" prevailed, and it was to Greece that Byron as a young man was to make his way, as he was to die there later in that country's struggle for liberty.

Georgian Homophobia

The purpose of this book is to analyze the homosexual side of Byron's temperament in the light of the attitudes toward such feelings in his day. A dawning awareness of his bisexual nature troubled Byron's adolescence and was important in inspiring his first trip to Greece and Turkey. After his separation from his wife, rumors of his erotic adventures in the East began to circulate in England and helped create the hostile atmosphere that drove him abroad once again. During his second exile his passion for boys seems to have been in abeyance. But in the last months of his life, in peculiarly tense and trying circumstances, this strain in his nature reasserted itself, like a thread of lost color reemerging at the edge of the cloth. The evidence—conclusive at some points, obscure and ambiguous at others—that elucidates this aspect of Byron is to be found throughout the poet's numerous letters, journals, and poems, as well as in the diaries and memoranda of his enemies and friends. These documents will be considered in due course in later chapters.[1] Before we can fully understand them, we must first enlighten ourselves about the views on homosexuality held by the society into which Byron was born.

Much has been written about the fate of such despised or feared groups as Jews, witches, and heretics in Euro-

---

1. G. Wilson Knight discusses Byron's bisexuality at length in *Lord Byron's Marriage: The Evidence of Asterisks* (New York: Macmillan, 1957); see esp. chaps. 1, 5, 7. Much new evidence has, however, come to light as a result of the researches of Leslie Marchand and Doris Langley Moore. For a good, brief account that considers later findings, see Moore's "Appendix 2: Byron's Sexual Ambivalence," in *LBAR*, pp. 437–59.

pean history, far less about homosexuals. Indeed, until recent decades a kind of taboo excluded consideration of such matters outside of medical or legal texts. In England, Havelock Ellis's pioneering work, *Sexual Inversion*, which contained some social history, was banned under the obscenity statutes in 1898, a few months after it was published, and more than half a century passed before scholars dared take up the tale again. Even now few educated men and women realize that from the start the medieval and Spanish Inquisitions ranked homosexuals with heretics as a class of persons to be sought out and destroyed.[2] Secular legislation, frequently drawing its justification from religious sanctions, also made sexual relations between men and between women capital offenses throughout Europe and its colonies. As a symbolic reminder of the fate of Sodom, burning was the classical punishment. But hanging and drowning, burial alive, and dismemberment—even starvation—were other fates prescribed by law or meted out at the discretion of judges. In Spain, Italy, France, Switzerland, Germany, and Holland, certainly hundreds, and probably thousands, of men and women were put to death by these means.[3] In Scotland, during Byron's boyhood, legal tomes still identified burning as the national remedy, citing Leviticus as a sanction for such executions, which were to be carried out early in the morning, apparently to avoid giving too great publicity to so

2. For a description of how the thirteenth-century Inquisition organized groups of local citizens to ferret out homosexuals in Italian cities, see Michael Goodich, *The Unmentionable Vice: Homosexuality in the Later Medieval Period* (Santa Barbara, Ca.: ABC-Clio, 1979), p. 82. Executions under the Spanish Inquisition are documented in Henry Charles Lea, *History of the Inquisition of Spain*, vol. 4 (New York: Macmillan, 1907), 361–71.

3. Surveys of such executions are included in Louis Crompton, "Gay Genocide: From Leviticus to Hitler," in *The Gay Academic*, ed. Louie Crew (Palm Springs, Ca.: ETC Publications, 1978), pp. 67–91; and Louis Crompton, "The Myth of Lesbian Impunity: Capital Laws from 1270 to 1791," *Journal of Homosexuality* 6 (Fall-Winter 1980–1981): 11–25, which adds further cases for both women and men.

heinous a sin.[4] The jurist David Hume defended the law as one that "justly expose[s] the offender to be punished with death as one whose very presence is a pollution to the society of his fellow-creatures."[5] The last known burning in Scotland had taken place more than a century earlier. In England, on the other hand, where the rope had replaced tinder, the law was still very much alive. In other countries executions for sodomy reached their height during the sixteenth and seventeenth centuries, at the same time as witch hunts and heresy trials. But the death penalty in England seems to have been most rigorously enforced during the early nineteenth century. In the age of Castlereagh and Wellington, while Wordsworth, Coleridge, Byron, Shelley, and Keats lived and wrote, homosexuals suffered regularly upon the gallows or stood at the mercy of ill-wishers in public pillories.

Parliament had made male homosexuality a capital offense in 1533. William Blackstone, whose *Commentaries* appeared in 1765–1769, emphasized the biblical source of this statute and seemed to regret the desuetude of the tradition of fire. Byron, who boasted that he had read Blackstone as a schoolboy, would have been familiar with his paragraphs on sodomy:

> This the voice of nature and of reason, and the express law of God, determine to be capital. Of which we have a signal instance, long before the Jewish dispensation, by the destruction of two cities by fire from heaven: so that this is an universal, not merely a provincial, precept. And our antient law in

4. John Erskine, *An Institute of the Law of Scotland*, ed. J. B. Nicolson (Edinburgh: Bell & Bradfute, 1871), 2:1203.

5. *Commentaries on the Law of Scotland Respecting Crimes* (Edinburgh: Bell & Bradfute, 1844), 1:469. This David Hume was not the philosopher but a Baron of the Exchequer. His *Commentaries* were first published in 1797 when Byron was nine and at school in Aberdeen. In its entry for "Sodomy," the third edition of the *Encyclopaedia Britannica* (Edinburgh, 1797) noted: "There is no statute in Scotland against Sodomy; the libel of the crime is therefore founded on the divine law, and practice makes its punishment to be burnt alive."

some degree imitated this punishment, by commanding such miscreants to be burnt to death.[6]

The language of the criminal indictment was appropriately archaic, sonorous, and theological:

> The Jurors of our Sovereign Lord the King upon their oath present that [the name of the accused] . . . wickedly, devilishly, feloniously, and against the Order of Nature, . . . did and committed with the said [person] that sodomitical, detestable, and abominable Sin called Buggery, (not to be named among Christians), to the great Displeasure of Almighty God, and to the Disgrace of all Mankind, and against the Peace of our said Sovereign Lord the King, his Crown and Dignity, and against the Form of the Statute in such Case made and provided.[7]

Charges of this sort were common during Byron's day. We have few records of any use of the law in Tudor England, and only a few executions are at present known to have taken place before the eighteenth century.[8] It was not until that age that the law appears to have been seriously enforced. Then in 1726, according to a contemporary source, "a great Number of these Wretches" were convicted and three put to death.[9] There was a lull at mid-century, but when a Captain Robert Jones was pardoned in 1772, a furor broke out. The strength of popular feeling at that date may be inferred from a report in the London Evening Post: "The concourse of people about Newgate this morning, in ex-

6. Commentaries on the Laws of England, vol. 4 (Oxford: Clarendon Press, 1769), 216.

7. W. Nelson, The Office and Authority of a Justice of the Peace (London: R. Gosling et al., 1736), 1:140–41.

8. See B. R. Burg, "Ho Hum, Another Work of the Devil: Buggery and Sodomy in Early Stuart England," Journal of Homosexuality 6 (Fall-Winter 1980–1981): 69–78. The flippancy of this title seems oddly out of keeping with the two trials it chiefly deals with, that of Lord Castlehaven and of John Atherton, Bishop of Waterford, both grim affairs that led to executions. Burg does, however, make the legitimate point that executions were rare in Stuart England.

9. Giles Jacob, Every Man His Own Lawyer (London: J. Hazard, S. Birt, & C. Corvett, 1736), p. 444.

pectation of seeing Jones go to Tyburn, was amazing. There was a universal murmer, when it was learned that a respite had been received. It was thought impossible, and the execrations of the populace were pretty liberally poured forth upon a certain Great Personage."[10] The editor reminded George III that the Bible condemned kings of Judea who tolerated "Sodomites in the land."[11] Thereafter, and throughout Byron's lifetime, that is, from 1788 to 1824, pardons were extremely rare. By 1806 the number of executions had risen to an average of two a year and remained there for three decades, though executions for every other capital offense decreased dramatically.[12]

In this, England contrasted markedly with the Continent. In 1730, a wave of religious hysteria, strikingly akin to that which had affected Salem, Massachusetts, a generation earlier during its witch hunts, swept Holland and led to the hanging, drowning, and burning of a hundred men and boys.[13] But later in the century, as the influence of the Enlightenment spread, executions were rare. In *The Spirit of the Laws* (1748) Montesquieu decried homosexuality as effeminizing, but by placing it in the same category as heresy and witchcraft, he implied that it was an archaic ecclesiastical offense too severely punished.[14] In Italy, Cesare

10.   August 8–11, 1772, p. 4.

11.   Ibid.

12.   The *Report of the Select Committee on Criminal Laws*, issued by the House of Commons in 1819, gives the following number of hangings carried out: 1806, 6; 1807, 0; 1808, 2; 1809, 2; 1810, 4; 1811, 2; 1812, 1; 1813, 1; 1814, 5; 1815, 1; 1816, 2; 1817, 1; and 1818, 1 ([British Sessional Papers, 1819], 17:312). The *Tables Showing the Number of Criminal Offenders Committed for Trial or Bailed . . . in the Year 1836* supplements these figures with hangings up to that year, at which point they appear to have ceased: 1819–1825, 15; 1826–1832, 7; 1831, 1; 1832, 0; 1833, 3; 1834, 4; 1835, 3; and 1836, 0 ([British Sessional Papers, 1837], 46:9).

13.   Crompton, "Gay Genocide," pp. 73–77, 85–91. The tables show only sixty deaths but are incomplete according to recent unpublished research by Leo Boon.

14.   Book XII, trans. Thomas Nugent (New York: Hafner, 1949), pp. 189–90.

Beccaria, whose *Essay on Crimes and Punishments* (1764) was
to have immense influence on European and American reformers, speculated that in sodomy cases "tortures . . .
often triumph over innocence" and hinted that a society
that fostered such behavior through sexually segregated
boarding schools had no right to exact penalties.[15] In the
famous disquisition "Socratic Love" in his *Philosophical Dictionary* (1764), Voltaire had reiterated the popular fear that
homosexuality threatened the existence of the race and
decried such behavior as an unseemly anomaly in north-
ern Europe. But in a later essay he unequivocally opposed the death penalty. Such a crime, he wrote, should be
"shrouded in the shadows of oblivion, rather than illuminated by flaming brands in the eyes of the crowd."[16] In
1786, Quaker humanitarianism and the new penology combined in the wake of the American Revolution to effect the
abolition of the death penalty for sodomy in Pennsylvania;
other American states then followed this lead.[17] By the end
of the century, Catherine the Great, Joseph II, Frederick
the Great, and Leopold of Tuscany had all adopted new
liberal laws, which achieved the same result.[18] France in
1791 went still further. A reformed code inspired by the
Declaration of the Rights of Man decriminalized same-sex
relations entirely. No executions are known to have taken
place in Europe thereafter. It was totally out of keeping
that England, under the circumstances, should have invoked its parliamentary statute to hang sixty men in the

15. Chap. 36, "Crimes Difficult to Prove," trans. K. Forster and
J. Grigson (New York: Oxford University Press, 1964), p. 83.
16. "Prix de la justice et de l'humanité," in *Oeuvres complètes* [ed.
P. A. Caronde Beaumarchais, M. J. A. N. Caritat, Marquis de Condor-
cet, and L. P. Decroix] ([Kehl]: L'Imprimerie de la Société Littéraire-
Typographique, 1785), 29:322.
17. Louis Crompton, "Homosexuals and the Death Penalty in Colo-
nial America," *Journal of Homosexuality* 1 (1976):277–93.
18. Leon Radzinowicz, *The Movement for Reform*, Vol. 1 of *A History of
English Criminal Law and Its Administration from 1750* (London: Stevens &
Sons, 1948), pp. 286–97.

first three decades of the nineteenth century and have
hanged another score under its naval regulations.[19]

When we consider that England's gay male minority at
this time must have numbered several hundred thousand
(if we use modern statistics as a guide), it is obvious that
only a tiny proportion were touched by the law in its
severest form. Yet the threat of the gallows was always
present to darken these men's perception of themselves as
outcasts and to justify a multitude of lesser, but still oner-
ous, forms of persecution. As one of Byron's closest friends
at Cambridge put it in a letter to the poet about their
shared inclinations: "We risque our necks."[20] At the time
this letter was written, Byron was on his way back from his
first journey to Greece. Charles Skinner Matthews's remark was inspired by a visit he had made with their common friend Scrope Davies to see two convicted men, an
army lieutenant and a sixteen-year-old drummer, in Newgate. The man and boy were hanged shortly after before a
huge crowd, which included a royal duke, who had himself recently figured in a scandal that had encouraged
alarming rumors.[21]

It was anomalous that England, in many respects the
most liberal country in Europe, should at the end of the
eighteenth century have had a criminal code with more
than two hundred capital offenses. Europe's enlightened
despots had been much quicker to respond to the wave of
criminal law reform that swept Europe in the 1780s than
the British Parliament. Having failed to act at this time,
that body found it impossible to do so in the wave of reaction provoked by the wars with France. But even if war had
not intervened, it seems unlikely that England would have
abolished the death penalty for homosexual relations. The

19. Arthur N. Gilbert, "Buggery and the British Navy, 1700–1861,"
Journal of Social History 10 (1976):72–98.
20. MS, John Murray collection. This letter is cited at length on
pp. 160–62.
21. See p. 171, n. 18.

hard fact was that both learned and popular opinion in England was overwhelmingly on Blackstone's side.

This benightedness appalled England's leading law reformer. Jeremy Bentham, who was born in 1748, began drawing up arguments for a more humane and rational criminal code early in his twenties. His efforts were not to bear fruit in his native land for another fifty years though his reputation soared in Europe. Indeed, his most important writings were first published in French translations. Madame de Staël thought the era should be called not the age of Napoleon or the age of Byron but the age of Bentham.[22] In Spain and Spanish America, where his ideas were popular with reforming jurists, Bentham was hailed as "el legislador del mundo." But if Bentham's compatriots were slow to follow him in the direction of the utilitarian reform of law generally, they would have found his views on homosexuality unimaginably daring.

It is doubtful that many even of his closest friends knew of his consuming interest in the subject or read the hundreds of pages Bentham wrote on it. Cerebration this extensive and this radical on the matter of sexual nonconformity was unheard of in England. At the beginning of the eighteenth century an Italian canonist had included ninety-two paragraphs on male and female homosexuality in a treatise on criminal law.[23] In contrast, an English judge in Bentham's day who wrote two pages to justify hanging a man for sodomy in a doubtful case was twitted by a commentator for showing a "very indelicate profusion of learning."[24] Blackstone himself had set his seal on the British

22.   Bentham's ideas on law reform had significant influence on the Napoleonic Code. Napoleon called Bentham's *Traités de législation* "un ouvrage de génie" (Radzinowicz, *Movement for Reform*, p. 359, n. 5); chap. 11 of Radzinowicz's work examines Bentham's influence in detail both in England and abroad.

23.   Ludovico Maria Sinistrari, "Sodomia," in *De Delictis et Poenis* (Venice: Albriccio, 1700).

24.   William Eden, *Principles of Penal Law* (London: B. White, 1771), p. 245n. The reference was to J. Fortescue Aland's report of the Wiseman

tradition of reticence, which had almost the force of a tribal taboo, by introducing his few lines in the *Commentaries* with the remark: "I will not act so disagreeable a part, to my readers as well as myself, as to dwell any longer upon a subject, the very mention of which is a disgrace to human nature. It will be more eligible to imitate in this respect the delicacy of our English law, which treats it, in it's very indictments, as a crime not fit to be named: '*peccatum illud horribile, inter christianos non nominandum.*'"[25] In light of this national bias toward silence, Bentham's voluminous analyses are, to say the least, remarkable. Bentham first jotted down about fifty pages of notes in 1774 when he was twenty-six. In 1785 he completed a somewhat longer formal essay. In 1814 and 1816 he filled almost two hundred pages with another impassioned indictment of British attitudes. Two years later he produced several hundred more pages of notes on homosexuality and the Bible, and in 1824, eight years before his death at the age of eighty-four, he wrote a final short synopsis of his ideas on sodomy law reform. All in all, this adds up to a sizable book on a subject that British jurists usually dismissed in a paragraph or page.

What moved Bentham to these labors, which consumed months, even years, of his life? His style is for the most part cool, logical, and dry, his vocabulary abstract and periphrastic to the point of obscurity. But beneath the pedantic and turgid prose there is a sense of outrage that from time to time bursts forth. Something like fierce indignation steeled the jurist who could write of the treatment of homosexuals in England: "The propensities in question have, in the British Isles, beyond all other countries, been the object of the violence of that thirst which

---

case, which involved an act of sodomy performed on a twelve-year-old girl.

25.   "The horrible sin not to be named among Christians" (*Commentaries*, 4:215–16).

nothing less than the heart's blood of the victims marked out for slaughter by the dissocial appetite has hitherto been able to satisfy."[26] The intensity of his countrymen's bigotry appalled Bentham; in a few dramatic lines written in 1816 he tells how he had encountered it face to face in a self-satisfied judge:

> By the eyes by which this pen is guided, an instance of this sort was once seen in the person of a Judge. He had just come from the Circuit. For an offense of the sort in question he had just been consigning two wretches to the gallows. Delight and exultation glistened in his countenance; his looks called for applause and congratulations at the hands of the surrounding audience. The recollection he awakened was that of Jeffries [sic], upon his return from his campaign relating the history of his exploits.[27]

It was not only the hangings that dismayed Bentham. Foreign visitors to England were struck by another form of punishment for homosexual offenses. This was the pillory. Standards of proof were high in sodomy cases: until 1828, courts required evidence both of penetration and emission. But if these were missing, men were convicted of the lesser offense of "assault with the attempt to commit sodomy." This charge might be based on nothing more than a solicitation invited by a plain-clothes man who had gone to some homosexual rendezvous for the purpose of entrapping men. Convicted men were placed in the pillory and exposed to the wrath of the mob, who were allowed to pelt them. Such events attracted thousands, sometimes tens of thousands of spectators. The pelting of the men often took on an organized form under the supervision of the police. There was a tradition that women of the street—fishwives, vendors of produce, and "Cyprians" (as the press euphemistically called prostitutes)—should have ˜

---

26.   Code Penal, April 25, 1814, box 74a, folio 119. See the appendix.
27.   August 26(?), 1816, box 74a, folio 186. The reference is to Judge Jeffreys at the "Bloody Assizes," which ferociously punished those involved in the Monmouth Rebellion of 1685.

pride of place in these orgies of ill-will, and some of the most abused members of British society revenged themselves for the contempt they received from others by the violence with which they attacked the helpless sodomites. A Prussian officer, visiting England in the 1780s, reported: "Since English women are so beautiful and the enjoyment. of them is so general, the revulsion of these Islanders against paederasty passes all bounds. Attempted homosexuality is punished by the pillory and several years of imprisonment, the act itself by the gallows. The pillory, however, is almost as good as death." [28] Bentham tells us that a man in the pillory might easily have "a jaw broken or an eye beat out." [29] On occasion, men were killed by the crowd. The French annotators of an edition of Voltaire published in 1785 felt moved to protest in a footnote to his appeal for sodomy law reform: "The law of England, which exposes guilty men to all the insults of the mob, and above all the women who torment them, sometimes to death, is at the same time cruel, indecent, and ridiculous." [30] Reacting against the theological bias they perceived behind such legislation, the editors remind the reader that Europe owed such laws to "superstition."

In the same letter that told of his visit to see the condemned men in Newgate, Charles Skinner Matthews reported to Byron on the exposure of the so-called "Vere Street coterie," the most sensational pillorying in the Regency period. The press routinely reported such brutality with equanimity or approbation. Their accounts employed a stereotyped lexicon of abuse—from "miscreant" (at the mildest) to "monster." But this bludgeoning style was not limited to newspapers. It was endemic in the learned as well as the popular literature of the age. It is instructive,

28. J. Wilhelm von Archenholz, *England und Italien* (Leipzig, 1787), 2:267, as cited in Ivan Bloch, *A History of English Sexual Morals*, trans. William H. Fostern (London: Francis Aldor, 1936), p. 389.

29. April 24, 1814, box 74a, folio 117.

30. *Oeuvres complètes*, 29:323, n. 17.

for instance, to look at the language and rhetoric of so so-
phisticated a spokesman of the Enlightenment as Edward
Gibbon, in the pages he devoted to Justinian's laws in his
Decline and Fall of the Roman Empire in 1776.

At the start, Gibbon pays his respects to the "unspeak-
ability" tradition so strong in England, in a style Dickens
was later to purloin for Mr. Pecksniff: "I touch with reluctance, and dispatch with impatience, a more odious vice,
of which modesty rejects the name, and nature abominates
the idea."[31] In two long paragraphs Gibbon finds space for
at least a dozen opprobrious terms—"odious vice" and
"abomination" are succeeded by "infection," "degeneracy,"
"the indelible stain of manhood," "unmanly lust," "sin
against nature," "licentiousness," "impure manners," "disease," "corruption," and "moral pestilence." Only once
does he relent to the extent of calling gay men "lovers of
their own sex." Was it his personal feelings against homosexuals—which were strong—that moved Gibbon to these
paroxysms, or did he feel it unsafe to venture on the topic
at all without this rhetorical overkill? Despite his avowals,
the evidence suggests that Gibbon found the subject fas-
cinating and had read widely in it. Perhaps this was the
price he felt he must pay for revealing the scope of his
erudition. His compact summary is replete with learning
about homosexuality in the classical and early Christian
worlds. Within a few lines he reviews biblical laws, seven
ancient and four Byzantine historians, five Roman poets
and orators, three German jurists, an Italian commentator
on Roman law, a French historian, Montesquieu, and some
contemporary travel writers. It is amusing to see him begin
a note with the comment that "a curious dissertation might
be formed"—that is, on Greek pederasty—only to break
off as he reminds himself again that the subject is taboo.[32]

31. *The History of the Decline and Fall of the Roman Empire*, ed. J. B. Bury
(London: Methuen, 1900), 4:504.
32. Ibid., pp. 504–06.

Gibbon thought Roman law (which fined men for relations with free-born boys) too lenient and regretted that
"the practice of vice was not discouraged by the severity
of opinion." He deplores the homoerotic inclinations of
Catullus and Juvenal and slyly reminds his readers that
Ovid in his *Art of Love* did not quite reject the love of boys
but merely declared that he liked them *less* than girls. Only
once, in commenting on the reign of terror instigated
by Justinian, does he don the mantle of a humanitarian
philosopher:

> The same emperor declared himself the implacable enemy of
> unmanly lust, and the cruelty of his persecution can scarcely
> be excused by the purity of his motives. In defiance of every
> principle of justice, he stretched to past as well as future of-
> fenses the operations of his edicts, with the previous allow-
> ance of a short respite for confession and pardon. A painful
> death was inflicted by the amputation of the sinful instrument,
> or the insertion of sharp reeds into the pores and tubes of most
> exquisite sensibility; and Justinian defended the propriety of
> the execution, since the criminals would have lost their hands,
> had they been convicted of sacrilege. In this state of disgrace
> and agony, two bishops, Isaiah of Rhodes and Alexander of
> Diospolis, were dragged through the streets of Constantinople,
> while their brethren were admonished, by the voice of a crier,
> to observe this awful lesson, and not to pollute the sanctity of
> their character. Perhaps these prelates were innocent. A sen-
> tence of death and infamy was often founded on the slight and
> suspicious evidence of a child or a servant; the guilt of the
> green faction, of the rich, and of the enemies of Theodora, was
> presumed by the judges, and paederasty became the crime of
> those to whom no crime could be imputed.[33]

In England, in the sixty years following the publication
of Gibbon's history, scores of men were to be hanged,
many more pilloried, and dozens of others prominent, like
Byron, in politics and letters, ostracized or driven into exile. A British bishop was to succeed Justinian's prelates as
an object of infamy, and a powerful foreign minister com-

33. Ibid., pp. 505–06.

mitted suicide under the pressure of blackmail threats. One wonders if the measure of suffering the late eighteenth and early nineteenth centuries exacted did not exceed that of the age of Justinian, and one wonders also what Gibbon would have made of the situation if he could have foreseen it. However, he declined to accept the lead of his fellow intellectuals in France on law reform: "The favorable persuasion of [Montesquieu] that a legislator may confide in the taste and reason of mankind is impeached by the unwelcome discovery of the antiquity and extent of the disease."[34] In a famous aside on Hadrian, Gibbon had remarked: "Of the first fifteen emperors Claudius was the only one whose taste in love was entirely correct."[35] Now he notes the prevalence of homosexuality in Palestine and in Gaul, China, India, and pre-Columbian America (unaccountably omitting Islam and Japan) and ends with a sanctimonious touch: "I believe, and hope, that the Negroes, in their own country, were exempt from this moral pestilence."[36] It is notable that Gibbon (who was perhaps fortunate in being spared the discoveries of nineteenth-century anthropologists about Africa)[37] uses the cross-cultural argument, so often employed to call European prejudices into question, to oppose an argument against punishment. So deeply ingrained are his preconceptions that he can coolly declare the whole world, past and present, out of step without any awareness of the paradox. Nor was his homophobia insincere. When William Beckford, fleeing hostile England, took refuge in Switzerland a few years later, Gibbon opposed receiving him there.

34. Ibid., p. 506.
35. Ibid., 1:75n.
36. Ibid., 4:506n.
37. These findings are catalogued for about forty different Negro peoples in Africa by Ferdinand Karsh-Haack, *Das gleichgeschlechtliche Leben der Naturvölker* (1911; rpt. New York: Arno Press, 1975), pp. 116–80. For homosexuality in native African cultures, see also Gwen J. Broude and Sarah J. Greene, "Cross-Cultural Codes on Twenty Sexual Attitudes and Practices," *Ethnology* 15 (1976):419.

The young Bentham wrote his notes of 1774 two years before Gibbon published the first volume of his history, fully aware of the chasm that lay between his opinions and those of his fellow countrymen. These miscellaneous fragments cover a striking range of topics and contain in embryonic form much that was to preoccupy Bentham's thinking about homosexuality during the next fifty years. He takes note of newspaper controversies, the writings of Greek historians, medieval canonists, and French philosophers and discusses such disparate topics as Scripture, animal behavior, the psychology of homophobia, the purported threat to pupils, the effect of homosexuality on population, etc. At every point Bentham goes out of his way to challenge received opinion. Sixty years later, an anonymous poet, writing of Byron's homosexuality and the need for law reform, referred to love between men as a "vice"

Which none so brazened e'er presume to own.[38]

In his notes, Bentham made himself the spokesman of a silent and invisible minority. First, he rejects the silence taboo. "It seems rather too much," he remarks with dry irony, "to subscribe to men's being hanged to save the indecency of enquiring whether they deserve it."[39] Then, in a passage that might have served as a rebuke to Gibbon, he pleads for a more rational mode of debate, which would scrutinize the purported social evils of forbidden sexual conduct rather than give rein to fervid rhetoric: "If you would prove to the Legislator the necessity of his interposition to proscribe a practise, do not exhaust your invention to belabour it with hard names but point out and ascertain with calmness and perspicuity the species and proportion of misery it occasions. It is thus and thus only you can vindicate yourself from the charge of empty and irrational

38.   Don Leon, in A Homosexual Emancipation Miscellany, c. 1835–1952 (1866; rpt. New York: Arno Press, 1975), p. 7.
39.   "Nonconformity," box 74a, folio 25.

declamation." [40] But, most of all, he insists that we should establish that an act really does cause social harm before we criminalize it: "The extreme horror and indignation with which this Vice is regarded by the generality of people in this country will occur obviously enough as a reason for continuing the punishment for it." [41] But an emotional prejudice is not enough. We must remember "that it is a crime, if a crime it is to be called, that produces no misery in Society." [42] "A Man's own feelings, tho' the best reason in the world for his abhorring the thing, are none at all for his abhorring the Man who does it—how much less then are they for destroying him?" [43] Only once does Bentham imply that others share his views, but it is not clear if he means other English thinkers. If so, it is hard to guess who made up this antihomophobic party:

> More than a few who are as far from the misfortune of being infected with that odious taste as those who choose the most extravagant expressions to vent their antipathy against it, and who think that there are other methods of displaying their virtue than pouring forth their fury at free cost against a Vice of which they are secure from the temptation, scruple not to avow their sentiments that a bad taste is a very bad reason for a man's being thrust into perdition with the vilest, and that to thirst after a man's blood who is innocent, if innocence consists in the doing of no harm to anyone, is a much worse taste. [44]

Bentham objected to laws that criminalized acts on the grounds of taste alone: "To destroy a man there should certainly be some better reason than mere dislike to his Taste, let that dislike be ever so strong." [45]

As a philosophical hedonist, Bentham had no a priori aversion to sexual pleasure; as a utilitarian, he was com-

40. Box 74a, folio 7.
41. Box 74a, folio 5.
42. Ibid.
43. Box 74a, folio 6.
44. Box 74a, folio 3.
45. Box 74a, folio 6.

mitted to the "greatest happiness principle" and was convinced that only deeds manifestly harmful to society should
be made crimes. Most of the shibboleths of traditional legal
theory—the law of nature, the moral sense, good order,
etc., Bentham rejected as mere phantoms, which disguised
unanalyzed assumptions or cloaked outmoded prejudices.
From Cesare Beccaria he took the idea that social utility
was the test to distinguish genuinely pernicious behavior
from "imaginary" (i.e., harmless) crimes. Nowhere did
utilitarian ethics yield more devastating results than in its
application to sexual morality. This was particularly true of
the idea of "crimes against nature," which had entered
legal tradition through patristic theology. In a comment
on the *Law of Nations* (1672) by the German jurist Samuel
Pufendorf, a writer much esteemed in Bentham's day, he
took exception to the author's equating all nonprocreative
sexual acts with "Brutal Lust" and to his denouncing "all
those Pollutions which we justly call unnatural":

> It is curious to observe the efforts that writers on this subject
> make to keep up the semblance of an argument and to find a
> pretence not to shock popular prejudices, and the dictates of
> their own passions. "To carry on our enquiries as clearly as
> may be (says Puffendorf [*sic*] in his Chapter of Matrimony),
> this in the first place we take to be most evident, that all those
> impure pleasures are repugnant to the Laws of Nature, which
> aim at no other satisfaction but Brutal Lust. For the more
> warmly the appetite of Love stirs in the Human Breasts, the
> more is Nature and Reason concerned to provide that the ir-
> regularities of its motions do not prejudice comely order,
> which is the very life of Society, and that it be rather made to
> contribute to the maintenance of decency and Peace."—From
> these [premises] there follows one conclusion: "Whence ap-
> pears the detestable sinfulness of those Pollutions which we so
> justly call unnatural." In order to support this conclusion,
> which somehow or other was at any rate to be supported, we
> may observe how he has conjured up on purpose this Phan-
> tom of comely order, which having performed this office is
> blown away and returned to its primitive nothing—for in fact
> we hear of it no more throughout the book.—I call it a Phan-
> tom for either it is the same with "general Happiness" or it is

nothing. Now to have asserted that it is prejudicial to general happiness is an assertion that evidently is either false or at least requires a long course of argument to prove it otherwise. He was forced to have recourse to this vague expression to cover the vacuity of the argument from his own observation and his readers'.[46]

Bentham regarded the consequences of Europe's sodomy laws as calamitous—"death to a human creature, confusion, reproach and anguish to an innocent family," all to no purpose.[47] What provoked such an excess of punitiveness? In trying to fathom the psychology of homophobia, Bentham recalled an episode from his own life. A female relative had once shocked him by asking him to kill a toad simply because she found the animal ugly. It occurs to him that the feelings of most people toward these "unhappy wretches" are not unlike the woman's—a blind, unreasoning hatred or antipathy, which they then try to rationalize. "They may give an answer to their judgments and those of other men with the notions of this prejudice to population, & of the supposed warrant from scripture so to serve them, considerations which upon other occasions perhaps shall influence them but little: but it is this [i.e., blind hate] which occupies indeed their hearts."[48]

The problem was how to inaugurate a discussion on a subject about which emotions ran so high. It was in fact not until 1957 that the publication of the Wolfenden Report finally laid the basis for a rational public debate in England. Two centuries earlier the case seemed hopeless. Over and over again, a sense of urgency possessed Bentham with the conviction: "I must speak out." Humanity aside, the very soul and logic of his new legal philosophy required him to repudiate laws penalizing the sexual relations of consenting adults in private. But when he weighed the consequences, something like panic seized him:

46. Box 74a, folio 8.
47. Box 74a, folio 6.
48. Box 74a, folio 14.

A hundred times have I shuddered at the view of the perils I was exposing myself to in encountering the opinions that are in possession of men's minds on [this] subject. As often have I resolved to turn aside from a road so full of precipices. I have trembled at the thoughts of the indignation that must be raised against the Apologist of a crime that has been looked upon by many, and those excellent men, as one among the blackest under Heaven. But the dye is now cast, & having thus far adhered with that undeviating fidelity [to] the principles of general utility I at first adopted, I will not at last abandon them for considerations of personal danger. I will not have to reproach myself with the thought that those principles which my judgment has approved, my fears have compelled me to abandon.[49]

His dilemma was this: to have publicly admitted that utilitarianism and the "greatest happiness principle" led logically to the decriminalization of sodomy would have given Bentham's opponents a powerful weapon for discrediting his whole program of reform.[50] We must sympathize with his predicament even if we deplore his need for silence. He had forged a strong instrument for abolishing the worst outrages of the criminal system. Yet if he used it against one of the least defensible of them, it would break in his hands. Under the strain, Bentham became uncharacteristically self-dramatizing, declaring at one point: "Even this dangerous & bitter cup would I not put from me."[51]

But a page later he recovered his sense of humor. He recalls reading about the terrifying initiation rite of some Brazilian pirates and remarks apropos of law reform:

Should it ever be desired to subject to a probation as trying to the fortitude of the mind, as this to the patience of the body, those whose ambition leads them to be ranked among the teachers of critical Jurisprudence, let this subject be given him

49. Box 74a, folio 4.
50. Though Bentham clearly favored decriminalization, he was apparently willing to accept banishment as a compromise; "Nonconformity," Box 74a, folio 4.
51. Box 74a, folio 23.

to treat of & let him be honest. The [prejudices of men] are phantoms more dangerous than any that the imagination of monastic fablemongers sent to terrify their legendary Saint. After this, he might bear any thing, no danger nor any sacrifice in the pursuit of the great interest of mankind would be too dear.[52]

He then made a list of other points to be explored. But fear held him back. "Perhaps I have gone too far already. . . . Perhaps I have gone too far in proposing topics for inquiry, for inquiry supposes certainty to be wanting."[53] Bentham's rough notes give a vivid picture of conscience at war with discretion. Discretion won out. After two more pages, he broke off and did not return to the subject for another ten years.

Meanwhile, pilloryings continued, with much brutality and occasional deaths. In 1780, an exceptionally grim episode led a famous member of Parliament to utter a unique protest. On April 10 of that year, a coachman named William Smith and a plasterer named Theodosius Reed had been exposed in the pillory at St. Margaret's Hill in London for attempted sodomy. Though their punishment did not take place until nearly noon, nevertheless, according to one newspaper: "A vast Concourse of People had assembled upon the Occasion, many by Seven o'Clock in the Morning, who had collected dead Dogs, Cats, &c. in great Abundance, which were plentifully thrown at them; but some Person threw a Stone, and hit the Coachman on the Forehead, and he immediately dropped on his Knees, and was to all Appearance dead."[54] Smith did, in fact, die though there was some uncertainty whether the cause of his death was the violence of the crowd or the tightness of the pillory about his neck. Edmund Burke, learning of the case the next day, was moved to expostulate in the House of Commons:

52. Ibid.
53. Ibid.
54. *Daily Advertiser*, April 11, 1780, p. 1, col. 2.

He said, the matter which had induced him to make these reflections was the perusal of a melancholy circumstance stated
in the newspapers of that morning. . . . The relation he alluded to, was that of the unhappy and horrid murder of a poor
wretch, condemned to stand in the pillory the preceding day.
The account stated that two men (Reed and Smith) had been
doomed to this punishment; that one of them being short of
stature, and remarkably shortnecked, he could not reach the
hole made for the admission of the head, in the awkward and
ugly instrument used in this mode of punishment; that the officers of justice, nevertheless, forced his head through the hole,
and the poor wretch hung rather than walked as the pillory
turned round: that previous to his being put in, he had deprecated the vengeance of the mob, and begged that mercy,
which from their exasperation at his crime, and their want of
considering the consequences of their cruelty, they seemed
very little to bestow. That he soon grew black in the face and
the blood forced itself out of his nostrils, his eyes, and his ears.
That the mob, nevertheless, attacked him and his fellow criminal with great fury. That the officers seeing his situation,
opened the pillory, and the poor wretch fell down dead on the
stand of the instrument. The other man, he understood was so
maimed and hurt by what had been thrown at him, that he
now lay without hope of recovery.[55]

After the mandatory deprecation of sodomy as a crime
that "could scarcely be mentioned, much less defended or
extenuated," Burke protested that the pillory existed to expose men to contempt and not to kill them by a punishment "as much more severe than execution at Tyburn, as
to die in torment, was more dreadful than momentary
death." Burke then seized the occasion to propose that a
bill be introduced to abolish the pillory since it was open to
such abuse. Burke's brave and unprecedented raising of
the issue prompted others to voice their own misgivings.
Another member told how a man he had known at Bury,
condemned for the same crime, had swallowed poison

55.   April 11, 1780, *Parliamentary History of England* (London: Hansard, 1814), vol. 21, cols. 388–89. The attorney-general proposed an in-
vestigation to determine if the officers were guilty of neglect of duty and
who in the mob might be "most immediately concerned in the murder."

fearing "that the populace would be so exasperated against him, that they would take his life." He was exposed the next day and was "so severely treated by the populace that he died that night in gaol, and whether he died from the poison, or in consequence of his ill treatment from the mob, had never been ascertained."[56]

Burke had the satisfaction of seeing the undersheriff for Surrey tried for murder;[57] not surprisingly, the jury acquitted him. Burke himself, though complimented in the House on his humanity, suffered much abuse in the press for his stand. The *Morning Post* complained: "Every *man* applauds the spirit of the spectators, and every *woman* thinks their conduct right. It remained only for the patriotic Mr. Burke to insinuate that the crime these men committed should not be held in the highest detestation, and that it deserved a milder chastisement than ignominious death."[58] Four years later, the *Public Advertiser* also attacked Burke maliciously for showing sympathy for homosexuals. In both cases Burke sued for libel and won. He was able to obtain a pension for the dead coachman's widow, a circumstance that suggests that not all levels of British officialdom were as passionately homophobic as the press.[59]

But prejudice ran high at the popular level and affected most of the intelligentsia. What inspired it? What had led England and Europe alike for so many centuries to condemn homosexuals to death? Undoubtedly, much of this feeling, like anti-Semitism and the fear of witchcraft, was religious in origin. Leviticus had prescribed capital punishment, and its lethal verse (20:13) was cited by innumerable jurists on the Continent and in the British Isles. The Sodom story added a dramatic threat of destruction to terrify the

56.   Sir Charles Bunbury, in ibid., col. 391.
57.   *Correspondence of Edmund Burke*, ed. John A. Woods, vol. 4 (Cambridge: Cambridge University Press, 1963), 230.
58.   Quoted in ibid., p. 350.
59.   Ibid., p. 230.

superstitious. St. Paul, in his Epistle to the Romans, expressed his detestation of men and women who manifested "vile affections." [60] Early Christian emperors incorporated the death penalty into Roman law, which in the Middle Ages and the Renaissance was revived first in Italy, France, and Spain, and later even in Germany and Scotland. [61]

Religious hysteria over sodomy was still very much alive in the eighteenth century. The persecutions of 1730 in Holland were sanctioned by a national proclamation warning that God would destroy Holland as He had destroyed the Cities of the Plain if they did not stamp out this vice. [62] As we have seen, Blackstone felt an appeal to the Sodom legend to be conclusive in his defense of Henry VIII's statute of 1533. It is scarcely surprising that English clergy in the eighteenth century repeatedly whipped up animosity against the nation's gay minority in essays, sermons, and scriptural commentaries. The church historian Joseph Bingham, after taking note of early Christian legislation condemning homosexuals to death, complaisantly declared: "Thus the civil and the ecclesiastical laws combined together to exterminate all sorts of uncleanness; deterring men from such acts of impurity as were a scandal to the Christian profession, by such penalties, temporal and spiritual, as were thought the most proper to be inflicted." [63] The reforming clergyman Jeremy Collier, responding to a

60. Romans 1:26–27.
61. See Crompton, "Myth of Lesbian Impunity," p. 16.
62. One lengthy proclamation was translated in full in an appendix to the *Monthly Chronicle*, July 1730, pp. 49–50. The "Placat" is also translated in Crompton, "Gay Genocide," pp. 86–87. English papers gave much attention to the Dutch persecutions and recorded the hostile reception refugees from the persecution received in England. See, e.g., the *York Courant* for June 9, June 23, July 7, July 28, Sept. 1, and Sept. 8, 1730. The Sept. 8 *York Courant* refers to the pillorying of a Dutch refugee in London.
63. *The Antiquities of the Christian Church* (1708–1722), in *Works*, ed. R. Bingham (Oxford: Oxford University Press, 1855), 6:434.

current of moral conservatism that swept England early in the eighteenth century, made a passionate plea for the enforcement of the law in his essay on "Whoredom" in 1720: "This Wickedness is Felony, without Benefit of Clergy, by our *Statutes*. And in ancient Times, these Criminals were burnt by the Common Law. Indeed, such Monsters ought to be the Detestation of Mankind, pursued by Justice, and exterminated the Earth."[64] The willingness of Christians to kill homosexuals in the name of morality was often cited as proof of the superiority of Christianity over the religions it had superseded. In 1795, the Scottish divine James Macknight, commenting on Romans 1:26–27 in a new translation of Paul's epistles, wrote: "The Gospel, by its Divine light, hath led the nations to correct their civil laws; so that in every Christian country these enormities are prohibited, and when discovered are punished with the greatest severity. The Gospel, therefore, hath made us far more virtuous than the most enlightened and most polished of the Heathen nations were formerly."[65]

How religious scruples worked in private life can be seen from the journals of Samuel Johnson's friend, Hester Thrale. Thrale was a cultivated literary woman, witty and warm-hearted—except where homosexuals were concerned. Her love of gossip has preserved a surprising amount of information about how gay men were perceived in a pious, conservative English household. A few months before the outbreak of the French Revolution, she was moved to philosophize: "Nature does get strangely out of Fashion sure enough: One hears of Things now, fit for the Pens of Petronius only, or Juvenal to record and satyrize: The Queen of France is at the Head of a Set of Monsters call'd by each other *Sapphists*, who boast her Example; and

---

64. *Essays upon Several Moral Subjects*, 3rd ed. (London: George Strahan, 1720), p. 154.

65. *A New Literal Translation from the Original Greek of All the Apostolical Epistles* (Edinburgh: James Macknight, 1795), 1:160.

deserve to be thrown with the *He* Demons that haunt each
other likewise, into Mount Vesuvius."⁶⁶ When a preacher
at St. Asaph's ventured the opinion that "the Vices of the
Ancients were *unknown* to Modern Times," Thrale reacted
with patronizing indignation to his naïveté: "poor Dear
Man!" "'Tis now grown common to suspect Impossibilities—(such I think 'em)—whenever two Ladies live
too much together; the Queen of France was all along accused, so was Raucoux the famous Actress of the Paris
Stage: & 'tis a Joke in London now to say such a one visits
Mrs. Damer."⁶⁷ The actress Sarah Siddons had confided to
her that her sister "was in personal Danger once from a female Fiend of this Sort." "Bath is a Cage of these unclean
Birds."⁶⁸ Male acquaintances with mannerisms were also
suspect; in private discourse Thrale and her friends referred to sodomites as "Finger twirlers."⁶⁹ She noted the
effeminacy of the dramatist Richard Cumberland and the
"luscious fondness" in his descriptions of his heroes, a
quality she also saw in the writings of William Beckford,
whom she identified, *tout court*, as "a Professor of
Paederasty."⁷⁰ Thrale also joked about the sentencing of
Captain Jones and criticized Gibbon's comments on Justinian's laws as too lenient in their tendency.⁷¹

It is especially interesting to see her reaction to homosexuality in a man she loved and appreciated. In January
1794, she reported (prematurely) that George James had
been guillotined in Britanny and that Neddy Onslow
had been massacred in Paris. Both men were homosexuals

66. April 1, 1789, *Thraliana: The Diary of Mrs. Hester Lynch Thrale,
1776–1809*, ed. Katharine C. Balderston, 2nd ed. (Oxford: Clarendon
Press, 1951), 1:740.

67. December 9, 1975, in ibid., 2:949. "Raucoux" is an error for
"Raucourt," the famous tragedienne.

68. Ibid.

69. March 29, 1794, in ibid., p. 875n.

70. November 1796, in ibid., p. 969.

71. March-April 1778, in ibid., 1:246; and December 9, 1795, in ibid.,
2:948.

who had fled to France: James, a painter, had been her particular friend. Given her strong opposition to the Revolution, one might expect some sympathy for its victims, but
Hester Thrale merely remarks: "See how Vengeance does
pursue the Guilty!!!"[72] About a year later she returned to
the subject of James in a passage that mingled personal affection and moral animosity:

> Death of two Friends! oh how unlike each other! put every-
> thing else out of my Head. Venerable, virtuous, pious, ex-
> emplary Mr. Hutton, elegant, sprightly, chearful, charming
> Mr. James. They both loved *me* exceedingly—'twas all they
> had in common—but humanity: they both contributed to
> sweeten *my* Existence . . . who will ever hope to equal the ex-
> cellence of one, the social Gayety of the other? Had not his
> atrocious Vice forced him to hide from public Notoriety—
> James must have been actually the delight of every Circle
> where Pleasure is sought in the Company of airy good humour,
> & elegant Hilarity . . . *Poor* Fellow! now perished almost for
> Want in a french Prison, where Debts had driven and Preju-
> dice [i.e., political prejudice] confined him: for those he lived
> among there did not—I dare say—detest his odious Propen-
> sity—as much as those who drove him from Society in England
> did; probably not at all; and as to Politics, he was Democrate
> enough I believe, but Heaven pursues such horrid Violation of
> its Laws with Vengeance first or last.[73]

Hester Thrale's remarks illustrate how much the English
prided themselves on maintaining a sterner sexual morality than the French, above all, with respect to homosexuality. By 1794, of course, the Revolution was well into its
radical phase, and the subsequent outbreak of war left England isolated from the Continent for a generation. Parliament was moved to follow neither the new liberal *Code
pénal de la Révolution Française*, promulgated in 1791, which
decriminalized sodomy, nor the Napoleonic Code of 1810,
which preserved this reform and eventually set the standard for most of Europe. But to the English, these changes

72. January 25, 1794, in ibid., 2:868.
73. May 11, 1795, in ibid., pp. 926–27.

in the law appeared only as another example of the way French immorality went hand in hand with French infidelity, which now replaced French Catholicism as a threat. Wartime fears intensified the demand for social discipline. Arthur Gilbert has explained the unusually harsh treatment of homosexuals in England during the period 1805–1815 as due to the exacerbated tensions and hysteria of war.[74] With respect to hangings in the navy, which were indisputably more frequent during the war years, this was no doubt the case. But though the war certainly made things worse, such an explanation fails to take into account the strong animosity toward homosexuals that existed before military hostilities began. Then again, after Waterloo, executions continued at the same average rate (about two a year) for another two decades. During the period 1805–1835, when the annual number of executions for all crimes dropped from about seventy to about thirty, sodomy was the only crime for which the number of hangings remained more or less constant.[75]

It took Bentham's distinguished mind to understand, even in his own day, that the homophobia behind this policy was itself a social phenomenon that required explanation. While writers like Swift, Defoe, Collier, Smollett, and Gibbon simply assumed that homosexuality was an abomination from which all men would instinctively recoil in horror, Bentham felt it was hostility *to* homosexuals that challenged analysis. Such a view put him some two centuries ahead of his contemporaries. When we consider that he was the first social scientist to perceive the problem, his grasp of the issues still seems remarkably broad and suggestive. Though one might say, without exaggeration, that

74.   "Sexual Deviance and Disaster During the Napoleonic Wars," *Albion* 9 (1977):98–113.

75.   Radzinowicz, *Movement for Reform*, p. 153, for the period 1805–1810; for the period 1832–1835, see Leon Radzinowicz, *Grappling for Control*, Vol. 4 of *A History of English Criminal Law and Its Administration from 1750* (London: Stevens & Sons, 1968), p. 309.

the question obsessed him for half a century, his fullest treatment of homophobia appears in his notes of 1814–1816 where a score of pages are devoted to it. At this point, it may be appropriate to depart from strict chronology and draw together his ideas on the subject from manuscripts written at widely different dates.

To begin with, Bentham was fully aware of the difference Christianity had made in European morals. On two occasions he enumerates famous Greeks and Romans who might have faced penalties in postclassical times. "What would have become," he asks rhetorically, "of Aristides, Solon, Themistocles, Harmodius and Aristogiton, Xenophon, Cato, Socrates, Titus—the delight of Mankind, Cicero, Pliny, Trajan, Adrian &c., &c.—these idols of their Country and ornaments of human Nature? They would have *perished on your Gibbets.*"[76] The fall of classical civilization and the rise of medieval theology had completely changed the moral climate of Europe, a fact he notes with some bitterness. The blame, he wrote, lay with "a cluster of barbarians, pushed by Priests worse than blind as laboured Error is worse than Ignorance."[77]

In 1814 Bentham set out systematically to analyze in detail what he thought lay behind the new attitudes. The ascetic side of religion, he conjectured, had grown out of the superstitious idea that sacrifice was necessary to appease and bribe an irascible deity. Fear and hope led men at first to sacrifice food to the gods. From this they went on to sacrifice or forego other sources of pleasure (especially sexual pleasure) and then to the sacrifice, as victims, of men and women who partook of pleasures the majority themselves did not favor.[78] This had the double advantage of propitiating God and ridding the world of people who were unpopular because their tastes differed from their neighbors'.

76. "Nonconformity," box 74a, folio 7.
77. "Code Penal," April 22, 1814, box 74a, folios 106–07.
78. April 22, 1814, box 74a, folio 108.

Moses (to whom Bentham, ignorant of the more advanced biblical scholarship of his day, ascribed the authorship of the Pentateuch) had, he thought, converted the idea of physical impurity into moral impurity and by this illegitimate equation of "filth" with "vice" gave a sanction to the punishment of harmless forms of sexual behavior.[79] Such a proliferation of legal taboos, he suggested presciently, immensely strengthened the hands both of priestly and secular rulers: "The more extensive and, above all, the more indefinite the system of penal law, the more transgressions on the part of the subject many; the more the transgressions, the more fear; the more fear in the breasts of the subject many the more power in the hands of the ruling few. When the people are in a shivering fit, the physician of their souls is absolute."[80] Bentham did, however, make a distinction between the religion of Jesus and what he perceived as the asceticism of Moses and Paul:

> On this whole field in which Moses legislates with such diversified minuteness and such impassioned asperity, Jesus is altogether silent. Jesus from whose lips not a syllable favourable to ascetic self-denial is by any of biographers represented as having ever issued . . . Jesus has on the whole field of sexual irregularity preserved an uninterrupted silence. Jesus was one person, Paul was another. The religion of Jesus was one thing, the religion of Paul another; where Jesus had been silent, Paul was vehement.[81]

In the case of the "pleasures of the table," Protestants no longer make the eating of forbidden foods a moral issue; men may exercise this faculty for pleasure within limits short of excesses that injure health. In the case of the "pleasures of the bed," it is different. Both Protestants and Catholics observe the old prohibitions without asking what real harm these outlawed pleasures do.[82]

79.   April 20, 1814, box 74a, folio 103. See C. K. Ogden's transcriptions in his edition of *Theory of Legislation* (London: Kegan Paul, Trench, Trubner, 1931), pp. 496–97.
80.   April 20, 1814, box 74a, folio 103.
81.   "Nonconformity," box 74a, folio 104.
82.   "Not Paul but Jesus," December 1818, box 161b, folios 251–56.

Bentham, of course, was quite aware that ascetic tendencies in European morals had secular as well as religious roots. He thought that many of the traditional negative attitudes toward pleasure in general and sexual pleasure in particular could be traced to the kind of "philosophical pride" that characterized moralists like the Stoics, who, in his point of view, were not far from the Pharisees in their pretenses. To many, the thought that "I am not as other men are" is a gratifying one, and ascetic styles of life have been the basis of social prestige in many ages.[83] As a philosopher devoted to championing the pleasure principle over asceticism, Bentham was appalled at what he saw as a needless and perverse tendency to puritanism in the human race.

Bentham imagined that some prejudice against homosexuals might arise from simple envy on the part of men and women unable to share their pleasures.[84] A more potent temptation to moralists, however, was the chance to gain a reputation for virtue by condemning sins they were free from and not to be suspected of. Several times he quotes Samuel Butler's couplet from *Hudibras* about those who

Compound for sins they are inclined to,
By damning those they have no mind to.[85]

But this was a reputation for virtue cheaply won and as open to profligates as to saints. Occasionally, Bentham

83.   Bentham noted, however, that though moral philosophers of the Greco-Roman period often tended toward asceticism, they did not show any special animus against homosexuality per se:

In the past, among the philosophic ascetics, in a word, among *the Stoicks*, . . . pleasure belonging to this appetite and clothed in these irregular forms seems scarcely to have been distinguished from the crowd of other pleasures. Contempt, rather than hatred, contempt and that of but a moderate degree seems to have been the strongest moral feeling they displayed in such matters. ("Code Penal," April 22, 1814, box 74a, folio 111)

84.   April 19, 1814, box 74a, folio 99.
85.   See "Nonconformity," box 73, folio 90; "Code Penal," July 31, 1816, box 74a, folio 222; "Sextus," August-September 1817, box 161a, folio 17.

thinks, men with homosexual tendencies may decry the "vice" in order to avoid suspicion.[86] Bentham repeatedly cites, with some indignation, the case of James I, who, though passionately attracted to handsome young men, nevertheless, in his *Basilikon Doron*, ostentatiously listed sodomy as one of the half-dozen capital crimes that a king should never on any account pardon.[87]

Bentham also understands that hatred for another may rest on nothing more tangible than a difference in preferences. In 1785, he wrote: "As in so many other cases the disposition to punish seems to have had no other ground than the antipathy with which the persons who had punishment at their disposal regarded the offender."[88] "Look the world over, we shall find that differences in point of taste and opinion are grounds of animosity as frequent and as violent as any opposition in point of interest."[89] Antipathy leads men to feel justified in finding pleasure in the suffering of others—a highly illicit gratification when the behavior punished causes no real mischief. But if emotional antipathy were adequate justification for inflicting pain on others, this would surely be enough to warrant the destruction of religious heretics: "I see not, I must confess, how a Protestant, or any person who should be for looking upon this ground as a sufficient ground for burning paederasts, could with consistency condemn the Spanish for burning Moors or the Portuguese for burning Jews: for no paederast can be more odious to a person of unpolluted taste than a Moor is to a Spaniard or a Jew to an orthodox Portuguese."[90]

86.   "Code Penal," April 1814, box 74a, folio 118.
87.   See James I, *Political Works*, ed. Charles Howard McIlwain (Cambridge: Harvard University Press, 1918). James advised his son Prince Henry: "Some horrible crimes . . . yee are bound in conscience neuer to forgive: such as Witch-craft, wilfull murther, Incest, . . . Sodomie, poisoning, and false coine" (p. 20).
88.   Louis Crompton, ed., "Jeremy Bentham's Essay on 'Paederasty,' Part 2," *Journal of Homosexuality* 4 (1978):94.
89.   Ibid.
90.   Ibid., p. 98.

Bentham's interest in the nature and causes of homophobia was wide-ranging. His analysis includes not only what may be called the primary causes of intolerance but also those secondary channels through which antipathy was popularly communicated. Though Bentham's literary background was not exceptionally broad, it was wide enough for him to instance works of English, French, and German fiction, which, by their patently prejudiced references to relations between men, had fed, in his view, the fires of popular hostility:

> Not inconsiderable is the number of Novels and other works having amusement for their object, in which the danger of loss by the introduction of a topic which no person charged with the care of a youth of either sex would naturally expose to the view of a pupil . . . has not been sufficient to let slip the occasion of giving vent and increase to the popular antipathy of which these propensities are the object.[91]

Bentham gives as examples the beating of a homosexual in *Joseph Andrews* (1742),[92] the Lord Strutwell episode in Chapter 51 of *Roderick Random* (1748),[93] and the horror expressed in Christoph Wieland's *Agathon* (1773) by the hero, a native of ancient Greece, when he is solicited by a pagan priest—a horror "as well adapted to the time and place at which the story was written as ill-suited to that in which the scene is laid."[94] Bentham also mentions a pseudo-Oriental tale,

91.   September 3, 1816(?), box 74, folio 95.
92.   Bentham remarks: "In Fielding's Life of Joseph Andrews, by one of the dramatis personae a similar proposal is made to the suppositious brother of the virtuous Pamela. He comes not off so cheaply as the Scottish Earl: he gets a good drubbing for his pains" (ibid.). I have not been able to identify such an episode in the novel.
93.   Bentham adds an interesting note that suggests that Smollett had in mind a particular model in creating Strutwell: "Much about the time when this novel was first published a Scotch Earl was detected in the consummation of an amour after the manner of Tiberius with two of his servants at the same time. The affair getting around[?], he found himself under the obligation of going off to the Continent where at the close of a long life he died not many years since." In the margin Bentham identifies the aristocrat as "Earl Tylney" (ibid.).
94.   Christoph Martin Wieland's *Agathon* was a widely read romance

written in French, in which "some horrible catastrophe is brought to view" of which "the sort of propensity here in question is the cause."[95] In another note, a year later, he again lists the same works, now identifying the Oriental collection as the *Peruvian Tales*, and deplores the influence of their homophobic episodes.[96]

Nevertheless, the influence of these authors was trifling compared with the press in England. It was seemingly impossible for a newspaper or magazine to report an arrest or a trial for sodomy without laying down a barrage of scurrilous epithets. Bentham pointed out how much this must exacerbate sentiment and inhibit thoughtful discussion of the subject:

> In all other parts of the field of morality—public and established religion out of the question—the press has for this century or more been practically free. But, in effect, upon this it neither is nor ever has been practically free. A battery of grapeshot composed of all the expressions of abhorrence that language has given or can give birth to is by each newspaper and every other periodical kept continually playing upon this ground. No wonder that down to this instant no man with the torch of reason in his hand should have found nerve to set foot

with a Greek setting. Shelley, like Bentham, complained of Wieland's misrepresentation of Greek life in his "Discourse on the Manners of the Antient Greeks." In Book VII, chap. 2, of vol. 2, Agathon's mentor, Theogiton, a priest of Apollo, disguises himself as the god in a nocturnal vision and tries to seduce him. Agathon then "reproached him for his wickedness with a spirit of indignation, which enabled me to break off all connection with him" (*The History of Agathon* [London: C. Heydinger, 1773], 2:156).

95.   At this point (folio 95) the work is vaguely described as "one of the numerous European imitations which the original Oriental work known by the name of the Arabian Nights Entertainments has produced—the Persian Tales is it not?" In "Sextus" (box 161a, folio 18), Bentham identified the stories as by "Madam Graffigny, or who ever else was the author of the Peruvian Tales." But Madame Graffigny's work was the *Lettres d'une Péruvienne* (1747); the *Peruvian Tales* were by Thomas Gueulette. An English version by Samuel Humphreys appeared in 1734. It was republished in 1764 and 1786 and was included in *Walker's British Classics* in 1817.

96.   "Sextus," box 161a, folio 18.

on it. Miscreant! You are one of them then! Such are the thanks
he would receive, such the bad thanks which any man [would
receive] who should attempt to carry upon this part of the field
of morality those lights to which all other parts are open.[97]

But how to combat the staunch conviction held in England that a sexual relation between men was the crime of
crimes? Bentham was appalled by the intensity of feeling
he perceived but baffled as to how to deal with it. He saw
the problem as urgent though he hardly guessed its extent
since he held the common pre-Kinsey view that homosexual behavior was rare. On this point he ventured the speculation that relations between men were, in his day, common in Rome, not so common in Paris, and less common
still in London.[98] This being the case, he did not realize
how widespread the suffering must have been that flowed
from England's refusal to tolerate her homosexual sons and
daughters. It did not occur to him or his contemporaries
that the invisibility of England's gay minority was the result, not of its small size—there is no reason to believe it
was actually smaller than in other countries—but of the
high level of public feeling.

Most of Bentham's voluminous writings on homosexuality are in the form of unorganized notes and jottings. In
1785, however, he produced a coherent and polished essay
of some sixty folio pages. What moved him to put his
thoughts together at this point we can only conjecture. Perhaps it was the strong movement toward law reform then
agitating Europe and sending ripples to England. Perhaps
it was the sensational and well-publicized scandal that
had overwhelmed William Beckford the year before and
sent that literary millionaire into exile; Bentham had met

97. "Code Penal," March 24, 1816(?), box 74a, folio 168.
98.   Jeremy Bentham, "Offences Against One's Self: Paederasty, Part
1," *Journal of Homosexuality* 3 (1978):392. These estimates probably reflected the views of most educated Europeans of Bentham's day. In the
eighteenth century, Rome was regarded as the "gay capital" of Europe,
just as Florence had been in the Renaissance, and as Berlin and Amster-
dam were to be, respectively, in the pre- and post-Hitler eras.

Beckford in 1780, when his entertainments were the height of fashion, and had admired his harpsichord playing. We do know that a less well-publicized scandal, which took place a few years before Beckford's and involved another member of Parliament, had made a lasting impression on him. Forty years later he wrote to Beckford about this episode:

> The case of poor Sir William Meredith has never been out of [my] mind: what an excellent Statesman that man was: how well disposed, and how well qualified, to render in various ways important service to his country and mankind; and how he was driven into exile and for no other cause than his having partaken of gratifications, the innoxiousness of which it is one main business of this work in question to demonstrate.[99]

Meredith, like Bentham, had had a serious interest in law reform.[100] But whatever the immediate incentive, the manuscript of Bentham's essay all too clearly reveals the pains it cost him. He began with eight pages of miscellaneous paragraphs, the substance of which is indicated by the marginal headings he added—"Distinction between physical impurity and moral," "Antipathy no sufficient warrant" (i.e., for punishment), "Whether it is an affront to God?," "God's burning Sodom—whether a sufficient warrant"

---

99. "Sextus," box 161a, folio 14. "Sextus" was, in fact, a prospectus addressed to Beckford; see p. 270.

100. The *Dictionary of National Biography* (*DNB*), which began publication in 1882, is often evasive or obfuscatory in its treatment of homosexuals. Sometimes scholars or legislators famous in their time are totally omitted, as in the case of the early nineteenth-century humanitarian and parliamentary reformer, Henry Grey Bennett. More often, entries simply make no mention of ostracism or exile, as with William Beckford, Richard Heber, the bibliophile, or Byron's school friend, William Bankes. The *DNB* does, however, provide some facts about Meredith's life. He was born about 1725 and sat in Parliament from 1754 to 1780, holding posts as a lord of the admiralty and privy councilor. He tried to abolish the subscription of the Thirty-Nine Articles required at Oxford and Cambridge and campaigned energetically against the death penalty. The *DNB* is vague about the end of his career. It says only that he "withdrew from public life" in 1780 and "dropped into obscurity." The latter detail, with the fact that he died abroad in France in 1790, suggests some scandal.

(a brilliant counterargument to Blackstone's use of Genesis 19), and "Zeal shewn against it in the English Marine Law." Apropos of the last, he remarked: "Of all the offenses of which a man in the maritime service can be guilty . . . this is the only one which it was thought necessary to exclude from mercy. The safety of the fleet and of the Empire were in the eyes of the legislator objects of inferior account in comparison with the preservation of a sailor's chastity." [101]

Despite such sallies—written one imagines less with an eye to publication than in an effort to keep a personal sense of sanity and proportion—the strain shows. Bentham's hand, though generally difficult to the point of illegibility as a result of the haste with which his pen flew across the page, is generally even and regular. But at this point, before beginning his formal essay, Bentham breaks off to produce a page of crowded, irregular, and almost miniscule notes, in which he expresses his anxieties. "To other subjects," he writes, "it is expected that you sit down cool: but on this subject if you let it be seen that you have not sat down in a rage you have *given judgment against* yourself at once." Once again he is assailed by his fears of a decade earlier: "I am ashamed to own that I have often hesitated whether for the sake of the interests of humanity I should expose my personal interest so much to hazard as it must be exposed to by the free discussion of a subject of this nature." Then he adds, rather wistfully: "At any rate when I am dead mankind will be the better for it." Did Bentham mean that he intended his essay not to appear until after his death, or was he merely making a pessimistic estimate of the length of time it would take for his ideas to be accepted in England? Looking realistically at the facts, he lamented: "There is a kind of punishment annexed to the offence of treating [this crime] with any sort of temper, and that one of the most formidable that a man can be sub-

101.   Crompton, ed., "Jeremy Bentham's Essay on 'Paederasty,' Part 2," p. 106.

jected to, the punishment of being suspected at least, if not accused, of a propensity to committ it." Finally, his fear is mixed with a kind of helpless indignation: "When a man attempts to [touch] this subject it is with a halter about his neck. On this subject a man may indulge his spleen without controul. Cruelty and intolerance, the most odious and most mischievous passions in human nature, screen themselves behind a mask of virtue." In this instance, men "make a merit of discarding all reason and all humanity."[102]

Bentham's rhetorical strategy in his essay is perhaps a measure of his despair. Obviously, what Bentham was facing in England was crude hate and rancorous religious prejudice. But instead of addressing these issues, he replies instead to contemporary objections to homosexual behavior that seemed to him to have at least some measure of rationality. In essence, his appeal is not to the hostile many but to the enlightened few who may be open-minded. (Perhaps he meant this essay, like some of his other works, to circulate in French on the Continent.) Consequently, he limits himself to refuting three arguments commonly used against homosexuality, arguments which he thought would indeed, if valid, justify sanctions from a utilitarian point of view. These are: (1) Voltaire's opinion that homosexuality "would destroy mankind if it were general," (2) Montesquieu's contention that "it gives to one sex the weaknesses of the other," which Bentham interprets as meaning that homosexuality enervates men and weakens the power of the state to resist enemies, and (3) the idea that male homosexuality threatens the status of women in society.

Discounting the threat to population, Bentham argues that only a tiny fraction of heterosexual couplings lead to childbirth. With this overplus of procreative energy, population is not likely to suffer if part is diverted to male relations. Ancient Greece, where they were common, suffered

102. Louis Crompton, "Jeremy Bentham's Essay on 'Paederasty': An Introduction," *Journal of Homosexuality* 3 (1978): 384–85.

from over- rather than underpopulation and, despite de-
pleting wars, was repeatedly forced to send an excess out
to found colonies. Paradoxically, he also maintains that by
diverting men from the seduction of women, relations
between males lessen the number of women degraded
into the prostitute class, a notoriously infertile one, and
may thereby actually arrest a tendency that diminishes
population.[103]

To refute Montesquieu, Bentham appeals to what we
know of the manners of classical civilization:

> In Athens and in ancient Rome in the most flourishing periods
> of the history of those capitals, regular intercourse between
> the sexes was scarcely much more common. It was upon the
> same footing throughout Greece: everybody practised it; no-
> body was ashamed of it. They might be ashamed of what they
> looked upon as an excess in it, or they might be ashamed of it
> as a weakness, as a propensity that had a tendency to distract
> men from more worthy and important occupations, just as a
> man with us might be ashamed of excess or weakness in his
> love for women.[104]

Far from diminishing military prowess, it had strengthened it, as in the case of the famous Theban Band who
fought as pairs of lovers. "Agesilaus and Xenophon, . . .
Themistocles, Aristides, Epaminondas, Alcibiades, Alexander and perhaps the greatest number of the heroes of
Greece were infected with this taste."[105] So were many Romans and the gods of the classical pantheon. Indeed, Montesquieu's concern that homosexuality effeminizes men by
placing them in the role of women hardly makes sense unless we limit it to those who play the passive role in sodomy. But even if we look only at such men, we see that, in
the ancient world, Alcibiades "was not remarkable either
for weakness or for cowardice," Clodius was "one of the
most daring and turbulent spirits in all Rome," and "Julius

103. Bentham, "Offences Against One's Self: Paederasty," pp. 396–98.
104. Ibid., p. 392.
105. Ibid., p. 393.

Caesar was looked upon as a man of tolerable courage in his day, notwithstanding the complaisance he showed in his youth to the King of Bithynia, Nicomedes." [106]

Of all the apparently rational objections to male homosexuality, Bentham treats most seriously the idea that it produced indifference to women and thereby robbed them of their rights. This is an idea that seems strange to us. Nowadays, women and homosexuals tend to make common cause politically on the ground that both suffer from invidious sex-role stereotyping. The argument had, however, a great vogue in the eighteenth century when it appears in a remarkably wide range of contexts, from philosophy to pornography. John Cleland, for instance, has Fanny Hill, his prostitute-heroine, complain that "this practice took away not only our own living, but something from all womankind which nature intended them to have." [107] Sometimes, as formulated by male writers with a heterosexual bias, the argument seems like nothing more than the voice of wounded pride, offended that its pleasures are not appreciated by others.

The most popular compendium of English statutes in Bentham's day, Matthew Bacon's *New Abridgement of the Law*, which went through seven editions between 1736 and 1832, eschewed Blackstone's theological argument for an apparently utilitarian rationale based on this idea:

> If any crime deserve to be punished in a more exemplary manner this does. Other crimes are prejudicial to society; but this strikes at the being thereof: it being seldom known that a person who has been guilty of abusing his generative faculty so unnaturally has afterwards a proper regard for women.
>
> From that indifference to women, so remarkable in men of this depraved appetite, it may fairly be concluded that they are cursed with insensibility to the most extatic pleasure which human nature is in the present state capable of enjoying.

106. Ibid., p. 395.
107. *Memoirs of Fanny Hill* (Privately printed, Kamashastra Society, 1907), p. 246.

It seems a very just punishment that such wretches should
be deprived of all taste for an enjoyment upon which they did
not set a proper value; and the continuation of an impious disposition, which then might have been transmitted to their children, if they had any, may be thereby prevented.[108]

But if Bacon seems to suggest that homosexuals should be
punished merely for failing to appreciate heterosexual
pleasures, the "neglect of women" argument was, nevertheless, held by thinkers who were thoughtful and committed feminists. Shelley, for example, was later to use it in
his "Discourse on the Manners of the Antient Greeks." It
was, no doubt, because the argument had weight in the
eyes of social theorists sincerely concerned for the rights of
women that Bentham chose to treat it seriously and at
length.

Bentham admits that pederasty may compete with pre-
or extramarital heterosexual relations, but he does not
think it discourages men from marrying. Only matrimony
can gratify the desire for children, for family alliances, and
for lifelong companionship. The love of boys is notoriously
brief—it is notable that Bentham thinks of homosexuality
here only in terms of man-boy relations—and does not
outlive the short term of adolescent beauty. In Greece, men
who had pederastic affairs regularly married. In Rome, the
population did eventually decline, but this was because
men preferred "the convenience of a transient connection
to the expense and hazard of a lasting one."[109] Philosophical Europe had been much struck by the discovery of the
paradise of Tahiti in 1767. But in Tahiti, where both kinds
of sexuality are freely indulged, women are by no means
neglected. (Elsewhere, Bentham was to note that the low
status of women in Moslem countries was not due to
the homosexuality common in these lands but to male jeal-

---

108.   7th ed., ed. C. E. Dodd (London: J. & W. T. Clarke et al., 1832),
p. 374.
109.   Bentham, "Offences Against One's Self: Paederasty," p. 401.

ousy, which insisted on sequestration.)[110] Classical poets,
such as Virgil and Horace, were in fact bisexual, the common pattern of their day. Though men call sodomites "misogynists," the term is really more appropriate to religious
celibates. However, it is understandable if some men do indeed develop an aversion to women as a result of being
persecuted on their behalf: "It would not be wonderful if
the miserable pederast should look upon every woman as
a merciless creditor at whose suit he is in continual danger
of being consigned not to a prison only but to the gallows
or the stake." "A ribbon or ringlet is a much more suitable
and not less powerful tie to bind a lover than the hang-
man's rope of the executioner."[111]

Bentham must have known that such arguments would
cut little ice with his countrymen. His rational rebuttals
were not likely to touch biases so deep and emotional as
the average Englishman's and Englishwoman's. Many nations have ascribed native "vices" to foreign influences,
sexual "vices" most of all. Few, however, have carried the
tendency quite so far as the English did with homosexuality. The passion for ascribing it to a Continental source
can be traced back at least as far as the fourteenth century.
In 1376, members of the Parliament of Edward III had accused Italian merchants of introducing the practice into England. Edward Coke treated this theory seriously in his *Institutes*, even to the point of (falsely) deriving the legal term
buggery from an Italian root.[112] This need to find a Mediter-

110.   "Not Paul but Jesus," January 3, 1818, box 161b, folio 285.
111.   Crompton, ed., "Jeremy Bentham's Essay on 'Paederasty,' Part
2," p. 107.
112.   "Of Buggery or Sodomy," in *Third Part of the Institutes of the Laws
of England* (London: E. & R. Brooke, 1797), chap. 10, p. 58. The Anglo-
French of fourteenth-century parliamentary documents is idiosyncratic,
but the relevant passage in the Rolls of Parliament might be approxi-
mately construed as follows:

The Commons beg that all the Lombards who follow no other calling but that of
merchants [Brokours] be made to leave the country. . . . They are wicked usu-

ranean origin for same-sex relations in England moved
Bentham to ridicule:

> The same Jurist, very well read in the Rolls of Parliament, but
> very ill read in the great Book of Human Nature, informs us
> upon the authority of those Rolls, that this vice was brought
> into England by the Lombards. I had as a lief have said, that
> the use of women was brought in by the Lombards, as if the
> same nature which first taught it to the people of one country,
> was not able to teach it afterwards to the people of another. So
> strong is the madness for running round in the circle of ety-
> mology, both for words & manners, that reasoners like Dr. Coke
> would fetch over instruction in this mystery upon rafts from
> Florida or Mexico if they did not hear by good luck of its being
> practised a little nearer.[113]

Yet Bentham, for all his perspicuity, failed to understand
how English xenophobia intensified English feelings about
sodomy. In particular, he failed to see its peculiar connection with English Protestantism. The national tendency to
what may be called moral chauvinism had been greatly intensified by the Reformation: the temptation to reaffirm
the traditional association of sodomy with Italy was too
powerful for Protestant polemicists to resist. For instance,
the violently anti-Catholic bishop, John Bale, made much
of the point in a satire he concocted in 1538, under the title
*A Comedge, Concernynge Thre Lawes, of Nature, Moyses, and
Christ, Corrupted by the Sodomytes, Pharysies, and Papistes
Most Wicked*. The allegorical figure of "Sodomismus," in
the guise of a monk, declares: "I dwelt amonge the Sodomytes, / The Beniamytes, and Madyanytes, / And nowe
the popysshe hypocrytes / Embrace me every where."[114]
Henry VIII used accusations of sodomy to counter popular

---

rers and employ all the subtle wiles of such men. . . . They have now lately introduced into the land a very horrible vice which is not to be named, because of
which the Realm cannot fail to be destroyed if swift[?] punishment be not or-
dained. (*Rotuli Parliamentorum . . . Tempore Edwardi R. III*, vol. 2 [1767], 332)

113.   "Nonconformity," box 73, folio 91.
114.   (London: Thomas Colwell, 1562), p. [16].

support for the monasteries he meant to pillage.[115] In his satire Bale indicts "Pope July" (Julius II) as a debaucher of boys. John Donne endorsed the tradition by rhyming "sodomy" and "Italy" in his second satire, a license that appealed strongly to later poets. Thus, Daniel Defoe, assigning various vices to various realms in *The True-Born Englishman* (1701), could write:

Lust chose the torrid zone of Italy,
Where blood ferments in rapes and sodomy.[116]

This faith in the absolute foreignness of same-sex attractions inevitably became an argument for punishing them with special harshness. A generation after Defoe, the poetaster John Armstrong wrote an incongruous poem called *The Oeconomy of Love*, in which he delivered Ovidian advice in Miltonic measures. At the end of his manual on seduction he warned against "unnatural pleasures":

Britons, for shame! Be Male and Female still.
Banish this foreign Vice; it grows not here,
It dies, neglected; and in Clime so chaste
Cannot but by forc'd Cultivation thrive.
So cultivated swells the more our Shame,
The more our Guilt. And shall not greater Guilt
Meet greater Punishment and heavier Doom?[117]

115.   In 1543 Henry wrote to Earl Arran, Regent of Scotland, advising him to send commissioners "most secretly and groundly to examine all the religious of their conversation and behaviour in their livings, whereby if it be well handled, he shall get knowledge of all their abominations," as a first step toward confiscating monastic wealth in that country (Dom David Knowles, *The Religious Orders in England*, vol. 3 [Cambridge: Cambridge University Press, 1959], 204). Henry's own commissioners of 1535 compiled the *Compendium Compertorum*, which listed 181 cases of "sodomy"; it is unclear how many of these cases referred to homosexuality and how many to other sex acts (ibid., pp. 296–97). Such information gave Thomas Cromwell and others interested in suppressing the monasteries a powerful weapon.
116.   *The Novels and Miscellaneous Works of Daniel De Foe*, ed. Walter Scott (Oxford: Thomas Tegg, 1841), 20:12.
117.   (London: T. Cooper, 1736), p. 42. I am indebted to Robert F. Oaks for this reference.

Armstrong's point was that a tolerant England would collectively merit a fate worse than Sodom; it was an easy step from this to justifying exemplary punishment for the individual who strayed so far from the national norm. Tobias Smollett, with his characteristic mixture of spleen and prejudice, added another voice to the chorus. His first published work was a verse satire called "Advice," a substantial portion of which was devoted to attacking homosexuals under real or invented names. In *Roderick Random*, inveighing against this "spurious and sordid desire" as personified in Lord Strutwell, he put four lines from his own diatribe into the mouth of his hero:

> Eternal infamy the wretch confound
> Who planted first that vice on British ground!
> A vice, that 'spite of sense and nature reigns,
> And poisons genial love, and manhood stains![118]

This popular combination of xeno- and homophobia reached its zenith in a vitriolic anonymous pamphlet entitled *Satan's Harvest Home*, published in London in 1749. The writer was particularly incensed at the fashion of men kissing in the streets, a custom he denounced for its sodomitical tendencies:

> Damn'd *Fashion*! Imported from *Italy* amidst a Train of other *unnatural Vices*. Have we not *Sins* enough of our own, but we must eke 'em out with those of *Foreign Nations*, to fill up the Cup of our Abominations, and make us yet more ripe for *Divine* Vengeance?
>
> 'Till of late years, *Sodomy* was a *Sin* in a manner unheard of in these Nations; and indeed, one would think that where there are such *Angelic Women*, so foul a Sin should never enter into Imagination: On the contrary, our *Sessions-Papers* are frequently stained with *Crimes* of these *beastly Wretches*; and though many have been made an Example of, yet we have too

118. "Advice: A Satire" (1746), in *The Works of Tobias Smollett* (Westminster: Archibald Constable, 1901), 12:7; *The Adventures of Roderick Random*, ed. Paul-Gabriel Boucé (Oxford: Oxford University Press, 1979), pp. 310–11. The first line varies slightly in the two versions.

much Reason to fear, that there are Numbers yet undiscov-
er'd, and that this *abominable Practice* gets Ground ev'ry Day.

Instead of the Pillory, I would have the *Stake* be the Punishment of those, who in Contradiction to the Laws of *God* and
Man, to the Order and Course of *Nature*, and to the most
simple principles of *Reason*, preposterously *burn* for each
other, and *leave* the *Fair*, the *charming Sex*, neglected.[119]

The anonymous pamphleteer writes as a robust man of
the world and no doubt hoped to sell his wares by spicing
them with strong condiments. But the level of chauvinism
in Hester Thrale's genteel private journals is quite as high.
Thrale married a music teacher, Gabriel Piozzi, and made a
wedding journey to Italy, an experience that only served
to confirm her convictions about the un-Englishness of
homosexuality:

> Our *Beckfords* & *Bickerstaffs* too run away at least from the origi-
> nal Theatre of their Crimes, & do not keep their Male Mis-
> tresses in Triumph like the Roman Priests & Princes. This Italy
> is indeed a Sink of Sin; and whoever lives long in it, *must* be a
> little tainted. . . . External Rites of Worship here are supposed
> a complete Compensation for the utter Absence of all Moral
> Virtue, & all Sense of honor. England . . . though wickeder
> than one would wish it, & more defective in Faith & Works—I
> verily do believe . . . is the *best* part of Europe to live in, for
> almost every Reason.[120]

Bentham, after the typical fashion of an eighteenth-
century philosopher, tried to account for homophobia in
terms of universal human psychology rather than looking
for causes that were specific, historical, concrete, and local.
Though he was keenly aware of its unusual force in his native land, he did not explain why this trait should have developed so potently in England and to such deadly effect.
This is a surprising oversight in a mind so analytical. Obviously, Bentham failed to understand fully its connection
with xenophobia and with anti-Catholic prejudice. More

119.   (N.p.), p. 51.
120.   June 27, 1786, *Thraliana*, 2:640.

striking was his failure to realize what the punitive traditions of his day owed to a campaign by religious leaders and laymen conducted energetically in the early part of the eighteenth century.

Perhaps his blindness stemmed from the fact that the work of this earlier group—the so-called Society for the Reformation of Manners—had ceased a few years before he was born and later attracted little attention from historians. Yet it was the forces set in motion in the moral-judicial sphere by the Society and nurtured by its powerful later successor that Bentham had to contend with during his long career. The Society for the Reformation of Manners had, in fact, been founded in 1691. It was an alliance of pious Churchmen and like-minded Dissenters, who set aside their political animosities to wage the first important morals campaign since the Puritan Revolution, aimed in effect at countering the freedom of the Restoration period. It received the blessing of several archbishops and found a warrant for its efforts in the curious late-Stuart tradition of royal proclamations against vice, issued first by Charles II, and, later, with more credibility, by Mary II, William III, and Queen Anne. For forty-six years it proved remarkably effective; its published annual reports show that its informers succeeded during that period in prosecuting over 100,000 men and women.[121]

The Society's manifesto of 1694, entitled *Proposals for a National Reformation of Manners*, is a significant document, which social historians seem unaccountably to have overlooked. It throws much light on the mentality of the age. First, the anonymous writer plays on popular fears: an earthquake had devastated Jamaica, tremors had been felt in London, and these are interpreted as divine protests

121. See the summary of the statistics in "Annual Reports, 1715–1738," in the table following p. 254, in Garnet V. Portus's *Caritas Anglicana: or, An Historical Inquiry into Those Religious and Philanthropical Societies That Flourished in England Between the Years 1678 and 1740* (London: A. R. Mowbray, 1912).

against "prophane conduct," that is, against "Swearing,
Cursing, Drunkenness, Revilings, Lasciviousness, Whore-
doms, Riot," and "Blasphemies." England's national destiny, the author proclaims, is under the direct protection of
God: "What *Jerusalem* was of old unto *Judea*, and *Judea* unto
other Nations, in like manner *London* is unto *England* and
England unto CHRISTENDOM. A *City* and a *Nation* more
favoured of God, (and more envied by the Common Ad-
versary) there is not to be found under the whole heav-
ens." [122] Such divine attention, however, was the occasion
for as much apprehension as congratulation. England had
escaped the threats of the Armada and of the Gunpowder
and Popish Plots and had been delivered from James II, but
profane lifestyles may cost it this divine favor. [123] In this
way, public morals were linked in the popular mind both
with anxiety over the nation's fate and with pride in England's success in keeping the papists at bay.

But England had been xenophobic and anti-Catholic for
centuries, during which the death penalty for sodomy was
used sparingly. [124] What caused the change? The *Proposals*
give only the faintest hint in this direction. Near their conclusion the writer advocates "searching out the lurking
Holes of Bawds, Whores and other Filthy Miscreants." [125] In
the early eighteenth century social clubs abounded in London; some of these catered to homosexuals. That the word
miscreants here likely refers to men who frequented such
places is suggested by its common use in this sense in
popular and legal literature. [126] Still, the attack on homosex-

122.   *Proposals for a National Reformation of Manners, . . . to Which Is
Added . . . the Black Roll, Containing the Names and Crimes of Several Hundreds Persons, Who Have Been Prosecuted by the Society, for Whoring, Drunkenness, Sabbath-breaking, &c.* (London: John Dunton, 1694), pp. 8, 2.

123.   The author asks rhetorically how else, apart from divine inter-
vention, one can interpret England's deliverance from these repeated
threats (ibid., p. 3).

124.   The last known hanging was in 1640 when the Bishop of Waterford, John Atherton, was executed in Dublin.

125.   *Proposals for a National Reformation of Manners*, p. 29.

126.   See the quotation from Blackstone (p. 15, above) and Bentham's

uals was at first muted. Perhaps the Society, aware of the rumors current about the sexual orientation of their patron and "deliverer," William III, was hesitant to take up an issue that might have invited ironic ripostes from the Jacobites and Louis XIV.[127] After the succession of Anne, no such inhibition existed, and the Society's chief defender, John Disney, a former magistrate turned clergyman, felt free to campaign against homosexuals in his *Second Essay upon the Execution of the Laws Against Immorality and Prophaneness* (1710). In this treatise he advances sodomy to second place (after blasphemy) among the Society's concerns, invoking the traditional threats of divine vengeance.[128] We have seen how Jeremy Collier, joining the hew and cry of the age, raised his voice to demand the extermination of homosexuals a decade later. Within a few years the tradition of almost a century was set aside. In 1726, through the efforts of informers working for the Society, there were many arrests, and three men were hanged at Tyburn.[129]

The Society for the Reformation of Manners became increasing unpopular as time went by. Its system of infor-

---

use of the term as an epithet in his description of the homophobia of the English press (p. 45, above). The word was very common in early nineteenth-century newspaper accounts. The anonymous annotator of the anonymous poem *Don Leon* refers to "two gangs of miscreants (as they were called when this poem was written)," i.e., ca. 1833 (*Don Leon*, in *A Homosexual Emancipation Miscellany*, p. 91; see also nn. 27 and 56 to *Don Leon*).

127.   Henri Van Der Zee and Barbara Van Der Zee, who speculate about William's homosexuality in *William and Mary* (New York: Knopf, 1973), pp. 422–24, conclude that there likely was a homosexual element in his personality, especially in his relations with Arnold van Keppel, Earl of Albemarle.

128.   "Where we are able to form a Conviction of the horrid Sin of *Sodomy* or *Bestiality*, we should by no means suffer it to escape in any Instance whatsoever: Because this Sin draws down the Judgments of God upon the Nation, where 'tis suffered, in a very particular Manner" (*Second Essay* [London: Joseph Downing, 1710], pp. 206–07). Disney repeatedly makes the point that the whole nation will suffer at the hands of God if immorality is not punished.

129.   See Edward Bristow, *Vice and Vigilance: Purity Movements in Britain Since 1700* (London: Gill & Macmillan, 1977), p. 29. The three men who

mers was resented, its attacks on the pastimes of the poor were seen as discriminatory, its efforts to close brothels led to riots, and two of its agents were killed. Perhaps the hostility of its foes led it more and more to concentrate on the prosecution of sodomy cases as less likely to cause antagonism. In the pillorying of homosexuals, it was possible for rakes, ruffians, and men of religion to unite in expressing their detestation of an unpopular minority who had no public defenders and were themselves silent. The protests of foreign observers, who were shocked by this ferocity, went unheeded. England's claim that its religion was purer than that of Catholic France seemed confirmed by its victories under Marlborough and in the Seven Years' War. Its claim to be superior to France in morality, and especially sexual morality, appeared shakier. The multitude of prostitutes on the streets of London, the high level of illegitimacy and of infanticide, and the adulterous intrigues of the aristocracy could all be interpreted as calling this claim into question. But the hanging, pillorying, and ostracism of homosexuals were incontrovertible facts to which the nation could point to assure itself of its superiority to Catholic Europe in at least one respect. In this way, as in Spain under the Inquisition, intolerance became a badge of virtue and brutality a point of national pride.

It is perhaps not a coincidence that the harsher measures toward homosexuals in England marked the early Hanoverian period and the arrival of a new dynasty. The accession of George I in 1714 symbolized, by the act of Parliament that legalized it, the ultimate triumph of Protestant-

---

were hanged were Gabriel Lawrence, 43, a milkman; William Griffin, 43, an upholsterer; and Thomas Wright, 32, a woolcomber. Accounts of their trials are to be found in *Select Trials at the Sessions-House in the Old-Bailey* (London: James Hodges, 1742), 2:362–69. Griffin, at his trial, mentioned two informers named Willis and Williams, employed by the Society for the Reformation of Manners, who effected the arrests.

ism after the equivocal Tudors and Stuarts. With the relaxa-
tion of severity in Catholic Europe, persecution moved
north to Holland and England in the eighteenth century.
Growing tolerance in Italy and France was seen as striking
proof of Protestantism's claim to moral superiority over
these decadent lands. In England, an ancient xenophobic
tradition, traceable back to the Middle Ages, had at first
linked itself with Italy in the case of the Lombard merchants. Then, with the coming of the Reformation, its basis
ceased to be economic, and antihomosexualism became a
stock ingredient of antipapal propaganda. Though anti-
clerical lawyers reacted against ecclesiastical tradition in
Catholic countries and achieved decriminalization, first in
France in 1791 and, later in Italy and Spain, nevertheless,
Protestant England, Germany, Scandinavia, and the United
States held aloof, regarding such changes as moral backsliding. So in Germany, Catholic Bavaria followed the
Napoleonic Code in 1813 while Protestant Prussia kept its
sodomy law, which was finally imposed on the united
country after 1870. When Hitler came to power, this north-
south split took on a new perspective. Nazi jurists looking
for justification for severe new antihomosexual laws in the
Third Reich saw the pattern in racial terms. In their eyes,
"Teutonic" England, America, and Germany had taken the
right course; the liberalism of the Catholic south was now
seen as a sign of a specifically Latin degeneracy.[130]

The moral crusade of the Society for the Reformation of
Manners came to an end in 1738 when the Society expired.
But William Wilberforce had its example in mind when he
prevailed upon George III to revive the tradition of issuing
royal proclamations against vice in 1787. The next year he
founded the Proclamation Society. Fourteen years later it
chose a new name, the Society for the Suppression of Vice,

130.   See Rudolf Kläre, *Homosexualität und Strafrecht* (Hamburg: Hans-
eatische Verlagsanstalt, 1937), chaps. 6, 7.

and under that designation it pursued a vigorous course in Georgian and Victorian England. With the coming of the new century, hangings of homosexuals increased in number and became more or less annual events. We do not know what administrative decisions by the police, judiciary, and higher authorities determined this rate of executions, but its regularity suggests that those in power had reached a tacit understanding that such a level of enforcement was desirable. Did the Society for the Suppression of Vice use its potent influence here? Its publicly declared aims were the suppression of obscene publications, Sabbath-breaking, and cruel sports, matters in which English opinion was by no means unanimous. But its emphasis on enforcing morals legislation set the tone for the new century and strongly influenced the administration of justice. Popular sentiment against homosexuals, worked up to such a pitch during earlier morals campaigns, seems not to have subsided; in this new moral climate, with England isolated by war and politics from Continental liberalism, it was easy for authority to assume an unprecedented harshness. It was an irony of fate that the year of Byron's birth coincided with Wilberforce's founding of the Proclamation Society and his puberty with its metamorphosis into its powerful successor. Byron and the nation's determination to suppress sexual vice by every social and legal means came of age together.

· 2 ·

Byron at School

We have suggested that the proportion of men and women who were attracted to their own sex in early nineteenth-century England was not much different from today. But the effect of severe laws and strongly hostile public opinion made it more difficult for homosexuals to meet and give one another support. If sensational punishments advertised the fact that others of their kind at least existed, newspaper rhetoric implied that they were monsters whose rarity matched their enormity. Self-awareness brought pain and fear. For a homosexual or bisexual, the discovery of his (or her) identity was an experience that must often have made adolescence a long agony. To be a sodomite in England was to be a double anomaly, violating both the natural and the national order.

Most such men and women inevitably lived obscure lives. What they thought and felt we will never know. One of the effects of persecution is to destroy knowledge of the persecuted. This is especially true when the unpopular group is invisible, has much to lose by ceasing to be silent, and has no family tradition to preserve records. Only in exceptional cases will it be possible to reconstruct the past. Such a coincidence, nevertheless, did occur in the Romantic period, when fate decreed, by an ironic twist, that the Englishman most in the world's eyes should be a bisexual.

Byron was of course exceptional in every way, most notably on account of his rank, his beauty, and the talent that won him fame. Only his lameness marred the gifts of fortune. But these advantages made him as sensitive as he was proud, and his sense of belonging to a despised minority must have rankled cruelly. Nor could he count on his privileges to protect him. In some times and places they would have. In seventeenth-century France, for instance, though homosexuals of the lower and middle class faced the stake, aristocrats, even when their tastes were widely known, were secure from the law and ostracism.[1] Princes, dukes, and generals might be the object of jeering gossip, but they did not risk their lives or status or even their posts; England in the same age, by contrast, had hanged a bishop and beheaded a peer. Byron's forebears had already faced a measure of public unpopularity and private distress. The great-uncle from whom he inherited his title ("The Wicked Lord") had killed a neighbor in a drunken fight that was more a brawl than a duel; his father, a rake and wastrel who had run through the fortunes of two heiresses, had had to flee to France to avoid arrest. But the great-uncle's seclusion at Newstead Abbey seems to have been largely a self-imposed eccentricity, and Jack Byron wanted only a new supply of cash to return to English society. By contrast, identification as a homosexual, in the press or by mere rumor, put one, whatever his rank, beyond the pale. The list of suspected peers and men of distinction who sought refuge on the Continent was long and continually growing in Byron's day. Above all and most notably, there was William Beckford. Beckford was the wealthiest man in England, but neither his wealth nor his aristocratic connections nor his talents as a writer and musician could save him from ten years of exile and a life of lonely ostracism once he was publicly accused of the

1. See, e.g., Marc Daniel, "A Study of Homosexuality in France During the Reigns of Louis XIII and Louis XIV," *One Institute Quarterly: Homophile Studies* 4 (1961):77–93, 125–36. Daniel's study first appeared in French in *Arcadie*, December 1956–September 1957. For the situation in France in a later period, see D. A. Coward, "Attitudes to Homosexuality in Eighteenth-century France," *Journal of European Studies* 10 (1980): 231–55.

"nameless crime."[2] The phrase was Byron's, and, as we shall see, Byron must have been strongly struck by the parallels in their situations.

Secular England condemned homosexuals for their "neglect" of women. Byron's good looks, title, and glamour as a poet were to attract women powerfully, and he was far from unresponsive: his love affairs were many and famous. But if a failure to copulate heterosexually was an ostensible matter for criticism, orthodox amorousness could not save a man. Beckford was happily married and a father. Probably the majority of men pilloried or exiled were heads of families. Bentham had noted in 1774:

> A proof that it is not any apprehension of the crime's occasioning women to be neglected that occasions the abhorrence of this crime is, that a man who should be known to be indifferent, or even averse to women would not be the object of any such abhorrence, at least of any abhorrence near equal to it, if he were exempt from any suspicion of this crime: on the other hand, a man supposed to be guilty of it, though he were known to have a connection with never so many women would not find the detestation of him anything if at all abated by it.[3]

As for literary genius weighing in the balance, the English have never been inclined to show the indulgence for art's sake that France showed, for example, to Gide and Genet. The conviction and imprisonment of Oscar Wilde was to demonstrate this in the nineties, and E. M. Forster never dared publish his homosexual novel or his homosexual short stories during his long life.

Yet his fame has enabled us to determine the truth about Byron. He was the center of a remarkable amount of contemporary attention. Curious journalists culled every bit of gossip and jotted down all his opinions. More important still, his intimate friends and acquaintances wrote letters,

2. See p. 120.
3. "Nonconformity," box 74a, folio 25.

diaries, and reminiscences, recorded conversations, and captured rumors. His wife, after he left her, had a potent incentive to horde every bit of damaging information she could against the possibility of a suit for the custody of their daughter. It was an articulate age when men and women wrote voluminously, often in an elaborately circumspect way that now seems absurdly stilted, but sometimes with a telling trenchancy. Byron himself was endlessly self-expressive in his poetry, letters, and journals. Most of what he hinted about the homosexual side of his nature was deliberately vague and mysterious: genders were changed in poems, codes used in letters, references made purposely ambiguous in autobiographical notes. As a result, what he wrote was almost certain to be read by the unaware reader, as Byron intended, in heterosexual terms. For someone as communicative and as naturally candid as Byron, these disguises must have cost some effort as he sought at once to celebrate and obscure, to share and disguise his feelings. One recalls Beckford's words about the discomfort of having to wear a mask that made his face ache.[4] But Byron's obsessive need for confession has provided the evidence that has enabled us finally to grasp the complexity of his sexual being.

Punitiveness toward homosexuals and bisexuals in Byron's age was a public melodrama. But to understand how such men and women felt about themselves in private, we must be prepared to analyze the most delicate hints and subtlest nuances of human feeling and to draw conclusions with a full awareness of unresolved ambiguities. Our task is to catch the slow degrees by which Byron moved to an awareness of his identity as a bisexual. To do this, we must sift clues and interpret emotions that Byron himself probably did not understand at first. There is, to

---

4.   "How tired I am of keeping a mask on my countenance. How tight it sticks—it makes me sore" (May 27, 1787, *The Journal of William Beckford in Portugal and Spain, 1787–1788*, ed. Boyd Alexander [New York: John Day, 1955], p. 41).

begin with, the problem of his precocity. Byron became heir to the family title at eight when the Wicked Lord's son died. His own father had died when Byron was three, leaving only debts and a wife with a drastically diminished fortune. In 1798 Byron became a lord, and he and his mother escaped from a pinched life in Aberdeen, where he had attended grammar school, to comparative affluence in England. He was a peer at ten, and his emotional and sexual life seems to have developed correspondingly early. He fell in love with one female cousin, Mary Duff, when he was seven and another, Margaret Parker, when he was twelve. Of his initiation into sexual experience, he wrote darkly years later: "My passions were developed very early—so early—that few would believe me—if I were to state the period—and the facts which accompanied it."[5] He appears to be referring to his seduction at the age of nine by his Scottish nursemaid, May Gray, a devout Calvinist, who had also taught him his Bible lessons. Byron eventually complained of her attentions to the family lawyer, John Hanson, who had her dismissed. Byron speculated that this early introduction to sex had influenced him negatively: "Perhaps this was one of the reasons which caused the anticipated [i.e., precocious] melancholy of my thoughts— having anticipated life.—My earlier poems are the thoughts of one at least ten years older than the age at which they were written,—I don't mean for their solidity, but their Experience."[6]

Byron entered Harrow in 1801. At first he did not especially like the school. Two years later he drove his mother (with whom his relations were to become increasingly strained) to despair by adamantly refusing to return for the

5. "Detached Thoughts," October 15, 1821, in *BLJ*, 9:40.
6. Byron's negative reaction was somewhat unusual. In a survey of 796 college students, David Finkelhor found that 66 percent of the girls who had had sexual relations with adults as children had reacted negatively, but only 38 percent of the boys. "Boys report feeling more interest and pleasure at the time, and girls remember more fear and shock" (*Sexually Victimized Children* [New York: Free Press, 1979], p. 70).

autumn term. His intransigence was the result of frustrated love. He had become desperately enamored of a Notting-hamshire neighbor, Mary Chaworth, a relative of the man his great-uncle had killed. Mary was a pretty and flir-tatious young woman, two years older than Byron and en-gaged to be married. She did not take him seriously and on one occasion referred to him disparagingly as "that lame boy" on account of his club foot. When she married John Musters, Byron was heartbroken. As if to prove the rule that unconsummated love affairs are the most inspira-tional, she continued to haunt his imagination and poetry for many years.

When Byron returned to Harrow for a final year and a half, his emotional life centered on his relations with the school's younger boys. Later he was to recollect that "Hunter, Curzon, Long and Tatersall, were my principal friends, Clare, Dorset, Cs. Gordon, De Bath, Claridge and Jno. Wingfield, were my juniors and favourites, whom I spoilt by indulgence."[7] The chief clues we have as to the nature of these relations are the poems Byron published after he had left Harrow for Cambridge. Byron's first col-lection, *Fugitive Pieces*, was privately printed in 1806 when he was eighteen; Byron suppressed it when a friend sug-gested that one poem portrayed heterosexual passion too candidly, and Jerome McGann, in his edition of Byron's poems, lists only four known copies. A second edition to which he added a number of new pieces appeared as *Poems on Various Occasions* in 1807, again privately printed. Later that year, his first published collection, *Hours of Idle-ness*, reprinted about half the poems in *Fugitive Pieces*, eight selections from the 1807 *Poems*, and a dozen new pieces. In 1808, three months after he had left Cambridge, Byron published a fourth collection, *Poems Original and Translated*, which added a few new compositions and dropped others.

Of these poems, a significant number are amorous

7.   *LJL*, 1:43.

verses conventionally addressed "To Caroline," "To Eliza," "To Mary," etc. The next largest group are the poems of friendship. These fall into three distinct classes: (1) poems to particular individuals, (2) poems on the psychology of friendship ("Childish Recollections" and "L'Amitié Est L'Amour Sans Ailes"), and (3) classical translations with possible homoerotic overtones. The majority belong to the first category. These include "To E——," "To D——" (i.e., Delawarr), "Epitaph on a Friend," "To the Duke of Dorset," "To Edward Noel Long," "To George, Earl Delawarr," and "To the Earl of Clare." Finally, there is one poem, published then suppressed, to his Cambridge friend, the choirboy John Edlestone: "The Cornelian." The dates of the first four imply they were written at Harrow; the rest appear to belong to Byron's college years.

Byron was later to tell his friend William Harness that his first poems (at age fourteen) were written to him.[8] Harness was a Harrow boy two years younger than Byron, also lame, whom Byron befriended and protected from a school bully. None of these verses, however, survives. The earliest extant poem, dated November 1802, "To E——," addresses someone below Byron's state in society. He expects this will cause comment, "Yet virtue will have greater claims / To love, than rank with vice combin'd."[9] Thomas Moore thought the poem was inspired by the son of one of Byron's tenants at Newstead Abbey, his family estate,[10] but Leslie Marchand thinks that it was deliberately misdated and that "E" stands for John Edlestone, whom Byron did not meet until October 1805.[11] "To D——" is a

8. February 16, 1808, *BLJ*, 1:156.
9. *CPW*, 1:124.
10. *LJL*, 1:44n.
11. *BB*, 1:109n.; Marchand thinks the date should not be "November 1802" but "November 1805," i.e., shortly after Byron met Edlestone. Jerome McGann offers a theory to reconcile Moore and Marchand. He thinks the poem is "almost certainly addressed to John Edlestone" but that it may have been originally written in 1802 for the "unknown person (also of low birth) eulogized in 'Epitaph on a Friend'" (*CPW*, 1:376–77).

reflection of one of Byron's deepest and most troubling Harrow attachments. Its dedicatee, the Earl of Delawarr, seems to have had a potent hold on Byron's affections though their friendship did not run smoothly. "To D——" speaks of an estrangement; "envy" has somehow separated them. But they will be united in the afterworld: "On *thy dear* breast I'll lay my head, / Without *thee! where* would be *my Heaven?*"[12] A year and a half later Byron, then sixteen, wrote to Augusta about the thirteen-year-old:

> You tell me you don't know my friend Ld. Delawarr. He is considerably younger than me, but the most good tempered, amiable, clever fellow in the universe. To all which he adds the quality (a good one in the eyes of women) of being remarkably handsome, almost too much so for a boy. He is at present very low in the school, not owing to his want of ability, but to his years. I am nearly at the top of it. By the rules of our Seminary he is under my power but is too goodnatured ever to offend me, and I like him too well ever to exert my authority over him.[13]

Then, after relating some difficulties with his mother over Lord Grey de Ruthyn, their tenant at Newstead Abbey, he continues: "You Augusta are the only relation I have who treats me as a friend . . . if you desert me, I have nobody I can love but Delawarr. If it was not for his sake, Harrow would be a desart, and I should dislike staying at it."[14] Byron testily forbids Augusta to burn his letters, but two later lines referring to Delawarr are crossed out. This is in itself a curious detail, which makes one wonder about the motive for the erasure.

Byron's letter to his sister was written two months after his return to Harrow following the Chaworth affair. Byron, reversing his early dislike, now fell in love with the school and a year later grieved at leaving it. His friendship with Delawarr, however, did not go well, and the later poem "To

12.   February 1803, *CPW*, 1:126.
13.   November 2, 1804, *BLJ*, 1:54.
14.   Ibid.

George, Earl Delawarr," written in 1807 and added to *Hours of Idleness*, records a new, more lasting estrangement, which Byron nevertheless hopes time will heal. But Clare, Dorset, and Harness still claimed his heart. Byron was seriously upset when Clare on one occasion addressed him as "my dear Byron" rather than "my dearest Byron." Indeed, Clare retained a unique place in Byron's affection not only through college but up until the last years of his life, when he noted with surprise how strong the emotion he felt for his old friend was.

But what are we to make of these poems? Conventional, even banal in expression, does their phrasing give any significant hint of Byron's later homosexual involvements? First, we must note how much they vary in tone with the subject. "Epitaph on a Friend" (originally "Epitaph on a Beloved Friend") gives sentimentalism free rein in not very inspired verse. Like many in his age, Byron felt that death enhanced pathos, and weakened the taboo that set limits on protestations of devotion between males. Other poems, such as the verses to Edward Noel Long, fall clearly into the category of affectionate friendship, with no deeper overtones. Nevertheless, there is some evidence that Byron himself found the intensity of his emotions both puzzling and troubling. This comes out most clearly in "Childish Recollections," which he wrote when he was a sophomore at Cambridge looking back at his Harrow attachments. It was first published in *Poems on Various Occasions* and then suppressed in *Poems Original and Translated* because of a satirical sally he came to regret.

In this poem Byron nostalgically apostrophizes Harrow as "Ida," the mountain from which Jupiter carried off Ganymede. (Later he visited the region in his Eastern travels but reported seeing no eligible young shepherds.) Using classical epithets for each, he recalls his feelings for John Wingfield, John Tattersall, Clare, and Long. He now calls Delawarr "Euryalus" after the boy in an episode from the *Aeneid* he was sufficiently struck by to translate in full shortly afterward. Despite their estrangement he declares:

> That name is yet embalm'd, within my heart;
> Yet, at the mention, does my heart rebound,
> And palpitate, responsive to the sound.[15]

Today, this sounds to us more like the language of love than friendship; we feel affection for our friends, we hardly "palpitate" at their names. Byron himself felt uncomfortable about his emotions and wondered why he should feel so attracted by his schoolfellows a year and a half after leaving Harrow. Even women's love and beauty cannot, he tells us, extinguish what he has experienced. Surely this marks him as different from others:

> Yet, why should I alone with such delight,
> Retrace the circuit of my former flight?
> Is there no cause beyond the common claim
> Endear'd to all in childhood's very name?[16]

Byron tries to explain his obsession on the ground that he has no father, brother, or sister at home, pointedly omitting the mother he was now at odds with over his extravagant spending.

The difficulties we face in interpreting these lines reveal the ambiguities that inevitably arise in any attempt to write about feelings between members of the same sex in other historical periods. How, in reading the poems or letters or fiction of the past, are we to distinguish between romantic friendship and homosexual love? Both may speak with intense devotion, both reflect strong passion. Can we ever be sure the feeling has or has not an erotic side to it? Modern "scientific" psychology is not always useful. By extending the term *homosexual* to include all affective relations between men or between women, Freud has obfuscated rather than clarified the issue. Usually friendship does not

15.   *CPW*, 1:168.
16.   Ibid., p. 165.

have an erotic basis. Occasionally it does, and in the latter case the relationship belongs to gay history.

We must, of course, recognize that different ages have different vocabularies for expressing emotion. *Lover* in Elizabethan English often meant only friend. Fashions in the expression of romantic friendship have varied. In early nineteenth-century England, as in France and Germany, such feelings were much in vogue and often found literary expression. This may seem paradoxical in the light of the strong taboo against homosexual relations, but a little reflection shows that it is not. Just as the incest taboo makes it possible in our society for near relatives to live together without censure or suspicion, so by treating homosexuality as something unthinkable, earlier ages in effect facilitated the expression of sentiment between members of the same sex. Romantic friendship did not disappear from modern literature until Krafft-Ebing and Freud began to be widely read. Relations that once seemed innocent now became equivocal and problematic in the light of contemporary sexology. Three disparate examples will demonstrate this. The first has a comic side. The Weimar monument to Goethe and Schiller shows the poets holding hands. In 1907 a cartoon appeared in the German magazine *Jugend*, which represented Schiller, on his pedestal, as anxiously detaching himself. The caption makes him say: "Wolfgang, let go of my hand! Here comes Magnus Hirschfeld!"[17] The squib was meant to satirize the propensity of Hirschfeld (who was a percursor of Kinsey and the leader of the German homosexual rights movement) to find homosexuality everywhere. But it also marked, significantly, a growing self-consciousness about how men expressed their affection for each other. The same development took place in female friendships. Lillian Faderman has amply docu-

17.   James D. Steakley, *The Homosexual Emancipation Movement in Germany* (New York: Arno Press, 1975), p. 39. This study includes a valuable history of the Nazi persecutions of the 1930s and 1940s.

mented this in her comprehensive study of romantic friendship and love between women during the last four hundred years. For instance, sentimental love stories about
schoolgirls' affection for each other were not uncommon in
late nineteenth-century family magazines in America and
appeared up until the time of World War I.[18] After that date
they faded from the scene as popular awareness of lesbianism grew and sophistication bred fear and shyness.
Ernest Hemingway demonstrates this development clearly,
on the male side, in *The Sun Also Rises*. There, another man,
wishing to express his feelings for the hero on a fishing trip
in Spain, tells him: "Listen. You're a hell of a good guy, and
I'm fonder of you than anybody on earth. I couldn't tell you
that in New York. It'd mean I was a faggot."[19] There follow
a series of extravagant whimsicalities; for instance, Abraham Lincoln loved Robert E. Lee, which caused the Civil
War. Homosexuality is so threatening that the suspicion
must be exorcised by elaborate jokes that demonstrate that
the speaker is not naïve about the subject.

   These anxieties were far rarer in Byron's day. Byron copied a line from Jean François Marmontel on the flyleaf of
one of his notebooks: "Friendship, which in the world is
scarcely even a sentiment, is a passion in cloisters."[20] No
doubt he saw a parallel between the monastery and the

   18.   See esp. Part IB, chap. 2, "The 'Fashion' of Romantic Friendship
in the Eighteenth Century," in Lillian Faderman, *Surpassing the Love of
Men: Romantic Friendship and Love Between Women from the Renaissance to the
Present* (New York: William Morrow, 1981). Faderman quotes from correspondence between Lady Mary Wortley Montagu and her sister-in-law to-
be, between Elizabeth Carter and Catherine Talbot, Anna Seward and
Honora Sneyd, and Mary Wollstonecraft and Fanny Blood. She concludes
that these passionate friendships did not necessarily carry any sexual
overtones, being part of the accepted style of the day. Chaps. 1 and 2 of
Part IIIA show the growing tendency to label such relations lesbian in the
early twentieth century and to discourage them on this account.
   19.   *The Sun Also Rises* (New York: Charles Scribner's Sons, 1926),
chap. 12, p. 119.
   20.   Byron transcribed the passage in French and dated it 1808 (*LJL*,
1:42n.).

British public school. Nineteenth-century novels portrayed fervid schoolboy friendships in a style unimaginable today. In 1844 Disraeli could write quite un-self-consciously in his novel *Coningsby*:

> At school, friendship is a passion. It entrances the being, it tears the soul. All loves of after-life can never bring its rapture, or its wretchedness; no bliss so absorbing, no pangs of jealousy or despair so crushing and so keen! What tenderness and what devotion; what illimitable confidence; infinite revelations of inmost thoughts; what ecstatic present and romantic future; what bitter estrangements and what melting reconciliations; what scenes of wild recrimination, agitating explanations, passionate correspondence; what insane sensitiveness, and what frantic sensibility; what earthquakes of the heart and whirlwinds of the soul are confined in that simple phrase, a schoolboy's friendship![21]

Obviously this is a different world of feelings and manners from our own. If a modern novelist describes such friendships in our time, he feels constrained to call them "special." Yet two of Byron's friends, Shelley and Leigh Hunt, put on record such experiences as an important part of their youth. Here are Hunt's recollections in his *Autobiography*:

> If I had reaped no other benefit from Christ Hospital, the school would be ever dear to me from the recollection of the friendships I formed in it, and of the first heavenly taste it gave me of that most spiritual of the affections. I use the word "heavenly" advisedly; and I call friendship the most spiritual of the affections, because even one's kindred, in partaking of our flesh and blood, become, in a manner, mixed up with our entire being. . . . If I ever tasted a disembodied transport on earth it was in those friendships which I entertained at school, before I dreamt of any maturer feeling. I shall never forget the impression it first made on me. I loved my friend for his gentleness, his candour, his truth, his good repute, his freedom even from my own livelier manner, his calm and reasonable kindness. . . . I smile to think of the perplexity (though he

21. (London: Longmans, Green & Co., 1877), Book I, chap. 9, pp. 43–44.

never showed it) which he probably felt sometimes at my enthusiastic expressions, for I thought him a kind of angel.[22]

Shelley's account of a schoolboy friendship in his notebooks is similarly celebratory, but more sophisticated and discriminating. In his case there is a difference. Shelley was quite aware of the possibility of sexuality entering into the picture and deliberately denies its influence:

> The nature of Love and Friendship is very little understood, and the distinction between them ill established. This latter feeling—at least a profound and sentimental attachment to one of the same sex, wholly divested of the smallest alloy of sensual intermixture, often precedes the former. It is not right to say, merely, that it is exempt from the smallest alloy of sensuality. It rejects, with disdain, all thoughts but those of an elevated and imaginative character and the process by which the attachment between two persons of different sexes terminates in a sensual union has not yet begun. I remember forming an attachment of this kind at school. I cannot recall to my memory the precise epoch at which this took place, but I imagine it must have been at the age of eleven or twelve.
>
> The object of these sentiments was a boy about my own age, of a character eminently generous, brave, and gentle; and the elements of human feeling seem to have been, from his birth, genially compounded within him. There was a delicacy and simplicity in his manners, inexpressibly attractive. . . . The tones of his voice were so soft and winning, that every word pierced into my heart; and their pathos was so deep, that in listening to him the tears have involuntarily gushed from my eyes.[23]

Byron's relations with younger boys are often touchingly paternal. Their weakness seems to have regularly appealed to his protective instincts. But there are a few ominous notes. Editors have long debated who was the object of the satire in the sketch "Damaetas," E. T. Coleridge,

22. Ed. Roger Ingpen (Westminster: Archibald Constable, 1903), 1:92–93.

23. "An Essay on Friendship," in *Complete Works*, ed. Roger Ingpen and Walter E. Peck, vol. 7 (New York: Charles Scribner's Sons, 1930), 143.

in particular, arguing that the poem was not a self-portrait. But Jerome McGann has now discovered a manuscript of the poem in Byron's hand. It is headed "My Character," which clearly indicates that Byron was describing himself at nineteen in these lines:

> In law an infant, and in years a boy,
> In mind a slave to every vicious joy, . . .
> Damaetas ran through all the maze of sin,
> And found the goal, when others just begin.[24]

And "To the Duke of Dorset," addressed to Byron's ten-year-old "fag" when Byron was about to leave Harrow, though it begins with conventional advice to study and avoid flatterers, sounds a prophetic warning:

> Tho' ev'ry Error stamps me for her own
> And dooms my fall, I fain would fall alone.[25]

Byron obviously responded fully and passionately to the contemporary cult of friendship and felt licensed, by its conventions, to give full expression to such sentiments in his poetry. But were these experiences sexless? Or did Harrow see the first burgeoning of his homoeroticism, which was later to flower in Greece? The statistics published by Kinsey in our day show that a significant number of adolescent boys do indeed have sexual encounters with other males.[26] There seems to have been little public discussion of this phenomenon in England in Byron's day when homosexuality was regarded as a heinous foreign importation. To admit that English schoolboys entered into such vice with no external prompting would have run counter to this theory. On the Continent, writers were more candid.

24. CPW, 1:51–52, and the notes on pp. 51, 367.
25. Ibid., p. 67.
26. Michael Schofield, in a study published in 1965, found that 28 percent of the boys at English boarding schools admitted taking part in homosexual relations, compared with 5 percent at coeducational schools. He implies these figures may be low (The Sexual Behavior of Young People [Boston: Little, Brown, 1965], p. 58).

Voltaire, in his essay in the *Philosophical Dictionary*, pours scornful contempt on adult male homosexuals but waxes almost lyrical over schoolboys:

> How did it come about that a vice which would destroy man-kind if it were general, that a sordid outrage against nature, is still so natural? It seems the highest degree of deliberate cor-ruption, and yet it is the ordinary lot of those who have not yet had time to be corrupted. . . . When the young males of our species, brought up together, feel the force which nature be-gins to unfold in them, and fail to find the natural object of their instinct, they fall back on what resembles it. Often, for two or three years, a young man resembles a beautiful girl, with the freshness of his complexion, the brilliance of his col-oring, and the sweetness of his eyes; if he is loved, it's because nature makes a mistake; homage is paid to the fair sex by at-tachment to one who owns its beauties, and when the years have made this resemblance disappear, the mistake ends.[27]

Beccaria, we saw, explained the prevalence of male ho-mosexuality in Italy as due to "those institutions, packed with hot-blooded youth [whose] natural vigour, as it devel-ops, is faced with insurmountable obstacles to every other kind of relationship."[28] This was also the view of Montes-quieu: "The crime against nature will never make any great progress in society unless people are prompted to it by some particular custom, as among the Greeks, where the youths of that country performed all their exercises naked; [or] as amongst us, where domestic education is disused."[29] In England, though attacks were made on the prevalence of homosexuality at the universities, little was said in pub-lic in the eighteenth century about the public schools. But Bentham in his essay of 1785 endorsed Montesquieu's opinion. Pointing to the strict segregation of boys and girls

27. "So-called Socratic Love," trans. Peter Gay (New York: Harcourt, Brace & World, 1962), pp. 76–77.

28. Cesare Beccaria, *Of Crimes and Punishments*, trans. K. Foster and J. Grigson (London: Oxford University Press, 1964), p. 83.

29. *The Spirit of the Laws*, trans. Thomas Nugent (New York: Hafner, 1949), p. 189.

and comparing England with ancient Greece, he remarked: "On the present plan [boys] are often forced together under circumstances still more favourable to it [i.e., homosexuality] by the custom of lying naked together in feather beds, implements of indulgence and incentives to the venereal appetite with which the antients were unacquainted."[30] Presumably, Bentham had in mind the tradition of boys sharing beds in boarding schools. At Eton it was the custom for masters to lock boys into dormitories at eight o'clock and to leave them unattended: the authorities took no responsibility for their behavior "after school." The liberal clergyman Sydney Smith described the typical English public school in 1810 as "a system of premature debauchery that only prevents men from being corrupted by the world by corrupting them before their entry into the world."[31] His language is deliberately vague and general but was meant no doubt to cover both hetero- and homosexual experimentation. The language of schoolboys was less philosophical than Bentham's and Smith's. Thackeray has left it on record that on his arrival at Charterhouse in 1817 the first order he received from a schoolmate was "Come & frig me."[32] As to Harrow, a note to *Don Leon* appended in 1842 recorded: "Some twenty years ago . . . an allusion was made in the public papers to certain rumours which had spread about concerning the unnatural propensities of the boys in Harrow school."[33] John Addington Symonds, who arrived at Harrow about a decade later, painted a lurid picture. Montgomery Hyde, paraphrasing Symonds's un-

30. Louis Crompton, ed., "Jeremy Bentham's Essay on 'Paederasty,' Part 2," *Journal of Homosexuality* 4 (1978):92.

31. A. D. C. Peterson, *A Hundred Years of Education* (London: Gerald Duckworth, 1952), pp. 90, 92. Nathaniel Brown discusses homosexuality in nineteenth-century English public schools in *Sexuality and Feminism in Shelley* (Cambridge: Harvard University Press, 1979), pp. 141–43.

32. Gordon Ray, *Thackeray: The Uses of Adversity, 1811–1846* (New York: McGraw-Hill, 1955), p. 452, n. 39.

33. In *A Homosexual Emancipation Miscellany, c. 1835–1952* (1866; rpt. New York: Arno Press, 1975), p. 70.

published autobiography, tells us: "Every boy of good looks had a female nickname, and a boy who yielded his person to an older lover was known as the elder lad's 'bitch.'" According to Symonds: "The talk in the dormitories and studies was of the grossest character, with repulsive scenes of onanism, mutual masturbation and obscene orgies of naked boys in bed together."[34]

From the very first, Byron's biographers were forced to take note of his large number of schoolboy favorites and the intensity of his passion for them. Thomas Moore, writing in 1830, a few years after Byron's death, must have felt he was facing a delicate and embarrassing topic in broaching the subject. But Byron's poems were in everyone's hands, and his relations with boys like John Edlestone and Nicolo Giraud obviously called for some kind of comment. It is not surprising that Moore in his *Life* of Byron should have invoked the contemporary cult of romantic friendship to explain such passions:

> One of the most striking results of the English system of education is, that while in no country are there so many instances of manly friendships early formed and steadily maintained, so in no other country, perhaps, are the feelings towards the parental home so early estranged, or, at the best, feebly cherished. Transplanted as boys are from the domestic circle, at a time of life when the affections are most inclined to cling, it is but natural that they should seek a substitute for ties of home in those boyish friendships which they form at school, and which, connected as they are with the scenes and events over which youth threw its charm, retain ever after the strongest hold upon their hearts. . . . [Moore then notes that in France and Ireland this is not so.]
>
> To a youth like Byron, abounding with the most passionate feelings, and finding sympathy with only the ruder parts of his nature at home, the little world of school afforded a vent for his affections, which was sure to call them forth in their most ardent form. Accordingly, the friendships which he con-

34.   H. Montgomery Hyde, *The Love That Dared Not Speak Its Name: A Candid History of Homosexuality in Britain* (Boston: Little, Brown, 1970), p. 110.

tracted both at school and college were little less than what he
himself describes them, "passions." [35]

This plausible and eloquent paragraph drew forth a
skeptical retort from John Cam Hobhouse, who, on reading it, wrote in the margin of his copy of Moore's *Life*:
"M. knows nothing, or will tell nothing of the principal
cause & motive of all these boyish friend[ships]." [36] Hobhouse, a lifelong friend of Byron, undoubtedly knew more
about Byron's bisexuality than anyone else of whom we
have any record. He thought it was an open question
whether Moore was writing in innocent naïveté or in a deliberate attempt to obfuscate the issue. But evidence has
now come to light that Moore was neither naïve nor ignorant. In the published memoirs of Charles Fulke Greville,
we learn that Moore spoke at length about his forthcoming
biography with Greville on November 9, 1829. After a discussion of Byron's orgies with women in Venice, the conversation turned to another question: "Moore *said* he did
not believe in the stories of his fancy for Boys, but it looked
as if he does believe it from his manner." [37] Apparently
Moore tried to dismiss the matter lightly, but his lack of
ease on a subject of such momentous significance in England betrayed him.

In his authoritative biography of Byron, Marchand took
the position that Byron might "possibly" have recognized
the "sexual implications of these passionate friendships
. . . before he left Harrow, probably while he was at Cambridge, and certainly while he was in Greece on his first
pilgrimage." [38] Four years later, in 1961, Doris Langley
Moore published excerpts from the Lovelace papers, which

35.   *LJL*, 1:43–44.
36.   *BB*, 1:90n.
37.   *The Greville Memoirs, 1814–1860*, ed. Lytton Strachey and Robert
Fulford (London: Macmillan, 1938), 1:325–26.
38.   *BB*, 1:90n. This is the only place in his 1,264-page biography
where Marchand speaks directly of Byron's homosexuality and uses the
word, though his work implies throughout a keen awareness of this side
of Byron's life.

were not available to Marchand. These contain a memorandum by Lady Byron of Byron's purported confession to Lady Caroline Lamb that "from his boyhood on he had been in the practice of unnatural crime. . . . He mentioned 3 schoolfellows whom he had thus perverted. (N.B. two of their miniature pictures were burnt with a curious remark)." [39] Lady Caroline's strong animus against Byron after he had broken with her must be taken into account in evaluating this purported confession. Nevertheless, I am inclined to think that here she is reporting him, in the main, accurately. It seems highly likely, given Byron's precocious sexual nature, that he did give some physical expression to it before leaving Harrow. This, and the pull on his affections, may explain why, though he was unwilling to return to school in 1804, he was even more loath to leave in 1805.

At this point, it is perhaps appropriate to consider another puzzle in Byron's early life, his contretemps with Lord Grey de Ruthyn. Byron and his mother, being in serious want of money, had rented the ancestral home, Newstead Abbey, to Lord Grey while they lived in nearby Southwell. During his emotional crisis over Mary Chaworth, Byron was a frequent overnight guest at the Abbey. Grey was kind to him, but being a typical country squire, bored Byron by his obsession with shooting and his lack of intellectual or literary interests. In November 1803, during his truancy from Harrow, Byron had stayed with Grey, who was twenty-four. He had meant to prolong his visit until his birthday on January 22, though he did not, as it turned out, stay so long. His letters to his sister are full of mysterious hints on the subject of his consequent break with the older man. In March he wrote her: "I am not reconciled to Lord Grey, *and I never will*. He was once my *Greatest Friend*. My reasons for ceasing that Friendship are such as I cannot explain, not even to you my Dear Sister . . . but they will

39.   *LLB*, p. 243.

ever remain hidden in my own breast." In November he still speaks of his "cordial, deliberate detestation" for Lord Grey.[40] Matters were not eased by his mother, who had, absurdly enough, fallen in love with Grey and insisted, in a stormy scene, that Byron make up the quarrel. What had caused the fracas? Marchand thinks that "the sensuous young lord had made some kind of sexual advance which disgusted his younger companion."[41]

This is the usually accepted interpretation, which has been endorsed by Doris Langley Moore, herself a scholarly and astute interpreter of Byron's character. However, some difficulties present themselves if we assume that Byron merely repulsed Grey's overtures. Thomas Moore, who does not mention the break between the men, simply tells us that "an intimacy . . . soon sprung up between [Byron] and his noble tenant." To this innocuous remark, the vigilant Hobhouse, however, added another comment in the margin of his copy of Moore's biography: "A circumstance occurred during [this] intimacy which certainly had much effect on his future morals."[42] This suggests that Byron in later life told Hobhouse that something sexual had taken place. It seems, however, difficult to imagine how Hobhouse could have asserted that the episode affected Byron's later behavior if he had not been a willing participant.[43]

40.   March 26, 1804, *BLJ*, 1:46; November 2, 1804, *BLJ*, 1:54. See also Byron's letters to his mother expressing the same sentiments, in *BLJ*, May 1–10, 1804?, 1:49–50; and other letters to Augusta, November 11, 1804, 1:55, and November 21, 1804, 1:59.

41.   *BB*, 1:80.

42.   *LJL*, 1:53; *LBAR*, p. 77.

43.   Doris Langley Moore recognizes this difficulty and seeks to explain it on the grounds that Byron was not attracted to older men: "It is odd to find Grey credited—or debited—with Byron's phase of cheerful abandonment, six years afterwards, to adventures with youths in the Near East, seeing that his reaction to the approaches had been horrified recoil; but perhaps in his account of this juvenile ordeal, he did not, considering his own deviations, lay much emphasis on the repugnance he had felt when obliged to resist a man eight years his senior" (*LBAR*, p. 77). This is perceptive, but it does not, I think, account for the tone and substance of Grey's letter cited below.

Four years later, after he had graduated from Cambridge, Byron wrote to Grey on business, mentioning, in conclusion: "Circumstances, which though now long past, and indeed difficult for me to touch upon, have not yet ceased to be interesting.—Your Lordship must be perfectly aware of the very peculiar reasons that induced me to adopt a line of conduct, which however painful, and painful to me it certainly was, became unavoidable." [44] Byron's earlier animus has declined: he is now willing to meet but not to resume their earlier friendship. Grey's reply is curious:

> With respect to that part of your letter which recals to my recollection the days of our Youth, I can only say it will ever be the farthest from my wish to assume any character to Your Lordship but that of a friend, but as you seem to suppose me so well acquainted with the cause of your sudden secession from our former friendship I must beg leave to assure you that, much as I have reviewed[?] every circumstance and given to each its most full & weighty import, still I am now at a loss to account for it. We parted in 1804 the best of Friends, your letters were afterwards most affectionate, nay, I have even now a trifling pledge of your esteem which your mother gave me and therefore under all these counts you cannot wonder at my being somewhat surprised.
>
> You say the break was painful to yourself, I need not say to you who know I have not the power to command my feelings when deeply wounded what my sensations were. [45]

Doris Langley Moore remarks that "the absurdity of writing in one sentence that they had parted the best of friends and, in the next, that he had been deeply wounded by the break, must cause us to question the balance of [Grey's] mind." [46] She also questions the existence of the "affectionate letters." But there is no necessary inconsistency if we assume Byron did not assume his hostile attitude until some time *after* he had parted from Grey. Had Grey been

44.   August 7, 1808, *BLJ*, 1:168.
45.   Undated MS letter in Meyer Davis, Jr. Collection of Lord Byron, University of Pennsylvania library.
46.   *LBAR*, p. 82.

writing to someone else, he might have misrepresented the mood of their parting and the tone of Byron's letters, but it is hard to imagine that, knowing Byron's mettle, he would make assertions to him that were patently false when he is trying to conciliate him. One can only wonder what did happen. Did Grey anger Byron by boasting of his "conquest" to some mutual acquaintance? Until further evidence turns up, we must remain in the dark.

Byron's early poems and his passions for Mary Chaworth and other women reveal a sensibility that was already fully developed on the heterosexual side. But when and how did he come to understand the other part of his nature? Men who eventually identify themselves as bisexual come to self-awareness through various paths, some of which are neither comfortable nor easy. In Byron's day, one of the commonest, for the educated, was through the study of the classics that made up the core of a gentleman's education. Byron boasted with pride in later life that he had thirteen years of classical studies behind him. In his account of his early experience with literature, he recorded that he had read Greek and Latin poets "without number" and had "translated a good deal from both languages, verse as well as prose." [47] Though hardly a model student, his interest seems to have been genuine and lasting. His enthusiasm for Greek history and literature was a potent influence in drawing him to Greece first as a visitor and later as a liberator. But what exactly would he have read and what knowledge of homosexuality would this have given him in a culture where scholarly discussions of the subject were rigorously tabooed?

Byron began to write when the so-called Greek revival was at floodtide. Pope and his age had looked to Augustan Rome for its models and knew Greek art mainly through late Roman copies. But after 1760, Europe turned to Athens to imbibe the Greek spirit at its source. James Stuart and

47. *LJL*, 1:97.

Nicholas Revett's *Antiquities of Athens* (1762) provided the first engravings of the Parthenon and the Erechtheum. In literature and even on the musical stage, new currents flowed from Grecian springs. Gluck's *Orfeo* and, still more, his *Alceste* took opera back to its origins in Greek tragedy. Thomas Gray studied Greek assiduously and imitated Pindar. In Germany, Johann Joachim Winckelmann's *History of the Art of Antiquity* (1764) aroused a new enthusiasm for Greek sculpture, inspiring Goethe, Lessing, and Hegel. These influences combined with an idealistic desire to free Greece from Turkish rule to produce the movement we call philhellenism. Shelley summed up the sentiment of two continents when he declared, in his preface to *Hellas*: "We are all Greeks." [48]

A culture thus enamored of ancient Greece might have been expected to come to terms with Greek homosexuality, perhaps to have modified its censoriousness in the light of the important role it played in a nation so admired. Such a readjustment took place only to a limited extent on the Continent and in England not at all. In Germany the high prestige of classical scholarship led eventually to candid translations and learned essays on Greek pederasty. These in turn helped pave the way for the German homosexual emancipation movement that was born with the twentieth century. But in England religious and national sentiment precluded such a development: north of the channel, Paul triumphed over the Greek Anthology. Clergymen like James Macknight, annotating the Epistle to the Romans, indicted Socrates, Aristotle, and Zeno as homosexual pagans. Thomas Scott, explicating the same passage in his influential and much reprinted commentary, deplored the homoerotic tendencies in ancient poetry:

> Those unnatural crimes and vile affections, which are most scandalous at present, and carefully concealed, or most se-

48.   For the Greek revival in the plastic arts, see Mario Praz, *On Neo-classicism*, trans. Angus Davidson (Evanston, Ill.: Northwestern University Press, 1969).

verely punished, were openly avowed among the Greeks and Romans, even in their politest ages; and their most elegant and celebrated poets have defiled their compositions by the mention of such detestable amors, without any expressions of abhorrence, or even of disapprobation; nay, often in a way, which sanctions them, and almost wins the unwary reader to palliate, or even approve them![49]

Shelley was to protest, when he came to write on the subject, that his contemporaries seemed to be engaged in a conspiracy to keep an important side of Greek life a secret from modern readers who could not read the original documents.[50] He was particularly disappointed that men of philosophical temperament, such as Barthélemy in France and Christoph Martin Wieland in Germany, ignored or bowdlerized Greek manners.[51] In the case of Winckelmann, it is arguable that his own homosexuality helped fire his enthusiasm for Greek marbles. In his "Essay on the Beautiful in Art" (1763) he had declared: "Those who are only aware of beauty in the female sex and are hardly or not at all affected by beauty in *our* sex, have little innate feeling for beauty in art in a general and vital sense."[52] At the end of the preface to his *History*, Winckelmann suggested that there was an intimate connection between Greek art and Greek homoeroticism: "I should have been able to say more if I had written for the Greeks, and not in a modern tongue, which imposes on me certain restric-

49. Scott's remarks appear in his notes on Romans 1:24–27 in *The Holy Bible*, first published in 1788–1792. I have used the American reprint of the fifth London edition, vol. 6 (Boston: Samuel T. Armstrong, 1830), 11.

50. "A Discourse on the Manners of the Antient Greeks Relative to the Subject of Love," in *The Platonism of Shelley*, ed. James A. Notopoulos (Durham, N.C.: Duke University Press, 1949), p. 407.

51. Abbé Jean-Jacques Barthélemy's *Voyage du jeune Anacharsis en Grèce dans le milieu du quatrième siècle avant l'ère vulgaire* was published in French in 1787; an English version, *Travels of Anacharsis the Younger in Greece*, appeared in 1796. Shelley read it in 1813. We have noted earlier Bentham's objections to Wieland's misrepresentation of Greek manners in *Agathon* (see p. 43).

52. *Winckelmann: Writings on Art*, ed. David Irwin (London: Phaidon, 1972), p. 92.

tions. For this reason, I have, although reluctantly, left out a *Dialogue upon Beauty*, after the manner of the *Phaedrus of Plato*, which would have served to elucidate my remarks when speaking of it theoretically." [53] But though Shelley was to be profoundly influenced by Winckelmann's view of the Greeks and their art and Byron was to echo the German's famous paragraphs on the Apollo Belvedere and the Laocoön, there is no hint that either had an inkling of this side of his personality. [54]

Shelley's response to Winckelmann is clear in his own voluminous notes on classical sculpture, which warmly echo Winckelmann's appreciation of androgynous male beauty. Byron is more shy. In some famous stanzas near the end of Canto IV of *Childe Harold*, he turns from "Laocoon's torture dignifying pain" to the Apollo. But though he finds something Byronic in his proud glance, he feels free to appreciate his beauty only through the eyes of a woman:

> Or view the Lord of the unerring bow,
> The God of life, and poesy, and light—
> The Sun in human limbs arrayed, and brow
> All radiant from his triumph in the fight;
> The shaft hath just been shot—the arrow bright
> With an immortal's vengeance; in his eye
> And nostril beautiful disdain, and might,
> And majesty, flash their full lightnings by,
> Developing in that one glance the Deity.
>
> But in his delicate form—a dream of Love,
> Shaped by some solitary nymph, whose breast
> Long'd for a deathless lover from above,
> And madden'd in that vision—are exprest
> All that ideal beauty ever bless'd
> The mind with in its most unearthly mood,
> When each conception was a heavenly guest—
> A ray of immortality—and stood,
> Starlike, around, until they gathered to a god! [55]

53.   Ibid., pp. 105–06.
54.   Winckelmann's influence on Shelley is discussed by Nathaniel Brown in *Sexuality and Feminism in Shelley*, p. 19.
55.   Stanzas 161, 162, *CPW*, 2:178–79.

In Victorian times a young student would most likely have found enlightenment about Greek sexuality by reading translations of the *Symposium* and the *Phaedrus*. This is how John Addington Symonds, at seventeen, first became aware of the ideal side of Greek love.[56] But this possibility did not exist in Byron's day. First, as we shall see, Plato was little read. This general ignorance is reflected by Bentham's writings on Greek homosexuality. Though one might have expected Plato to have been a prime source, Bentham does not cite him at all. When he speaks of Socrates, it is always the Socrates of Xenophon's *Memorabilia* he has in mind.[57]

The other reason for popular ignorance of Plato's views on homosexuality was the misleading nature of the one translation that did exist. The first English rendering of the *Symposium* was published by Floyer Sydenham in two parts in 1761 and 1767. Despite Plato's lack of vogue, this was an ambitious work of philological and historical scholarship, in which a line of text may be accompanied by a page of notes. But Sydenham took drastic measures to assure that the reader who knew no Greek would not guess at the nature of the love celebrated in the panegyrics of Phaedrus and Pausanias that open the dialogue. Achilles, in Sydenham's version, becomes not the lover of Patroclus, but his "admirer."[58] The Greek word *eromenos* (male beloved) is regularly rendered as "mistress," and Phaedrus's famous boast—"I know not any greater blessing to a young man who is beginning life than a virtuous lover, or to

56. Phyllis Grosskurth, *John Addington Symonds* (New York: Arno Press, 1975), p. 34.

57. Bentham was well trained in Greek and Latin at Westminster School. While there he wrote letters in both languages and considerable verse. When he entered Oxford at twelve, his library contained Archbishop Potter's *Antiquities of Greece*, Horace, Virgil, Juvenal, Pliny, Anacreon, Aeschines, and Lucian's *Dialogues*. A list of classical citations on homosexuality appears in the margin of his notes of 1774 (box 74a, folio 7a).

58. Sydenham, *The Banquet: A Dialogue of Plato Concerning Love. The First Part* (London: W. Sandby, 1761), p. 57.

a lover than a beloved youth"[59]—becomes: "I know no greater Good than Love; to the Party Beloved, if she has a worthy Lover; or to the Lover himself, if his Mistress be worthy."[60] As a result, Phaedrus's "army of lovers," soon after to be realized in the famous Theban Band, becomes by implication an army of knights and ladies, turning a practical suggestion into a romantic fantasy. Later he boldly translates "boy" in the Greek as "maiden" or "woman." Only when he comes to the speech of Aristophanes does he find himself inescapably forced to refer, once, to "Sapphic Lovers" and then to men who are attracted sexually to men.[61] Sydenham gives no apology for his bowdlerizations, nor does he hint, in his lengthy preface, that he is changing anything. At the conclusion of this "incomparable Dialogue," as he calls it, he was naturally acutely embarrassed by the speech of Alcibiades, in which the young rake tells of his failure to seduce Socrates. In his 1761 preface Sydenham calls this speech *"one of the most essential Parts, without which the Work had been wholly defective in the End for which it was framed; as will presently appear."*[62] But when he came to publish the second part of his edition six years later, extreme pressure was put on him to suppress it. Consequently, he ends his translation with the speech of Socrates and then adds an "Advertisement," in which he tells the reader how he was

> almost unanimously advised by such of his Friends, as are acquainted with the Original, not to publish his Translation of the last Speech in this Dialogue, that of *Alcibiades*, for fear of the Offence it may reasonably give to the Virtuous from the gross Indecency of some Part of it, the Countenance it may possibly give to the Vicious from the Example of *Alcibiades*, and the Danger into which it may bring the Innocence of the

59. *Dialogues of Plato*, trans. Benjamin Jowett, 4th ed. (Oxford: Clarendon Press, 1953), 1:510.
60. Sydenham, *The Banquet*, p. 53.
61. Ibid., p. 93.
62. Ibid., pp. 12–13.

Young, by filling their Minds with Ideas which it were to be
wished they could always remain Strangers to.[63]

That some youths might have needed and welcomed information about a society in which they were not outcasts did
not occur to Sydenham. He sees the matter solely in the
light of national morality. The reformation of the stage
effected by Addison and Steele, he tells us, has been thrown
back by the "licentious Comedy" of Gay and Fielding.
A new effort at reform is under way. "It would therefore be
the more unpardonable in the Translator of *Plato* to inter-
rupt this beginning Reformation, by presenting to View of
his English Readers a Character fit only for the Plays of an
Aristophanes." [64] Morality took precedence over truth.

But if Plato was a closed book, the gardens of poetry
were open. The classical curriculum in England, as John
Stuart Mill was to complain, ignored history and philosophy in favor of philology and poetry.[65] In the case of poetry,
the readings encompassed an odd mixture of the heroic
and the rococo, the former represented by Homer, the latter by the erotic poets. It was a paradox that an age that
would have rejected formal sex education as shocking
should have prescribed amorous Latin and Greek poetry as
a staple of education. Lady Byron (a quintessential Victorian even before Victoria) was to complain late in life to
Harriet Beecher Stowe that "there was everything in the

63.   *The Banquet: A Dialogue of Plato Concerning Love. The Second Part*
(London: W. Sandby, 1767), p. 247. That Socrates rejected the advances of
Alcibiades was not enough. That Alcibiades should have made them at all
and implied that such relations were common in his culture was sufficient
to damn the speech. The first complete edition of Plato in English, prepared by Thomas Taylor in 1804, used Sydenham's translations of the dialogues (where they existed). Though he left the bowdlerized text of the
Symposium unrevised, Taylor was brave enough to add a translation of
the speech by Alcibiades. The first candid and complete translation of the
Symposium in English was made by George Burges for the Bohn Classical
Library in 1850. Henry Carey's *Phaedrus* was added in 1858. These versions were then superseded by Benjamin Jowett's in the 1870s.

64.   Ibid., p. 249.

65.   See pp. 286–87.

classical course of the schools to develop an unhealthy growth of passion, and no moral influence of any kind to restrain it." [66] Byron himself was keenly aware of the irony. In Canto I of *Don Juan* he satirizes Lady Byron in the person of Juan's mother, Donna Inez. The latter wants to keep her son ignorant of "natural history" but finds her aims subverted by the standard schooling of the day. Byron had only to recite a typical list of classroom poets to make his point:

> Ovid's a rake, as half his verses show him,
>   Anacreon's morals are a still worse sample,
> Catullus scarcely has a decent poem,
>   I don't think Sappho's Ode a good example,
> Although Longinus tells us there is no hymn
>   Where the sublime soars forth on wings more ample;
> But Virgil's songs are pure, except that horrid one
> Beginning with *"Formosum Pastor Corydon."* [67]

Ovid, of course, wrote no love poems to boys, though at the beginning of the *Amores* he mentions them as eligible addressees. Anacreon's morals are "worse" because of his bisexuality. Catullus writes to Juventius in much the same vein as he writes to Lesbia. Virgil's second eclogue dramatizes the love of Corydon for Alexis, a beautiful young shepherd. This reference and Sappho's Ode leave no doubt as to Byron's point. Indeed, by implying that Longinus singled out the Ode for praise on ethical rather than aesthetic grounds, Byron manages to give an extra measure of dignity to Sappho's lesbianism.

In addition to these bisexual or homosexual Latin poets, Byron might have mentioned also Lucretius, Horace, and Tibullus. He does refer to Martial in a note. Byron would have known most of this literature as a schoolboy. His li-

66. Stowe, *Lady Byron Vindicated* (London: Sampson Low, Son, & Marston, 1870), p. 164.

67. *Byron's "Don Juan": A Variorum Edition*, ed. Truman Guy Steffan and Willis W. Pratt, 2nd ed. (Austin: University of Texas Press, 1971), 2:45.

brary in England included Latin editions of Xenophon, Athenaeus, Catullus, Virgil, Horace, Tibullus, Propertius, Petronius, and Martial, and English translations of Anacreon, Herodotus, Lucretius, Juvenal, and Tacitus, all of whose writings touch on the subject of homosexuality in Greece and Rome.[68]

Lucretius speaks of men being impelled by Venus toward women or boys indifferently at the beginning of *De Rerum Natura*. Horace addresses love poems to Lysicus and Ligurinus, Tibullus to Marathus. Martial writes of boys in a style explicitly sexual. Juvenal, who was widely admired, translated, and imitated in Byron's day, attacked effeminate homosexuals in his second satire, but at the end of Satire VI he recommends boys as less dangerous bedmates than women. Petronius was a byword for homosexuality in the eighteenth century. Propertius has no poems addressed to boys but shows the typical Roman acceptance of bisexuality by giving sympathetic advice to a friend who is wooing a boy. Tacitus, like Suetonius, uses homosexual scandals to denigrate the emperors.

The contemporary English versions were, of course, often misleading. For instance, Robert Bland's *Translations Chiefly from the Greek Anthology* (1806), which Byron owned, omits all the poems from Book XII (the *Mousa Paidikē*). It reprints Ambrose Philips's seventeenth-century translation of Sappho's prayer to Aphrodite, which turns Sappho's lover into a "youth." Nevertheless, Thomas Moore's popular translation of Anacreon's odes, which Byron much admired, included "To Bathyllus," a poem Coleridge deplored in the *Biographia Literaria* as demonstrating that good poetry may be morally unacceptable. Moore deprecated any discussion at all of Anacreon's homosexuality in

68. See William H. Marshall, "The Catalogue for the Sale of Byron's Books [1816]," *Library Chronicle of the Friends of the University of Pennsylvania Library* 34 (1968): 24–50. A reprint of the *Catalogue of the Library of the Late Lord Byron* for the sale of July 6, 1827, ed. Gilbert H. Doane (Privately printed, 1929), adds Suetonius in Latin and Petronius in Italian.

his preface; in a remark that ranked virtuous misapprehen-
sion above candor, he declared: "Whatever is repugnant to
modesty and virtue is considered in ethical science, by a
supposition very favourable to humanity, as impossible;
and this amiable persuasion should be much more strongly
entertained, where the transgression wars with nature as
well as virtue."[69] Obviously, poetry had a license prose
lacked.

What influences from this reading show up in Byron's
first schoolboy verses? To begin with, there is a translation
of Sappho's Ode, published in *Fugitive Pieces* in 1806, but
Byron's translation does not purport to be from the Greek
but from Catullus's version, "To Lesbia," a Latinization and
heterosexualization of the original. More interesting is
Byron's translation of one of Catullus's love poems to the
boy Juventius (Carmen 48, "Mellitos oculos tuos, Juventi"),
dated November 16, 1806, and published in the same
collection:

> Oh! might I kiss those eyes of fire,
> A million scarce would quench desire;
> Still, would I steep my lips in bliss,
> And dwell an age on every kiss;
> Nor then my soul should sated be,
> Still, would I kiss, and cling to thee;
> Nought should my kiss from thine dissever,
> Still, would we kiss, and kiss for ever.[70]

For more than a year, as we shall see, Byron had been ex-
changing chaste kisses with a boy at Cambridge he had
fallen in love with. But he thought it advisable to call his
version "To Ellen"; translations of homoerotic classics were
more acceptable with the genders disguised.

Byron, like many of his contemporaries, repeatedly
praised the *Anacreon* of his friend and future biographer,

69. *Odes of Anacreon*, trans. Thomas Moore, 7th ed. (London: J. Carpenter, 1806), 1:9–10.
70. *CPW*, 1:72.

Thomas Moore. In *Hours of Idleness*, which appeared six
months later, in June 1807, Byron included his own version
of the ode that Moore had numbered twenty-three, but
which Byron calls "Ode 3." In it, a young boy knocks at the
poet's door on a stormy night:

> At this lone hour, the Paphian boy,
> Descending from the realms of joy;
> Quick to my gate, directs his course,
> And knocks with all his little force;
> My visions fled, alarm'd I rose,
> "What stranger breaks my blest repose?"
> Alas! replies the wily child
> In faultering accents, sweetly mild;
> "A hapless infant here I roam,
> Far from my dear maternal home;
> Oh! shield me from the wint'ry blast,
> The nightly storm is pouring fast,
> No prowling robber lingers here;
> A wandering baby, who can fear?"
> I heard his seeming artless tale,
> I heard his sighs upon the gale;
> My breast was never pity's foe,
> But felt for all the baby's woe,
> I drew the bar, and by the light,
> Young Love, the infant, met my sight. . . .
> With care I tend my weary guest,
> His little fingers chill my breast;
> His glossy curls, his azure wing,
> Which droop with nightly showers, I wring.

Then Cupid, reviving, fears his bow is unstrung from the
damp and asks to test it:

> With poison tipt, his arrow flies,
> Deep in my tortur'd heart it lies:
> Then loud the joyous urchin laught,
> "My bow can still impel the shaft;
> 'Tis firmly fix'd, thy sighs reveal it:
> Say, courteous host, canst thou not feel it?"[71]

71. Ibid., pp. 74–75.

The poem is of course allegorical, but Byron has managed nevertheless to give a vivid description of a man falling in love with a boy: the poet is smitten by Eros in two senses.

Anacreon's poems are playfully frivolous. So too are most of the other pederastic poems of the Greek Anthology, which in this respect parallel the poems to girls. But there was another tradition of Greek love, heroic rather than hedonistic, to which Byron was also powerfully drawn. Its most famous exposition occurs at the beginning of the *Symposium*, where Phaedrus speaks of Achilles and Patroclus as the great exemplars of this tradition.

Though Byron had not read Plato, he could have found much about this kind of heroic devotion in Books XIII and XV of the *Deipnosophists* of Athenaeus, a copy of which he owned. Athenaeus makes reference both to a lost play by Aeschylus, *The Myrmidons*, in which the love of Achilles, left uncharacterized in Homer, is made explicitly sexual, and also to a lost tragedy by Sophocles on a homoerotic theme, his *Niobe*. Athenaeus also lists famous pairs of heroic lovers, beginning with Aristogiton and Harmodius, who won a place in the history of Greece by dying while resisting tyrants. It would appear that this tradition of self-sacrificing love made a strong appeal to Byron's boyish idealism. Curiously enough, the most glowing account of Greek pederasty available in English was the work of an archbishop. John Potter's *Antiquities of Greece*, first published 1697–1699, was still widely read. Byron recorded it in a "List of Historical Writers Whose Works I Have Perused" drawn up when he was nineteen. In his chapter "On their Love of Boys," Potter repeats Athenaeus's praise, paraphrases fully Strabo's famous account of Cretan pederasty, and applauds the Theban Band, bound together by what he calls "this excellent passion." What allowed Archbishop Potter to write so enthusiastically was his rash assumption that all these loves were immaculately chaste. How Byron perceived the sexual side of Greek love at this point it is difficult to say. Later in life he persistently ridiculed all forms of "Platonism." But at this period he seems to have been fascinated by the idea of heroic love between males. One classical story that attracted him greatly was the episode of Nisus and Euryalus in Book IX of the *Aeneid*, a kind of Latin analogue of the Achilles-Patroclus romance. As we have seen, Byron had used "Euryalus" as an epithet for his friend Delawarr in "Childish Recollections." In *Hours of Idleness* he published what he called a "paraphrase" of Virgil's episode. Here is his description of the young Euryalus who inspires Nisus's love:

> With him Euryalus, sustains the post,
> No lovelier mien adorn'd the ranks of Troy,
> And beardless bloom yet grac'd the gallant boy;
> Though few the seasons of his youthful life,
> As yet a novice in the martial strife,
> 'Twas his, with beauty, valour's gifts to share,
> A soul heroic, as his form was fair;
> These burn with one pure flame of gen'rous love,
> In peace, in war, united still they move;
> Friendship and glory form their joint reward,
> And now combin'd they hold the nightly guard.

As Virgil tells the story, the lovers dare a foray into the enemy's camp. Euryalus is captured; Nisus surrenders in despair and pleads for the boy's life. When Euryalus is slaughtered before his eyes, Nisus, facing hopeless odds, attacks his slayers and is slain. In the final lines of the poem, Byron once more depicts a favorite fantasy of his early poems, the male *Liebestod*:

> Thus Nisus all his fond affection prov'd,
> Dying, reveng'd the fate of him he lov'd;
> Then on his bosom, sought his wonted place,
> And death was heavenly, in his friend's embrace![72]

By an interesting coincidence, when Bentham took up the subject of homosexuality again in 1814 and sought

72. Ibid., pp. 76–77, 89.

more evidence to counter Montesquieu's suggestion that pederasty effeminized men, he also turned to the story of Nisus and Euryalus. "In the Aeneid," he wrote, "the most distinguished exemplification of the union of bodily vigour with mental intrepidity is that exhibited by Nisus and Euryalus in the attack made by the two youths without other company upon the enemy's camp." But was their love to be regarded as sexual? Bentham thought Virgil's text invited this interpretation. "Of the bond of attachment by which the valorous pair were united in so desperate an enterprise, effectual indication[?] is given by the four words, 'Nisus, amore pio pueri,'" that is, "Nisus [notable] for his pious love of the boy." To the objection that the adjective "pious" makes their love nonsexual, Bentham might have pointed out that in Latin, as in modern Italian and Spanish, *pius* (or *pio*) when characterizing relationships means "devoted" or "affectionate" rather than "moral" or "religious." (Byron had translated it as "generous.") Instead, Bentham countered this argument by an appeal to Virgil's Corydon eclogue: the objection might have been valid, he argued, "had Virgil been a disciple of Paul or Moses, but Virgil was no such thing. Take the answer from himself. Note the pathos of his lamentations for the cruelty of the beautiful Alexis and think by what sort of denial that cruelty manifested itself."[73]

In April 1807, Byron wrote to his friend Edward Long that he was preparing "Nisus and Euryalus" for *Hours of Idleness*, which was to appear in June. In that same month he said farewell to the boy who seems to have inspired the poem. Byron had first met John Edlestone in October 1805. At that time, Edlestone was fifteen and Byron, who had just arrived at Cambridge, seventeen. Byron had become interested in Edlestone through hearing him sing in the Trinity College choir. The boy's background was humble, but he had some refinement of mind, and Byron assumed

73. "Code Penal," May 1, 1814, box 74a, folio 143. Bentham's phrase is quoted from line 296 of Book V of the *Aeneid*.

the role of aristocratic patron to a youngster of talent, calling him his protégé. This was a relation that Byron felt especially comfortable with in the case of younger boys, whom at a later date he made his pages or attendants. Edlestone was fair and thin, with dark eyes. One imagines him as rather diffident, perhaps somewhat feminine: frailness in younger males brought out the chivalric side of Byron's character.

Byron had arrived at Cambridge in a state of depression, unhappy at leaving Harrow. His lameness and his rejection by Mary Chaworth may have made him shy about exposing his heart to others. He tells us he was first attracted to Edlestone by his voice, then by his looks and personality. Finally, an inadvertent revelation of the boy's feelings crystallized his own into love. Byron, with his typical generosity, had probably made substantial presents of money to Edlestone. When the latter wished to reciprocate, he gave Byron an inexpensive stone, a cornelian. But fearing that Byron would despise his gift, he burst into tears. This in turn melted Byron, who shed tears of his own. Byron commemorated the occasion in two poems, "The Cornelian," which he included only in the privately printed *Fugitive Pieces* and *Poems on Various Occasions*, and "Pignus Amoris," which was not published until 1898. In the first he expresses a fear that others will sneer at his sentimental friendship. The second poem seems to have been written after he and Edlestone parted since he speaks of "visions of the past":

For these this toy of blushing hue
   I prize with zeal before unknown,
It tells me of a Friend I knew,
   Who loved me for myself alone. . . .

Through many a weary day gone by,
   With Time the gift is dearer grown;
And still I view in Memory's eye
   That teardrop sparkle through my own.

And heartless Age perhaps will smile,
   Or wonder whence those feelings sprung;

Yet let not sterner souls revile,
 For Both were open, Both were young.[74]

Byron felt shy about telling others of his love for Edle-stone. He seems especially to have feared the ridicule of the sophisticated and critical William Bankes, a fellow un-dergraduate, whom he looked up to as his "pastor, master and friend." Nevertheless, he did take at least two people into his confidence. One was Long, a sensitive fellow stu-dent whom Byron found congenial, who played the flute and cello and spent considerable time in his company. By-ron found the courage to tell him the truth about "The Cor-nelian." But in February 1807, a month after the poem had appeared in its second private printing, he wrote to Long: "Pray, keep the subject of my 'Cornelian' a Secret," and in May he explained that in the forthcoming Hours of Idleness: "The Cornelian (which you & all the Girls, I know not why think my best) will be omitted."[75] In his Ravenna journal of 1821 Byron wrote of Long: "His friendship, and a violent, though pure love and passion—which held me at the same period—were the then romance of the most romantic pe-riod of my life." Clearly, Byron is here making an impor-tant distinction. His friendship with Long was a romantic "friendship" of the sort characteristic of the period. But he recognizes that the "violent, though pure," love and pas-sion he felt for Edlestone was not friendship, but love.[76]

This realization must have made Byron anxious since such love was so little acceptable in England. It was about this time that Augusta became aware of a startling and mysterious change in Byron's temperament, a transforma-tion she was later, after Byron's marriage, to comment on to his wife. Augusta must also have mentioned this devel-opment in her letters to Byron because a few months after meeting Edlestone he wrote to her: "My melancholy pro-

74. CPW, 1:181–82.
75. February 23, 1807, BLJ, 1:110; May 14, 1807, ibid., p. 118.
76. January 12, 1821, BLJ, 8:24.

ceeds from a very different cause to that which you as-
sign. . . . I will not however pretend to say I possess that
Gaité de Coeur which formerly distinguished me, but as the
diminution of it arises from what you could not alleviate,
and might possibly be painful, you will excuse the Dis-
closure." He then gave a list of reassurances—he is not
worried about his health or his money difficulties, nor is he
about to fight a duel—which cannot have been very re-
assuring since the mystery was only deepened. He then
adds, probably ironically: "You know me too well to think
it is *Love*." [77] Augusta had, in fact, been well aware of the
Chaworth affair: Marchand thinks that this is a feint and
that the letter does indeed refer to Edlestone. His use of
"melancholy" is one clue. Fifteen years later, Byron said of
his Cambridge days: "I took my gradations in the vices—
with great promptitude—but they were not to my taste . . .
and my heart, thrown back upon itself, threw me into excesses perhaps more fatal than those from which I shrunk."
The fatality here was, presumably, his love affair with Edlestone. Then he writes: "People have wondered at the Melancholy which runs through my writings. . . . If I could
explain at length the *real* causes which have contributed to
increase this perhaps *natural* temperament of mine—this
Melancholy which hath made me a bye-word—nobody
would wonder—but this is impossible without doing much
mischief." [78]

Byron speaks of women who admired "The Cornelian."
One of these was Elizabeth Pigot, his mother's neighbor at
Southwell, with whom he was on friendly terms. On June
30, 1807, shortly before parting from Edlestone, he sent

77.   January 7 [1805], *BLJ*, 1:87–88. Byron also mentioned his sister's
awareness of his change in disposition in his "Detached Thoughts,"
which he began in Ravenna on October 15, 1821: "When we met again in
1805—(she tells me since) . . . my temper and disposition were so completely altered that I was hardly to be recognized.—I was not then sensible of the change—but I can believe it—and account for it" (*BLJ*, 9:25).
78.   *BLJ*, 9:37–38.

her a description of his musical friend. No doubt her curiosity had been piqued by the poem since he refers to Edlestone as "the *Hero* of my *Cornelian*." [79] Byron, whose weight
had shot up to 202 pounds, had since dieted so success-
fully, he tells her, that Edlestone had not at first recognized
him when he returned from Southwell to Cambridge.
When Pigot responded sympathetically, he poured out his
heart more fully five days later after Edlestone had left: "I
write with a *bottle* of *Claret* in my *Head*, & *tears* in my *eyes*,
for I have just parted from 'my *Cornelian*' who spent the
evening with me; as it was our last Interview, I postponed
my engagements to devote the hours of the *Sabbath* to
friendship, Edlestone & I have separated for the present, &
my mind is a *Chaos* of *hope* and *Sorrow*." Edlestone had
taken a post in a "mercantile house" in London. For whatever reason, they planned a separation of a year and a half:

> We shall probably not meet, till the expiration of my minority,
> when I shall leave to his *decision*, either *entering* as a *Partner*
> through my Interest, or residing with me altogether. Of course
> he *would* in his present *frame* of mind prefer the *latter*, but he
> may alter his opinion previous to that period, however he
> shall have his choice, I certainly *love* him more than any hu-
> man being, & neither *time* or Distance have had the least effect
> on my (in general) changeable Disposition.

Byron then supplies a remarkable catalogue of friendships
as analogues for his own:

> In short, We shall put *Lady E. Butler*, & Miss *Ponsonby* to the
> *Blush*, *Pylades* & *Orestes* out of countenance, & want nothing
> but a *Catastrophe* like *Nisus* & *Euryalus*, to give *Jonathan* & *David*
> the *"go by."*—He certainly is perhaps more *attached* to *me*, than
> even I am in *return*. During the whole of my residence at *Cam-
> bridge*, we met every day summer & Winter, without passing
> *one tiresome moment*, & separated *each time* with increasing Re-
> luctance. I hope you will *one day* see *us* together. He is the only
> *being* I *esteem*, though I *like many*.[80]

79.   *BLJ*, 1:123.
80.   July 5, 1807, *BLJ*, 1:124–25. In Lucian's *Amores*, a dialogue debat-
ing the respective merits of heterosexual and homosexual love, Orestes
and Pylades are named as heroic lovers in a speech defending pederasty.

Obviously, Byron gave his list of faithful couples, intending them to be taken as examples of romantic friendships. He was hardly making an avowal of homosexuality. But inevitably a certain ambiguity hovers over the names, as in the case of Nisus and Euryalus. The suggestion has been made many times—and as often contradicted—that Jonathan's love for David was homosexual. In a cynical-sentimental poem, "To Romance," Byron had used Pylades as the generic name for a friend whose attraction would match the romance of the love of women.

But the most interesting models Byron proposes for Edlestone and himself are contemporary, the so-called "Ladies of Llangollen." In 1778, Lady Eleanor Butler and Sarah Ponsonby, daughters of two prominent aristocratic families in Ireland, had eloped together. Eleanor was thirty-nine, Sarah twenty-three. They were captured by their families, berated, and restrained, but remaining adamant, they were finally allowed to leave the country. They settled in a picturesque house in a tiny village in Wales. Intensely snobbish and class-conscious in an age when such manners were taken as a matter of course, they nevertheless charmed the villagers and were seen as emblems of a self-sacrificing devotion that had renounced the world.

Four years after their flight, Lady Louisa Stuart wrote: "When I first heard of them I was disposed to be captivated by anything so romantic."[81] Eventually they became a national and even an international cult and their cottage the haunt of celebrities. (One thinks of Gertrude Stein and Alice B. Toklas in France in the 1920s.) Queen Charlotte corresponded with them, they received a government pension, and their guests included Sir Walter Scott and Robert Southey, William Wilberforce, Josiah Wedgwood, Sir Humphry Davy, the Duke of Wellington, and the young Charles Darwin. Prime ministers apologized for passing through

81.   Elizabeth Mavor, *The Ladies of Llangollen: A Study in Romantic Friendship* (London: Michael Joseph, 1971), p. 62. See also Faderman, *Surpassing the Love of Men*, pp. 120–25.

Wales without visiting them. Wordsworth addressed them in a sonnet as "Sisters in love." [82] The two women were to live together for fifty years until after Byron's own death. They dressed like men and shared a bed; today they would undoubtedly be perceived as a lesbian couple. But enthusiasm for them as popular favorites inhibited scandal though innuendoes occasionally appeared in the press. In 1790, some gossipy paragraphs in the *General Evening Post* described their flight and dropped hints that made them uncomfortable: "Miss Butler is tall and masculine, she wears always a riding habit, hangs her hat with the air of a sportsman in the hall, and appears in all respects as a young man, if we except the petticoats which she still retains." [83] Full of indignation, the ladies wrote to Edmund Burke, who, perhaps recalling his own difficulties a decade earlier, advised them not to sue. It was an irony that one of their most adoring friends was the ever-suspicious Hester Thrale, who wished to see all lesbians and male homosexuals consigned to volcanic fires.

Byron's own love for Edlestone seems to have been at once chaste and clandestine. Kinsey notes that young homosexuals commonly experiment in their mid-teens and then withdraw for a few years from such affairs as they become increasingly aware of social disapprobation, resuming them at a later date.[84] Something like this seems to have occurred in Byron's case if, as seems likely, he was sexually involved with his Harrow schoolmates. Ordinarily the

82.   The sonnet was published in 1827 with the title "To the Lady E. B. and the Hon. Miss P. Composed in the Grounds of Plass Newidd, near Llangollen, 1824."

83.   The ladies read this account on July 24, 1790 (Mavor, *Ladies of Llangollen*, p. 82).

84.   Alfred C. Kinsey, Wardell B. Pomeroy, and Clyde E. Martin, *Sexual Behavior in the Human Male* (Philadelphia: W. B. Saunders, 1948): "During their late teens, many males experience considerable personal conflict over their homosexual activities, because they have become more conscious of social reactions to such contacts. Particularly in that period, many individuals attempt to stop their homosexual relations, and try to make the heterosexual adjustments which society demands" (p. 629).

most unplatonic of lovers, Byron in this case achieved something like the palpitating restraint Socrates advocates in the *Phaedrus*, where the male lovers, though burning with erotic desire, restrict the expression of their emotions to "the sight, the touch, the kiss, the embrace." After Edlestone's death Byron was to write of their love in his famous elegy "To Thyrza," in which he disguised Edlestone's identity behind a feminine name. There he describes the amorous side of their life together at Cambridge:

> Ours too the glance none saw beside;
>   The smile none else might understand;
> The whisper'd thought of hearts allied,
>   The pressure of the thrilling hand;
> The kiss so guiltless and refin'd
>   That Love each warmer wish forbore;
> Those eyes proclaim'd so pure a mind,
>   Ev'n passion blush'd to plead for more. . . .
> The pledge we wore—I wear it still.[85]

Obviously, Byron was well aware of the part sexual passion played in this attraction. One is reminded inevitably of another clandestine and platonic Cambridge romance, the affair carried on by Clive Durham and Maurice Hall before the unseeing eyes of their relatives and friends at home and at college in E. M. Forster's novel *Maurice*.

Always in need of self-expression, Byron seems to have commemorated his feelings for Edlestone in another poem during his years at the university. Besides "The Cornelian" and "Pignus Amoris," Byron wrote some further lines, which he published a month after their parting. In this case he did what he was to do again more extensively in the Thyrza lyrics of 1811 and 1812—he pretended that the object of his passion was a girl. In July 1807 he sent to the editor of *Monthly Literary Recreations* a poem that was published over his name but never reprinted by him in his lifetime. These were the "Stanzas to Jessy," which Marchand thinks were inspired by the separation from Edlestone that

85. *CPW*, 1:347.

had just taken place. Their style and substance, I think, make Marchand's conjecture convincing. They have the facile expression and rhetoric of most of Byron's early lyrics, but they are also marked by the chastened, wistful note characteristic of Byron's love for the young choirboy:

There is a mystic thread of life
    So dearly wreath'd with mine alone,
That destiny's relentless knife
    At once must sever both, or none.

There is a Form on which these eyes
    Have fondly gaz'd with such delight—
By day, that Form their joy supplies,
    And dreams restore it through the night.

There is a voice whose tones inspire
    Such soften'd feelings in my breast,
I would not hear a seraph choir,
    Unless that voice could join the rest.

There is a face whose blushes tell
    Affection's tale upon the cheek,
But pallid at our fond farewell,
    Proclaims more love than words can speak.

There is a Lip which mine has prest,
    But none had ever prest before;
It vowed to make me sweetly blest,
    That mine alone should press it more.

There is a bosom all my own,
    Has pillow'd oft this aching head,
A mouth which smiles on me alone,
    An eye, whose tears with mine are shed.

There are two hearts whose movements thrill
    In unison so closely sweet,
That pulse to pulse responsive still,
    They both must heave, or cease to beat.

There are two souls whose equal flow
    In gentle stream so calmly run,
That when they part—they part?—ah no!
    They cannot part—those souls are one.[86]

86. Ibid., pp. 208–09.

· 3 ·

To the East

Within a few days of his farewell to John Edlestone, Byron found himself in a new circle of Cambridge students whom he had known only casually before. The coterie consisted of John Cam Hobhouse, who was to be his lifelong friend and defender; the witty, dissipated Scrope Berdmore Davies; and the scholarly but irreverent Charles Skinner Matthews. The group was liberal in politics, skeptical in religion, fiercely contemptuous of moral cant. Their literary tastes ran to Pope and Juvenalian satire, with no quarter given.

These views undoubtedly answered to something in Byron's own temperament. In this milieu of high-spirited raillery, Byron the satirist was born. The astringency of his most famous letters reflects their tone; so does the banter of *Don Juan*. Hobhouse was the steadiest of the quartet. His youthful revolt made him a radical member of Parliament; eventually, his fires banked down, he became a member of the cabinet and, under Victoria, a peer. Scrope Davies's liveliness dominated the others in conversation. But he wrote nothing, and later he was forced to flee to France to escape arrest for debt. In point of mind and scholarship, the most formidable of the quartet was Charles Skinner Matthews. Byron called Matthews

> a Man of the most astonishing powers as he sufficiently proved at Cambridge by carrying off more prizes & fellowships against the ablest candidates than any other Graduate on record. . . . There was the stamp of immortality in all he said or did. . . . To me he was much, to Hobhouse every thing.—My poor Hobhouse doted on M[atthews].—For me, I did not love quite so

107

much as I honoured him; I was indeed so sensible of his infinite superiority that though I did not envy, I stood in awe of it.

Byron acknowledged that he had taken Matthews, like William Bankes, as his "guide, philosopher, and friend."[1]

Matthews, though learned, was never solemn; he was given to pranks and fantastic clowning. He was also the most unorthodox in his opinions. Byron called him a "most decided Atheist,"[2] who was "very free in his speculations upon all kinds of subjects, although by no means either dissolute or intemperate in his conduct, and as I was no less independent, our conversation and correspondence used to alarm our friend Hobhouse to a considerable degree."[3] Byron later told John Murray that their letters were, in that age, unpublishable. On one occasion the two young men rode together from London to Cambridge talking "all the way incessantly upon one single topic."[4] Byron did not say what the topic was, though we may guess what engrossed them from some as yet unpublished letters in the Murray collection.

Thomas Moore deprecated Matthews's influence in his *Life*: "By singular ill-fortune, too, the individual who, among all his college friends, had taken the strongest hold on his admiration and affection, and whose loss he afterwards lamented with brotherly tenderness, was, to the same extent as himself, if not more strongly, a skeptic."[5] Hobhouse's comment on this in his journal for January 15, 1830, is interesting:

The most unjust of [Moore's] conclusions is that B's singularities both in conduct and opinion are chiefly to be ascribed to college associates. Certainly B had nothing to learn in the way of depravity either of mind or body when he came from Har-

1.   To R. C. Dallas, August 21, 1811, *BLJ*, 2:76; September 7, 1811, ibid., pp. 92–93.
2.   *BLJ*, 2:76.
3.   *BB*, 1:132.
4.   Ravenna, November 19, 1820, *BLJ*, 7:231.
5.   *LJL*, 1:124.

row. . . . A great deal of stress is laid on the influence of Matthews (Charles) on Byron's opinions—I do not believe he had
any—if he had that influence related more to practical debauchery than to metaphysical conjecture. Moore has delated
on B's unequal friendships such as for Eddlestone [sic] and
Rushton. He little knows the ground he treads.[6]

It is noteworthy that Hobhouse mentions Byron's involvement with boys such as his page, Robert Rushton, immediately after referring to the influence of Matthews on his
sexual behavior. Byron's one surviving letter to Matthews,
written as he was about to leave for Greece, is also revealing. It shows, as we shall see, that both anticipated that his
visit there would lead to homoerotic adventures.

But in England, as Byron waited for his twenty-first
birthday and his accession to the House of Lords, his involvements seem to have been all on the heterosexual side.
To the Reverend John Becher of Southwell he wrote that he
was suffering from "*too much Love*. . . . My Paphian God-
desses are [here], and I have sacrificed at their altar rather
too liberally.—In fact, my blue eyed Caroline, who is only
sixteen, has been lately so *charming* that, though we are
both in perfect health, we are at present commanded to *re-
pose*, being nearly worn out.—So much for Venus."[7] And
to Hobhouse next day he confessed more bluntly: "I am
buried in an abyss of Sensuality. I have renounced *hazard*
however, but am given to Harlots and live in a state of Con-
cubinage."[8] During the same period, Byron seems to have
become a father of a child by a servant in Nottinghamshire
named Lucy, though details about this purported illegitimate son are lacking.

Passionately drawn to women, Byron is sometimes (as
here) the jaunty rake, at others the tender lover. He could
be considerate, brutal, sentimental, enraged, playful, and,
at least sometimes, wracked by guilt and self-disgust. This

6.   *LLB*, p. 291.
7.   February 26, 1808, *BLJ*, 1:157.
8.   *BLJ*, 1:158.

last mood, absent from his letters or journals, is familiar only in his poetry, but it is wrong to discount it. Leslie Marchand posits some residual Calvinism, foreign to Byron's intellect but ingrained in his emotions from early years. But certain ambiguities appear in the period of Byron's life between his leaving Cambridge and departing for Greece. Though his involvements were overwhelmingly heterosexual, various stories circulated, all at second hand, about how he disguised his inamoratas as boys to deceive his mother or others. Thomas Medwin quotes Byron as saying he passed off one mistress as his brother Gordon.[9] Since Byron was often attracted by boys with girlish looks, Marchand suggests that some of the boys in his company were in fact mistaken for girls in disguise. Marchand notes also his interest in a tradesman's son at Brighton and his frequent visits to Harrow, now, presumably, the most innocent of his pastimes.[10]

Both Marchand and Doris Langley Moore have suggested that Byron's hectic involvement with women at this time may have been intensified by his fear of his homosexual impulses. Of course, such pursuits were common enough for wealthy young aristocrats in his day, and Byron's heterosexual instinct was inherently strong. But whatever inhibitions any teenage peer might have had in the reign of George III would have been countered by a realization that these pleasures were far less dangerous than any attraction to his own sex. Perhaps this anxiety did add to his fever. It was during these years that the hanging of homosexuals, sporadic earlier in the king's reign, now became regular annual events, and pilloryings seem to have increased in number and to have attracted increasingly larger and rowdier crowds.

9. *Medwin's Conversations of Lord Byron* (1824), ed. E. J. Lovell, Jr. (Princeton: Princeton University Press, 1966), p. 67.

10.   Marchand identifies the boy as John Cowell and says that Byron "later used his influence to have him admitted to Eton" (*BB*, 1:157).

But if Byron hoped by a plenitude of women to obliterate his desire for boys, he did not succeed. England, ac-
cordingly, began to appear a less and less attractive domicile. The conventional grand tour of France and Italy being
out of the question because of the war with Napoleon, Byron had first proposed to his mother that he visit Germany,
Austria, and Russia. But by January 1808 he had decided
upon the Orient instead and spoke of going as far as Persia
and India. He wrote to John Hanson, his attorney, of a
wish to study "India and Asiatic policy and manners."[11]
This sounds as if Byron may have had in mind a diplomatic
or administrative career in the empire. At various times he
thought seriously of becoming an Oriental scholar. If he
had not been a poet, it is possible to imagine him a scholar-
adventurer like Sir Richard Burton.

Was Byron's interest in the Islamic world influenced by
the difference between its moral climate and England's?
Bentham, writing about "Offences against Reputation" in
his essay "The Influence of Time and Place in Matters of
Legislation" had taken note of the contrast: "Among other
traits which discover the manners of the ancient Greeks,
we learn, from what Xenophon relates regarding himself,
that crimes against nature could be esteemed but a joke.
Even now, wherever the Mahometan religion prevails,
such practices seem to be attended with but little disrepute."[12] Byron must have been aware of this cultural an-
tithesis from an early age. He liked to boast of his expertise
in Turkish history and, in a note written in 1818, claimed to
have read "Knolles, Cantimir—De Tott—Lady M. W. Mon-
tague—Hawkins's translation from Mignot's History of the
Turks—the Arabian Nights—All travels or histories or

11.   November 18, 1808, *BLJ*, 1:175.
12.   *The Works of Jeremy Bentham*, ed. John Bowring (1838–1843; rpt.
New York: Russell and Russell, 1962), 1:175. Mary P. Mack, in *Jeremy
Bentham: An Odyssey of Ideas, 1748–1792* (New York: Columbia University
Press, 1963) dates this essay as belonging to the 1780s (p. 406, n. 50),
though it was not published until Bowring's edition of 1838.

books upon the East I could meet with, as well as Rycaut, before I was *ten years old*." [13] If Byron—and we have no reason to doubt his word—had indeed read Paul Rycaut before 1798, he would have been made dramatically aware of the way Islamic mores differed from England's. Rycaut's *Present State of the Ottoman Empire* is remarkably communicative on the subject of homosexuality, though strongly negative. Speaking of the influence of Persian literature on the education of the pages of the sultan's court, Rycaut remarks:

> It teaches them also a handsome and gentle deportment, instructs them in Romances, raises their thoughts to aspire to the generous and virtuous actions they read of in the *Persian* Novellaries, and endues them with a kind of *Platonick* love to each other, which is accompanied with a true friendship amongst some few, and with as much gallantry as is exercised in any part of the world. But for their Amours to Women, the restraint and strictness of Discipline, makes them altogether strangers to that Sex; for want of conversation with them, they burn in lust one towards another, and the amorous disposition of youth wanting more natural objects of affection, is transported to a most passionate admiration of beauty whereseover it finds it, which because it is much talked of by the *Turks*, we will make it a distinct discourse by it self. [14]

In the next chapter, "Of the Affection and Friendship the Pages of the *Seraglio* bear each other," Rycaut shows how these affairs, so reminiscent of those described in the dialogues of Plato and Plutarch, were reconciled in Turkish culture with the dictates of the Muhammadan religion: "They call it a passion very laudable and virtuous, and a step to that perfect love of God, whereof mankind is only capable, proceeding by way of love and admiration of his image enstamped on the creature." But since his view of

13. Isaac Disraeli, *The Literary Character of Men of Genius* (London: John Murray, 1822), 3rd ed., pp. 101–02. This is a marginal comment Byron wrote to the 1818 edition, which Disraeli incorporated as a note in 1822.
14. (London: John Starkey and Henry Brome, 1668), p. 31.

the matter is Paul's, and not Plato's, Rycaut proceeds to ex-
coriate this defense: "This is the colour of virtue, they paint
over the deformity, of their depraved inclinations; but in
reality this love of theirs, is nothing but libidinous flames
each to other, with which they burn so violently, that banishment and death have not been examples sufficient to deter
them from demonstrations of such like addresses." [15] Rycaut
then points out that such passions are shared not only by
the pages but by "Persons of eminent degree" and the sul-
tans themselves.

In the West, tradition condemned the kind of love the
Turks found celebrated in Persian literature. But most literary cultures outside Christian Europe did not. Medieval
Islamic poets, especially, wrote of homoerotic and heterosexual love indifferently. Jahiz, in his *Treatise on Love*, composed about 830 A.D., denies that "*ishq*," denoting passionate love, can be used for the feeling one man has for
another. But within a century this view had been superseded. Lois Anita Giffen, in her *Theory of Profane Love
Among the Arabs*, tells us that in the multitude of treatises
on erotic psychology that follow Jahiz, the rule is that love
may exist between men as well as between men and
women. [16] From the tenth century to the nineteenth, this is
the tacit assumption throughout the Islamic world. This
may be clearly perceived in the most famous of all these
books, Ibn Hazm's *The Ring of the Dove*, written in Arab
Spain about 1022. Ibn Hazm, far from being an Ovid or
Anacreon, writes as a devout Muslim and stern moralist,
who declares pointedly (if somewhat defensively) that he
is "a man of spotless innocence, pure, clean, and unde-
filed." Nevertheless, he is an ardent amorist on the purely
sentimental side since, as he tells us, "every heart is in
God's hands." [17] Indeed, a "hadith," or saying ascribed to

15. Ibid., p. 33.
16. (New York: New York University Press, 1971), pp. 3, 86.
17. *The Ring of the Dove: A Treatise on the Art and Practice of Arab Love*,
trans. A. J. Arberry (London: Luzac, 1953), pp. 235, 22.

Muhammad, declared that "he who loves passionately and remains chaste and dies, dies a martyr."[18] Many orthodox imams, according to Ibn Hazm, have been saints and martyrs of love.[19] (One can hardly imagine a Christian historian making such a boast about a pope or a bishop.) With this romantic ideal of Platonic love in mind, Ibn Hazm recites numerous stories and quotes many love poems, the object of the man's passion being sometimes female, sometimes male. Even when he tells of his own experiences, he is quite un-self-conscious about the gender of his beloveds; we learn about it only incidentally. We may compare this with the remark of the English general Henry Seymour Conway to his lifelong friend Horace Walpole, a remark that reflects the mores of Georgian England. Conway declares: "The avowing a passion for a youth (though not an uncommon thing with the Greek and Roman poets) is so notoriously impious and contrary to nature, as well as morality and religion, that it is impossible not to be offended at it."[20] In Ibn Hazm, by contrast, the emphasis is on the emotional suffering, or the temptation resisted, and the two kinds of love are in no way distinguished. This liberal tradition extended from the Pyrenees to the Himalayas. An examination of almost any classical anthology of Islamic verse, whether it originates in Delhi, Kabul, Shiraz, Baghdad, Damascus, Istanbul, Cairo, Fez, Cordova, or Seville, reveals the same intermingling of homo- and heteroerotic poems. Even so stern a jurist as the fourteenth-century philosopher, Ibn Khaldun, though he favors punishing homosexual acts by stoning to death, includes as a matter of course, in his *Universal History*, without apology or comment, as monuments of Arabic poetry, a significant

18.   *Theory of Profane Love*, p. 107.
19.   *Ring of the Dove*, p. 22.
20.   A. L. Rowse, *Homosexuals in History* (London: Weidenfeld and Nicolson, 1977), p. 83.

number of poems in which men express their amorous infatuation for each other.[21]

Could Byron have known any of this poetry? In the late
eighteenth century, Persian classics began to appear for the
first time in English translation. The major poets of this tradition—Attar, Hafiz, Sadi, and Jami—celebrate with the
same refined, subtle, and sensual imagery the charms of
young women and men and declare their devotion with in-
discriminate fervor. In the list of books he drew up at Cambridge in 1807, most of which he had read before he was
sixteen, Byron mentions "Sadi, and Hafiz, the immortal
Hafiz, the Oriental Anacreon. The last is reverenced beyond
any bard of ancient or modern times by the Persians, who
resort to his tomb near Shiraz, to celebrate his memory."[22]

How much of Sadi and Hafiz Byron had actually read is
a matter of dispute. Harold S. L. Wiener assumes that Byron had seen only the lyrics scattered through the thirteen
volumes of the great Orientalist, Sir William Jones.[23] These,
however, like Floyer Sydenham's translation of the *Symposium*, were thoroughly bowdlerized. However, there
were other translators who, if they followed Jones in revising the poetry, at least faced the issue candidly in their
prefaces. John Hindley, whose *Persian Lyrics, or Scattered
Poems from the Diwan-i-Hafiz* appeared in 1800, admits the

21. Ibn Khaldun, *The Muqaddimah: An Introduction to History*, 2nd ed.,
trans. F. Rosenthal (Princeton: Princeton University Press, 1967), 1:296.
22. *LJL*, 1:100.
23. Harold S. L. Wiener, "Byron and the East: Literary Sources of the
'Turkish Tales,'" in *Nineteenth-Century Studies*, ed. H. Davis et al. (Ithaca:
Cornell University Press, 1940), pp. 89–129. William Cable Brown as-
sesses Eastern travel literature in "Byron and English Interest in the East,"
Studies in Philology 34 (1937):55–64. More directly related to the present
study is Bernard Blackstone's "Byron and Islam: The Triple Eros," *Journal
of European Studies* 4 (1974):325–63. Blackstone reviews Byron's reading of
Oriental literature and his early aspirations to become an Oriental scholar.
He emphasizes the appeal Turkish tolerance of homosexuality must have
had for Byron and cites Rycaut. His essay is wide-ranging, speculative,
and hard to evaluate. One may agree with him that Byron had an *anima*

homoerotic nature of many of Hafiz's odes and recognizes the discomfort they will arouse in English readers:

> To avoid being suspected of disingenuousness, we must here also point out a blemish in our Author, too glaring for disguise, and which, if not explained away, must subject him to the same moral disgrace, which unfortunately attaches itself to some of the first poets, and even to some of the philosophers, of antiquity. Well aware of the dishonour reflected upon VIRGIL and ANACREON, from the names *Alexis* and *Bathyllus*, it is not without regret that we find HAFIZ, and indeed all the SUFI poets of this class, continually liable to the opprobrium of similar accusations. Happy should we be to join in the triumph of decorum and virtue, could the defence, which has been set up by the *Turkish commentators*, to rescue their favourite author from such degrading accusations be pronounced just and satisfactory. Whether it be possible that *the sovereign monarch, his ministers, approved and ancient friends, the mistress of a chaste affection, or even a beloved wife,* can be disguised under these allusions, or whether we must interpret them in that gross and masculine sense which shocks human nature, or through the medium of mysticism and allegory, is a point we leave for better judges to determine.[24]

After this ironic dismissal of attempts to explain away Hafiz's bisexuality, Hindley was still faced with the problem of translating poems addressed to beautiful cupbearers. Once again he chose to bowdlerize: "This disgusting object has, in obedience to decorum, been very properly translated by Sir William Jones . . . into a *damsel*, fair as a nymph of Paradise, by a licence of which we shall be found to have availed ourselves throughout these poems, and, we trust,

---

naturaliter Islamica without agreeing with all his conclusions. Blackstone makes much of parallels he finds between ideas and expressions in Byron's early poems and Stephen Weston's *Moral Aphorisms in Arabic, and a Persian Commentary in Verse, Translated from the Originals, with Specimens of Persian Poetry* (1805). He also attempts to link Byron with the "gnostic" thought of the Bekhashti dervishes through Ali Pasha.

24. (London: E. Harding, J. Debrett, & West & Hughes, 1800), pp. 8–9.

for reasons too obvious to need any formal apology on our part."[25]

If Byron had any doubts as to whether Eastern manners of earlier ages still persisted at the beginning of the nineteenth century, these must have been set at rest by his reading of his copy of Nicolas Sonnini's *Travels in Upper and Lower Egypt* (1799). In the days when Christianity and Islam were rival faiths competing for sovereignty in the Mediterranean world, Muhammadan tolerance of homosexuality was looked upon as proof of Christian superiority and was so cited in theological polemics.[26] With the coming of the enlightenment, religious rancor subsided, but the visibility of homosexuality in Oriental countries was taken as evidence of the moral, cultural, and, later, racial inferiority of these peoples, a condition that justified, by implication, the rights of European countries to suzerainty or conquest. Writing in French in 1799, Sonnini speaks not in the Pauline accents of Rycaut, but in the language of *sensibilité*:

> The passion contrary to nature which the Thracian dames avenged by the massacre of Orpheus, who had rendered himself odious by gratifying it, the inconceivable appetite which dishonoured the Greeks and Persians of antiquity, constitute[s] the delight, or, to use a juster term, the infamy of the Egyptians. It is not for the women that their amorous ditties are composed: it is not on them that tender caresses are lavished; far different objects inflame them. Sensual pleasure with them has nothing amiable, and their transports are merely paroxysms of brutality. This horrid depravation which, to the

25. Ibid., p. 33n.
26. See, e.g., *Passio S. Pelagii*, a narrative poem by the German dramatist and nun Hrosvitha (ca. 935–ca. 1002). Pelagius, a young Christian of noble birth, is held hostage by Abd-er-Rahman III (891–961), the great Caliph of Cordova. When the caliph, attracted by Pelagius's beauty, tries to kiss him, Pelagius strikes the Arab ruler and is condemned to death (*The Non-Dramatic Works of Hrosvitha*, ed. Sister M. Gonsalva Wiegand [St. Louis: n.p., 1936], pp. 129–58).

disgrace of polished nations, is not altogether unknown to
them, is generally diffused over Egypt; the rich and the poor
are equally infected with it; contrary to the effect it produces in
colder countries, that of being exclusive, it is there associated
with the love of women.[27]

What repelled Rycaut and Sonnini about Muhammadan
culture inevitably drew homosexual or bisexual writers to
it. One thinks of the experiences of Flaubert and Gide in
North Africa, of Burton and T. E. Lawrence in the Near
East, or, in Byron's own day, of the fiction of William Beckford. When Byron first read *Vathek, an Arabian Tale*, is
unknown; it was first published in 1786. But Beckford's
fantastic romance, purportedly the history of Haroun-al-
Raschid's grandson, fascinated him for a variety of reasons, not the least of which must have been its bisexual
ambiance. Henry Lansdown reported that Byron called
the book "his gospel"; and Medwin's *Conversations* speak of
a "very early admiration."[28] In his notes to *The Giaour*,
Byron acknowledged his debt to that "'sublime tale,' the
'Caliph Vathek.' . . . As an Eastern tale, even *Rasselas* must
bow before it; his 'Happy Valley' will not bear comparison
with the 'Hall of Eblis.'"[29] Three years later in a note to *The
Siege of Corinth*, Byron referred to it again as a work "I . . .
never recur to, or read, without a renewal of gratification."[30]

Byron was not only attracted to Beckford's prose romance: he was also fascinated by his life and fate. Born in
1760, the son of a popular Lord Mayor of London who,

27. *Travels in Upper and Lower Egypt*, trans. Henry Hunter (London:
John Stockdale, 1799), 1:251–52. The book was in Byron's library in 1816.
28. *Recollections of the Late William Beckford of Fonthill*, ed. Charlotte
Lansdown (n.p., 1893), p. 32; *Medwin's Conversations*, p. 258.
29. *CPW*, 3:423.
30. Ibid., p. 486. For an account of Byron's relations with Beckford,
literary and personal, see André Parreaux, "Beckford et Byron," *Etudes
Anglaises* 8 (1955):11–31, 113–32; for Beckford's homosexuality in the context of his age, see "Beckford et Sodome," in André Parreaux, *William Beckford: Auteur de "Vathek" (1760–1844)* (Paris: A. G. Nizet, 1960), pp. 54–69.

through his West Indian plantations, had amassed the largest fortune in England, Beckford, like Byron, looked forward to a life of luxury at the pinnacle of society. Bentham in his *Memoirs* recorded hearing "a trait of young Beckford's profusion. When about to sleep at an inn, he ordered it to be papered for him, at an expense of £10, like Wolsey, who travelled with a set of gold hangings." Beckford was not only a distinguished connoisseur of painting and architecture; he was also, as a writer and musician, an accomplished artist in his own right. When Bentham met him at Lord Pembroke's early in the 1780s, he noted that Beckford sat down at the harpsichord as soon as he entered the room and "played delightfully."[31] Beckford's mother had aristocratic connections, and Beckford was himself about to be named a peer when disaster struck. In October 1784, Beckford was accused of sexual relations with the sixteen-year-old William Courtenay while on a visit to Powderham Castle. The newspapers, egged on by his enemy Lord Loughborough, buzzed with scandal. Beckford tried to face down the affair, but a concerted campaign of ostracism finally drove him into exile the next summer. Lady Milbanke, Byron's mother-in-law-to-be, gives a sense of the atmosphere of the times in a letter written to a friend:

> What an infamous wretch is Beckford! & what a disgrace to the Age that he should be suffered to walk about! it is suspected that the Grande-monde mean to protect that vice *sourdement* [secretly], as in Italy, & if B is not universally shunn'd (is he?) it is too strong a confirmation of it.[32]

Beckford lived mainly abroad for the next decade. When he finally settled again in England, he was treated as a pariah for his remaining fifty years despite his fortune, the

31. *Memoirs and Correspondence*, in *Works of Jeremy Bentham*, 10:285, 122.
32. Malcolm Elwin, *Lord Byron's Wife* (New York: Harcourt, Brace & World, 1962), p. 69.

splendors of the immense Gothic abbey he raised at Fonthill, and his fame as the author of *Vathek*.[33]

When Byron left England on his first trip abroad, almost
his first act on the Continent was to visit the mansion
where Beckford had lived in exile at Cintra near Lisbon. He
described the palace in Canto I of *Childe Harold*. He had
also intended to include the following stanza on Beckford:

> Unhappy Vathek! in an evil hour
> Gainst Nature's voice seduced to deed accurst,
> Once Fortune's minion, now thou feel'st her Power!
> Wrath's vials on thy lofty head have burst.
> In wit, in genius, as in wealth the first,
> How wondrous bright thy blooming morn arose[!]
> But thou wert smitten with unhallowed thirst
> Of nameless crime, and thy sad day must close
> To scorn, and Solitude unsought—the worst of woes.[34]

These lines, suppressed and not published until 1833,
nine years after Byron's death, are interesting from several
points of view. They show how fully Byron was aware of
the social sanctions visited on homosexuals and bisexuals
by English society and how little wealth, talent, and position availed to protect any man who was once suspect. But
what strikes the reader especially is Byron's use of the con-

33.   The account of Beckford by Richard Garnett in the *Dictionary of
National Biography* is particularly egregious. No mention is made of the
Powderham episode of 1784. Garnett takes Beckford's life down to 1820
without a hint that he had been ostracized and forced to live abroad. At
this point, he feels he must make some reference to the decades of seclusion at Fonthill, which he treats as follows: "This seclusion may have been
partly owing to grave imputations upon his moral character, which, however, in the absence of any avowed accuser or attempt at proof, it is reasonable as well as charitable to regard as the consequence of his retire-
ment than the cause." No hint whatever is given as to the nature of
Beckford's offense, though the press of the day repeatedly referred to it
and it was everywhere understood in English society. One can imagine
with what sardonic bitterness Beckford might have commented on the
theory that his isolation was self-imposed.

34.   *CPW*, 2:18. McGann's transcription of the poem from Byron's
manuscript differs appreciably in its wording from the previously received version.

ventional homophobic language of the times—"Gainst
Nature's voice seduced to deed accurst"—"unhallowed
thirst / Of nameless crime." How are we to interpret this?
A. L. Rowse has scolded Byron for what he perceives to be
the poet's hypocrisy.[35] The impulse is understandable: Byron wrote these lines in Albania, ten weeks after visiting
Portugal, when he was on his way to Greece where he
hoped to have the same experiences for which Beckford
had been exiled. Is this another case of James I condemning sodomy? Or had Byron so internalized British values as
to feel a strong sense of guilt about his desires? Doris Langley Moore has taken the latter view: "Alluding to William
Beckford, he had written in *Childe Harold* of 'th' unhallowed thirst of crime unnamed,' and though he very properly cancelled the stanza, seeing that from his own glass
house . . . he was in no position to throw stones, it expressed an authentic feeling."[36]

It is hard to discount this view entirely. Byron, for all the
flippancy of his letters, seems to have felt considerable
guilt about most aspects of his sexual activity. But we must
also remember that violently condemnatory language was
the coin demanded of anyone who had the temerity to
mention homosexuality in print. This put both homosexuals and anyone who wished to defend them in a well-
nigh-impossible position. How was one to change or even
mitigate public prejudice if prejudicial language was *de
rigueur*? Bentham's case is particularly instructive. His 1785
essay on pederasty, though advocating reform and strongly
opposing popular attitudes, is couched in homophobic language throughout.[37] One might explain this as a rhetorical
strategy: an attitude of apparent moral disapprobation (at

35. *Homosexuals in History*, p. 114.
36. *LBAR*, p. 443.
37. E.g., he refers to homosexuality in this essay as "this kind of
filthiness" (p. 391), "this inconceivable propensity" (p. 392), "this abomination," a "depraved taste" (p. 393), etc. ("Offences Against One's Self:
Paederasty, Part 1," *Journal of Homosexuality* 3 [1978]:389–405).

least at the verbal level) may have been the price Bentham felt he had to pay to argue against hangings, perhaps also to deflect suspicion that he himself might harbor homoerotic feelings. But it is interesting that Bentham's notes of 1774, intended only for his own eyes, use similar language.[38] It was not until the more radical notes of 1814–1816 that Bentham consciously revolted against the traditional vocabulary and attempted to find neutral and nonpejorative language for same-sex relations. Since it took someone as sensitive to the nuances of moral discourse as Bentham this long to free himself from the linguistic conventions of the day, we should realize how great the difficulties were.

Though the homosexual side of *Vathek* is discreetly veiled, it is implicit in Beckford's description of the effeminately beautiful boy Gulchenrouz of whom the caliph is enamored, a description which the vigilant Hester Thrale characterized in her journal as suspiciously "luscious."[39] The homosexual theme is more explicit in the "Episodes from Vathek," tales meant to be added to his book, which Beckford completed but did not publish. Byron never met Beckford, though during his stay in Venice he expressed a desire for a meeting. He had heard about the episodes from his friend and fellow poet Samuel Rogers, who had visited Beckford in the seclusion of Fonthill in 1818. Byron subsequently wrote Rogers: "Could you beg of *him* for *me* a copy in M.S.S. of the remaining *tales*? I think I deserve them as a strenuous & public admirer of the first one;— I will return it—when read—& make no ill use of the copy."[40] Beckford, however, declined to part with his manuscript. Rogers had expressed disapproval of some of the

38. Bentham speaks of men "infected with this odious taste" (box 74a, folio 3), "this vice" (folio 16), "an act of this loathsome nature" (folio 19), etc.

39. November 1796, *Thraliana: The Diary of Mrs. Hester Lynch Thrale, 1776–1809,* ed. Katharine C. Balderston, 2nd ed. (Oxford: Clarendon Press, 1951), 2:969n.

40. March 3, 1818, *BLJ,* 6:17.

stories. Presumably, one that upset him was the tale of Prince Alasi, who falls in love with the stripling Firouz. Though Firouz later turns out to be a girl, Beckford makes no apology for Alasi's passion, which is presented as unabashedly pederastic.

There is no doubt that such associations were in Byron's mind when he prepared for his journey to Greece and Turkey. Byron had attained his majority in January 1809. As the date approached, did any recollection of his promise to Edlestone trouble his mind? It would be interesting to know what his feelings were, but the record is a void on Byron's side. Doris Langley Moore has, however, now published evidence that Edlestone, at least, had remembered the romantic promise. Byron had originally planned to sail for Greece in March. Shortly before this, Edlestone had written asking for some kind of help. Byron, always generous, and in this case, no doubt, feeling somewhat guilty, offered Edlestone "pecuniary assistance to form some permanent means of subsistence," presumably some kind of annuity.[41] Of their correspondence at this time, only Edlestone's reply has survived. Far from being a love letter, the note is punctiliously formal, declines Byron's offer, and asks merely for his "patronage" in finding employment. We do not know how Byron responded. Edlestone shortly afterward became a clerk in the Admiralty, though apparently not through Byron's efforts, and held the position through the rest of his short life.

Whatever his feelings about Edlestone, Byron at this point in his career suffered from intense paranoia. On April 16, six weeks after Edlestone wrote his second letter, Byron told John Hanson, his lawyer and agent, who had warned him about leaving England when his financial affairs were in so bad a state:

> If the consequences of my leaving England, were ten times as ruinous as you describe, I have no alternative. There are circumstances which render it absolutely indispensible, and quit

41. *LBAR*, pp. 89–90.

the country I must immediately. . . . I am pestered to death in country and town [by creditors] and rather than submit to my present situation, I would abandon every thing, even had I not still stronger motives for urging my departure.[42]

What was Byron so concerned about? Six months later, when he was traveling in Albania, he returned to the theme in another equally mysterious letter to Hanson:

I will never revisit England if I can avoid it. It is possible I may be obliged to do so lest it should be said I left it to avoid the consequences of my Satire [i.e., challenges to duels], but I will soon satisfy any doubts on that head if necessary & quit it again, for it is no country for me.—Why I say this is best known to myself. You recollect my impatience to leave it. You also know by what I then & still write that it was not to defraud my creditors. I think you know me well enough to think no motive of personal fear of any kind would induce me to such a measure; it was certainly none of these considerations, but I will never live in England if I can avoid it. *Why* must remain a secret.[43]

There is no open admission here on Byron's part (it is inconceivable he should have made one) that his bisexuality was the reason for his anxieties, but any reader must be struck by the parallels between these letters and those to Augusta about his melancholia. In each case Byron hints at an undisclosable secret and discounts the more obvious interpretations of his behavior to avoid misconceptions. He reassures Augusta about his health. He assures Hanson he is not acting dishonorably. But it seems likely his bisexuality explains the evasive vagueness in both cases.[44]

42. *BLJ*, 1:200–01.
43. Prevesa, November 12, 1809, *BLJ*, 1:232.
44. Marchand notes: "The secret reason for Byron's urgency to leave England . . . and his reluctance to return must remain a mystery. . . . It is tempting to speculate . . . that he had a wish to escape his own proclivities toward attachment to boys, or perhaps that he feared a closer connection with the Cambridge choirboy Edlestone, who had wanted to live with him in London. But there is no solid evidence of this" (*BLJ*, 1:232n.). It does not seem, however, that Byron meant to "escape" his homosexual

The expression of anxiety in his April letter is particularly striking. Byron was a very brave man, brave often to the point of recklessness, and fear is a rare emotion in his correspondence. But accusations of homosexuality were something even brave men flinched at in his day. So potent an instrument of terror were they that judges of the King's Bench ruled in 1779 that their use in extortion cases made the crime equivalent to highway robbery at pistol point.[45] Shortly after Byron departed for Greece, a wave of public hysteria in connection with homosexuals raised the number of blackmail cases to an unusual level.[46] Byron may have feared exposure for some indiscreet letter or act. To be "paragraphed" in the press as the Earl of Leicester had been in December 1808 or as Beckford had been thirty-five years earlier would have been an unpleasant experience.[47] In such cases it was necessary to bring, and win, a libel suit or else leave the country under a cloud of ignominy. Indeed, even though Leicester technically won in the courts, his victory was so equivocal that he was nevertheless forced to retire from England. Byron himself was engaged in a vendetta with a scurrilous journalist named Hewson Clarke for reprinting hostile reviews of *Hours of Idleness*. He had some thought of challenging him to a duel but instead attacked him in his new polemic, *English Bards and Scotch Reviewers*, as

---

impulses by traveling abroad—quite the contrary. He did, presumably, mean to escape the consequences of giving expression to them in England. On this point it seems to me the presumptive evidence is strong.

45.   H. Montgomery Hyde, *The Love That Dared Not Speak Its Name: A Candid History of Homosexuality in Britain* (Boston: Little, Brown, 1970), p. 69.

46.   Arthur Gilbert, "Sexual Deviance and Disaster During the Napoleonic Wars," *Albion* 9 (1977): 103.

47.   On December 3, 1808, the *Morning Herald* had reported (erroneously) that Lady Leicester was divorcing her husband on charges of sodomy. Two days later it published another false account that he had fled the country. Leicester sued for libel and won. The court, however, limited the damages because of the "flying rumors" concerning the earl's reputation. See *Annual Register* (1809), pp. 346–50.

A would-be satirist, a hired Buffoon,
A monthly scribbler of some low Lampoon.[48]

Clarke was more than willing to descend to personalities. The attack was, however, postponed to the eve of Byron's return from Greece. When it did come, he called Byron illegitimate and his father a murderer, without, as Byron remarked, probably with relief, hitting on "something like the shadow of truth."[49]

Byron and Hobhouse left for Falmouth on June 20. Since they missed the ship for Malta, they were obliged to wait until July 2 when the Lisbon Packet sailed. The letters Byron sent off while he was waiting have a strikingly euphoric ring, as if he were relieved from some strain and reveling in a new sense of freedom. Before this he had made no direct or open allusions to homosexuality in his correspondence; now he recurs repeatedly to the subject. In a letter to Francis Hodgson on June 25 he tells of a strange coincidence: "On Hartford Bridge we changed horses at an Inn where the great Apostle of Paederasty Beckford! sojourned for the night. We tried in vain to see the Martyr of prejudice, but could not; what we thought singular, though perhaps you will not, was that Ld. Courtney [sic] travelled the same night on the *same road* only one stage *behind* him."[50] The gossipy, mocking, supercilious tone—typical of Byron's epistolary references to contemporary homosexuals—is notably different from the portentous lines on Beckford he composed a few months later.

On the same day, in the same mood, he writes, jokingly but revealingly, to Henry Drury, a friend who was a master at Harrow, about Hobhouse's plan to keep a journal of their travels: "I have laid down my pen, but have promised to contribute a chapter on the state of morals, and a further

48. *CPW*, 1:259.
49. To Hobhouse, July 31, 1811, *BLJ*, 2:65.
50. *BLJ*, 1:210. Courtenay and Beckford had been estranged since the events of 1784. Byron's innuendo must be wide of the mark.

treatise on the same to be entituled [sic] 'Sodomy simpli-
fied or Paederasty proved to be praiseworthy from ancient
authors and modern practice.'" Byron is being facetious,
but one thinks of the essay on this theme Sir Richard Burton was to append to his translation of the *Arabian Nights*
some eighty years later. If the times had allowed, Byron
would surely have relished anticipating Burton. Then he
adds, more outrageously still: "Hobhouse further hopes to
indemnify himself in Turkey for a life of exemplary chastity
at home by letting out his 'fair bodye' to the whole Divan."[51] This fantasy of Hobhouse's alluring the sultan's
cabinet must have amused Drury, given Hobhouse's staid
demeanor. (Perhaps the Divan might have been responsive. During an interview with the Turkish Minister of the
Marine, the latter stared at a member of Byron's party and
remarked: "I love English seamen.")[52]

To another acquaintance, Edward Ellice, he remarked:
"The Inhabitants [of Falmouth], both female & male, at least
the young ones, are remarkably handsome."[53] It was, however, the male youths who particularly engaged his attention. Two years later, when Hobhouse had returned to England, Byron described for him a Greek boy who reminded
him of a mysterious "Abbé Hyacinth" he had met at Falmouth.[54] This reference is illuminated by a revealing letter
he dispatched on June 22 to Charles Skinner Matthews:

> My dear Mathieu,—I take up the pen which our friend has for
> a moment laid down merely to express a vain wish that you
> were with us in this delectable region, as I do not think Geor-
> gia itself can emulate in capabilities or incitements to the
> "Plen. and optabil.—Coit." the port of Falmouth & parts adja-
> cent.—We are surrounded by Hyacinths & other flowers of the
> most fragrant [na]ture, & I have some intention of culling a
> handsome Bouquet to compare with the exotics I hope to meet

51.   *BLJ*, 1:208.
52.   *BB*, 1:244.
53.   June 25, 1809, *BLJ*, 1:209.
54.   Athens, August 23, 1810, *BLJ*, 2:14.

in Asia. One specimen I shall surely carry off, but of this here-
after.—Adieu Mathieu![55]

Some of the allusions in this deliberately oblique letter
are readily intelligible. Georgia was the home of the Circas-
sians, famous for their beauty; the "Hyacinths" refer to the
legend of Apollo's love for a beautiful boy who, acciden-
tally killed by the god in a game of quoits (pronounced as,
and in Byron's day sometimes spelled, "coits"), was trans-
formed into the flower. The puzzling Latin quotation, however, baffled editors until 1957, when Gilbert Highet, in response to a query from Marchand, identified it. The phrase
"plenum et optabilem coitum" occurs in a tale in the Satyricon in which Eumolpus tells how, by several tricks, he
managed to obtain from the boy he was sleeping with "full
and to-be-wished-for intercourse."[56] The context of Byron's
letter is thus unmistakably homosexual. Byron, on the eve
of his departure, which he thought would be final, felt he
could make a candid, if cryptic, avowal of one of his reasons for traveling abroad.

Matthews's reply has until now not been published. Its
matter and tone reveal beyond a doubt the nexus binding
him with Byron and Hobhouse. On June 30 he responded
from London:

> In transmitting my dispatches to Hobhouse, mi carissime βυ-
> ρον [Byron] I cannot refrain from addressing a few lines to
> yourself: chiefly to congratulate you on the splendid success of
> your first efforts in *the mysterious*, that style in which more is
> meant than meets the Eye. I shall have at you in that style be-
> fore I fold up this sheet.
>
> Hobhouse too is uncommonly well, but I must recommend
> that he do not in future put a *dash* under his mysterious sig-
> nificances, such a practise would go near to letting the cat out
> of the bag, should the tabellarians [i.e., postmen] be inclined

55. *BLJ*, 1:206–07.
56. *BB*, 1:181n. The phrase occurs in *Satyricon* 86. For the full story,
see William Arrowsmith's translation (Ann Arbor: University of Michigan
Press, 1959), pp. 87–89.

to peep: And I positively decree that every one who professes *ma methode* do spell the term wch designates his calling with an e at the end of it—*methodiste*, not method*ist*, and pronounce the word in the French fashion. Every one's taste must revolt at confounding ourselves with that sect of horrible, snivelling, fanatics.

As to your Botanical pursuits, I take it that the flowers you will be most desirous of culling will be of the class polyandria and not monogynia but *no*gynia. However so as you do not cut them it will all do very well. A word or two about hyacinths. Hyacinth, you may remember was killed by a Coit, but not that "full and to-be-wished-for Coit."

Have a care your Abbey Hyacinth be not injured by either sort of coit. If you should find anything remarkable in the botanical line, pray send me word of it, who take an extreme interest in your anthology; and specify the class and if possible the name of each production. . . .

Adieu my dear Lord; I wish you, not as Dr. Johnson wished Mr. Burke, all the success which an honest man can or ought to wish you, but as grand founder and arch-Patriarch of the Methode I give your undertaking my benediction, and wish you, Byron of Byzantium, and you, Cam of Constantinople, jointly and severally, all the success which in your most methodistical fantasies, you can wish yourselves.[57]

This letter unequivocally reveals the homosexual bond in the Cambridge circle. It clearly implies something hitherto unsuspected, that Hobhouse shared Byron's and Matthews's tastes. Matthews takes the lead as patriarch of the Cambridge neo-Methodists but addresses the other two men as sympathetic disciples. In a sense, the three share what would today be called a gay identity, based on common interests and a sense of alienation from a society they must protect themselves from by a special "mysterious" style and mutually understood codes.

Byron and Hobhouse arrived at Lisbon on July 7, then visited the village of Cintra, a few miles away, and saw the

57. I am obliged to John Murray for providing copies of this and the second Matthews letter reproduced below. Some of Matthews's botanical allusions may need clarification: polyandrous flowers have male stamens; "monogynia" refers to the class of flowers with female stamens.

magnificent Moorish palace in which Beckford had lived during the first year of his bitter exile. "The first and sweetest spot in this kingdom," Byron wrote to Hodgson, "is Montserrat, lately the seat of the great Beckford."[58] It was ironic that Byron, on his first arrival in Europe, should have been immediately reminded of another wealthy and literate bisexual who had been forced to live abroad. When Byron commemorated the visit in Canto I of *Childe Harold* three months later, the excursion to Cintra inspired the stanza on Beckford that we have already quoted and which Byron suppressed. However, he did include the following lines on Beckford's ruined mansion:

> And yonder towers the Prince's palace fair:
> There thou too, Vathek! England's wealthiest son,
> Once form'd thy Paradise, as not aware
> When wanton Wealth her mightiest deeds hath done,
> Meek Peace voluptuous lures was ever wont to shun.

> Here didst thou dwell, here schemes of pleasure plan,
> Beneath yon mountain's ever beauteous brow:
> But now, as if a thing unblest by Man,
> Thy fairy dwelling is as lone as thou![59]

The moralizing tone could hardly contrast more strikingly with Byron's correspondence to Matthews. The future poet of *Don Juan* was still willing to compromise with convention.

Byron enjoyed Portugal; he was even more captivated by Cadiz and Seville, from which he sent home glowing letters on the beauty of Spanish women and their eagerness for intrigue. But when he was at Gibraltar waiting for a ship for Malta, an obscure crisis occurred. Byron had taken with him on the voyage, in the role of a page, Robert Rushton, the "Robin" of *Childe Harold*. This handsome boy stands behind Byron in the famous painting by George

---

58. July 16, 1809, *BB*, 1:187. Moore omitted this sentence when he quoted the letter in his *Life* (*LJL*, 1:193–94).
59. *CPW*, 2:19.

Sanders, "Byron Landing from a Boat," which the poet had commissioned before he left England. Byron had taken Rushton into his entourage when he repossessed New-stead from Lord Grey in the fall of the preceding year. Jerome McGann has transcribed a stanza, which appears near the beginning of the manuscript of *Childe Harold*, a stanza Byron did not publish, in which Rushton (here called Alwin) is described:

> Of all his train there was a henchman page
> A peasant boy who served his master well
> And often would his pranksome prate engage
> Childe Harold's ear when his proud heart did swell
> With sable thoughts that he disdained to tell
> Then would he smile on him, as Alwin smiled
> When aught that from his young lips archly fell
> The gloomy film from Harold's eye beguiled
> And pleased the Childe appeared, nor eer the boy reviled.[60]

Rushton had been the object of some jealousy. When Byron's valet, William Fletcher, took the boy to a brothel in London prior to their departure, Byron was furious at both of them and threatened to send Rushton home to his father. We recall that Hobhouse had linked Edlestone and Rushton as boys whose connection with Byron Moore had treated naïvely. Lady Caroline Lamb later told Lady Byron that Byron had confessed to her "that Rushton was one of those whom he had corrupted."[61]

Byron arrived at Gibraltar on August 4. At this point, he had some second thoughts. Perhaps the combination of close intimacy and lack of privacy while traveling was too much of a strain. Perhaps the discreet and antisentimental Hobhouse had delivered an ultimatum. Whatever the trouble, Byron sent Rushton back to England with an elderly servant, Joe Murray. Inevitably, he felt a need to ex-

60.   It is interesting that in the first version of this stanza the opening lines read: "Of all his train there was a *guilty* page / A dark-eyed boy who loved his master well" (*CPW*, 2:10–11, my emphasis).

61.   *LLB*, p. 243.

plain this decision to his mother, now managing Newstead for him: "I have sent . . . the boy back, pray show the lad any kindness as he is my great favourite. I would have taken him on"—here R. E. Prothero's 1898 edition of the letter ends, as if the sentence were incomplete. What Byron wrote and crossed out was "but you *know boys* are not *safe* amongst the Turks."[62] To Rushton's father he rephrased the matter more discreetly: "The country which I am now about to travel through, is in a state which renders it unsafe, particularly for one so young."[63] Since the "state" of Turkey was well known to Byron before he left England, these reasons must surely be factitious.

Rushton's departure plunged Byron into gloom. The novelist John Galt, who accompanied him on the packet to Malta, noted his moodiness: Byron was sociable by day, but "when the lights were placed, he made himself a man forbid, took his station on the railing . . . and there, for hours, sat in silence, enamoured it may be, of the moon."[64] Galt thought Byron's behavior affected and unaccountable. Hobhouse may have understood the cause, but obviously he would not have enlightened their fellow traveler. The parting had not been made easier by Rushton's marked unwillingness to return home.[65]

In Malta the ever-volatile Byron recovered sufficiently to fall in love with Constance Spencer Smith, a young married woman with a romantically adventurous past. Before he left the island, they had made an elaborate pact for a later reunion and elopement. The brief encounter ended when the young men sat sail for Greece and made plans to stop en route in Albania. Byron's imagination was immediately seized by the idea of an excursion to so romantic a

62. *The Letters and Journals*, ed. R. E. Prothero, vol. 1 (London: John Murray, 1898), 242. Marchand restored the erasure. Gibraltar, August 15, 1809, *BLJ*, 1:221–22.

63. August 14, 1809, *BLJ*, 1:222.

64. *Life of Lord Byron* (London: Colburn & Bentley, 1830), pp. 62–63.

65. To Mrs. Byron, Constantinople, June 28, 1810, *BLJ*, 1:252.

country. He wrote his mother excitedly: "I . . . embark to-
morrow for Patras from whence I proceed to Yanina where
Ali Pacha holds his court, so I shall soon be among the
Mussulmen."[66]

Albania, though only fifty miles from the heel of Italy,
was then, as now, the least known and least accessible part
of Europe. Few Britons had visited the country, and Byron
later boasted that he and Hobhouse had penetrated further
than any other Englishman, except the government's official envoy. The ruler, Ali Pasha, was a brigand warlord of
legendary fame, whose military prowess had won him the
soubriquet, "the Napoleon of the East." He was nominally
under the jurisdiction of the sultan but, in fact, independent through his clever balancing of England and France
against Turkey. Treacherous, ruthless, affable, and feared,
he had something about him of the tyrants of the *Arabian
Nights* and *Vathek* and contributed traits to Byron's own
Oriental tales.

Albania was remarkable in another respect. According
to one theory, the Dorian tribesman who in post-Homeric
times had introduced homosexuality into Greece as part of
their military regimen had come from this part of Europe.
In Byron's day, the culture, part Muslim and part Christian, was unique in that both factions preserved some aspects of this ancient tradition in an institutionalized form.
Havelock Ellis thought the phenomenon sufficiently notable to incorporate anthropological reports on Albania
into the first chapter of his *Sexual Inversion*. He cites Johann
Georg von Hahn's *Albanesische Studien* of 1853 to the effect
that "the young men between 16 and 24 love boys from
about 12 to 17. A Gege marries at the age of 24 or 25, and
then he usually, but not always gives up boy-love." Hahn
quotes one of these mountain tribesmen:

> "The sight of a beautiful youth awakens astonishment in the
> lover, and opens the door of his heart to the delight which the

66. September 15, 1809, *BLJ*, 1:224.

134   Byron and Greek Love

contemplation of this loveliness affords. Love takes possession
of him so completely that all his thought and feeling goes out
in it. If he finds himself in the presence of the beloved, he rests
absorbed in gazing on him. Absent, he thinks of nought but
him. If the beloved unexpectedly appears, he falls into confusion, changes color, turns alternately pale and red. His heart
beats faster and impedes his breathing. He has ears and eyes
only for the beloved. He shuns touching him with the hand,
kisses him only on the forehead, sings his praise in verse, a
woman's never."

Hahn's knowledge of Plato and Sappho may have led him
to emphasize elements in the man's speech that echoed the
erotic psychology of classical antiquity; if not, the parallels
are striking. Ellis reports Weigand's opinion in the *Rhein-
isches Museum für Philologie* (1907) that such affairs were
"really sexual, although tempered by idealism" and noted
that "while most prevalent among the Moslems, they are
also found among the Christians, and receive the blessing
of the priest in church."[67]

But the tone of popular travel accounts in Byron's day
differed from German scholarship on Albanian mountain-
eers. Napoleon's agent, François Pouqueville, whom Byron
quotes in his notes to *Childe Harold*, had reacted more typically in his *Travels in the Morea, Albania, and Other Parts of
the Ottoman Empire*, first published in English translation in
1806:

Why am I forced here to notice the deep offence against morality with which, in one respect, these people are to be charged?
But it seems as if a passion disowned by the first laws of our
nature is one of the ordinary concomitants of barbarism. The
Albanian is no less dissolute in this respect than the other inhabitants of modern Greece, without seeming to have any idea
of the enormity of his crime; especially since, far from seeing it
discredited, he finds it rewarded by the chief to whom he is
subjected. The wandering lives led by these people, their days

67.   Hahn and Weigand are quoted in Havelock Ellis, *Sexual Inversion*,
Vol. 2 of *Studies in the Psychology of Sex*, 3rd ed. rev. (Philadelphia: F. A.
Davis, 1920), p. 10.

being passed chiefly amid camps, perhaps encourage this re-
volting passion. It is general among all classes. The women are
not shut up under locks and bars, but in the mountains may be
seen walking about perfectly free and unveiled.[68]

Pouqueville's reference to the Albanians' chief doubtless
reflected his knowledge of Ali Pasha's court at Janina. Another French writer, General Guillaume de Vaudoncourt,
was more explicit in his *Memoirs on the Ionian Islands . . .
Including the Life and Character of Ali Pacha* (1816). Ali, he advised his readers, "is almost exclusively given up to Socratic pleasures, and for this purpose keeps up a seraglio of
youths, from whom he selects his confidants, and even his
principal officers."[69] This unusual system of government,
unknown in the West, except perhaps at St. Petersburg
under Catherine the Great, was not uncommon in Muslim
lands and was even more fully developed in the Japanese
shogunate of the seventeenth and eighteenth centuries.[70]

Both Byron and Hobhouse were to give accounts of their
Albanian visit to the British public, Hobhouse in his *Journey Through Albania* first published in 1813, Byron in *Childe
Harold*. In addition, we have Byron's personal letters to England. It is interesting to see the way they tried to convey
their knowledge of what were, to the English, unspeakable
habits. Hobhouse is circumspect and erudite. His remarks
in the *Journey* are meant to inform only the informed. Albanian soldiers, he tells us, live

independent of the other sex, whom they never mention, nor
seem to miss in their usual concerns or amusements. The
same habit is productive of a system, which is carried by them
to an extent of which no nation, perhaps, either modern or an-

68. Trans. Anne Plumptre (London: Henry Colburn, 1813), p. 405.
Byron was no doubt familiar with the French edition of 1805.
69. Cited in William A. Borst, *Lord Byron's First Pilgrimage* (New
Haven: Yale University Press, 1948), p. 84n.
70. See Donald H. Shively, "Tokugawa Tsunayoshi, the Genroku
Shogun," in *Personality in Japanese History*, ed. A. M. Craig and D. H.
Shively (Berkeley: University of California Press, 1970), pp. 97–99.

cient, unless we reluctantly except the Thebans, can furnish a similar instance. Not even the Gothic Taifali (I refer you to Gibbon for their depraved institution) could be quoted against this assertion, and you should have sufficient proof of its truth, were I not aware of the propriety of the maxim approved, or probably invented by the great Latin historian, "Scelera ostendi oporteat (dum puniuntur) flagitia abscondi."[71]

The least obscure reference in this tissue of obscurities is to the Sacred Band of Thebes, the regiment of male lovers who fought in Greece in Plato's time. Tacitus's maxim—"Crimes should be blazoned abroad by the retribution, but abomination hidden"—appears in his account of the drowning of homosexuals by the ancient Germans.[72] Hobhouse's most recherché allusion, from Gibbon's *Decline and Fall*, is to a tribe in ancient Rumania, whose military renown, Gibbon declares, "was disgraced and polluted by the public infamy of their domestic manners. Every youth, on his entrance into the world, was united in ties of honourable friendship, and brutal love, to some warrior of the tribe; nor could he hope to be released from this unnatural connexion, till he had approved his manhood by slaying, in single combat, some huge bear, or a wild boar of the forest."[73]

Ten years later, Hobhouse was imprisoned for a radical pamphlet he had written while electioneering for Parliament. When he was in Newgate, he heard an execution

71. (Philadelphia: M. Carey, 1817), 1:130.
72. *Dialogus, Agricola, Germania*, trans. Sir William Peterson (Cambridge: Harvard University Press, 1963), p. 231. In this passage, Tacitus describes how the ancient Germans plunged men who were *corpore infames* (sexually infamous) "in the mud of marshes with a hurdle on their heads" (*Germania*, 12). Heinrich Himmler, when told that homophobia had its origins in Judaism, apparently used this passage to justify the Nazi persecutions that sent thousands of homosexuals to death camps (Harry Wilde, *Der Schicksal der Verfremte* [Tübingen: Katzmann, 1969], p. 62). Tacitus was important to German racial theory because he described the ancient Germans as "a race untainted by marriage with other races" and "a people peculiar and pure" (*Germania*, 4).
73. *The History of the Decline and Fall of the Roman Empire*, ed. J. B. Bury (London: Methuen, 1900), 3:106.

outside his cell. The style of the account he wrote in his diary on December 29, 1819, contrasts markedly with the paragraph in his *Journey*:

> A man was hanged this morning for an unnatural crime. Had my windows fastened up but could not sleep. They began putting up the scaffold at 4 o'clock. The tolling of the bell at 8 was frightful. I heard the crash of the drop falling and a woman screetch violently at the same moment. Instantly afterwards, the sound of the pye man crying, "all hot, all hot." Tis dreadful hanging a man for this practise.[74]

The climax of Byron's journey was inevitably his meeting with Ali Pasha. If he had no previous knowledge of Ali's temperament, he was enlightened on his first day in Albania. His ship had landed at Prevesa, where he was shown Ali's local palace by the Albanian governor, "a most merry man who laughed much with little Signior Bosari and told him . . . 'avec une sourire impudent' that one of the rooms was for the 'boys.'"[75] After a stay in Janina, Byron and Hobhouse had to travel inland for eight days through rugged terrain to Tepelene to meet Ali, who was engaged in "a little war" and interested in cultivating English allies. Ali was capable of ordering a massacre on a whim, but Byron found him in a benevolent mood. Indeed, he received them standing in his audience chamber and overwhelmed them with amiability. But Byron soon became aware that Ali was as much struck by his person as his nationality. Byron was bemused: he had not counted on playing the part of the young Caesar in Bithynia. He obviously relished telling the story some three weeks later in a letter to his mother, which shows a remarkable talent for social comedy:

> The Vizier received me in a large room paved with marble, a fountain was playing in the centre, the apartment was surrounded by scarlet Ottomans. He received me *standing*, a won-

---

74.   Robert E. Zegger, *John Cam Hobhouse: A Political Life, 1819–1852* (Columbia: University of Missouri Press, 1973), p. 159.
75.   *BB*, 1:202.

derful compliment from a Mussulman, & made me sit down
on his right hand. . . . His first question was why at so early
an age I left my country? . . . He said he was certain I was a
man of birth because I had small ears, curling hair, & little
white hands, and expressed himself pleased with my appearance & garb.—He told me to consider him as a father whilst I
was in Turkey, & said he looked on me as his son.—Indeed he
treated me like a child, sending me almonds & sugared sherbet, fruit & sweetmeats 20 times a day.—He begged me to visit
him often, and at night when he was more at leisure.

Byron thought Albanian men were "the most beautiful
race in point of countenance in the world. Their women are
sometimes handsome also." If his mother read all this with
shocked amusement—the compliments on her family's aristocracy would have pleased her vanity—one wonders
what she made of Byron's declaration that he had "no desire to return to England, nor shall unless compelled by absolute want & Hanson's neglect." Or of his postscript on
Ali's grandsons—"They are totally unlike our lads, have
painted complexions like rouged dowagers, large black
eyes & features perfectly regular. They are the prettiest
little animals I ever saw." [76] Byron departed from Tepelene,
still *persona grata*, with letters for Ali's son, who lorded it
over the Peloponnesus.

On the same day he wrote to his mother, Byron reiterated his determination to avoid England to Hanson, with
the evasive reasons we have already quoted. About this
time he showed Hobhouse a journal he had kept at Cambridge. Hobhouse urged him to burn it—presumably it
was too candid about his feelings for Edlestone. [77] On their

76. Prevesa, November 12, 1809, *BLJ*, 1:227–28.
77. Thomas Moore, in the manuscript "Notes" for his *Life* of Byron,
recorded the episode in these words:

> He said that when he and Hobhouse were together in Albania, Hobhouse laid
> hold of a great quantity of manuscript paper, which had fallen out of his port-
> manteau, and asked what it was. On being told that it was an account of B.'s
> early life and opinions, he persuaded him to burn it, "For," said he, "if any sud-
> den accident occur they will print it, and thus injure your memory." "The loss,"
> he said, "is irreparable." (*Prose and Verse, Humorous, Satirical and Sentimental, with
> Suppressed Passages from the Memoirs of Lord Byron*, ed. Richard Herne Shepherd
> [London: Chatto & Windus, 1878], p. 439)

way back, at Janina on October 31, Byron began *Childe Harold*. Canto I expresses his guilt about his heterosexual promiscuity but gives no hint of Byron's most urgent reason for traveling to the East. These lines, including the stanza on Beckford's fall, were written just before the letters to his mother and to Hanson. Clearly, he had been meditating on English severity at the same time he was observing Albanian manners.

It was not until March 28 of the following year that Byron composed Canto II, the part of *Childe Harold* that contains his impressions of Albania and Greece. In some verses radically revised before publication, he wrote first of Ali's harem, with a truly Oriental complacency. There, the typical harem woman lived

> . . . apart,
> And scarce permitted, guarded, veil'd, to move,
> She yields to one her person and her heart,
> Tam'd to her cage, nor feels a wish to rove.

Then, more candidly, something nearer the truth about Ali's pederasty:

> For boyish minions of unhallowed love
> The shameless torch of wild desire is lit,
> Caressed, preferred even to women's self above,
> Whose forms for Nature's gentler errors fit
> All frailties mote excuse save that which they commit.[78]

These lines, like the Beckford stanza, were later omitted and replaced by some innocuous reflections on Oriental motherhood. At this stage of his career, Byron was still afraid to affront the British public by "improper allusions."

By a fateful coincidence, Byron's first visit to Greece began with a brief stay at the town of Missolonghi. Then he and Hobhouse traveled along the shores to the Gulf of Corinth, by way of Delphi, Parnassus, and Thebes to Athens, arriving on Christmas day, 1809. In Albania he had been still intermittently under the spell of Constance Spencer

78.   *CPW*, 2:63.

Smith and had expressed his feelings in several poems—
"To Florence," "Stanzas Composed . . . in a Thunder-
storm," and "Stanzas Written in passing the Ambracian
Gulph." In Athens, he recorded the dissipation of this passion in the lines, "The spell is broke, the charm is flown!"
The two Englishmen lodged at the house of Tarsia Macri,
the widow of the English vice-consul, and were waited on
by her three daughters. Byron was soon writing appre-
ciatively in his letters of these girls, especially the young-
est, Theresa, who was twelve. Everything in Athens con-
spired to charm Byron during what were probably the
happiest months of his life. The city had the air of a primitive small town with no hotels, no luxury, no social life. But
the historical and literary associations fascinated him, and
his excursions to Pentelicus, Sunium, and Marathon all
worked on his imagination. After England, the clear skies
and winter warmth seemed paradisiacal: Byron never lost
the predilection for the Mediterranean that his stay in
Athens awakened. Later, he declared that Greece had made
him a poet:

> Where'er we tread 'tis haunted, holy ground;
> No earth of thine is ever vulgar mould,
> But one vast realm of wonder spreads around,
> And all the Muse's tales seem truly told,
> Till the sense aches with gazing to behold
> The scenes our earliest dreams have dwelt upon:
> Each hill and dale, each deepening glen and wold
> Defies the power which crush'd thy temples gone.[79]

The political situation, on the other hand, looked depressing. The western European colony in Athens was
united on only one point: their conviction that the Greeks
were sunk irremediably in servitude through their "national and individual depravity." Byron thought them much
inferior to the Albanians and to their Turkish masters. But,
usually inclined to take the side of the underdog, he re-

79.   Ibid., p. 73.

acted in their favor: "It seems to me rather hard to declare so positively and pertinaciously, as almost every body has declared, that the Greeks, because they are very bad, will never be better."[80] He tried to steer a course between enthusiastic philhellenes like Nicolas Sonnini and William Eton and the Greeks' more vehement detractors. He thought, however, they would need Western aid: "The English have at last compassionated their Negroes, and under a less bigoted government may probably one day release their Catholic brethren: but the interposition of foreigners alone can emancipate the Greeks, who, otherwise, appear to have as small a chance of redemption from the Turks, as the Jews have from mankind in general."[81] Byron was a pessimistic optimist. But at a time of almost complete apathy and despair, the notes to *Childe Harold* held out a flicker of hope, pointing the way to the Greek independence movement that began a decade later.

But what of the "Hyacinths" Byron had hoped to find on classical soil? Inevitably, some scenes reminded him of homosexual associations with Greek history. Sailing south on the west coast from Prevesa, he passed the island of Levka or Santa Mauros, with the famous Leucadian cliff from which Sappho was supposed to have leaped to her death:

Dark Sappho! could not Verse immortal save
That breast imbued with such immortal fire?
Could not she live who life immortal gave?[82]

Byron visited Leuctra, where the Sacred Band defeated the Spartans in 371 B.C., and Chaeronea, where they were annihilated by Alexander, who built there a monument to their fame still standing in Byron's day—and ours. Athens itself must have called to mind Aristogiton and Harmodius. Hailed as the patron saints of Athenian democracy

80. Ibid., p. 201.
81. Ibid., p. 202.
82. Ibid., p. 56.

because they had sacrificed their lives in ending the reign of the tyrants, the lovers had been commemorated in poetry and by statues that stood within the Agora. Five years after his visit to Greece, Byron was to celebrate Harmodius as a liberator in stanza 20 of Canto III of *Childe Harold*.

One other famous instance of Greek love and sacrifice also caught his imagination. The emperor Hadrian had met the young Antinoüs in Bithynia. Struck by his beauty, he took him into his entourage. During a state visit to Egypt, Antinoüs was drowned in the Nile. Hadrian built a temple in his honor on the shore and then a city, "Antinoöpolis," and filled the empire with memorial statues. Later, a legend sprang up that Hadrian had heard a prophecy that he would succeed in his ambitions only if that which he loved most would die. Antinoüs, hearing this, is supposed to have drowned himself. Byron, as one might expect, was powerfully drawn to the story. Using the mandatory ambivalent language of the day, he speaks, in his notes to *Childe Harold*, of Antinoüs, "whose death was as heroic as his life was infamous." [83]

As a result of Byron's epistolary silence, there is no account of Athenian manners to match his letters from Albania. In March, he and Hobhouse visited Asia Minor. Almost immediately on arriving, Byron wrote to his mother: "Pray take care of Murray and Robert, and tell the boy it is the most fortunate thing for him that he did not accompany me to *Turkey*." [84] No doubt his mother caught the innuendo. In Smyrna Byron regularly frequented the Turkish baths he was afterward to describe as "marble palace[s] of sherbet and sodomy." [85] Then two months later, after visiting Ephesus and the Plains of Troy, he wrote again to Henry Drury, to whom he had written from Falmouth. He was elated over having just swum the Hellespont, and his

83. Ibid., p. 190.
84. Smyrna, March 19, 1810, *BLJ*, 1:235.
85. To John Murray, Bologna, August 12, 1819, *BLJ*, 6:207.

high spirits led him again to speak of Eastern mores to his old schoolmaster. He had just visited Mount Ida where, he lamented, "the Shepherds are nowadays not much like Ganymede."[86] Perhaps this reminded him of his facetious promise to write Drury an essay on pederasty. There follow these lines, which Moore printed in his *Life*:

> I see not much difference between ourselves and the Turks, save that we have * * and they have none—that they have long dresses, and we short, and that we talk much and they little. * * * * * They are a sensible people.[87]

Moore regularly indicated omissions in Byron's letters by asterisks, with which the *Life* abounds. R. E. Prothero in 1898 and Peter Quennell in 1950 reprinted the letter in this form. The full text, in the new edition of Marchand, shows that Byron fulfilled his pledge, after a fashion. The missing word in Moore's text was "foreskins." The sentence that followed read:

> In England the vices in fashion are whoring & drinking, in Turkey, Sodomy & smoking. We prefer a girl and a bottle, they a pipe and a pathic.—They are a sensible people. Ali Pacha told me he was sure I was a man of rank because I had *small ears* and hands and *curling hair*.[88]

Here is nothing of "unhallowed thirst" in the familiar rhetorical style. Byron ended his letter with the news that he was "dying for love of three Greek girls in Athens."

In Constantinople, Byron and Hobhouse were exposed to another side of Turkish culture regularly witnessed and as regularly abominated by Western visitors. In Islamic countries at that time and later, public performances by dancing girls—of the sort the European ballet or music hall provided—were proscribed as unthinkably indecent. Instead, transvestite boys performed in public places or at

86.   Dardanelles, May 3, 1810, *BLJ*, 1:238.
87.   *LJL*, 1:222.
88.   May 3, 1810, *BLJ*, 1:238; *Letters and Journals*, 1:266; Peter Quennell, *Byron: A Self-Portrait* (London: John Murray, 1950), 1:65.

weddings, circumcisions, and other family affairs. Byron and Hobhouse saw such dances in the coffee houses of Galata, the foreign suburb of the city. Hobhouse described the performance as "beastly."[89] Byron's reaction has not been recorded.

Constantinople, however, did not excite Byron the way Albania did. Near the end of his visit he became depressed and apologized to the English ambassador for his unsociability—"some particular circumstances" had affected his spirits.[90] Marchand conjectures that this was bad news about his financial affairs in England, which were forcing him to return earlier than he hoped. But he also draws attention to an entry in Hobhouse's diary for June 6: "Messenger arrived from England—bringing a letter from Hodgson to B—tales spread—the *Edlestone* accused of indecency."[91] Presumably the tales linked Byron's name with Edlestone's and arose because Edlestone had been apprehended by the metropolitan police. But if the accusation meant that Edlestone was in trouble with the law, Byron must have flinched at the possibility of his friend's exposure to the London mob in the pillory. The thought that any exertion on Edlestone's behalf would in turn have made Byron himself liable to more suspicion must also have tortured him: this is a common dilemma homosexuals and bisexuals face when their friends are in trouble. Later, Byron tells us, in one of the Thyrza lyrics, that Edlestone was much in his mind on the return voyage to Athens:

> On many a lone and lovely night
> It soothed to gaze upon the sky;
> For then I deem'd the heav'nly light
> Shone sweetly on thy pensive eye:
> And oft I thought at Cynthia's noon,
> When sailing o'er the Aegean wave,
> "Now Thyrza gazes on that moon."[92]

89. *BB*, 1:243.
90. Ibid., p. 247.
91. Ibid., p. 245n.
92. "One Struggle More, and I am Free." The next line is puzzling,

On their return to Greece on July 17, Hobhouse took ship for England from Zea. The usually unsentimental Hobhouse was much affected by their parting, but Byron had grown impatient of his company. He told his mother he was "very glad to be once more alone, for I was sick of my companion (not that he was a bad one) but because my nature leads me to solitude."[93] Hobhouse, devoted to Byron as he was, was not happy when Moore referred to this comment in his *Life*, even though Moore tried to soften the effect by rhapsodizing on Byron's poetic nature: "So enamoured . . . had he become of these lonely musings, that even the society of his fellow-traveller, though with pursuits so congenial to his own, grew at last to be a chain and a burthen on him; and it was not till he stood, companionless, on the shores of the little island in the Aegean, that he found his spirit breathe freely."[94] This effusion was too much for the down-to-earth Hobhouse, who underscored the passage in his copy of the *Life* and wrote angrily in the margin: "On what authority does Tom say this? He has not the remotest grasp of the real reason which induced Lord B. to prefer having no Englishman immediately [or] constantly near him."[95]

On June 7, 1810, Byron had written "A Farewell Petition to JCH Esq." in anticipation of their parting six weeks later. The poem was not published until 1887 when it appeared in *Murray's Magazine*. Byron bids Hobhouse return to England "And in my name the man of Method greet," that is, Charles Skinner Matthews. Until now the epithet has been unintelligible. Now we can understand it as referring to the "Methodism" Matthews had used as a code word for homosexuality in his letter a year earlier.

---

however, since it reads "Alas, it gleam'd upon her grave." Edlestone did not die before Byron sailed the Aegean but while Byron was in Malta on his way home (*CPW*, 1:351).

93. Patras, July 30, 1810, *BLJ*, 2:9.
94. *LJL*, 1:254.
95. *LLB*, p. 90.

Tell him, that not in vain shall I essay
To tread and trace our "old Horatian way,"
And be (with prose supply my dearth of rhymes)
What better men have been in better times.[96]

Byron's "old Horatian way" is, of course, a reference to
Horace's bisexuality, which Byron hopes to emulate like an
ancient Greek or Roman.

But if Byron did not want Hobhouse on the scene in
Athens, he was not at all shy about telling him of his amorous escapades once the latter had returned to England.
Indeed, the series of letters he now wrote to keep Hobhouse, and, through Hobhouse, Matthews, informed of
his adventures are crucial documents for our knowledge of
Byron's homosexual life in Greece. As soon as he was alone,
Byron left on a long-planned tour of the Morea. He went
first to Vostitza where he added to his suite a young boy
named Eustathius Georgiou, whom he had met there in
December 1809 when Hobhouse and he were en route to
Athens. A letter dated January 1, 1810, written in an illiterate hand either by the boy or a public scribe, indicates that
Byron had asked to have Eustathius sent to Athens but that
he was at that time too ill to come.[97] Another letter, dated
April 7, says that Eustathius understands that Byron is
about to travel again and wishes to accompany him. By
then, of course, Byron had left for Smyrna. But on July 29,
a week and a half after Hobhouse's embarcation, Byron
met Eustathius again at Vostitza and a few days later sent
Hobhouse a detailed account of their reunion. Eustathius
was a temperamental, effeminate youngster, whose relations with Byron were affectionate but by no means placid.
Byron was amused at the difficulties the affair landed
him in:

At Vostitza I found my dearly-beloved Eustathius—ready to
follow me not only to England, but to Terra Incognita, if so my

96. CPW, 1:283.
97. BB, 1:251n.

compass pointed that way.—This was four days ago, at present affairs are a little changed.—The next morning I found the
dear soul upon horseback clothed very sprucely in Greek Gar-
ments, with those ambrosial curls hanging down his amiable
back, and to my utter astonishment and the great abomination
of Fletcher, a *parasol* in his hand to save his complexion from
the heat.—However, in spite of the *Parasol* on we travelled
very much enamoured, as it should seem, till we got to Patras,
where Strané received us into his new house where I now
scribble.—Next day he went to visit some accursed cousin and
the day after we had a grand quarrel. Strané said I spoilt him, I
said nothing, the child was as froward as an unbroken colt,
and Strané's Janizary said I must not be surprised, for he was
too *true* a *Greek* not to be disagreeable.—I think I never in my
life took so much pains to please anyone, or succeeded so ill. I
particularly *avoided* every thing which *could possibly give* the
least offense in any *manner*. Somebody says that those who try
to please will please. This I know not; but I am sure that no
one likes to fail in the attempt.—At present he goes back to his
father, though he is now become more tractable.—Our *parting*
was vastly pathetic, as many kisses as would have sufficed for
a boarding school, and embraces enough to have ruined the
character of a county in England, besides tears (not on *my*
part) and expressions of "Tenerezza" [tenderness] to a vast
amount.

The lightheartedness with which Byron here touches on
contrasting English manners is amusing. Next day the
emotional weather cleared:

My new Greek acquaintance has called thrice, and we improve
vastly, in good truth, so it ought to be, for I have quite exhausted by poor powers of pleasing, which God knows are
little enough, Lord help me!—We are to go to Tripolitza and
Athens together. I do not know what has put him into such
good humour unless it be some Sal Volatile I administered for
his headach [*sic*] and a green shade instead of that effeminate
parasol, but so it is, we have *redintegrated* (a new *word* for you)
our affections at a great rate.—Now is not all this very ridiculous? Pray tell Matthews it would do his heart good to see me
travelling with my Tartar, Albanians, Buffo, Fletcher, and this
amiable παιδη [boy] prancing by my side.[98]

98. To John Cam Hobhouse, Patras, July 29, 1810, *BLJ*, 2:6–7.

Byron must have been reminded of the difficulties As-
cyltus had with the temperamental Giton in the *Satyricon*.
Two weeks later Byron describes their final parting:

> I have sent Eustathius back to his home. He plagued my soul
> out with his whims, and is besides subject to *epileptic* fits (tell
> M this) which made him a perplexing companion. In *other*
> matters he was very tolerable. I mean as to his *learning*, being
> well versed in the Ellenics—You remember Nicolo at Athens,
> Lusieri's wife's brother.—Give my *compliments* to *Matthews*
> from whom I expect a congratulatory letter.—I have a thou-
> sand anecdotes for him and you, but at present Τι να καμω?
> [What to do?] I have neither time nor space, but in the words
> of Dawes, "I have things in store."[99]

Doris Langley Moore in her essay "Byron's Sexual Ambivalence" interprets these lines to mean Byron is asking Matthews to congratulate him on an affair with Nicolo Giraud.
The passage is confusing since Byron is attempting to
squeeze in so many hints. Apparently Matthews had some
theory connecting sex and epilepsy. (Untreated epilepsy
can, on occasion, cause the erratic emotional behavior Byron was "plagued" by.) Byron's remark that the illiterate
Eustathius was versed in Hellenic (i.e., classical) Greek, as
opposed to the contemporary "Romaic," has undoubtedly
a sexual meaning.

One of the attractions of the Morea was a chance to meet
Ali Pasha's son, Veli Pasha, in his capital of Tripolitza. John
Galt, who had visited him shortly before, described Veli as
"free and affable, with a considerable tincture of humour
and drollery."[100] Byron also found him playful and, in one
respect, very much his father's son:

> Velly Pacha received me even better than his Father did, though
> he is to join the Sultan, and the city is full of troops and confu-
> sion, which as he says, prevents him from paying proper at-
> tention.—He has given me a very pretty horse and a most par-

---

99.   To John Cam Hobhouse, Tripolitza, August 16, 1810, *BLJ*, 2:10.
100.   *Letters from the Levant* (London: T. Cadell & W. Davies, 1813),
p. 86.

ticular invitation to meet him at Larissa [in northwest Greece], which last is singular enough, as he recommended a different route to Ld. Sligo who asked leave to accompany him to the Danube.—I asked no such thing, but on his enquiring where I meant to go, and receiving for an answer that I was about to return to Albania for the purpose of penetrating higher up the country, he replied, "No, you must not take that route, but go round by Larissa where I shall remain some time on my way. I will send to Athens, and you shall join me. We will eat and drink well, and go a hunting."—He said he wished all the old men (specifying under that epithet *North, Foresti,* and *Stranè*) to go to his father, but the young ones to come to him, to use his own expression, "vecchio con vecchio, Giovane con Giovane."

Byron was flattered by this attention, but a bit embarrassed when the young ruler threw his arm around his waist, squeezed his hand, and called him a εὔμορφω παιδί [beautiful boy], "with a variety of other sayings which made Stranè stare, and puzzled me in my replies."[101] No longer shy in the embraces of Oriental potentates, Byron made up his mind to join Veli at Larissa.

By August 19, Byron was back in Athens. Some tensions now developed between him and Tarsia Macri over her daughter Theresa. Throughout the nineteenth century the famous lines addressed to the "Maid of Athens" led visitors to regard this young girl as the focus of Byron's sentimental life in Greece. Countless tourists visited the Macri house, wrote passages in their journals, and kept alive an aura of romance. Thomas Moore played up this aspect of Byron's stay by making much of it in his *Life,* and Theresa, who afterward married a Mr. Black, basked in her fame and lived and died "in an odor of Byronism." But, in fact, Byron had a falling out with her mother, who must have thought his attentions were becoming dangerous. "Intrigue flourishes," Byron wrote Hobhouse on August 26; "the old woman, Theresa's mother, was mad enough to think I was going to

101. To John Cam Hobhouse, Tripolitza, August 16, 1810, *BLJ,* 2: 9–10.

marry the girl." Byron was aristocrat enough to dismiss all thought of any alliance that did not bring birth and money. He had by this time removed himself from the Macri household to a Franciscan convent where, as he put it significantly, he had found "better amusement." [102]

The "convent" was in fact a monastery, which did duty also as a hostel and a boy's school. Accommodation was scarce in Athens, but it was likely that Nicolo Giraud's residence as a scholar there drew Byron to this domicile. As he explained to Hobhouse:

> I am most auspiciously settled in the Convent, which is more commodious than any tenement I have yet occupied, with room for my *suite*, and it is by no means solitary, seeing there is not only "il Padre Abbate" but his "schuola" [school] consisting of six "Regatzi" [boys] all my most particular allies.— These Gentlemen being almost (saving Fauvel and Lusieri) my only associates, it is but proper their character, religion, and morals should be described. Of this goodly company three are Catholics and three are Greeks, which Schismatics I have already set a boxing to the great amusement of the Father who rejoices to see the Catholics conquer.—Their names are Barthelemi, Giuseppe, *Nicolo*, Yani, and two anonymous, at least in my memory.—Of these Barthelemi is a "simplice Fanciullo" [simple boy] according to the account of the Father, whose favorite is Giuseppe who sleeps in the Lantern of Demosthenes.—We have nothing but riot from Noon till night.—The first time I mingled with these Sylphs, after about two minutes reconnoitering, the amiable Signor Barthelemi without any previous notice seated himself by me, and after observing by way of compliment, that my "Signoria" [Lordship] was the "pieu bello" [most beautiful] of his English acquaintances saluted me on the left cheek, for which freedom being reproved by Giuseppe, who very properly informed him that I was a "μεγαλοσ" [great man], he told him I was his "φιλοσ" [friend] and "by his beard," he would do so again, adding to the question of "διατι ασπασετε?" [why did you kiss him?] you see, he laughs, as in good truth I did very heartily. But my friend, as you may easily imagine is Nicolo, who by the bye, is my Italian master, and we are very philosophical.—I am his "padrone"

and his "amico" and the Lord knows what besides. It is about two hours since that after informing me that he was desirous to follow *him* (that is me) over the world, he concluded by telling me it was proper for us not only to live but "morire insieme" [to die together].—The latter I hope to avoid, as much of the former as he pleases.[103]

Clearly, this high-spirited and affectionate playfulness was shot through on Byron's part, and on the part of the boys, by an undercurrent of amorous feeling.

Giraud now undertook the task of teaching Byron Italian. How interested Byron was in the language at this time and to what extent the lessons merely served as a pretext for their constant companionship, it is impossible to say. Byron jokingly calls their relation "very philosophical." Perhaps he had in mind Lucian's statement that the love of boys was "more philosophical" than the love of women, or he may have recalled Cicero's cynical remark that the Greeks pursued pederastic interests "under the thin veil of philosophy." At any rate, they spent many hours together. Byron took much pleasure in swimming at the Piraeus where, he noted, the Greek boys, unlike the Turks, swam trunkless: Giraud was "vergogno" ("shameless"). Byron called him a poor swimmer—like the mysterious "Abbe Hyacinth of Falmouth."

Thomas Moore was quite aware of Byron's close association with Giraud, and the relation was well enough known that he thought it worth some comment in his *Life*. This is the way he presented the friendship to the British public:

During this period of his stay in Greece, we find him forming one of those extraordinary friendships,—if attachment to persons so inferior to himself can be called by that name,—of which I have already mentioned two or three instances in his younger days, and in which the pride of being a protector, and the pleasure of exciting gratitude, seem to have constituted to his mind the chief, pervading charm. The person, whom he now adopted in this manner, and from similar feelings to

103. Ibid., 2:11–12.

those which had inspired his early attachments to the cottage-
boy near Newstead, and the young chorister at Cambridge,
was a Greek youth, named Nicolo Giraud, the son [*sic*], I
believe, of a widow lady in whose house the artist, Lusieri,
lodged. In this young man he appears to have taken the most
lively, and even brotherly, interest;—so much so, as not only
to have presented to him, on their parting, at Malta, a considerable sum of money, but to have subsequently designed for
him, as the reader will learn, a still more munificent, as well as
permanent, provision.[104]

Moore was quite right in stressing the chivalrous, protective side of Byron's feeling for Giraud and other boys,
though one can detect behind the velvety manner a certain
apprehension about how his readers will interpret Byron's
generosity. Lusieri and Giraud's sister were gratified at the
English nobleman's patronage and appreciative of the interest he was showing in the obviously happy boy, who
was, in fact, Lusieri's brother-in-law and not his son, as
Moore supposed. If Lusieri suspected a sexual side to the
affair, he made no difficulties; perhaps his views were
those of the eastern Mediterranean. In the evening of the
same day in which he had written Hobhouse of his escapades with the boys, Byron added a postscript on further
developments:

I have employed the greater part of today in conjugating the
verb "ασπαζω" [to embrace, kiss] (which word being Ellenic as
well as Romaic may find a place in the *Citoyen's* [i.e., Matthews's] Lexicon). I assure you my progress is rapid, but like
Caesar, "nil actum reputans dum quid superesset agendum"
[considering nothing done while anything remained to be
done], I must arrive at the pl & opt C, and then I will write to
———, I hope I escape the fever, at least till I finish this affair,
and then it is welcome to try. . . . Take a quotation—"Et
Lycam *nigris* oculis, nigroque *Crine* decorum" ["And Lycus
beautiful for his black eyes and black hair"].[105]

104.   *LJL*, 1:243–44.
105.   August 23, 1810, *BLJ*, 2:14. The Latin is from Horace, *Odes* I, 32.

Marchand connects these lines with the melodramatic episode of Byron's rescuing a girl condemned to be drowned (which he used in *The Giaour*) in a way that suggests that Byron's mention of love-making here pertains to the girl. But the passage must surely refer to Giraud.

In September 1810 Byron set out for a second tour of the Morea with his young friend. He found him far more capable a person than the flighty Eustathius and gave him the responsibility of acting as major-domo of the expedition. Fletcher, the valet, was left behind; only Greeks and Albanians accompanied the pair. Unfortunately, the trip proved a disaster. The fever Byron had mentioned so lightly to Hobhouse did not wait until the end of the affair: Byron became seriously ill at Patras. Later, in England, three years after his return from Greece, he wrote to Lady Caroline Lamb's aunt, Lady Melbourne, who had become his confidante, about the near-lethal assault of this fever and noted, without specifying the gender of his bedmate, that it in no way abated his sexual passion; at one point, he told her, the disease was so severe that he thought he might expire *in coitu*.[106] He began a letter to Hobhouse on September 25 but was too ill to finish it until October 2. At this point he was nursing "poor Nicolo" who had "waited on me day and night till he is worse than I was." Even at this juncture Byron could not refrain from boasting of his sexual prowess. Two days later he asks Hobhouse to "tell M that I have obtained above two hundred pl & opt Cs and am almost tired of them. For the history of these he must wait my re-

106. January 12, 1814, *BLJ*, 4:26–27: "The last dangerous illness I had was a fever in the Morea in 1811—this very *month* [Byron has misremembered; this fever was in September 1810]—and what do you suppose was the effect?—I really *can't* tell you—but it is perfectly true—that at the time I myself thought & everyone else thought I was dying—I had very nearly made my exit like some 'just man' whom a King of Poland envied." The king was presumably Augustus, elector of Saxony, and later king of Poland, who reputedly fathered over 300 illegitimate children.

turn, as after many attempts I have given up the idea of
conveying the information on paper.—You know the monastery of Mendele. It was there I made myself the master of
the first." [107] By November 26 enthusiasm had given way to
satiety, and Byron was writing in a decidedly jaded tone:

> I have now seen the World, that is the most ancient of the an-
> cient part. I have spent my little all. I have tasted all sorts of
> pleasure (so tell the Citoyen). I have nothing more to hope,
> and may begin to consider of the most eligible way of walking
> out of it. . . . Mention to M that I have found so many of his
> antiques on this classical soil that I am tired of pl & opt Cs, the
> last thing I could be tired of. I wish I could find some of Soc-
> rates's hemlock but Lusieri tells me it dont poison people
> nowadays. [108]

Byron soon recovered from this depression. The remaining months in Greece were, in fact, his most social.
He now made friends with Frenchmen, Danes, and Germans in the foreign colony in Athens, went on historical
and archaeological expeditions, studied modern Greek literature, and collected the materials on Romaic and Albanian culture which were to make up the notes for Canto II
of *Childe Harold*. He also labored at one not very distinguished poem—*Hints from Horace*—and began another,
The Curse of Minerva, the latter an attack on Elgin's depre-
dations. It was a productive and happy time. He expati-
ated to his mother on the beneficent effects of foreign
travel—not the least of which was the counteracting of the
"bitter effects of staying at home with all the narrow prejudices of an Islander," [109] a reference which probably glances
at English homophobia. Unfortunately, his financial affairs
continued to look bad. More pressing was the case of
Scrope Davies, from whom he had earlier borrowed a substantial sum and who was now facing serious difficulties.

107.   Patras, October 4, 1810, *BLJ*, 2:23.
108.   Athens, November 26, 1810, *BLJ*, 2:28–29.
109.   Athens, January 14, 1811, *BLJ*, 2:34.

Byron felt he must return to England to find money to repay him. Reluctantly, in April 1811, he set sail for home.

He did not forget Giraud, whom he took to Malta on his
return trip. During his month's stay there, Byron had to
make embarrassed explanations to Constance Spencer
Smith, who had, to his distress, lived up to her name and
remained expectant. He remained on good terms with
Lusieri, who was also with them, and made provision for
Giraud by placing him in a religious school under the supervision of a Father Vicenzo Aquilina in Malta. Doris
Langley Moore has translated letters from Malta that detail
Giraud's progress as a scholar. Since he knew Greek well,
he was to be taught English, arithmetic, and calligraphy
and to polish his Italian. Probably Byron had in mind that,
like Edlestone, he would enter on a career in business.
Giraud wrote Byron a number of letters in Greek, in which
he promised to study hard and hoped for his continued
protection, so he would be "like your son and Your Excellency like my kindly father." [110] By October he was writing
in English. Byron had apparently dictated a letter to Giraud
to his Greek servant Demetrio Zograffo, acknowledging
the receipt of two letters in Greek and asking Giraud to
write in English. Doris Langley Moore has published the
reply: Giraud indicates that Demetrio had informed him
that "Your Excellency will come back to Malta in June,
which gives me very great pleasure, and I shall begin now
to pay more attention to my studies, that when you come
you will find me as you wish." In December 1812 Giraud
wrote that he had been expelled from school for going
"with Mr. Cockerell to the play." He had moved in with a
Maltese family known to his brother-in-law, "with whom I
live happy, without being among so many priests, who
troubled my head every moment and taught me nothing."
Byron was by now famous as the author of *Childe Harold*.
At this point Giraud drops from sight.

110. *LBAR*, pp. 441–42.

Doris Langley Moore thinks Giraud did not hold a very important place among Byron's loves since he wrote no poems about him. It is true that frustrated love is notoriously more inspirational than love satisfied. Byron's love poems are "complaints," in the traditional sense, or laments over impossibilities. But Giraud left him nothing to complain about or to regret. He stirred his blood, won his respect, and moved him to take a paternal, protective interest on parting. On his return to England Byron made a bolder gesture still, hardly conceivable if he had planned to stay in the country. He made Giraud the beneficiary of £7000 (perhaps about $200,000 in today's inflated currency). Such bequests to young foreigners had been the occasion of scandal and litigation in some English families.[111] No doubt it was this gesture that made Thomas Moore think it necessary to give some explanation in his *Life*. Some years later Byron canceled the will. But his memories of Giraud seem to have remained tender and passionate. Late in 1812, after he had become famous, Byron met a woman in London who, he told Lady Melbourne, "does not speak English, & to me nothing but Italian, a great point for from certain coincidences the very sound of that language is Music to me, & she has black eyes & *not* a very white skin, & reminds me of many in the Archipelago I wish to forget, & makes me forget what I ought to remember."[112] The "music" was the Italian Giraud had first taught him. The "many" were the boys of Greece, with

111.   In 1811 the Earl of Findlater, a peer who had lived abroad for thirty years, died and left a large fortune to a young Saxon named Fischer, who had been his page and secretary. The earl's family contested the will on the grounds that the relation had been immoral. "But the scandal became so great, of a noble family attempting to fix such a stigma on the memory of their relative from pecuniary motives" that a compromise was reached, and Fischer received £60,000 (Pisanus Fraxi [pseud. of Henry Spencer Ashbee], *Index Librorum Prohibitorum*, Vol. 1 of *Bibliography of Prohibited Books* [1877; rpt. New York: Jack Brussel, 1962], p. 341).

112.   September 25, 1812, *BLJ*, 2:208.

Giraud at their head, who had made him forget his English inhibitions.

We do not know what became of Giraud, who at this point disappears from the purview of Byron scholarship. A good knowledge of Italian, English, and Greek would have prepared him for a responsible position in some trading company. He seems to have been a spirited lad: the boy who complained that the priests "troubled his head" had earlier (in 1810) been "taken up by the guard, perhaps for some mimicry of the Turkish authorities."[113] It seems a shame to lose sight of him. Perhaps the annals of Valletta or Naples or Athens will one day yield information. Did he ever come to identify his patron-lover with the famous poet and leader of the struggle for Greek independence? We do not know. But he may have remembered his liaison with the English lord as the happiest and most notable adventure of his boyhood. And Byron, who later managed to make the lives of so many women miserable, must have looked back on the affair with a certain satisfaction.

113. February 14, 1810, *BB*, 1:231.

· 4 ·

England and "Thyrza"

Byron proceeded home in a dejected mood, sorry to leave Greece and plagued by a variety of maladies. His fever returned; he had hemorrhoids and gonorrhea contracted from womanizing with Greek and Turkish paramours. He was much concerned for the literary and worldly affairs of his friend Hobhouse and filled his letters with advice on his friend's writing and military career. There is also much mention of Matthews, whom he calls the "Citoyen" because of his atheistic radicalism. The idea of returning to England seems to have cast a pall over Byron's spirits. This must have been due in part to his awareness of how unwelcome bisexuals were in that realm.

It may, in fact, be plausibly argued that homophobia had reached a zenith in the British Isles in 1810 while Byron was abroad. The year saw a constitutional crisis: George III was now irremediably mad, and the Prince of Wales was declared Regent. The war with Napoleon dragged on, with no end in sight. Reaction, in the person of Lord Castlereagh, was firmly in the saddle both at home and in foreign affairs. In the two preceding decades only one notable liberal measure had been passed: the abolition of the slave trade in 1807. But the Wilberforce who had led that effort had also, as we have seen, founded the Society for the Suppression of Vice, and England's moral climate had become increasingly puritan. The Society, as it was popularly called, attacked cruel sports such as bear or bull baiting, but the pillory still survived, long after it had passed out of use in the more enlightened states of the Continent. Through it, all classes, rich or poor, pious or profane, could vent their hostility to homosexuals, and their anger went publicly unrebuked either by conservative editors or liberal reformers.

We have seen to how high a level homophobia rose in eighteenth-century England, both among the populace and the learned. Nevertheless, though the Society for the Reformation of Manners was successful in its campaign to have the death penalty revived, hangings remained sporadic in this period, apparently averaging only one or two per decade during the last half of the century.[1] But after 1805 a change took place, and the statistics for the next thirty years show an average of about two hangings each *year*. What brought about this dramatic increase?

Unfortunately, in our present state of knowledge we can only speculate. There seems no doubt that public opinion in England was ready to accept an increase in hangings. Antihomosexual feeling and the fear of opposing it assured that there would be no protest. Most likely the restraining influences previously had been administrative and judicial. But political events at the opening of the nineteenth century had a tendency to counteract these. For one thing, England in 1800 was ruled by a government that, in reaction to the French Revolution, had turned away from the law reform sentiment that had gathered force in the 1780s. Then, when England renewed its war with Napoleon in 1803, after the brief Peace of Amiens, a panic swept the country as it became obvious that the French were massing

1. The *Report of the Select Committee on Criminal Laws* for 1819 gives statistics for executions for all crimes, including sodomy, for the eighteenth century. They are, however, incomplete; the figures for London and Middlesex cover the years 1699–1804, for the Home Circuit (another assize circuit with its center in London) 1689–1803. But many of the other circuits have no figures for the early eighteenth century, and some have none before 1800. No executions are listed for areas outside of London before 1800, and we may assume they were rare. The London and Middlesex Circuit hangings are listed as 1725–26, 2; 1727–28, 1; 1729–30, 1; 1776, 2; and 1796, 1; in the Home Circuit single hangings took place in 1761, 1764, 1776, 1786, and 1799 ([British Sessional Papers, 1819], 8:143–63, 168–73). See above, chap. 1, n. 12, for the nineteenth-century figures.

troops for an invasion. This popular hysteria strengthened the government and turned the country in a still more conservative direction. England's blockade of the Continent and Napoleon's counterblockade of England hurt trade and caused much economic suffering. Cotton strikes broke out in 1808, and pauperism spread. In 1810, the year the Regency was declared, riots took place in London when Sir Francis Burdett, a radical member of Parliament, was arrested in connection with a freedom-of-the-press issue. Next year Luddite riots erupted in Byron's Nottinghamshire; men were killed and mills burned: eventually seventeen men were hanged at York. In the midst of this civil unrest, the government no doubt found the hangings and pilloryings of men belonging to an unpopular minority a safe diversion for the rough energies of London's impoverished mobs. But executions were not simply a wartime phenomenon limited to the decade of the Regency, though feeling probably reached its height in that period. Hangings continued after Waterloo; indeed, more men were hanged in the twenty years following the Congress of Vienna than during the war.

Byron and his circle were keenly aware of these sentiments. This is amply attested by a second, much longer, letter from Matthews that survives in the Murray collection. Dated from Trinity College, Cambridge, on January 13, 1811, and addressed to Byron in Malta, it answered a letter (now apparently lost) that had reached Matthews in England. Previously unpublished and uncited, it throws a flood of light on the personal interests within Byron's coterie. The letter opens in the vein of Matthews's Falmouth greeting:

> I am very happy to hear that you have been so well amused in Greece; and your plans for the future are so promising that I have no doubt your amusement will be progressive. A thousand thanks for your letter, of which I had given up all hopes. Cam did me great injustice when he said I was particular. Twould be the height of impudence in me, who am so indulgent towards myself. In one sense of the word, I would you

were a little more *particular;* that is to say, minute. In some of
your passages I desiderate volumes of commentary. Not that
there is any obscurity—the commentary I should require
would be illustrative not explanatory. I ought to recollect, however, as you justly remind me, that Cam will prove a living
commentary. And what he cannot fill up of your outline I shall
hope for from you yourself when you gratify my eyes by your
return.

In other words, Matthews has had no trouble deciphering
Byron's code, but he wants more details. He tells Byron he
has been amusing himself at Cambridge with feasting,
card playing, and reading:

But no *quoits* [i.e., "coits" or coitus], the lack of wch I feel
acutely. However, the sports I have mentioned, the tranquillity
of academic bowers, & the congeniality of old scenes eke me
out a tolerable existence. Quant à ma methode, my botanical
studies have been sadly at a stand. I have however added a
specimen or two to my anthology, but I have contemplated
them only at a distance. So you can see I am still as ignorant as
when you left me.

Then after an account of the king's madness, the new
Regency, and a good deal about boxing, Matthews goes on
to summarize the "gay news" of the day, mocking the
stereotyped contemporary expressions of horror:

But the grand feature, I take it, in the last year of our history, is
the enormous increase of Παιδεραστία [paiderastia] (that
damn'd vice). Good God! were the good old times of Sodom &
Gomorrah to return, fire not water w^d be the Englishman's element. At no place or time, I suppose, since the creation of the
world, has Sodomy been so rife. With your friends the Tur-
comans to be sure, it's value (compared with fornication) is as
5 to 2. But that wch you get for £5 we must risque our necks for;
and are content to risque them.
   Your Lordship's delicacy w^d I know be shocked by the pil-
lorification (in the Hay M.) of a club of gents who were wont to
meet in Vere Street (St. Clement's)—how all London was in an
uproar on that day, & how the said gents were bemired and
beordured. . . . Every Newsp that one casts one's eye upon,
presents one with some instance. Take a few that just occur to
my recollection. A sandman for pedicating one of his boys.

A sailor at *Falmouth* for forcible ditto of a boy. John Cary Cole, usher of a school, for ditto with some of his pupils, some of the "victims to his brutish passion" being under age of admissibility to take an oath. An officer was s^d to have cut his throat on a charge of this kind.

Obviously, Matthews meant to inform and titillate Byron with this account of pederasty in England, the topic to which he devoted by far the most space in his letter. He pokes fun at the rhetoric of the day—"damn'd vice," "will be shocked"—and tries to maintain a light tone. There is, however, a grim touch in his calligraphy. The initial capital "Π" at the beginning of "paiderastia" is enlarged to form a gallows, from which a man dangles. His statement that sodomy has increased enormously was a standard journalistic cliché of the day. What he and the newspapers in fact reported was an upsurge of police surveillance and activity. The census of 1811 numbered over 12 million in Great Britain, 1 million of whom lived in London. If we accept Kinsey's estimate of 10 percent, this would mean there would have been about 400,000 adult male homosexuals in the country and over 30,000 in London. Given the Draconian laws, there may have been less actual sexual behavior, but the number of self-identified homosexuals may have approximated to these figures. Undoubtedly the score or so of arrests in 1810 could have been multiplied a hundredfold had the authorities pursued their policy of entrapment vigorously enough. Living a quiet life in a university town, Matthews followed the metropolitan police news with obvious avidity. In the days before gay liberation, this was almost the only way an isolated homosexual could assure himself that he and his friends were not alone in the world. To be in the public eye meant to be the object of scandal or of criminal proceedings threatening jail, the pillory, or the gallows. It was chiefly through a sense of common danger —"*we* risque our necks"—that homosexuals like Matthews affirmed a sense of what would today be called gay solidarity.

The most notable of the episodes Matthews refers to was the Vere Street case, which probably attracted more publicity than any trial for homosexuality before Oscar Wilde. On July 8, 1810, the police had raided the White Swan in Vere Street, a popular gay tavern. The *Alfred and Westminster Evening Gazette* gave details that throw light on police methods and show how dangerous it was for homosexuals to congregate socially, even in a private club. Plain-clothes officers had "gained admittance by some finesse, into the back parlour, which was the principal rendezvous of these miscreants; and after being at first a little suspected of coming there as spies, they were at last considered as persons of the same propensity, and treated without reserve."[2] Most of the men were charged with "assault with the intention to commit sodomy," and six were sentenced to stand in the pillory.

Another pillorying before the Lord Mayor's residence at Cornhill on September 25 gave some hint of what was to follow two days later. So great was the crowd that the balustrades of the Mansion House collapsed, and six or seven spectators broke their legs. The "unfortunate sufferers," an anonymous contemporary account tells us, "were taken into the Mansion-house by the Lord Mayor's private door, where they received personally from his Lordship every kind attention." Of Joshua Viguers, the man who was pelted, the journalist noted in conclusion: "The head of this wretch when he reached Newgate, was compared to a *swallow's nest*. It took three buckets of hot water to restore it to any thing like a human shape. Though much bruised and battered, the fellow is in no danger, but he is at present totally blind."[3]

In Regency London, the news that a homosexual suspect had been apprehended was enough to bring a hostile

2. September 24, p. 4, col. 2.
3. *Trying and Pilloring of the Vere Street Club* (London: J. Brown, 1810), pp. 27–28. Viguers's name is misspelled in this account as "Wygoss."

mob to the scene. Repeatedly, press accounts stress that arrested men were in danger of their lives. Large bodies of police were required to escort them to the courts. The same journalist tells us that when the occasion of the Vere Street arrests was known, it was with "the [ut]most difficulty the prisoners could be saved from destruction."[4] Those dismissed without conviction were immediately attacked: "A numerous crowd of people, who had collected at the door, assailed them with sticks and stones, which the constables could not completely prevent, though they were about forty in number."[5]

On September 27 the pillorying of the Vere Street "miscreants" attracted an enormous crowd in London, variously estimated at from thirty to fifty thousand. The center of the city was paralyzed for a day; shops were shut from Newgate to the Haymarket, where the men were to be exposed. The fullest account of the event is given in a pamphlet entitled *The Trying and Pilloring of the Vere Street Club*. Since this book is rare and no copy exists at the British Library, I shall quote it at some length. It describes in unique detail the ritual of degradation.

> At an early hour, the Old Bailey was completely blockaded, and the increase of the mob about 12 o'clock put a stop to the business of the Sessions. . . . Shortly after 12, the *ammunition waggons* from the neighbouring markets appeared in motion. These consisted of a number of carts which were driven by butchers' boys, who had previously taken care to fill them with the offal, dung, &c. appertaining to their several slaughter-houses. A number of hucksters were also put in requisition, who carried on their heads baskets of apples, potatoes, turnips, cabbage-stalks, and other vegetables, together with the remains of divers dogs and cats. The whole of these were sold to the public at a high price, who spared no expence to provide themselves with the necessary articles of assault.
>
> A number of fishwomen attended with stinking flounders and the entrails of other fish, which had been in preparation several days. These articles however were not to be sold, as

4. Ibid., p. 6.
5. Ibid., pp. 13–14.

their proprietors, hearty in the cause, declared they wanted them for their own use.[6]

The occasion was attended with a good deal of ceremony, much of it protective and intended to constrain the mob's violence within the prescribed limits:

> The Sheriffs and City-Marshalls arrived about half-past 12, with more than 100 constables, mounted and armed with pistols, and more than 100 on foot. This force was ordered to rendezvous in the Old Bailey Yard, where a caravan, used occasionally for the purpose of conveying prisoners from the gaols of London to the hulks, waited to receive the culprits. The caravan was drawn by two shaft-horses, led by two men, armed with a brace of pistols. The gates of the Old Bailey Yard were shut, and all strangers turned out, after which the miscreants were all brought out, and placed in the caravan. *Amos* began a laugh, which induced his vile companions to reprove him, and they all sat upright, apparently in a composed state; but, having cast their eyes upwards, the sight of the spectators on the tops of the houses operated strongly on their fears, and they soon appeared to feel terror and dismay. Directly the church-clock went half-past 12, the gates were thrown open, the mob at the same time attempting to force their way in, but they were repulsed. A grand sortie of the police was then made, and about 60 officers, armed and mounted as before described, went forward with the City-Marshalls. The caravan went next, followed by about 40 officers and the Sheriffs. The first salute received by the offenders was a volley of mud, and a serenade of hisses, hootings and execration, which compelled them to fall flat on their faces in the caravan. The mob, and particularly the women, had piled up balls of mud, to afford the objects of their indignation a warm reception: indeed, the depots in many places appeared like pyramids of shot on a gun-wharf. These were soon exhausted, and, when the caravan passed the old house which once belonged to the notorious Jonathan Wild, the prisoners resembled bears dipped in a stagnant pool.[7]

What is striking is the way in which the authorities, in effect, facilitated the expression of popular rancor. Foreign visitors were reminded, when they saw streetwomen tor-

6. Ibid., pp. 15–16.
7. Ibid., pp. 16–18.

menting the prisoners, of the women of the French Revolution. Here, however, the police organized the semilynch-
ing, which was supposed to stop short of killing, though it
was never certain that the exposed men would survive
their ordeal.

> It is impossible for language to convey an adequate idea of the
> universal expressions of execration which accompanied these
> monsters on their journey. It was fortunate for them that the
> weather was dry; had it been otherwise they would have been
> smothered. From the moment the cart was in motion, the fury
> of the mob began to display itself in showers of mud and filth of
> every kind. Before the cart reached Temple-bar, the wretches
> were so thickly covered with filth, that a vestige of the human
> figure was scarcely discernible. They were chained, and placed
> in such a manner, that they could not lie down in the cart, and
> could only hide and shelter their heads from the storm by
> stooping, which, however, could afford but little protection.—
> Some of them were cut in the head with brickbats, and bled
> profusely; and the streets, as they passed, resounded with the
> universal shouts and execrations of the populace. . . .
> Before any of them reached the place of punishment, their
> faces were completely disfigured by blows and mud; and be-
> fore they mounted, their whole persons appeared one heap of
> filth. Upwards of fifty women were permitted to stand in the
> ring, who assailed them incessantly with mud, dead cats,
> rotten eggs, potatoes, and buckets filled with blood, offal,
> and dung, which were brought by a number of butchers' men
> from St. James's market. These criminals were very roughly
> handled.[8]

The unprecedented sensation caused by the Vere Street
pillorying tempted newspapers to discuss a topic usually
reported only tersely in the crime columns. Almost every
London paper had a substantial report. Many felt the need
to editorialize, and their comments provide a rare survey
of opinion on a matter not often openly discussed. Some
antiwar papers, like the *Morning Chronicle*, tried to exploit
English xenophobia by ascribing homosexual conduct to
foreign influence, calling it a crime "horrible to the nature

8. Ibid., pp. 21–22, 19.

of Englishmen, the prevalence of which we fear we must ascribe, among other calamities, to the unnecessary war in which we have been so long involved. It is not merely the favour which has been shewn to foreigners, to foreign servants, to foreign troops, but the sending our own troops to associate with foreigners, that may truly be regarded as the sources of the evil."[9] (Nearly all the Vere Street men, in fact, belonged to the English working class.) None of the papers expressed any sympathy with the battered men. Two thought "some of them . . . cannot survive the punishment; and should it prove their death, they will not only die unpitied, but justly execrated by every moral mind throughout the universe,"[10] the last phrase demonstrating the difficulty Regency England had in imagining standards different from its own. When editors did comment on the severity of the ordeal, it was to complain that it had not been sufficiently harsh. The *Morning Advertiser* thought "the annals of the pillory never furnished an instance in which popular vengeance was carried to greater extent." But this was not enough: it hoped "to see an Act passed in the ensuing Session [of Parliament] to make the attempt of this abominable offence capital."[11] In effect, this would have made any homosexual who responded to a stranger's advances liable to hanging, should the stranger be a masquerading officer. The call for the extension of the death penalty was echoed by the *Morning Post*, the *Observer*, the *Stateman*, the *News*, and *Bell's Weekly Messenger*.

The anonymous author of *Trying and Pilloring* pleaded for a change in the law on religious grounds:

> In the name of decency and of morality, for the sake of offended Heaven itself, we exhort our Legislators to take this

9. September 28, 1810, p. 3, col. 5. The *General Evening Post* for September 27–29, 1810, repeats this language.

10. *General Evening Post*, September 27–29, 1810; and *Bell's Weekly Messenger*, September 30, 1810, p. 311.

11. September 28, 1810, p. 5, col. 2.

subject into their most serious consideration in the ensuing Session. The monsters must be crushed, or the vengeance of Heaven will fall upon the land. Annihilation to so detestable a race can no otherwise be effected than by making every attempt of this abominable offence punishable with instant death, without benefit of Clergy. The present punishment cannot surely be deemed commensurate to an offence so abhorrent, and shocking to human nature; besides, is it not dreadful to have female delicacy and manly feeling shocked, and the infant mind perhaps polluted by such disgusting spectacles, and the conversation to which they unavoidably give rise?[12]

The call for "annihilation" suggests the spirit behind such persecutions as the killing of early Christians in Rome, or anti-Semitic pogroms, or Hitler's genocidal measures. Liberal papers such as the *Examiner* uttered no protest, describing the occasion without comment. If they had any doubts, they were not willing to voice them in the face of popular hostility.

The *Morning Chronicle*, at the end of its editorial, informed its readers that some unidentified "illustrious personages," presumably legislative leaders or jurists, had at first objected to the proposed extension of the death penalty as "illiberal." But these men were apparently not able to withstand the hysteria of the times, for the writer boasts that they are "now convinced of the right view" and are "zealously disposed to stemming a torrent of corruption that threatens to involve us in the gulph of infamy as well as ruin."[13]

Though no public protest was heard, some misgivings were voiced in private. Foreign observers who did not share English prejudices were appalled, rather after the fashion of the Western press reporting Islamic severity in our own day. Louis Simond, a French visitor who learned of the event while visiting Southey and Coleridge in the Lake District, wrote in his journal:

12. P. 22.
13. September 28, 1810, p. 3, col. 5.

We have just read in all the newspapers a full and disgusting account of the public and cruel punishment on the pillory of certain wretches convicted of vile indecencies. I can conceive of nothing more dangerous, offensive, and unwise, than the brutality and unrestrained publicity of such infliction. The imagination itself is sullied by the exposition of enormities, that ought never to be supposed to exist; and what are we to think of a people, and women too, who can for hours indulge in the cowardly and ferocious amusement of bruising and maiming men tied to the stake, and perfectly defenceless![14]

A month later when Simond was in Edinburgh, "one of the Scotch judges (Lords of Session) expressed his marked disapprobation of the prosecution and punishment, and declared their courts would not countenance any such proceedings." Simond complained that such prosecutions strengthened the hands of blackmailers and noted that "several persons of distinction were mentioned, now prosecuted in England, or threatened with vexatious charges of the same nature; which, false or true, inflict provisionally shame, ridicule and exile."[15] We shall identify one shortly.

The Vere Street prosecutions led to more serious sentences for a man and a boy. Matthews had visited the pair, accompanied by another member of Byron's Cambridge circle, Scrope Davies, and described the occasion for Byron near the end of his long letter of January 13:

> Lastly I will mention a lieutenant Hepburn, for amusing himself with Thomas White (16), a drummer boy. These two last I saw in Newgate, where they lie under sentence of death. Davies, who accompanied me, agreed with me that the lieutenant's piece was scarcely worth hanging for. There are a few curious circumstances relating to this last affair. The lieut. was first smitten in the Park, employed another drummer boy to bring T. W. to him. T. W., who appears to have been a practised *cinaed* (ready made to his hand) answered him "that if he wished to do anything with him he had better meet him at

14.   October 15, 1810, *Journal of a Tour and Residence in Great Britain During the Years 1810 and 1811*, 2nd ed. (Edinburgh: Constable, 1817), 1:470.

15.   November 17, 1810, ibid., p. 494.

a house in Vere Street." And the constupration actually appears to have taken place in the very room where the above-mentioned friends were dining, nor does s^d Hep^n. appear to have at all regarded them. We also saw Pol Fox and Pol Lane [two of the Vere St. coterie]. Such is the depraved state of our island. Nay, I am even informed, & yr lordship will hear with horror, that even the women rival our sex in irregularity of passion & that there are many among them, in the higher classes, who find in their own gender all that they wish for. A Lady of very high rank is mentioned to be very strongly thus addicted. By the way I should mention a report current this last day or two that Ld. Courtenay has set sail on his Yacht for America. His Devonshire exploits have become so notorious that the magistrates have intimated to him that he is in considerable danger.

No doubt Matthews's jaunty style was intended to bolster and to maintain his morale (and Byron's) by refusing to be intimidated. Nevertheless, his man-of-the-world pose is chilling. He has no word of pity for Hepburn and White, who were hanged two months later. And his cold-blooded reference to the boy as the older man's "piece" reflects the same cynicism Regency bucks showed in speaking of one another's mistresses.

The two victims were executed on March 7, 1811. The system required that persecuted men confirm its justice by showing contrition and remorse on the scaffold. The account in the *Morning Chronicle* was calculated to achieve this effect:

Yesterday morning, about five minutes before 8 o'clock, Ensign Hepburn, and —— White, the drummer, a lad, only 16 years of age, for the perpetration of an unnatural crime, were brought on the scaffold, in front of the Debtor[s'] door, Newgate, and executed pursuant to their sentence. Their conduct since condemnation has been such as to evince a sincere contrition, and a just sense of the heinousness of their offence. They behaved in a manner becoming their unhappy situation; and after spending a few moments in fervent prayer and devotion, with the Rev. Dr. Ford, the Ordinary of Newgate, were launched into eternity amidst a vast concourse of spectators.[16]

16.   March 8, 1811, p. 3, col. 4.

Clearly, the *Morning Chronicle* reporter thought it his duty to extract all of the edification he could from the hangings, which he may not have witnessed. It was no doubt gratifying for readers to hear that homosexuals recognized the justice of society and could be brought to a desirable mental state by the noose. The less stereotyped *Times* account rings truer:

> Yesterday morning, *Hepburn* (late an Ensign), and *White*, the drummer, for an abominable offence, were executed before the Debtors' door, Newgate. *White* came out first; he seemed perfectly indifferent to his awful fate, and continued adjusting the frill of his shirt while he was viewing the surrounding populace. About two minutes after, *Hepburn* made his appearance, but was immediately surrounded by the clergyman, the executioner, his man, and others, in attendance. The executioner, at the same time, put the cap over Hepburn's face, which of course, prevented the people from having a view of him. White seemed to fix his eyes repeatedly on Hepburn. After a few moments prayer the miserable wretches were launched into eternity. A vast concourse of spectators attended, The duke of CUMBERLAND, Lord SEFTON, Lord YARMOUTH, and several other noblemen were in the Press-yard.[17]

The *Times* report that the Duke of Cumberland was in the crowd is interesting. He was a younger brother of the Regent, who would have inherited the English throne (as he did that of Hanover) if the Duke of Kent had not been recalled from Quebec to marry and sire Victoria. Nine months earlier, his valet had been found murdered; in later years the radical press insinuated that the duke had killed him to hush up a homosexual intrigue with another servant.[18]

17. March 8, 1811, p. 2, col. 2.
18. On the night of May 31, 1810, the duke had been found badly bloodied in his apartments at St. James's Palace. His valet, Sellis, was shortly after discovered in his room with his throat slit. One theory was that the valet had known of the duke's "unnatural propensities" and had been killed to silence him. An investigating jury, led by the radical Francis Place, exonerated the duke of any guilt: the evidence pointed to the valet's having committed suicide. However, rumors persisted for decades and led to a libel suit (which the duke won) in 1833 when a radical editor ac-

Hearing of these events in Malta, Byron can scarcely have felt encouraged on his homeward voyage. We know he received Matthews's letter from some lines he wrote to Hobhouse. It may have inspired the whimsical musings on the subject of suicide Byron jotted down on May 22 as "Four or Five Reasons in Favour of a Change," which begin:

> 1st At twenty three the best of life is over and its bitters double. 2ndly I have seen mankind in various Countries and find them equally despicable, if anything the Balance is rather in favour of the Turks. 3rdly I am sick at heart.
>
> Me jam nec *faemina* . . .
> Nec *Spes animi credula mutui*
> Nec *certare* juvat *Mero*.
>
> [Neither maid . . .
> Nor the credulous hope of mutual hearts
> Nor drinking bout delights me now.][19]

And so on, through not four or five but seven half-serious reasons. The abbreviated line from Horace's "Prayer to Venus" reads in the original: "Neither maid *nor youth* . . . delights me now." By the ellipsis Byron emphasized what he omitted.

At sea three weeks later, Byron recounted to Hobhouse a startling experience he had had in Athens with Michael Bruce, a young Englishman who was traveling in the East with William Pitt's eccentric niece, Lady Hester Stanhope: "He made me a profession of Friendship, on the extremity of the Piraeus, the only one I ever received in my life, and certainly very unexpected. . . . [But] I am too old for a Friend, at least a new one. Tell M I have bade adieu to every species of affection, and may say with Horace 'Me jam nec Faemina' &c—he will finish the lines." Was Bruce's

cused him of having been "surprised in an improper and unnatural situation with this Neale [another servant] by . . . Sellis" and of having murdered Sellis out of fear of exposure (*Annual Register* [1833], p. 92).
    19.   *BLJ*, 2:47.

emotional outburst a veiled declaration of love? Byron explained that "he is a little chivalrous & romantic and is smitten with unimaginable fantasies ever since his connection with Lady H. Stanhope.—However both her Ladyship & He were very polite, and asked me to go with them a 2d. time to Constantinople, but having been there once, and preferring *philosophy* at Athens, I staid in my Convent."[20] For "philosophy" we are no doubt meant to understand something else.

Hobhouse had left Byron in July 1810 and had arrived home just in time to encounter what Matthews called the "uproar" over the Vere Street scandal. He must have been appalled at the mood of the country. When Byron returned a year later, Hobhouse wrote to warn him the day after he landed, knowing how keen Byron was to share details of his life abroad with his close friends: "I sent a letter to you a month ago—in that I told you to keep the *Mendeli Monastery story* and every thing entirely to yourself. I have not opened my mouth to Charles Skinner on any of those branches of learning. I will give you a good reason when we meet."[21] What was the reason? Was Byron's name still linked with the compromised Edlestone?

Byron's long-looked-for reunion with Matthews never took place. On the first of August Byron's mother died. Two days later Matthews was drowned. He had been swimming in the river at Cambridge, dived beneath some weeds, surfaced struggling among them, and was pulled down to his death. On the tenth Byron wrote to console Hobhouse, and on the twelfth, shaken by these intimations of mortality, made a will leaving "to Nicolo Giraud of Athens, subject of France, but born in Greece, the sum of seven thousand pounds sterling."[22] He asked R. C. Dallas, his literary agent, to delay publishing Cantos I and II of *Childe*

20. June 19, 1811, *BLJ*, 2:49–50.
21. July 15, 1811, *LLB*, p. 90, n. 2.
22. "Directions for the Contents of a Will," August 12, 1811, *BLJ*, 2:71.

Harold so that he could add a memorial note on Matthews.

Perhaps Byron felt some debt to Matthews for helping him arrive at whatever degree of self-acceptance was possible in his day and age. Entertaining a high estimate of Matthews's intellectual attainments, he naturally took an interest in his literary remains. But, he reported to Hobhouse: "Not a scrap of paper has been found, at Cambridge, which is singular." [23] When, eight years later, Byron wrote a long letter to John Murray from Ravenna, proposing some kind of memoir, he again took note of this mystery: "What became of his *papers* (and he certainly had many), at the time of his death, was never known. I mention this by the way, fearing to skip it over, and *as* he *wrote* remarkably well, both in Latin and English." [24] Did some disapproving relative destroy his work? Byron himself was edgy about using their letters in any sketch: "I am afraid that the letters of Charles's correspondence with me . . . would hardly do for the public—for our lives were not over strict—& our letters somewhat lax upon most subjects." [25] Given Regency attitudes toward homosexuality, Byron was putting the matter mildly. The memoir was never written.

On his return to England Byron took Hobhouse's cautions seriously and tried to repress his pederastic side. The evidence suggests this cost him some struggle. What his intentions were in the case of Edlestone is unclear. He seems to have acquiesced to the view that it would be imprudent to see him again since the mysterious scandal of 1810 had set whispers circulating. Then, three months after his return, Byron received another shock. On September 22 Ann Edlestone wrote that her brother had died of consumption in May and assured Byron of his continuing place in the young man's affections. Byron read her letter on October 9 and the next day wrote veiledly to his

23. August 30, 1811, *BLJ*, 2:83.
24. November 19, 1820, *BLJ*, 7:231.
25. November 9, 1820, *BLJ*, 7:224–25.

friend Francis Hodgson: "I heard of a death the other day that shocked me more than any of the preceding, of one whom I once loved more than I ever loved a living thing, & one whom I believe loved me to the last, yet I had not a tear left for an event which five years ago would have bowed me to the dust; still it sits heavy on my heart & calls back *what I wish to forget*, in many a feverish dream." [26] Presumably Byron had made a confidant of Hodgson and expected him to pick up the reference to 1806 when his feelings for Edlestone were most intense. This semiconfession seems also meant to assure him that he hoped to avoid such involvements henceforth.

One of the fascinations of Byron's letters is the way in which he subtly shifts his tone—or premises—in addressing different correspondents. On the next day Byron wrote to R. C. Dallas of his grief for someone "very dear to me in happier times" but gives no hint as to the sex of the person or of anything undesirable about the affair. Clearly, he did not feel secure enough to take the pious clergyman into his confidence. More revealing is the apologetic note of his announcement of Edlestone's death to Hobhouse. He was reluctant to reveal the news, as if he feared that Hobhouse would interpret his grief as a form of backsliding: "At present I am rather low, & dont know how to tell you the reason—you remember E. at Cambridge—he is *dead*—last May—his Sister sent me the account lately—now though I should never have seen him again, (& it is very proper that I should not) I have been more affected than I should care to own elsewhere." [27]

Two days after receiving Ann Edlestone's letter, Byron wrote "To Thyrza," the first of what was to become a series of elegies to his dead friend. Then, on October 14, he sent Dallas a new stanza to be placed near the opening of Canto II of *Childe Harold*:

26. My italics, October 10, 1811, *BLJ*, 2:110.
27. October 13, 1811, *BLJ*, 2:114.

There, thou!—whose love and life together fled,
    Have left me here to love and live in vain:—
Twined with my heart, and can I deem thee dead,
    When busy Memory flashes o'er my brain?
Well—I will dream that we may meet again,
    And woo the vision to my vacant breast:
If aught of young Remembrance then remain,
    Be as it may Futurity's behest;
For me 'twere bliss enough to know thy spirit blest![28]

But on this occasion, apparently regretting his earlier candor, Byron added a false statement to throw Dallas off the track: "I think it proper to state to you, that this stanza alludes to an event which has taken place since my arrival here, and not to the death of any *male* friend."[29]

How deep Byron's turmoil was at the time and how chary he felt about giving direct and candid expression to his feelings can be deduced from another literary effort, his "Epistle to a Friend, in Answer to Some Lines Exhorting the Author to be Cheerful, and to 'Banish Care.'" This poem was enclosed in a letter to Hodgson written the same day Byron wrote "To Thyrza." The first sixteen lines of this curious effort express his grief that "all I loved is changed or gone" and are clearly inspired in part by Edleston's death; the next twenty speak of an earlier frustration, his disappointment at losing Mary Chaworth to John Musters; the strange conclusion envisions a time when Britain will be engulfed in revolutionary chaos and Byron will play a bloody part, "rank'd in some recording page / With the worst anarchs of the Age."[30] Here Byron looks forward glancingly to the desperado mood of *The Corsair* and *Lara*.

On October 31, Byron sent Dallas more stanzas on Edlestone for inclusion in *Childe Harold*, along with a cryptic note designed to discourage further inquiry or speculation:

28.   *BLJ*, 2:116. This became stanza 9 of Canto II.
29.   October 14, 1811, *BLJ*, 2:116.
30.   *CPW*, 1:346.

"They refer to the death of one to whose name you are a *stranger*, and, consequently, cannot be interested. I mean them to complete the present volume. They relate to the same person I have mentioned in canto 2d, and at the conclusion of the poem."[31] In sending these lines for insertion as stanzas 95 and 96 Byron forgot he had earlier stated that his beloved had died after his return to England and now depicted "her" (for he intended the reader to assume he was speaking of a woman) as failing to live "to welcome here thy wanderer home." All this must have made his earlier disavowal look gratuitous and self-contradictory. The new lines ran:

> Thou too art gone, thou lov'd and lovely one!
> Whom youth and youth's affections bound to me;
> Who did for me what none beside have done,
> Nor shrank from one albeit unworthy thee.
> What is my being? thou hast ceas'd to be!
> Nor staid to welcome here thy wanderer home,
> Who mourns o'er hours which we no more shall see—
> Would they had never been, or were to come!
> Would he had ne'er return'd to find fresh cause to roam!
>
> Oh! ever loving, lovely, and belov'd!
> How selfish Sorrow ponders on the past,
> And clings to thoughts now better far remov'd!
> But Time shall tear thy shadow from me last.
> All thou couldst have of mine, stern Death! thou hast;
> The parent, friend, and now the more than friend:
> Ne'er yet for one thine arrows flew so fast,
> And grief with grief continuing still to blend,
> Hath snatch'd the little joy that life had yet to lend.[32]

To the modern ear these lines sound vapid and conventional, but they exactly suited popular taste during the Regency period.

Byron was now to write—in October 1811 and over the

---

31. *BLJ*, 2:121.
32. *CPW*, 2:75.

next five months—a series of seven elegies for the dead boy.[33] "To Thyrza," the first, longest, and most elaborate of these memorials, was the most specific about the intimate side of the love affair:

> Ere call'd but for a time away,
>   Affection's mingling tears were ours . . .
> Ours too the glance none saw beside;
>   The smile none else might understand;
> The whisper'd thought of hearts allied,
>   The pressure of the thrilling hand.[34]

Byron's readers, of course, understood him to be writing about a woman since he used a feminine title and feminine pronouns throughout the poem.

Barely ten days after he had written "To Thyrza," Byron apologized a second time for his feelings for Edlestone. From Cambridge, where he was reveling with the irrepressible Scrope Davies at King's College, Byron confessed to Hobhouse: "The event I mentioned in my last has had an effect on me, I am ashamed to think of, but there is no arguing on these points. I could 'have better spared a better being.'" This reference to Falstaff seems puzzling since all the Thyrza poems idealize Edlestone. Perhaps this is simply Byron's way of agreeing with Hobhouse that some cloud of public obloquy hung over his lover and of assuring him that he realized the wisdom of not identifying

33. These include "To Thyrza," "Away, away, ye notes of woe!" (written shortly before December 8, 1811), and "One struggle more, and I am free" (written, McGann conjectures, in December 1811 or January 1812), all published at the end of the first edition of *Childe Harold*; and "And thou are dead, as young and fair" (February 1812), "If sometimes in the haunts of men" (March 14, 1812), and "On a Cornelian Heart Which Was Broken" (March 16, 1812), which were added to the second edition. McGann adds a newly discovered Latin elegy (first published in 1974) mourning Edlestone. The manuscript of this poem has Edlestone's name written three times at the top. It begins "Te, te, care puer!" ("Thee, beloved boy"). McGann prints the text and a translation (*CPW*, 1:354, 459). This is the only poem in the series that uses the masculine gender.

34. *CPW*, 1:347.

himself with him. He goes on to confess: "Wherever I turn, particularly in this place, the idea goes with me. I say all this at the risk of incurring your contempt, but you cannot despise me more than I do myself." [35] How much of this guilt was real, one wonders, and how much assumed to placate a man who looked at all sentimental involvements with high disdain? Byron himself was still sentimental enough to write to Elizabeth Pigot's mother a week later asking for the return of Edleston's cornelian, which Byron had entrusted to Elizabeth when he found she was sympathetic to his love.

Another letter to Hobhouse a few days later strikes a different note, this time unmistakably paranoid. He describes a convivial after-dinner party with Hodgson and their common friend, the garrulous James Wedderburn Webster:

> He [Webster] made one cursed speech which put me into a fever, about ἕνα παιδί [a boy] & made Hodgson nearly sink into the earth, who unluckily recollected our telling him the "two hundred a year" proffer pro ιακίνθος [for a "hyacinth"]. —He then to mend matters entered into a long defence of his brother in law [George Annesley, Lord Valentia], without any occasion as nobody had mentioned his name, persisted in spite of all endeavours to make him change ye. subject, & concluded by saying that Ld. Courtney was "called Cousin by the King of Prussia!!!" Now all this is verbatim conversation by Bold W[ebster]. You will think me Banksizing but it is a fact Per Dio! [36]

The context of this letter remains, like so much else touching on Byron's involvement with homosexuality, somewhat mysterious. Webster was a crony of Byron's with a reputation as a womanizer and a fool, whose wife Byron was later to flirt with. But what cause had Hodgson, in particular, to be embarrassed by a reference to a boy? Apparently

35. October 22, 1811, *BLJ*, 2:117.
36. November 2, 1811, *BLJ*, 2:124.

Hobhouse and Byron had told him about some boy who was for sale. Could this have been a price that Lusieri set on Nicolo, similar to what Madame Macri had asked for Theresa? Or had the offer been made in England? We have no clue. But Webster's indiscretion must have made Byron nervous about his own candid letters from Athens. "Pray," he asks Hobhouse, "what are become of *all* my *Greek* epistles?" He ended with another reference to his recent visit to Cambridge, which, he confessed "made me 'lemancholy' for many reasons, & some d——d bad ones." [37]

Byron's anxieties about his continuing interest in boys could only have been exacerbated by fuller knowledge of the recent Courtenay scandal, of which Matthews had earlier apprised him. William Courtenay had never lived down the notoriety of his affair with Beckford, despite his being only sixteen at the time of the famous scandal. This and his marked effeminacy made him a dubious figure in British society, accepted in some circles, shunned in others. Late in 1810, however, he was driven into exile. A contemporary diarist, Joseph Farington, gives a detailed picture of the machinations that brought about his flight:

> Mr. Morton of Exeter, an excellent magistrate, was alone the person who by His determined conduct brought the proceedings against Lord Courtney [*sic*] to a point which obliged Him to secure His safety by leaving the Kingdom. Mr. Morton had solicited other magistrates to concur with Him in His exertion for this purpose but they on one pretence of another declined it. He took the Depositions against His Lordship, one of them was to a fact,—the other to an attempt,—Lord Courtney had affected to disregard any proceedings against Him, saying that should He be accused before the Lords they most of them He said were like Himself [and] would not decide against Him. Thus shameless was He in His mind; but when He was informed that the Officers of Justice were ordered to pursue Him, He lost all resolution,—wept like a child, and was willingly taken on board a vessel, the first that could be found, an American Ship, and passed there under a feigned name.

37.   Ibid.; "lemancholy" is not given in the *Oxford English Dictionary*. It appears to be a coinage from "leman," a lover.

> After He had been on board sometime He asked whether
> He might not be called by His own name, but was told it
> would be dangerous on acct. of the Sailors whose prejudice
> against [him] might have bad effects.[38]

When Byron later contemplated, in bitterness of heart,
the necessity of his own self-exile, he must have thought of
Courtenay's flight as an unhappy precedent, though he
himself faced only ostracism and not a trial by the House of
Lords. Courtenay, on reflection, must have recalled that
that body, after all, had voted to behead Lord Castlehaven.
No doubt this jury system, instituted at first to obviate
class bias, worked to reinforce the harsh English system of
ostracism. No thoughtful lord relished the prospect of trying a fellow peer on a criminal charge, where he would
be forced to choose between acquittal (which might lead to
popular criticism) and voting to hang a friend or acquaintance. Far better to force the man to leave the country.

Unlike other minorities, who inevitably formed social
groups, homosexuals in Byron's age were too intimidated
to risk associating freely and openly with each other. In
this respect their position was like that of blacks or Jews
who have "passed" as members of the dominant culture.
Hobhouse was acutely anxious that Byron should not associate with any man who was suspect. He warned him that
Webster's brother-in-law was indeed a man to avoid. Byron,
however, thought his anxiety excessive: "I see nothing
very 'cativo'" in Lord Valentia, he wrote, "as every body
speaks to him, one can't very well avoid it." When Hobhouse was intolerant toward other homosexuals (an all too
common minority failing), Byron was not above adopting a
supercilious tone to deflate him: "Sir W. [William Ingilby]
with whom you are so wrothfully displeased, is going to
Edinbug—burgh. I tell you, he is not what you take him
for, but is going to be married, reformed, and *all that*."
Byron then twitted Hobhouse about an indiscretion of

38. May 17, 1811, *The Farington Diary*, ed. James Greig, vol. 6 (London: Hutchinson, 1926), 273.

his own: "I give you joy of your dinner with the *Bishop* of *Fernes*. Was not 'Atherton' a Bishop? What says the Dean? —What a proper Scoundrel that same Serving man must have been. I thought better of the Irish."[39] As we have noted, John Atherton, Bishop of Waterford, had been hanged in Dublin in 1640 after being convicted of sodomy with his tithe collector. The ecclesiastic whom Hobhouse was to meet was, as chance would have it, another Irish bishop, Percy Jocelyn, of Ferns and Leighlin. In 1810, when his brother's coachman had threatened to accuse him of a solicitation to sodomy, Jocelyn had the man arrested. False accusations of sodomy, or the "attempt," were punished severely in Great Britain, and the man was subsequently whipped through the streets and imprisoned. Twelve years later, Jocelyn, who had since been transferred to the see of Clogher, was to figure in another homosexual episode of unprecedented notoriety. The cautious Hobhouse had not chosen well.

Byron's temperament was nothing if not kaleidoscopic. While he wrote cynical banter to Hobhouse, he was quite capable of confessing sentimental feelings to other correspondents, and even of engaging in flirtations with younger men. The day after he had expressed concern about his letters from Greece, he had rallied Hobhouse for an unwontedly sentimental moment of his own. Hobhouse had recommended John Claridge, a common schoolfriend, to Byron on the basis of Claridge's "attachment" to him, prompting Byron to reply:

> Claridge my *dearest* friend (for he cost me much more than *fifteen* shillings) is indeed dull, as to his "attachment," will attachment keep one awake? or say pleasant things? or even soar beyond an execrable Oxonian pun? and at our time of life, to talk of "attachment!" when one has left School, aye and College too. Sdeath one would think you were like Euripides who admired the Autumn of Agatho.[40]

39. November 17, 1811, *BLJ*, 2:131–32.
40. November 3, 1811, *BLJ*, 2:126–27.

The love of Euripides for his fellow dramatist Agathon had been proverbial in ancient Greece where love between men had meant ordinarily the love of an adult male for a beardless adolescent.[41]

While Byron was teasing one correspondent, he was at the same time showing an emotional side to another. To the more sympathetic Hodgson he sent a new Thyrza lyric inspired by hearing a song he associated with Edlestone:

> Away, away, ye notes of woe!
>   Be silent thou once soothing strain,
> Or I must flee from hence, for, oh!
>   I dare not trust those sounds again.
> To me they speak of brighter days:
>   But lull the chords, for now, alas!
> I must not think, I may not gaze
>   On what I am, on what I was.
>
> The voice that made those sounds more sweet
>   Is hush'd, and all their charms are fled;
> And now their softest notes repeat
>   A dirge, an anthem o'er the dead!
> Yes, Thyrza! yes, they breathe of thee,
>   Beloved dust! since dust thou art;
> And all that once was harmony
>   Is worse than discord to my heart![42]

Did Hodgson guess who Thyrza was? Byron dropped a hint by telling him in the same letter that "the organ at Cambridge is a sad remembrancer." Then, in a sentence that would have made Hobhouse smile and perhaps raised some alarm if he could have read it, he confessed: "Master William Harness and I have recommenced a most fiery correspondence; I like him as Euripides liked Agatho, or Darby admired Joan, as much for the past as the present."[43] William Harness, the object of Byron's new—or rather, resuscitated—attention was the lame Harrow boy whom he

41. See "The Dialogue on Love," in *Plutarch's Moralia*, trans. W. C. Helmbold, vol. 9 (Cambridge: Harvard University Press, 1969), 435.
42. *CPW*, 1:349–50.
43. December 8, 1811, *BLJ*, 2:140.

had befriended when Harness was eleven and Byron four-teen. Since Byron's letters to him are the only surviving examples of what may be called his sentimental correspon-dence with schoolboy friends, it may be interesting to com-pare them with his usual man-of-the-world epistolatory style.

The first set of letters, written in 1808, before Byron had gone to Greece, and two months after Byron had left Cam-bridge, begin formally. Obviously, Byron is sounding Har-ness out to see if any of his old feelings have survived. He must have responded encouragingly since Byron in his next letter expresses his regret that time and a dissipated life have led him to neglect "an Intimacy, which Affection urged me to continue." [44] In what reads like a muted love letter, he tells Harness that his first poems were addressed to him, though Harness never saw them. Then before he sailed for Greece, Byron asked for a miniature to take abroad since "I am collecting the pictures of my most inti-mate Schoolfellows." [45] Later, as we have seen, Lady Caro-line Lamb was to connect these miniatures with boys she claimed Byron had admitted having sexual relations with, though it seems unlikely that the sedate Harness was one of them.

Byron's use of the word "fiery" to describe the corre-spondence when it was resumed after his return in 1811 seems oddly self-conscious. More often than not the letters are marked by a touching tone of solicitude. Sometimes they are bantering and only lightly colored by feeling: "And now don't give way to your imaginations & the bal-ancing of 'words' & 'looks' (to use your own expression). I cant say much for either of mine, but if ever they seem cold to you believe them at variance with my heart, which is as much yours as it was in the fourth form." [46] Occasion-

44. February 16, 1808, *BLJ*, 1:156. Byron had first written on Feb-ruary 11.
45. March 6, 1808, *BLJ*, 1:197.
46. December 6, 1811, *BLJ*, 2:137.

ally he calls Harness "Child" or "mio Carissimo" or addresses him as "Dearest William." Then in mid-December
he makes a confession, which must have puzzled the boy.
Apologizing for some harshness in an earlier letter Byron
told Harness:

> The latter part of my life has been a perpetual struggle against
> affections which embittered the earlier portion, & though I
> flatter myself I have in great measure conquered them, yet
> there are moments (and this was one) when I am as foolish as
> formerly.—I have never said so much before, nor had I said
> this now if I did not suspect myself of having been rather sav-
> age in my letter, & wish to inform you of the cause.[47]

What were the "affections which embittered the earlier
portion" of Byron's life? Were these the same bitter influences he told his mother were the results of "insular nar-
rowness"? Perhaps, but it is just as likely he had in mind
his rejection by Mary Chaworth, which, as we have seen,
still rankled.

How easily homo- and heterosexual feelings could co-
exist in Byron is demonstrated by his new liaison with a
young Welsh servant named Susan Vaughan. She figures
frequently in Byron's letters to Hobhouse during these
months, no doubt as a reassurance to that strict mentor.
But though Byron seems to have been genuinely involved
emotionally with Susan Vaughan, he broke with her after
a few weeks on discovering she was no more capable of
monogamy than he was. Her infidelity shook his self-
esteem and threw him into a self-pitying mood. "I do not
blame her," he told Hodgson, "but my own vanity in fancy-
ing such a thing as I could ever be beloved."[48] It was his
unwavering certainty that Edlestone had indeed loved him
that had given that relation such importance in his eyes.
By the middle of February he was writing Hodgson in a
misogynist vein: he begs him "never to mention a woman
again in any letter to me, or even allude to the existence of

47. December 15, 1811, *BLJ*, 2:148–49.
48. January 28, 1812, *BLJ*, 2:159.

the sex. . . . In the spring of 1813 I shall leave England for
ever. . . . I believe the only human being, that ever loved
me in truth and entirely, was of, or belonging to, Cambridge, and, in that, no change can now take place."[49] Obviously, the effect of the Vaughan affair was to throw him
back once more on his memories of Edlestone. In this same
month he wrote what is probably the best of the Thyrza
lyrics, "And thou art dead, as young and fair":

The love where Death has set his seal,
Nor age can chill, nor rival steal,
    Nor falsehood disavow:
And, what were worse, thou can'st not see
Or wrong, or change, or fault in me.

The better days of life were ours;
    The worse can but be mine:
The sun that cheers, the storm that lowers,
    Shall never more be thine.
The silence of that dreamless sleep
I envy now too much to weep;
    Nor need I to repine
That all those charms have pass'd away:
I might have watch'd through long decay.

The flower in ripen'd bloom unmatch'd
    Must fall the earliest prey,
Though by no hand untimely snatch'd,
    The leaves must drop away:
And yet it were a greater grief
To watch it withering, leaf by leaf,
    Than see it pluck'd to-day;
Since earthly eye but ill can bear
To trace the change to foul from fair.

I know not if I could have borne
    To see thy beauties fade;
The night that follow'd such a morn
    Had worn a deeper shade:
Thy day without a cloud hath past,
And thou wert lovely to the last;

49. February 16, 1812, *BLJ*, 2:163–64.

Extinguish'd, not decay'd;
As stars that shoot along the sky
Shine brightest as they fall from high.[50]

The pederast's love is often evanescent, like the particular kind of youthful beauty that inspires it. But this hard condition, which would have doomed the lover, inspired the poet. In these lines the facile emotionalism of the other elegies is reined in, and Byron's verse achieves precision and an almost Caroline sweetness. A month later he completed the two final elegies—"If sometimes in the haunts of men" and "On a Cornelian Heart Which Was Broken," the last in reference to Edlestone's emblematic gift.

Taken as a whole, the half-dozen Thyrza lyrics contain more sentimentality than the twentieth century relishes, though they made a powerful appeal to Byron's contemporaries. Occasionally they rise to the level of accomplished verse. The cadences of the second stanza of "Away, Away, Ye Notes of Woe" sank deep into the sensibility of the adolescent Tennyson, who read them about a decade after they appeared: they are echoed unmistakably in *In Memoriam*. But all too often the poems hover on the edge of that funeral bathos Mark Twain made fun of in *Huckleberry Finn*. What interests us most today is not the quality of the verse but rather what the nineteenth century would have been most uneasy about, namely, the relation they celebrate. For the question inevitably arises: why did Byron not address his lines to Edlestone openly, as poems inspired by the death of a male friend? After all, the most famous elegies in English have all been written by men about men: "Lycidas," "Adonais," "Thyrsis," *In Memoriam*. What prevented Byron from writing about John Edlestone as Milton had written about Edward King, and as Shelley and Arnold and Tennyson were to write about Keats and Arthur Clough and Arthur Henry Hallam? Byron's letters,

50.   *CPW*, 3:5–6.

so candid on so many subjects, throw no light on his decision to pretend he was mourning a woman.

Several considerations come to mind. The classical English elegiac tradition, though distinguished on its literary side, had been markedly impersonal, as Samuel Johnson complained of Milton. Most often poets wrote of men who were not close to them, or if they were close, showed marked reserve in their expression of feeling. For the homosexual poet, the form has always posed difficulties. Thomas Gray's most famous elegy is wholly generalized; the sonnet on Richard West, whom Gray indeed felt deeply about, may suffer from the stiltedness Wordsworth thought damned it just because Gray felt he had to conventionalize his feelings. Christopher Isherwood has explored the problem of mourning a male lover in his novel *A Single Man*; he reveals how awkwardly our society accommodates itself to such bereavements by the restraints it imposes. Above all, Byron's deepest need on this occasion was to give vent to his emotions freely and fully.

Edlestone's clouded reputation would in itself have made it difficult for Byron to address him directly in any dedication. He could of course have indicated he was writing about a man without identifying him. But no doubt he felt it would be easier to be evasive about a woman. Delicacy has traditionally sanctioned reticence about a poet's inamoratas: mysterious Lesbias, Stellas, Lucys, and Marguerites have abounded in literary history.

The most cogent comparison is, of course, with Tennyson, who also used the elegiac form to memorialize a deeply felt Cambridge friendship. Unlike Milton, Shelley, and Arnold, he writes personally and exposes a devastating grief. But, though the poem quickly became the quintessential testament of the Victorian age, Tennyson was at first blamed for overstepping the limits of propriety. An anonymous review in the *Times*, now presumed to be by Manley Hopkins, father of the poet Gerard Manley Hopkins, scolded him for striking what the critic chose to call a note of "amatory tenderness." Hopkins stressed the un-Englishness of such sentiments, which he deplored as "unpleasantly familiar" in classical and Oriental poetry.

Tennyson, of course, had been acutely aware of the controversy over Shakespeare's sonnets. This dispute had first erupted in 1780 when George Steevens, in editing the poems, decried the notorious Sonnet 20, in which Shakespeare calls his beautiful young friend "the master-mistress of my passion." "It is impossible," Steevens had complained, "to read this fulsome panegyrick, addressed to a male object, without an equal mixture of disgust and indignation." [51] Edmond Malone, in reply, argued that expressions of friendship were warmer in Elizabethan times. But Steevens's opening shot began a battle that has continued warmly, not just through Byron's age, but down to ours. The situation was made especially difficult for Tennyson since Henry Hallam, the father of his dead friend and a distinguished literary historian in his own right, had expressed the wish, in his history of Renaissance literature, that "Shakespeare had never written" his sonnets and had deplored their vogue "among young men of poetical tempers." [52] But Tennyson, deferential to the elder Hallam's prejudices in other matters, threw down the gauntlet when he deliberately invoked the suspect poems in section 61 of his elegy:

> I loved thee, Spirit, and love, nor can
> The soul of Shakspeare love thee more.

The result of this emotional openness was that Tennyson received "shameful letters of abuse." [53] He was compared

51. Cited in Hyder Rollins, *A New Variorum Edition of Shakespeare: The Sonnets* (Philadelphia: J. B. Lippincott, 1944), 1:55. See also Rollins's interesting review of the history of the controversy in "The Question of Homosexuality," in ibid., 2:232–39.

52. *Introduction to the Literature of Europe in the Fifteenth, Sixteenth, and Seventeenth Centuries* (New York: Harper, 1842), 2:179–80.

53. Noel Garde, *Jonathan to Gide: The Homosexual in History* (New York: Vantage Press, 1964), p. 591.

by the *Times* reviewer with Shakespeare, whose "mysterious sonnets present the startling peculiarity of transfer-
ring every epithet of womanly endearment to a masculine
friend,—his master-mistress, as he calls him by a compound epithet, harsh as it is disagreeable."[54]

Hopkins (if he was the critic) devoted several paragraphs of his review of *In Memoriam* to driving home this
point:

> We should never expect to hear a young lawyer calling a mem-
> ber of the same inn his "rose" [Hallam was studying for the
> bar at the time of his death], except in the Middle Temple of
> Ispahan, with Hafiz for a laureate. . . . Many of these poems
> seem to be contrived . . . "a double debt to pay," and might be
> addressed with perfect propriety, and every assurance of a
> favourable reception, to [a] young lad[y] with melting blue
> eyes and a passion for novels. . . . The taste is displeased
> when every expression of fondness is sighed out, and the only
> figure within our view is Amaryllis of the Chancery Bar.

"Amatory tenderness" for another male was, of course,
exactly the emotion Byron wished to express. He was quite
clear in his mind that what he experienced with John
Edlestone was love and not mere friendship. Writing of his
Cambridge experiences thirteen years later in his Ravenna
journal, he distinguished the two most intense relationships of his college days quite pointedly as, first, "romantic" friendship (i.e., with Edward Noel Long) and, second,
a "violent, though *pure*, love and passion." For Byron this
was one of the inescapable facts of his youth, but he could
not share it with the British public. Tennyson celebrated
Hallam's intellectual and literary interests and dramatized
his religious struggles. *In Memoriam* reveals nothing physical in their relation, no clandestine kisses or hand-holdings.
But what Byron remembered was Edlestone's beauty, his
delicacy and tenderness, and the emotional experience we
call being "in love." Byron might have written about him as

54. "The Poetry of Sorrow," *Times*, November 28, 1851, p. 8, col. 2.

Tennyson wrote of Hallam if he had been willing to represent *eros* as *philia*. But rather than misrepresent or disguise
his feelings, he chose to disguise their object, to falsify
Edlestone's gender rather than to falsify the emotion.

What had the experience meant to him that he felt compelled in 1811 and 1812 to write of it at such length? We
catch some sense of this in the fluctuations of his feelings
in the Vaughan affair and the distrust of women it revived.
His mother had had his welfare much at heart and was
sorely tried when he seemed to be repeating his father's
ruinous extravagances. But she was also an insensitive and
hot-tempered woman who had berated him as a "lame
brat." Later, Mary Chaworth had dismissed him from consideration as "that lame boy." It was surely no coincidence
that Byron wrote the "Epistle to a Friend" with its bitter
recollections of Mary Chaworth on the same day that he
wrote "To Thyrza," for the loss of Edlestone reopened the
old wound. The unique significance of Edlestone's love
was the reassurance it gave him. The anxiety that caused
Edlestone to burst into tears when he feared Byron would
reject his gift had revealed to the seventeen-year-old that
someone did indeed love him disinterestedly. When he
held the stricken boy in his arms and broke down himself,
he felt whole at last: Euryalus had rescued Nisus.

Naturally enough, the mystery in which Byron wrapped
the Thyrza poems piqued the curiosity of his friends and
contemporary commentators. The first readers of *Childe
Harold*, who found the first three Thyrza poems at the end
of the volume, naturally assumed that they referred to
some real person whom Byron had loved and lost through
death. Interest in the subject ran high during his lifetime
and, indeed, throughout his century. With Byron's own
death there had inevitably been some hope of revelations.
Thomas Moore was acutely aware of this fact. As in all the
episodes in Byron's career where a homosexual element is
involved, it is instructive to look at his *Life*. He had come to
know Byron just when the latter was writing the Thyrza

poems, and the vulgarly curious hoped that this intimacy would enable him to lift the veil or at least furnish some cogent hints. During the writing of the biography Moore must have been queried on the point ad nauseam. But his elaborate paragraph on the poems is a tour de force designed not to clarify the mystery but to deny there was one. With magisterial suavity he labored to convert Thyrza into a myth. After quoting the lines to Mary Chaworth from the "Epistle" to Hodgson, Moore remarked:

> It was about the time when he was thus bitterly feeling, and expressing, the blight which his heart had suffered from a *real* object of affection, that his poems on the death of an *imaginary* one, "Thyrza," were written;—nor is it any wonder, when we consider the peculiar circumstances under which those beautiful effusions flowed from his fancy, that of all his strains of pathos, they should be the most touching and most pure. They were, indeed, the essence, the abstract spirit, as it were, of many griefs;—a confluence of sad thoughts from many sources of sorrow, refined and warmed in their passage through his fancy, and forming thus one deep reservoir of mournful feeling. In retracing the happy hours he had known with the friends now lost, all the ardent tenderness of his youth came back upon him. His school-sports with the favourites of his boyhood, Wingfield and Tattersall,—his summer days with Long, and those evenings of music and romance which he had dreamed away in the society of his adopted brother, Eddlestone [*sic*],—all these recollections of the young and dead now came to mingle themselves in his mind with the image of her, who, though living, was, for him, as much lost as they, and diffused that general feeling of sadness and fondness through his soul, which found a vent in these poems. No friendship, however warm, could have inspired sorrow so passionate; as no love, however pure, could have kept passion so chastened. It was the blending of the two affections, in his memory and his imagination, that thus gave birth to an ideal object combining the best features of both, and drew from him these saddest and tenderest of love-poems, in which we find all the depth and intensity of real feeling touched over with such a light as no reality ever wore.[55]

55.   *LJL*, 1:302–03.

It is amusing to imagine what Byron, in a ribald mood, might have said about this torrent of eloquence. Was Moore being uncommonly ingenious or uncommonly disingenuous? Did he believe what he wrote, or was he simply trying to throw readers off the track? Moore argues that the poems are too passionate to be addressed to a male and too chaste to be addressed to a woman. The parallel between Moore and those critics of Shakespeare who have interpreted the sonnets as mere literary exercises is striking and demonstrates how difficult it has been for Anglo-Saxons (or Celts) to accept the idea that a love at once passionate and ideal can exist between men. Moore sees a relation between the Thyrza poems and the unhappy Chaworth affair, but he uses the latter to obfuscate the issue. In fact, obfuscation seems to have been Moore's real aim. One can sympathize with his dilemma. He could not be candid without incriminating his friend and raising a furor among Byron's friends and defenders. On the other hand, he could not be silent on an issue where there was so much pointed interest. Moore moved freely in English high society and was subject to constant interrogation about Byron's amours. He needed to say something on the matter; whether or not people believed him was a secondary concern. There is evidence that perceptive readers didn't. He had quoted Byron's October 11 letter to Dallas about a new "death," and commentators immediately seized the point that this suggested that Thyrza was a real person. One commentator quoted Dallas's already published letter of condolence, in which the latter clearly indicated that he understood the Thyrza stanzas to refer to a real loss.[56]

With the publication of *Childe Harold*, Byron, as he put it, awoke to find himself famous. It was, however, not just

56.   Dallas had replied to Byron's letter of October 11 ("I have again been shocked by a death and have lost one very dear to me in happier times") on October 17: "How truly do I wish that the being to whom that verse now belongs had lived and lived yours!" (R. C. Dallas, *Correspondence of Lord Byron with a Friend* [Paris: Galignani, 1825], 2:150–51).

as an adventurous traveler, pessimistic philosopher, or
jaded roué that he impinged on the popular imagination. It
was also as Thyrza's lover. The *Edinburgh Review*, where
Henry Brougham had earlier attacked *Hours of Idleness*,
singled out the Thyrza lyrics for special praise. Calling
them "a kind of elegies in honour of the same lady whose
loss is deplored in the concluding stanzas of the Pilgrimage," the reviewer found in them "great beauty and feeling." [57] The evangelical *British Review* called them "replete
with tenderness and grace." [58] Even the *Satirist*, previously
Byron's unrelenting foe, melted and selected the lines
"Ours too the glance none saw beside" as the most exquisite in the volume. [59]

In 1812, Byron's reflections on religion scandalized many,
and his philhellenism was still controversial. Only as a
tender lover who had lost the woman he cherished did he
make a nearly universal appeal. One critic, who took exception to his attack on female venality in the opening
stanzas ("Mammon wins his way where Seraphs might despair"), issued an oddly prescient warning: "Fie, my Lord!
the lyre of Orpheus was divinely strung; your own boasts
equal harmony, but, oh! remember, and beware that Poet's
fate!" [60] (Orpheus was killed by the Bacchantes when he
forsook women and turned to the love of boys after he had
lost Eurydice for a second time.) But for most female readers
"To Thyrza" canceled the misogyny of the poem's opening
and revealed a man who needed only another Thyrza to
redeem him.

Byron had originally planned to place near the opening

57. Francis Jeffrey, "Childe Harold's Pilgrimage," *Edinburgh Review* 19
(February 1812):475.
58. "Childe Harold's Pilgrimage," *British Review* 3 (June 1812):299.
59. "Review of Lord Byron's *Childe Harold's Pilgrimage*," *Satirist* 11
(December 1812):546.
60. "Critique on Lord Byron's 'Romaunt of Childe Harold's Pilgrimage,'" *La Belle Assemblée*, 2nd ser., 6 (supplement for 1812):349.

of *Childe Harold* the lines on Beckford dramatizing how social wrath threatened the exposed pederast:

Gainst Nature's voice seduced to deed accurst.

Instead, he published at the end of the volume the love
poems to John Edlestone. We may imagine the irony with
which he read the praise heaped on them as the most sympathetic revelation of his art. The paradox reveals how
deep the need was in his personality to assert his identity as a bisexual—he included also "To Florence" and
other poems inspired by his fleeting passion for Constance
Spencer Smith. It was entirely characteristic of Byron to
wear his heart on his sleeve: he was the most confessional
of poets. But the gesture also reveals his desperado side,
his fatal determination to risk everything, in this case by
making himself vulnerable to one of England's most deeply
held aversions. His dishonest honesty proved in fact to be
more daring than he intended. At the time he did not
mean to linger in England, nor did he anticipate that he
would become at once the center of national, European,
even worldwide attention. But this notoriety made his position, in effect, more dangerous once he had published his
semiconfession. The stage was set for misunderstanding
and disaster: it appeared in the guise of a romantic young
aristocrat, one of whose whims was to pursue Byron in the
costume of her pageboy attendants.

· 5 ·

Fame and Exile

With the publication of *Childe Harold*, Byron, until then known only as the author of a minor satire, became the center of what his contemporaries called the "Byrono-mania." No poet before or since has ever caught the imag-ination of so many readers in so many lands. No doubt his aristocratic status and his romantic looks helped his suc-cess, as well as his exotic subjects—Spain, Albania, and Greece. What is surprising is that the admixture of rakish cynicism and self-dramatizing guilt does not seem to have weakened the effect. But a taste for hero-villains was part of the literary fashion of the day, and in this respect, too, Byron was a storybook hero come alive. Then, finally, the Thyrza lyrics humanized him.

How potently the Thyrza myth worked can be seen in the case of Lady Falkland. This young widow, whom Byron had helped financially before he left for Greece but did not know personally, wrote from Derby: "Surely I cannot be mistaken! Byron, my adored Byron, come to me. . . . Tell me, my Byron, if those mournful, tender effu-sions of your heart to that Thyrza . . . were not intended for myself?"[1] Not surprisingly, Byron declined to answer her letters. But others of her class were more of a tempta-tion to a young man whose intimate experiences with women in England had previously been confined to ser-vants and prostitutes. The chief of these, drawn to him by his new fame, was Lady Caroline Lamb, who was to be,

1. *BB*, 1:346–47.

during the four succeeding years he spent in England, his
nemesis; indeed, her famous remark after meeting Byron
—"mad, bad, and dangerous to know"—proved in this affair even more applicable to herself.

Like Lady Falkland, she was literary, self-obsessed, and
romantic in the extreme. She had been born Caroline Ponsonby; her father was a second cousin of Sarah Ponsonby,
whose elopement with Lady Eleanor Butler she had much
admired. A relative had complained that the Irish Ponson-
bys were always making sensations, and Caroline was
equally intent on defying convention. At first Byron was
flattered by her infatuation. This was his first *grande affaire*,
played before the world's eyes with a lady of rank and fashion. For a man of Byron's insecurities, it was a flattering experience. William Lamb did not try to restrain his wife,
whose conduct, in their circles, was only remarkable for its
open daring, and for two months Byron seems to have enjoyed Caroline's love and returned it.

She did not entirely fulfill his idea of feminine beauty:
her figure he complained was not sufficiently "rounded."
But her elfin charm fascinated him and her devil-may-care
defiance of the world at whose social pinnacle she moved.
Perhaps her peculiar vulnerability also touched his heart.
But for someone struggling to emerge from an idealized devotion to "Thyrza," the affair had ironic overtones. Caroline
was diminutive and epicene, her nickname was "Ariel," and
she has been described as looking like a fourteen-year-old
boy. Her most famous portrait shows her dressed as a
page. Indeed, one of her principal fads was to collect attractive young pages and to fit them out in splendid uni-
forms of her own design. Occasionally she herself adopted
this disguise for clandestine visits to Byron. Her love of
masquerade and intrigue comes out in a letter of instructions she wrote to Byron's valet, William Fletcher:

> I also want you to take the little Foreign Page I shall send you
> in to see Lord Byron. Do not tell him before-hand, but, when
> he comes with flowers, shew him in. I shall not come myself,

unless just before he goes away; so do not think it is me. Besides, you will see he is quite a child, only I wish him to see my Lord if you can contrive it, which, if you tell me what hour is most convenient, will be very easy.[2]

The punctiliousness of this plan to deceive Byron into thinking she is a boy, and then revealing herself, has an air of erotic fantasy about it.

R. C. Dallas, who had arranged for the publication of *Childe Harold*, had also appointed himself Byron's moral mentor, a role he filled with a certain pomposity. In a book published shortly after the poet's death, he lamented that Byron had "gained some important conquests over his senses" (under Dallas's tutelage), but he had had "these avenues of destruction to the soul . . . again . . . thrown open by the publication of the poem." One day he was perturbed to find Byron busy composing a letter to his mistress (i.e., Lady Caroline Lamb). When he returned next day:

the lady's *page* brought him a new letter. He was a fair-faced delicate boy of thirteen or fourteen years old, whom one might have taken for the lady herself. . . . He was dressed in scarlet hussar jacket and pantaloons. . . . He had light hair curling about his face, and held a feathered fancy hat in his hand, which completed the scenic appearance of this urchin Pandarus. I could not but suspect at the time that it was a disguise; if so he never disclosed it to me. . . . I do not precisely recollect the mode of his exit.[3]

At one point, Byron and Caroline were close to eloping, but her public scenes, private tantrums, and jealous spying tried him sorely. Eventually her complete lack of discretion led him to break with her. Her mother and husband finally got her off to Ireland, but when she returned, she continued to harass him for years with passionate letters and unexpected visits.

At some point in the course of this romance or its dis-

2.   Byron, *The Letters and Journals*, ed. R. E. Prothero, vol. 2 (London: John Murray, 1898), 116n.

3.   R. C. Dallas, *Correspondence of Lord Byron with a Friend* (Paris: Galignani, 1825), 3:41–42.

solution Byron was moved to tell Caroline about his bisexuality. We know of the scene not at first hand from either
of the participants but from an account of Caroline's revelations to Lady Byron recorded by the latter shortly after her
separation from her husband. Caroline also told Lady
Byron that Byron had spoken of his incest with his sister
Augusta, presumably some time after his affair with Caroline had cooled:

> Since *that* avowal—Ly C—— L—— never suffered any inti-
> macy with Ld B—— though she had been prevailed upon to
> forgive "other & worse crimes"—. . . .
>   Of these she gave the following account—that he had (after
> touching distantly on the subject at different times, by allu-
> sions which she did not understand till subsequently) con-
> fessed that from his boyhood he had been in the practice of
> unnatural crime—that Rushton was one of those whom he
> had corrupted—by whom he had been attended as a page, &
> whom he loved so much that he was determined Ly C——
> L—— should call her page Rushton—which she owned with
> shame she had done.
>   He mentioned 3 schoolfellows whom he had thus per-
> verted. (N.B. two of their miniature pictures were burnt with a
> curious remark.). . . .
>   Ly C. L—— did not believe that he had committed this
> crime since his return to England, though he practised it unre-
> strictedly in Turkey—His own horror of it appeared to be so
> great that he several times turned quite faint & sick in alluding
> to the subject—
>   He concluded by threatening her in the most terrific man-
> ner, reminding her of Caleb Williams, and saying that now she
> knew his secret, he would persecute her like Falkland—he
> then endeavoured to regain her affection, whilst she sat filled
> with dread—and when he said "but you love me still"—an-
> swered "yes" from terror—he thrice obliged her to take the
> most solemn vow never to reveal—[4]

Lady Caroline was not always a woman to be trusted
where testimony about Byron was concerned. But these
revelations have generally the ring of truth, even in their

---

4. *LLB*, pp. 242–44. Falkland, the villain of William Godwin's novel
Caleb Williams, threatens to retaliate against his servant, Caleb, if the latter
reveals his knowledge of a murder Falkland has committed.

apparent contradictions. We may wonder, however, at what point of their relation Byron made his confession. Presumably it was in the summer of 1812 when the affair was still mutual since she says that at that time he had prevailed upon her to forgive these "worse crimes" (worse, i.e., than the incest she was to learn about later when his feelings had waned), and he seems to have been concerned to keep her love. But what prompted this admission, which was to have such devastating consequences later? No doubt she had queried him about Thyrza—she speaks in one letter of taking Thyrza's place in his life—and this may have inspired some of the hints.[5] Most likely, Byron was seeking sympathy and understanding. Perhaps he saw in this unconventional rebel another semioutlaw before whom he might drop his mask and reveal his tormented spirit.

In Lady Caroline, the heterodox rebel who admired "the Ladies" and such radicals as Mary Wollstonecraft and William Godwin, he had hoped to find a sympathetic confidante. As events were to prove, he could hardly have chosen worse. At first, she was shocked into speechlessness. Thereupon Byron's trust in her loyalty and discretion vanished, and his paranoia took over. Hence his attempt to terrorize her into silence. Eventually she must have recovered from her shock since she "forgave" him and even humored him by renaming her page, an odd bit of diablerie. (One recalls, by way of parallel, the way Beckford's infatuated cousin Louisa abjectly condoned his obsession with the young William Courtenay.) It would be interesting to know whether Caroline's assumption of her pageboy disguise antedated or followed his confession.

Though Byron finally became disgusted with her unbalanced and uninhibited pursuit, Caroline was determined at all costs not to be read out of his life. His damning con-

5. On August 9, 1812, Caroline sent Byron an envelope containing her pubic hair with the inscription "next to Thyrsa Dearest" (Malcolm Elwin, *Lord Byron's Wife* [New York: Harcourt, Brace & World, 1962], p. 146).

fession was, she felt, one link he could hardly dare to ignore. Early in 1813, months after his passion had dissipated, she had with typical impertinence invaded Byron's quarters while he was away and written, in a copy of *Vathek*, "Remember me!"—the ghost's plea in *Hamlet*. Undoubtedly her choice of book and author implied a threat. Though the Beckford scandal had erupted four years before Byron was born, Beckford's name was still a byword for the homosexual who had been driven from English society. Given Caroline's reckless and vindictive temperament, her words must have struck Byron as unpleasantly ominous. This awareness explains the bitterness of the famous lines he wrote in reply:

> Remember thee! remember thee!
>   Till Lethe quench life's burning stream,
> Remorse and shame shall cling to thee,
>   And haunt thee like a feverish dream!
>
> Remember thee! Ay doubt it not;
>   Thy husband too shall think of thee;
> By neither shall thou be forgot,
>   Thou *false* to him, thou *fiend* to me![6]

Just how fiendishly Caroline was capable of behaving Byron was to discover later. Betrayal by spurned lovers has always been a danger for homosexuals and bisexuals, and Caroline's visit to Byron's estranged wife was only one stroke in a long campaign. On January 3, 1813, Byron wrote to Francis Hodgson: "You can have no idea of the horrible and absurd things she has said and done . . . since I withdrew my homage,"[7] and by April 6 he told Lady Melbourne that he held Caroline in "utter abhorrence," with a feeling so strong "it has poisoned my future existence."[8] Three weeks later, she became sufficiently menacing for him to write in this vein:

6. *CPW*, 3:84; for McGann's dating of the poem, see ibid., p. 424.
7. *BLJ*, 3:7.
8. Ibid., pp. 35–36.

If you still persist in your intention of meeting me in opposition to your own friends & of mine—it must even be so—I regret it & acquiesce with reluctance.—I am not ignorant of the very extraordinary language you have held not only to me but others—& your avowal of your determination to obtain what you are pleased to call "revenge"—nor have I now to learn that an incensed woman is a dangerous enemy.—Undoubtedly those against whom we can make no defence—whatever they say or do—must be formidable—your words & actions have lately been tolerably portentous—& might justify me in avoiding the demanded interview—more especially as I believe you fully capable of performing all your menaces—but as I once hazarded everything *for* you—I will not shrink *from* you—perhaps I deserve punishment—if so—you are quite as proper a person to inflict it as any other. You say you will *"ruin me"*—I thank you but I have done that for myself already— . . . it is in a great measure owing to this persecution—to the accursed things you have said—that I again adopt the resolution of quitting this country.[9]

By this time, Byron had, of course, embarked upon a new affair with Jane Elizabeth, the Countess of Oxford. Cool and experienced, Lady Oxford was the opposite of the hysterical Caroline in everything except her amorous self-indulgence. The affair, however, brought no respite from Caroline's histrionics, which troubled both the lovers. Byron can hardly have been tempted to repeat his experiment of telling his new mistress the facts about his sexual nature. He may, however, have given her some indication of the kind of thing Caroline might accuse him of without committing himself on the truth of the accusations.

Our chief knowledge of these matters comes from Byron's numerous letters to Lady Melbourne, who did her best to keep Caroline, who was her daughter-in-law, in line. It had been proposed that Lady Melbourne be a third party at Caroline's canvassed interview, but Byron had explained that he would prefer Lady Oxford. It would be "less awkward for me," he wrote, "you will wonder why—

9. Ibid., p. 43.

& I cant tell you more than that she might make some brilliant harangue to which [Lady Oxford] would be a less embarrassed listener than you could possibly be." [10] This news must have puzzled Lady Melbourne, who, with voluminous epistolary accounts of Byron's entanglements with women before her, must have wondered what more there was about Byron's life to know.

Since his return to England, Byron had spoken repeatedly of retiring again to the Mediterranean. In the spring of 1813 these plans took on a more serious color: he would probably have left then for the East if the plague had not broken out there. But something else also held him in England: he had begun an affair with his half-sister, Augusta Leigh. In part, the very forbiddenness of such a relation made it attractive to Byron. Yet if it was, to use his own words, the "most perverse" of his entanglements, it was also the deepest and most serious. Augusta seems to have been the very opposite of the *femme fatale* type. Neither beautiful nor clever, she was, like Byron, shy, but unlike him she was timid and conventionally pious in a somewhat shallow fashion. Her friends considered her good and dowdy, and she was worriedly devoted to a spendthrift husband and a brood of troublesome children. But she had humor and charm and the rare gift of being able to handle Byron in his difficult moods. If she had been an unmarried cousin or if England had been ancient Egypt or classical Greece, she might have made him a reasonably satisfactory wife.

Her feeling for her brother seems to have been less romantic than protective. Did she know the troubling secret of his homosexuality? The evidence on this matter is teasingly vague. G. Wilson Knight has argued that she did. He notes the anxious concern for her brother that commences about the time of his encounter with Lord Grey. Living in London, moving in court circles, and reading the papers of

10.   March 14, 1813, *BLJ*, 3:26.

the day, she must have been keenly aware of the stigma any suspicion of homosexuality carried. Of the evidence cited by Knight, the most significant appears to be a letter Lady Byron wrote to Augusta on September 21, 1816, some eight months after she had left Byron. For the sake of intelligibility, I shall quote the passage at somewhat greater length than Knight does:

> As to the impressions of my parents towards you, I feel that I ought to say a few words on their accounts, lest they should appear to have been actuated by an irrational spirit of resentment. After they became acquainted with what had been *his* habits of life, and decided propensities, previous to my marriage, and during a time when his general proceedings must have been known to you (and indeed he made it clear that they *were* known), it was their opinion that in allowing any young woman to be united to him, and still more in endeavoring to smooth the apparent obstacles, you were sacrificing her to the most remote possibility of doing him service in any but a worldly point of view.[11]

Lady Byron's style is maddeningly prolix and vague, but a reasonable interpretation of her words is that her parents resented Augusta's promoting her marriage with Byron, whom Augusta knew to be homosexual, when the marriage was not likely to change him but only to serve as a cover. Of course, everything here depends on how one interprets the word "propensities." Obviously, this cannot refer to incest, and though it might in another context mean sexual activity in general, Byron's womanizing was so widely known and self-professed that it could hardly have been regarded as a secret known only to his sister. It is interesting to note Lady Byron's assertion that Byron told her of his sister's knowledge after this marriage had taken place.

Another passage Knight calls attention to is even more vague. But since it throws much light on the confidence that existed between Augusta and Byron and reveals clearly

11. *Letters and Journals*, ed. Prothero, 3:328.

what he sought in a relation with a "good" woman, it is
worth considering. Lady Blessington, who interviewed
Byron in Italy in 1823, reports him as saying:

> To my sister, who, incapable of wrong herself, suspected no
> wrong in others, I owe the little good of which I can boast; and
> had I earlier known her, it might have influenced my destiny.
> Augusta has great strength of mind, which is displayed not
> only in her own conduct, but to support the weak and infirm
> of purpose. . . . Augusta knew all my weaknesses, but she
> had love enough to bear with them. I value not the false senti-
> ment of affection that adheres to one while we believe him
> faultless; not to love him would then be difficult: but give me
> the love that, with perception to view the errors, has sufficient
> force to pardon them,—who can "love the offender, yet detest
> the offence"; and this my sister had.[12]

Obviously, Byron wanted "good" women to act as con-
fessors and confirm his sense of guilt. Given the intimacy
between them on matters that deeply troubled him, it
seems reasonable to assume that he communicated to
Augusta his homosexual anxieties and found her sympathetically alarmed. It was also important to Byron that any
confidante confirm his self-condemnation, and if Augusta
sounds like a conservative Christian in her moral stance,
we must realize that this is presumably what Byron wanted.
But Byron was unorthodox on one point: he regarded
his sins as inexpiable. Augusta complained that he had
no belief in religious salvation; the damnation was self-
damnation. This was difficult for her to bear and still more
for his wife later.

The mental strain of his liaison with Augusta reveals itself in the narrative poems Byron wrote in 1813 and 1814.
These are the melodramatic Oriental tales, sensationally
popular in their day, rarely read or admired now. Byron
himself did not value them as poetry and excused them as
necessary forms of psychological release. Of the second

---

12. *Lady Blessington's Conversations of Lord Byron*, ed. E. J. Lovell, Jr.
(Princeton: Princeton University Press, 1969), p. 198.

tale—*The Bride of Abydos*—he remarked to Moore: "I have written this, and published it, for the sake of the *employment*,—to wring my thoughts from reality, and to take refuge in 'imaginings,' however 'horrible.'"[13] On the same day he wrote to Madame de Staël that the poem had been composed "in some of those moments when we are forced by reality to take refuge in Imagination—I am much more obliged to it than I ever can be to the most partial reader—as it wrung my thoughts from selfish & sorrowful contemplation—& recalled them to a part of the world to which I am indebted for some of the brightest and darkest but always the *most living* recollections of my existence."[14]

Because he regarded these poems as exercises in therapy rather than literature, Byron was remarkably coy about their personal significance—even beyond his usual wont. *The Giaour*, *The Bride of Abydos*, *The Corsair*, and *Lara* present the archetypal Byronic hero, adumbrated in Canto I of *Childe Harold* in his full colors—brooding, remorseful, proud, misanthropic, and wracked by the recollection of some mysterious guilt. In *The Bride of Abydos*, Byron introduced the theme that was troubling him most—brother-sister incest, but with numerous equivocations. Though he had originally intended to make Zuleika and Selim siblings, he retreated from this plan so that while Zuleika at first believes her love for Selim is incestuous, she finds out later that they are only cousins.

In relation to this study, it is *Lara*, the last of the four tales, that is of most interest. If *The Bride of Abydos* toys with the possibility of incest and then tactfully negates it, *Lara* is a story that has suggestive pederastic overtones, though the hints, as befits this even more controversial subject, are more delicately developed. Strictly speaking, of course, it is not quite an Oriental tale. Its hero, Lara, has just returned from the Orient, but the setting is univer-

13. November 30, 1813, *BLJ*, 3:184.
14. Ibid., p. 185.

salized. Lara's name is Spanish, his page's Arabic (Kaled), and his foe's Italian (Ezzelin). Byron tells us the action is set in "no country and no age," though the feudal background suggests western Europe.

In *Lara*, the Byronic hero appears in his most developed guise: he is violent and melancholic, and though capable of love and generosity, he is inexplicably alienated from his fellows,

> Cut off by some mysterious fate from those
> Whom birth and nature meant not for his foes.[15]

Augusta, in a letter to Francis Hodgson, found the hero "wonderfully *ressemblant*" to her brother,[16] and Lady Byron recorded a conversation on the subject that her grandson, Lord Lovelace, later published:

> One of the conversations he then held with me turned upon the subject of his poems, and—tacitly between us—of their allusions to himself. He said of "Lara," "There's more in *that* than any of them," shuddering and avoiding my eye. I said it had a stronger mysterious effect than any, and was "like the darkness in which one fears to behold spectres." The remark struck him as accidentally more characteristic than he thought I could know it to be—at least I presume so from his singular commendation of it with the usual mysterious manner. He often said that "Lara" was the most metaphysical of his works.[17]

The poem hints at some unnamed crime committed in the East:

> All was not well they deemed—but where the wrong?
> Some knew perchance—but 'twere a tale too long;
> And such besides were too discreetly wise,
> To more than hint their knowledge in surmise.[18]

15. *CPW*, 3:243.
16. November 14, 1816, *Athenaeum*, no. 3021 (September 19, 1885), p. 370.
17. Ralph Milbanke, Earl of Lovelace, *Astarte: A Fragment of Truth Concerning George Gordon Byron, Sixth Lord Byron*, ed. Mary, Countess of Lovelace (London: Christophers, 1921), pp. 20–21.
18. *CPW*, 3:219.

Lara is attended by a beautiful page, Kaled, who has left his Eastern home out of devotion to his master:

> Light was his form, and darkly delicate
> That brow whereon his native sun had sate,
> But had not marr'd, though in his beams he grew,
> The cheek where oft the unbidden blush shone through;
> Yet not such blush as mounts where health would show
> All the heart's hew in that delighted glow;
> But 'twas a hectic hint of secret care
> That for a burning moment fevered there. . . .
> Nor mark of vulgar toil that hand betrays,
> So femininely white it might bespeak
> Another sex, when matched with that smooth cheek.[19]

Byron, in the preface to the anonymous first edition, equivocally hinted that the reader "may probably regard it as a sequel to a poem that recently appeared."[20] This has suggested to commentators that Lara's crime, like Conrad's in *The Corsair*, was piracy. But Byron's analysis of Lara's psyche suggests something more inward than this:

> But haughty still, and loth himself to blame,
> He called on Nature's self to share the shame,
> And charg'd all faults upon the fleshly form
> She gave to clog the soul, and feast the worm;
> 'Till he at last confounded good and ill,
> And half mistook for fate the acts of will.[21]

These lines certainly would fit a sexual proclivity better than an act of plunder. Byron's prefatory hint may perhaps be taken as a piece of deliberate obfuscation.

The action of *Lara* is, as Byron admitted, very slight. At a feast of nobles, Ezzelin suddenly recognizes Lara and threatens to expose his (unspecified) secret to the world. A time is appointed for the confrontation, but Ezzelin does not appear, and foul play is suspected. Civil war breaks out, and Lara, more for revenge on the society that treats

19. Ibid., pp. 232–33.
20. Ibid., p. 453.
21. Ibid., p. 225.

him as an outcast than for any love of democracy, takes the popular side, playing the vengeful political role Byron had imagined for himself in his "Epistle to a Friend." He is killed fighting against great odds and dies touchingly in the arms of his page, who himself succumbs to grief—and is discovered to be a girl.

All this takes place amid dark hints and calculated ambiguities. Some parallels with Byron's life are unmistakable: the situation of a man fearing imminent exposure and ruin was one Byron had lived with for two years since his ill-advised confession to Lady Caroline. The epicene page has been compared to the page in Sir Walter Scott's poem *Marmion* (also a woman in disguise), to a girl in boy's clothes Byron was reputed to have kept in Brighton, and to Lady Caroline herself. However, it is hard to believe this relation did not have some homoerotic significance for Byron. The tradition of transvestite pages and warriors is a venerable one in European romance and sometimes has a detectable homosexual overtone. In Sir Philip Sidney's *Arcadia* (1590), Philoclea falls in love with the disguised Pyrocles and is appalled to think she is experiencing lesbian emotions.[22] In Ariosto's *Orlando Furioso* (1532), Flordespine is attracted to Bradamante in her soldier's armor, but since Ariosto is Italian, she is less discomfited on discovering that her beloved is a woman. The ambiguities of Shakespeare's transvestite roles are well known. In Théophile Gautier's *Mademoiselle de Maupin* (1835), the hero of the novel falls in love with the eponymous heroine, whom he thinks is a boy; "he" plays Rosalind in *As You Like It*, who disguises herself as Ganymede, who then plays a girl's part for Orlando. Mademoiselle de Maupin herself later turns out to be bisexual, though she is less a believable character than an erotic fantasy of Gautier's. These stories of confused genders were sometimes clearly heterosexual in their titilla-

22.   Jeanette H. Foster, *Sex Variant Women in Literature* (London: Frederick Muller, 1958), pp. 36–38.

tions—a woman in man's clothes was erotically exciting on account of her daring and her revealing costume, though the "actresses" who revealed their feminine charms by dressing as boys in Shakespeare's day *were* boys. But in societies where straightforward representation of same-sex love was taboo, they also gave homosexual writers a chance for surreptitious romance. William Beckford used this device in his "Story of Prince Alasi," where the "boy" with whom the prince falls pederastically in love turns out to be a girl.

Byron, of course, does not go nearly as far as Beckford and indeed does not specifically make the relation an amatory one until the end. But there are hints that man and "boy" share a secret more damning than any heterosexual attachment. At one point, when Lara faints after a mysterious vision:

> His page approach'd, and he alone appear'd
> To know the import of the words they heard;
> And, by the changes of his cheek and brow,
> They were not such as Lara should avow,
> Nor he interpret.[23]

To the other possible inspirations for the Lara-Kaled story we must add Byron's love for Nicolo Giraud, whom he here seems to fantasize as his attendant and as the partner in the final love-death.

Byron published *Lara* in August 1814, five months before his marriage. He had first proposed to Annabella Milbanke in September 1812, using her aunt, Lady Melbourne, as his intermediary. Byron entertained two different plans at this time. One, repeatedly considered, was to live abroad. The other was, if he remained in England, to marry. Did a concern about his homosexual impulses play any part in his decision to marry if he stayed in his native land? There is some evidence that it did. When An-

23. *CPW*, 3:222.

nabella rejected his first proposal, he appeared to take it calmly, telling Lady Melbourne: "She is perfectly right in every point of view, & during the slight suspense I felt something very like remorse for sundry reasons not at all connected with C[aroline] nor any occurrences since I knew you or her."[24] Here Byron seems to be saying that something in his early life still troubled him. His remark suggests that his bisexuality propelled him toward marriage as a mode of escape. At the same time he was troubled about marrying a woman who was ignorant of his real nature. This is of course the eternal dilemma facing the male bisexual. Conventional friends and moralists frequently urge him to marry as a "cure" or a way of avoiding social difficulties; but others may condemn him with equal fervor as a monster if he does, especially if his wife is ignorant. As we have seen, Lady Byron's parents adopted the latter stance. In such cases marriage is seen as a salvation, a pitfall, or a damnable crime, depending on its often unforeseeable outcome.

At the same time, men in this dilemma are often temptations to women who wish to help them, who are naïve about the power and persistence of bisexual feelings. Annabella Milbanke, before she married Byron, was unaware of this aspect of his nature but nursed a mixture of sympathy and troubled hope, which has facilitated many doomed marriages. Sharing the passion for moral reform typical of her age, she has been called a "Victorian before the Victorians," though in fact her "pre-Victorianism" was characteristic of a formidable faction in late Georgian society. With this mental outlook, Annabella was naturally fascinated by the idea of Byron as a moral client and piqued by the challenge of "saving" the foremost literary rake of the day, whose sensitivity and remorse she read as favorable prognostications.

After her refusal, Byron did not entirely lose interest. In

24.   October 17, 1812, BLJ, 2:226.

August 1813, Lady Melbourne, now fearful of the consequences of Byron's affair with Augusta (which he had
hinted to her), encouraged her niece to reopen a correspondence. It is worth noting that Annabella's salvation-
ism, though bearing a certain resemblance to evangeli-
calism, was not quite orthodox but was marked by attitudes
that had more in common with early nineteenth-century
universalism. But this heterodoxy in no way diminished
Annabella's fervor as a moral missionary.

> Early in our acquaintance [she wrote Byron in 1813], when I
> was far from supposing myself preferred by you, I studied
> your character. I felt for you, and I often felt with you. You
> were, as I conceived, in a desolate situation, surrounded by
> admirers who could not value you, and by friends to whom
> you were not dear. You were either flattered or persecuted.
> How often have I wished that the state of Society would have
> allowed me to offer you my sentiments without restraint. As
> the language of Truth I was not too humble to think them
> more worthy of you than the worldly homage of persons who
> were my superior in Talent. My regard for your welfare did
> not arise from blindness to your errors; I was interested by the
> strength & generosity of your feelings, and I honored you for
> that pure sense of moral rectitude, which could not be per-
> verted, though perhaps tried by the practice of Vice. I would
> have sought to rouse your own virtues to a consistent plan of
> action, for so directed, they would guide you more surely than
> any moral counsel.[25]

In short, Annabella, in reopening their correspondence,
was clearly expressing her desire to become Byron's spiritual mentor. Byron should have been warned off by her
complacency ("I studied your character"), her priggish-
ness, and the pat program she offered for his reformation.
Yet while perceiving all this, he still played up to her, de-
ploring his "ill-regulated conduct," assuring her that for all
his misogyny he thought "the worst woman that ever existed would have made a *man* of very passable reputation,"
and at the same time scandalizing her in a way calculated

25. *Lord Byron's Wife*, p. 167.

to bring her moralism to the fore by averring that "the great object of life is Sensation—to feel that we exist."[26] He tempted her by telling her he had no "skeptical Bigotry," that he believed in God, and "should be happy to be convinced of much more,"[27] protesting that he would listen to her on sacred topics with pleasure. In the end Byron, usually the liveliest of letter writers, was composing epistles almost as solemn and serious as Annabella's. Occasionally, he wrote in a breezier style, as when he recommended her to read René de Vertol's history of revolutions in ancient Rome, which he had "met with by accident at Athens in a Convent Library," without, of course, explaining to her what this convent experience had meant to him.[28] But eventually his moral seduction proved irresistible. Annabella finally accepted him as her fiancé in September 1814.

Obviously, Byron's sense of guilt and hope for redemption propelled him toward this marriage. It was as though he were hypnotized by Annabella's virtue. But both had severe misgivings. His unmanageable moodiness was a problem. At one point during their engagement, when Annabella pressed him to reveal his troubles, Byron turned livid and fainted. She later described the "frenzy of despair" in which he referred to "the Past as involving some fearful mysteries. A burthened conscience or an overwrought imagination were the only causes I could conceive. There was too much unequivocal mental excitement to make it possible for these expressions to be from the mere love of producing effect. I walked firmly on to the Goal, but with the conviction I had linked myself to Misery if not Guilt."[29] Byron himself had doubts and wrote to break the engagement, but Augusta, anxious about her own situation and hoping to find in marriage a solution for her brother's manifold problems, dissuaded him from

26. September 6, 1813, *BLJ*, 3:109.
27. September 26, 1813, *BLJ*, 3:120.
28. August 18, 1814, *BLJ*, 4:161.
29. *Lord Byron's Wife*, p. 231.

sending the letter. Irresolutely resolved, Byron proceeded at a snail's pace from London to Annabella's home at Seaham. Hobhouse, who accompanied him, noted that the bridegroom was "more and more *less* impatient."[30]

The ceremony was scarcely over when the storm broke, and Byron's pent-up guilt, rage, and frustration overwhelmed him. In a dramatic scene the day after their marriage Byron told Annabella: "I have done that for which I can never forgive myself," and "I am more accursed in marriage than in any act of [my] life." "I am a villain—I could convince you of it in three words."[31] He was too upset to discuss his troubles, and we are left to guess at what the mysterious words might have been. He dropped hints— one was "murder"—by remarking portentously that there were unpunished murderers walking freely in society.[32] Byron implied that the deed had taken place in Greece and that Hobhouse knew the facts. One crime, he told her, was "another person's secret."[33] This would seem to be a reference to his love affair with Augusta and suggests that the second word was "incest." When Annabella tried to get him to relieve his mind by talking during the early weeks of their marriage, he told her that she "could know nothing of the things to which he alluded—good women could know nothing."[34] From this it appears that the third "crime" torturing his memory was "sodomy."

With so many sources of agitation, it is a difficult task to assess exactly what role homosexuality played in the fiasco of Byron's marriage. Doris Langley Moore has suggested that Byron's sense of his bisexual identity was threatened by his marital tie. As she notes in a subtle analysis in her essay "Byron's Sexual Ambivalence": "It seems . . . that bisexuality may be at times a less bearable state than homo-

30.   *BB*, 2:503.
31.   *Lord Byron's Wife*, p. 252.
32.   Ibid., p. 258.
33.   Ibid., p. 257.
34.   Ibid.

sexuality, since, whatever fulfillment is attained, the lover in some strange spirit of contradiction is liable to feel that he is being false to his nature." [35] There is certainly evidence that Byron's homosexual past continued to haunt him poignantly during his married life. But his love for Augusta was a much more immediately disturbing element. Whether or not he had shared Augusta's anticipation that marriage would end the affair, once wed he seems to have passionately resented the barrier Annabella posed to its continuance. When he and his wife visited Augusta at her home at Six Mile Bottom, Byron made his preference for his sister all too clear through insinuating behavior. Once he realized Augusta regarded the physical side of their relation as at an end, Byron angrily turned against her also. Augusta had treated Annabella in a sisterly fashion from the start: Byron's cruel and resentful behavior now drew the two women closer together. Annabella, for her part, was won over by the older woman's kindness and solicitude. Nevertheless, when Augusta came to visit them in Piccadilly in April, Annabella was relieved to see her depart since she was sufficiently alarmed by Byron's hints to be fearful that he would cajole his sister into resuming relations.

Given Byron's premarital declaration that he meant to take Annabella for his spiritual guide, one might have expected some effort on his part, however feeble, to conform to her way of thinking. But naïveté and provinciality hobbled her. By taking an anthropological and historical view of morals, Byron soon put Annabella on the defensive. The ministering angel was invited to become the devil's disciple. As Annabella wrote in a statement after their separation:

> In his endeavours to corrupt my mind he has sought to make me smile first at Vice. . . . There is *no* Vice with which he has not endeavoured in this manner to familiarize me—attributing

35. *LBAR*, p. 456.

the condemnation of such practices merely to the manners of different Countries, & seeking either to ridicule or reason me out of *all* principle. He has said a wife was only culpable towards her husband if her infidelity were practised openly.[36]

To Annabella, whose sense of "moral rectitude" was the very essence of her being, this rational libertinism must have been profoundly shocking.

Undoubtedly the "vices" about which he now sought to enlighten her included homosexuality. His travels and his wide reading of classical and Oriental literature gave him an advantage, which he did not fail to press. Apparently, he did not limit himself to a diabolist stance but tried to make her sympathize with customs different from those she knew. Not surprisingly he ran into strong resistance:

He laboured to convince me that Right & Wrong were merely Conventional, & varying with Locality & other circumstances —he clothed these sentiments in the most seductive language—appealing both to the Heart and Imagination. I must have been bewildered had I not firmly & simply believed in one Immutable Standard. . . . It would have required an abler logician than I was to expose the fallacy, when he stated such facts as that morality was one thing at Constantinople, another in London—& the requirements of Divine Law different in the time of Abraham & of Christ.[37]

The juxtaposition of London and Constantinople, of course, inevitably suggests the difference between Turkish and English attitudes toward homosexuality. The "seductive" language and appeals to the heart suggest that Byron told Annabella something of the idealistic side of Greek love. But Annabella was not one to let a sentimental appeal threaten her "one Immutable Standard."

Though Byron made no explicit personal confession to Annabella of his homosexual impulses, he seems to have dwelt on such matters often enough to have aroused her

36. *Lord Byron's Wife*, p. 349.
37. *LBAR*, p. 443.

suspicions. How much he told her about his friendships at Harrow is not clear. Puzzled as she was by Byron's hints and intrigued by clues that might explain his psychology, Annabella did, however, take a keen interest in the letters from Harrow and Cambridge that Augusta showed her. "His earliest letters to A—— from school were romantic & open-hearted—by no means sensible, but their affectionate character was highly interesting." These were the letters in which Byron spoke repeatedly of his love for Delawarr and his detestation of Lord Grey. "It [i.e., Byron's tempera- ment] changed between the age of 16 & 17, and she has often dwelt upon this change both to him—& to me in his absence—and he has acknowledged it with mysterious horror." This period, which included his last year at Harrow and his arrival at Cambridge, was when Byron seems to have realized the sexual nature of his feelings for school- boys and for Edleston and the social disapproval such ap- petites might bring. "It took place in an interval of a part- ing and meeting between them, and the first letter in that altered style is short mysterious, & cold, with a tinge of malignity. He says—in another I think, for it appeared to mark some remarks of hers upon the change—that it was not owing to *love*—of this he solemnly assures her."[38] Au- gusta told Annabella: "From that time he was only a cause of misery to her."[39] Was Augusta referring solely to his fi- nancial difficulties, or was she indirectly hinting to Anna- bella that there was something in Byron's temperament that they must try to protect him against? Obviously she was trying to educate her and engage her sympathies by sharing the letters. She may also have been trying to imply that there was a disinterested side to her own affair with her brother.

Curious as she was about Byron's sentimental history, Annabella was inevitably fascinated by hints that he let fall about Thyrza. Nothing could demonstrate more tellingly

38. *Lord Byron's Wife*, p. 293.
39. Ibid., p. 294.

Byron's simultaneous need to confess and to conceal than the way in which he tantalized her with details while repelling cross-examination on the subject.

> The first time I remember his mentioning Thyrza by name was at Seaham [in February 1815, a month after their marriage]. When he was talking over the names he had given to the personages in his poems, he said, "I took the name of Thyrza from Gessner—She was Abel's wife"—and his tone of mysterious agitation precluded further inquiry, for I never had the disposition of Caleb Williams to kindle a consuming flame in the visible darkness of Suspicion. Another night (for he was always more open then than in the day) he said—after some expressions of affection which I hoped were genuine, though I felt all the misery by which they were overwhelmed—
> "I think I love you—better even than Thyrza"—but he lamented that he could not feel as once he felt.[40]

After expatiating on this emotional falling off, Byron told her that she could not possibly conceive "the oppression of his conscience—'What can *you* know (or what can a *good woman* know) of strong passions & c.'—and yet he was often on the brink of trying the effect of confession upon me." Later in the same statement, Annabella added more recollections:

> He told me he had never read over the last Stanzas of C[hilde] H[arold] since they were written. He alluded to those which have the character of despair, occasioned I believe by the death of Thyrza, & some remorseful recollections (from what causes I cannot tell, but they were plainly such) embittered & perpetuated his grief. . . . He mentioned Thyrza to me but two or three times, but I felt that several associations recalled that being to his mind—& always with the deepest emotion. The mention of *consumption* of its delusive bloom—"yes, I have seen that"—would he say in a tone that "echoed to the heart as from its own." Of fair hair—I thought that in a large collection of hair which he once showed me, there was a beautiful tress of Thyrza's by the feeling with which he regarded it.[41]

---

40.   Ibid., p. 282.
41.   Ibid.

Then again later:

> To return to Thyrza—He talked to me of her another time in
> London—at the period when A[ugusta] was absent, for I
> wrote it to her, said that he believed now she was gone, his
> breast was the sole depository of that secret—that he had
> never mentioned her name. He described *her* beauty as he has
> described beauty in the abstract—told me of the emotion with
> which he used to expect the hour of meeting, when he would
> walk up & down till he almost fainted, & said he was sure that
> such a state of excitation, if circumstances had not put an end
> to it, must have destroyed him.[42]

All this throws new light on the intensity of Byron's feeling for John Edlestone at Cambridge and after. Apparently
the latter had developed tuberculosis before he parted
from Byron. The parting may have been the result of the
high state of tension into which the unconsummated affair
had thrown Byron. As to the remorseful thoughts that embittered his grief, Byron seems to have regretted his ac-
quiescence in Hobhouse's determination that he should
shun Edlestone as a kind of betrayal; of this, however, we
cannot be sure. Another remark recorded by Annabella
tells us that Byron received a letter about Edlestone on his
way home from the East, presumably, like the "indecency"
letter, from Francis Hodgson:

> He spoke of the encreasing induration of his feelings—that he
> could not now feel even for her as he had done. He had heard
> of her being well at Malta on his return from Greece, and at his
> arrival in England he learned her death.[43]

After she had left her husband in January 1816, Annabella set about writing lengthy memoranda that might be
used should Byron attempt to gain custody of their infant
daughter. These are devoted largely to her suspicions
about Byron and Augusta, but occasionally references to

42.   Ibid., p. 283.
43.   Ibid., pp. 283–84.

other matters surface. The extracts from Annabella's voluminous writings published by Malcolm Elwin in *Lord
Byron's Wife* are necessarily selective, and it is hard to guess
whether further hints about Byron's homosexuality exist
among Lady Byron's papers. Elwin, unlike other leading
Byron scholars, regularly discounts the homosexual side of
Byron's life and fails to comprehend his experiences in
Greece, taking the code phrase from Petronius to refer to
conventional Casanovism. However, he does quote two interesting excerpts from Annabella's "Statement G," which
he describes as "her case against Augusta." One of the
things Annabella feared she might have to explain in court
was why she had invited her sister-in-law to Piccadilly Ter-
race on November 15 for her lying-in if she had suspected
an incestuous liaison:

> He told me to write to her of his vicious courses at the theatre,
> as if his taking a mistress was out of revenge *towards her*—& a
> greater injury to her than to me! . . . He desired me to send
> her some very unkind messages—and when she was come
> to Town said he did not want her then as he had formerly
> done. . . . I confess I had at that time so far lost the suspicions
> in which he was concerned [i.e., of incest] from the apprehen-
> sion of crimes on his part yet more dreadful, that my only
> scruple in requesting her to come was lest she should suffer in
> any way from her interest for *me*—& particularly as to the pe-
> cuniary prospects of her children.[44]

Later in the same statement Lady Byron claimed that
she feared Byron might commit suicide and encouraged
Augusta to stay with him on that account, referring once
again to mysterious "practices": "I had heard so much too
of his addiction to other amours—besides the worse practices I suspected—that there was no ground for alarm on
her account (vide her letters), & her remaining in Town
really afforded me comfort during the early time after I left
it."[45] Elwin interprets the "more dreadful" crimes as refer-

44.   Ibid., p. 330.
45.   Ibid., p. 348.

ences to homosexuality but thinks they were "alcoholic ramblings" that Byron indulged in to shock his wife, thus giving the impression that Annabella had taken him seriously when she should not have. It is interesting to note that Annabella represents herself as so terrified at the hints of homosexuality at this time that fears about Byron's incest receded into comparative insignificance.

Lady Byron never speaks of more than suspicions in these matters. On January 3, 1816, Byron told her of his affair with the actress Susan Boyce and of "his intention to continue those courses, though tired of her personally."[46] He took the position that a woman had no legal right to complain about her husband provided that he did not beat her or lock her up; and he added: "I have not done an act *that would bring me under the power of the Law*—at least on this side the water."[47] This last may be taken as an assertion that he had not committed sodomy since his return to England, though it suggests that the situation had been otherwise abroad.

On January 15 Lady Byron left Piccadilly with their five-week-old daughter, Ada, ostensibly to visit her parents in Leicestershire, but in fact she was determined not to return unless Byron's violent and abusive behavior was due to insanity, a possibility she took seriously enough to consult medical opinion. She wrote him a warm and affectionate note. But when the doctors in London reported that Byron was not demented, she allowed her father to send a request, which Byron received on February 2, for a separation. Byron, not surprisingly, found it difficult to reconcile this turn of events with the tone of her previous letter. He was much taken aback and wrote in a dignified and restrained style to inquire if these were indeed Annabella's own personal feelings.

At this point, Lady Caroline Lamb, desperate to thrust

46.   Ibid., p. 344.
47.   Ibid., p. 400.

herself back into Byron's life and willing to go to any
lengths, took advantage of the curiosity that was inevitably
aroused by the breakup of the marriage. She began to
spread stories of Byron's homosexuality, based on the ill-
advised confession he had made three years before. On
February 9, Hobhouse noted in his diary: "The Melbournes
are in arms against Lady B. G[eorge] L[amb] called her a
d'd fool, but added that C[aroline] L[amb] accused Byron
of ———, poor fellow, the plot thickens against him." [48]
Hobhouse was to employ a long dash, which of course
stood for the unspeakable vice of sodomy, repeatedly in
his notes and memoranda of the next few weeks. On the
twelfth, he repeated to Byron "what I heard *in the streets*
that day—he was astounded indeed—!" [49] Hobhouse now
confronted Byron with other reports that he had heard
from Byron's sister and cousin about his mistreatment of
his wife, to which Byron confessed. "He was dreadfully
agitated—said he was ruined, & would blow out his brains
—he is indignant but yet terrified." [50] Augusta, distraught
over Byron's repeated threats of suicide, unwilling to give
up the theory of madness, and still hoping for a reconcilia-
tion, wrote to Annabella on February 17:

> There are reports abroad of a nature *too horrible to repeat*. I had
> guessed them from G. B.'s *mysterious* manner & *excessive* annoy-
> ance for some days past. *He* [George Byron, Byron's cousin]
> sent for Hobhouse, who I find last night informed B. of them,
> and HE B has desired me to inform you of them. Of course this
> has added considerably to his agitations. Every other sinks
> into nothing besides this MOST horrid one. God alone knows
> what is to be the end of it all. [51]

Augusta expressed fears that Byron would poison himself
with laudanum. "He said to me last night in an agony,

48. *BB*, 2:576.
49. *Lord Byron's Wife*, p. 407.
50. Ibid.
51. Ibid., p. 413.

'Even to have such a thing *said* is utter destruction & ruin to a man, & from which he can never recover.'"[52]

Her lawyer had informed Annabella she had an adequate legal basis for a separation on the grounds of adultery and cruelty. But neither side wanted to go to court, and after elaborate negotiations, broken off and renewed, an "amicable" separation was arranged. In the meanwhile, Byron had to face a devastating trial at the bar of public opinion. Lady Caroline betrayed Byron a second time by adding to her first accusation the accusation of incest, which Hobhouse first recorded in his diary on February 29.[53] Accusations of incest, if credited, were, of course sufficient for social ostracism, but there is no doubt that the charge of homosexuality was far more serious. Incest, though sinful, was not unspeakable. It even had a certain vogue in the literature of the period. Schiller and Alfieri had based plays on the theme. In 1816, Leigh Hunt used it in his *Story of Rimini* and Byron in *Parisina*, in which the heroine, like Phaedra, falls in love with her stepson.[54] In the next year, Shelley pointedly defended sibling love in the first version of *Laon and Cythna*. Later Wagner was to compose his most compelling love music (barring *Tristan*) for Siegmund and Sieglinde. But none of these liberals dared dramatize a same-sex relation. As for penalties, homosexuality was a hanging matter; incest, though not legal as some writers on Byron have supposed, was punished far less severely. Blackstone complained in his *Commentaries* that offenders were liable only to "the feeble coercion of the spiritual [i.e., ecclesiastical] court."[55] In 1813, the sanction was further reduced by a new act of Parliament

52. Ibid.
53. *BB*, 2:583.
54. On February 7, during the separation crisis.
55. *Commentaries on the Laws of England*, vol. 4 (Oxford: Clarendon Press, 1769), 64. In England incest was not an offense at common law. No statute existed until 1908. Except for a brief time under the Common-

limiting sentences pronounced by ecclesiastical courts to six months' imprisonment.

On March 4 Lady Byron wrote to her mother: "The silence of my friends [who had refused to make public the grounds on which she was prepared to go to court] has been very disadvantageous to Lord B. in regard to opinion—since worse than the true causes are supposed." [56] Annabella, of course, had her suspicions of incest and homosexuality confirmed by Caroline's revelations of March 27, which we have already noted. Caroline pretended to be motivated by pious contrition and a concern for Ada's welfare, but in fact she was playing a double game. Caroline afterward wrote to Byron to say that if Byron asked her, she would "swear I did it [i.e., made the accusations of homosexuality and incest] for the purpose of deceiving her [Lady Byron]. There is nothing, however base it may appear that I would not do to save you." [57] Rarely has a lover scorned gone to such lengths of deviousness. But though the weapon of social accusation was wielded by someone half-demented, it was wielded to deadly effect. Two days before Caroline's visit to Annabella, Byron wrote to his wife:

> My name has been as completely blasted as if it were branded on my forehead. . . . you are understood to say—"that you are not responsible for these [rumors]—that they existed previous to my marriage—and at most were only *revived* by our differences." Lady Byron they did not exist—but even if they had—does their *revival* give you no feeling? . . . is it with perfect apathy you quietly look upon this resurrection of Infamy? [58]

---

wealth, it could be punished only by the ecclesiastical courts. (By contrast, under Scottish law it was theoretically punishable by hanging until 1887.) The new measure limiting the sentences of ecclesiastical courts (53 George III, c. 127) was passed on July 12, 1813. By chance, this is just when Byron was most deeply involved in his liaison with Augusta.

56. *Lord Byron's Wife*, p. 424.
57. Ibid., p. 419.
58. March 25, 1816, *BLJ*, 5:54.

Hobhouse, ever the loyal friend and tireless ally, set about to mitigate the damage. After much discussion with intermediaries, including Byron's cousin, John Wilmot, it was agreed that Lady Byron should sign a kind of disavowal of the rumors. This she did on March 9. In its final form, the much debated paragraph to which she affixed her name read as follows:

> In reference to a paper communicated by Mr. Wilmot, Lady Byron declares that she does not consider herself in any ways responsible for the various reports injurious to Lord Byron's character and conduct which may be circulated in the world. They have certainly not originated with or been spread by those most nearly connected with her. And the two reports specifically mentioned by Mr. Wilmot [i.e., the charges of incest and homosexuality] do not form any part of the charges which, in the event of a Separation by agreement not taking place, she should have been compelled to make against Lord Byron.[59]

This may have been strictly true, but the paragraph palpably left open a substantial question, that is, did Lady Byron, whether or not she intended to raise such issues, believe the charges to be justified by facts?

Byron signed the separation agreement on April 21 and four days later left England for an exile that was to last all his life. But in the meantime another storm had blown up, this time in the press. During the negotiations Byron had worked off the emotions developed by the tense situation in characteristic fashion, by writing two poems. One was the rhetorical and sentimental appeal to Lady Byron entitled "Fare Thee Well!"; the other was a rather vicious satire on her confidante, Mary Anne Clermont, which put special emphasis on her poverty and servant status. Byron indiscreetly ordered John Murray, his publisher, to print the poems and had them circulated widely, but he stopped

59. Sir John C. Fox, *The Byron Mystery* (London: Grant Richards, 1924), p. 112.

short of actual publication. However, by venturing into print, and especially by circulating the satire, Byron gave the hostile press the handle it was looking for.

Newspaper silence about his domestic affairs was broken by the *Champion*, apparently at the secret instigation of Henry Brougham, the radical member of Parliament, acting from motives that remain obscure. John Scott, the editor of the newspaper, published both poems and commented on Byron's personal situation: "Of many of the *facts* of this distressing case we are not ignorant: but God knows they are not for a newspaper. Fortunately they fall within very general knowledge, in London at least—if they had not, they would never have found their way to us."[60] The Tory press was more than glad to have a stick with which to beat a radical peer who had made himself unpopular by criticizing the Regent and praising Napoleon. But the *Champion* and Scott had a reputation for antigovernment liberalism, so politics was not ostensibly the motive for this attack.

Whether sincerely or not, the stance assumed by the *Champion* was that of guardian of national morals. The masthead of the paper included a sentence from Milton, "Let not England forget her precedence of teaching nations how to live," and this seems to have been interpreted in an ethical as well as a political sense. Byron's defenders (specifically the *Examiner*), it charged, sought "to destroy that moral strictness, which as a distinction between this country and others, is most scrupulously and fondly regarded." Byron was associated by Scott with "the Anglo-Gallic school who have tried to introduce French laxness into England."[61]

Commenting on press attacks at this period, Byron was later reported by Thomas Medwin as saying that he "once made a list from the Journals of the day, of the different

60. *Champion*, April 14, 1816, p. 118.
61. *Champion*, April 28, 1816, pp. 133–34.

worthies, ancient and modern, to whom I was compared. I remember a few: Nero, Apicius, Epicurus, Caligula, Heliogabalus, Henry the Eighth, and lastly, the King." [62] Nero, Caligula, and Heliogabalus were all notoriously homosexual or bisexual emperors. The purported writers may have intended innuendoes in their comparisons, but since these reports have not yet been identified, it is hard to be certain about the contexts. Leigh Hunt's *Examiner*, in coming to Byron's defense, deplored the "depraved speculations" of the "falsest and most brutal nature" that were circulating. Hunt referred to the "inconsistent and villainous accusations, some of them so monstrous, that even the first public propagators of the scandal professed the singular delicacy of being able only to hint at them. Hint at them however they did, and set the imagination of it's mongers afloat, without any warrant whatsoever." [63] But very few papers joined the *Examiner* on Byron's side.

Byron sailed for Ostend on April 25. Was his leaving England a forced or a free decision? This has been a much debated question. In his biography of 1830, Thomas Moore, who observed the public reaction at first hand, mentioned certain "rumors" and declared that "such an outcry was now raised against Lord Byron as, in no case of private life, perhaps, was ever before witnessed." [64] Byron's exile, he tells us, "had not even the dignity of appearing voluntary, as the excommunicating voice of society left him no other resource." [65] To this Hobhouse retorted in the margin of his copy of Moore's book: "*There was not the slightest necessity even in appearance for his going abroad.*" [66] But here Hobhouse must have been writing in a spirit of contradiction or out of

62. *Medwin's Conversations of Lord Byron*, ed. E. J. Lovell, Jr. (Princeton: Princeton University Press, 1966), p. 48.
63. "Distressing Circumstances in High Life," *Examiner*, no. 434 (April 21, 1816), pp. 249, 248.
64. *LJL*, 1:653.
65. *LJL*, 2:1.
66. *LLB*, p. 295.

a compulsive need to defend his friend and minimize his unpopularity. Only one hostess had dared to try to stem the tide by inviting Byron and his sister to a social gathering, and at Lady Jersey's famous party, they had to endure galling snubs.

An account of how Byron perceived his ostracism is given in Medwin's *Conversations*. There Byron is represented as saying: "I was abused in the public prints, made the common talk of private companies, hissed as I went to the House of Lords, insulted in the streets, afraid to go to the theatre, whence the unfortunate Mrs. Mardyn [erroneously believed to be his mistress] had been driven with insult."[67] In 1819, after three years in Europe, Byron gave a fuller and slightly different account of his ordeal in the reply he wrote (but did not publish) to an attack that had appeared in *Blackwood's Edinburgh Magazine*:

> I was advised not to go to the theatres, lest I should be hissed, nor to my duty in parliament, lest I should be insulted by the way; even on the day of my departure my most intimate friend told me afterwards, that he was under apprehension of violence from the people who might be assembled at the door of the carriage. However, I was not deterred by these counsels from seeing Kean in his best characters, nor from voting according to my principles; and with regard to the third and last apprehensions of my friends, I could not share in them, not being acquainted with their extent, till some time after I had crossed the Channel.[68]

Later, after Byron's death, Hobhouse published a refutation of many passages in Medwin's work. Ever reactive, he contradicted Medwin's report with the terse denial: "Lord Byron was never hissed as he went to the House of Lords; nor insulted in the streets."[69] This cool rejoinder makes ironic reading set against Byron's statement that his "most intimate friend," that is, Hobhouse, apprehended "vio-

67. *Medwin's Conversations*, p. 48.
68. *Letters and Journals*, ed. Prothero, 4:479.
69. *Westminster Review* 3 (January 1825):25–26.

lence from the people who might be assembled at the door of the carriage." Moreover, even this last statement does not quite give the full measure of Hobhouse's fears in April 1816. In a recently published letter to Scrope Davies, written in Venice on December 7, 1818, saying why he thinks it would be inadvisable to return to England to help Hobhouse in an election campaign, Byron explains to Davies that, when he left, "even Hobhouse thought the tide so strong against me—that he imagined I should be '*assassinated*.'"[70] Byron adds that he himself is not and "never was apprehensive on that point."

Hobhouse's hysteria in 1816 seems to us today so melodramatic as to strain credulity. Yet of all those in Byron's circle, Hobhouse was the most level-headed and sober, to such a degree that his later eventual elevation to the cabinet and the House of Lords seems quite in line with this side of his temperament. But we must recall the intensity of the animosity that the British public, and especially street mobs in the Regency period, showed to men convicted of or even suspected of homosexuality. The newspapers recorded as a matter of course the appearance in the streets of angry crowds who threatened men who had been arrested on homosexual charges and the beating of men whose cases had been dismissed. Repeatedly they note that police escorts of forty or fifty constables were required to conduct these men through the streets, who would otherwise have been in danger for their lives. After his arrest in 1822, the Bishop of Clogher was menaced by such a mob, and at the height of the excitement over the Vere Street case the news of another arrest a few days later was enough to attract, on very short notice, a crowd of 5,000 hostile men and women in central London. As late as 1895 Oscar Wilde was attacked by onlookers on the way to prison. Set against this background, Hobhouse's fears, though overwrought, do not appear wholly ridiculous.

70. *BLJ*, 11:169.

230 Byron and Greek Love

Teresa Guiccioli's account of Byron's "persecution" in her *Recollections* gives fuller details than Medwin and seems also to corroborate his report in the face of Hobhouse's demurrers:

> It was at this time that, going one day to the House, [Byron] was insulted by the populace, and even treated in it like an outlaw. No one spoke to him, nor approached to give any explanation of such a proceeding, except Lord Holland, who was always kind to him, and indeed to every one else. Others— such as the Duke of Sussex, Lord Minto, Lord Lansdowne and Lord Grey—would fain have acted in a like manner; but they suffered themselves to be influenced by his enemies, amongst whom more than one was animated by personal rancour because the young lord had laughed at them and shown up their incapacity.[71]

This ostracism in the Lords must have been a galling humiliation to the always sensitive Byron. It was an ironic coincidence that homosexuality was at this time on the minds of the legislators of both Houses. A bill to abolish the pillory had been introduced the year before: we shall trace its fortunes in a later chapter. The parliamentary debates in the winter of 1816 showed that it would likely pass and that the abolition of this ancient punishment would at last exempt homosexuals from public torment. The proposer of the bill had made clear that he wished the reform to extend even to "that abominable offence, which was so disgraceful to human nature, and to which it had been so often apportioned." Sir Robert Heron, in the debate in the Commons, regretted this change as a step toward moral decadence. Speaking on February 22, 1816, two weeks after Lady Caroline had first begun spreading rumors about Byron, he pled for rigorous ostracism of suspected men should abolition come about:

> The improved and mild morality of the present times had been disadvantageous so far as it was too lenient to crimes, and had

71. *My Recollections of Lord Byron* (London: Richard Bentley, 1869), 1:40n.

too much pity for former acquaintances and connexions. This sometimes paralyzed the arm of the law, and gave facilities for the escape of guilty persons. It sought to retain in society those who had disgraced it. . . . Certain offences [i.e., sodomy] had of late much increased, and, he feared, owing too much to the prevailing mildness and indulgence. . . . If such crimes were effectually checked in upper life, it would have a great effect. The wretch, who stood in little fear of imprisonment, pillory, or death, might perhaps be affected by the terror of perpetual disgrace and scorn.[72]

We must remember that the "mildness" Heron here refers to was embodied in a law code with over two hundred capital offenses, for which, on the average, seventy men and women a year were hanged, including some for sodomy. Heron's speech was reported verbatim the next day in the *Times*. It must have had an intimidating effect on men like Sussex and Grey. Given this moral climate, Byron's chilly reception in the House of Lords was unavoidable.

Not all the comment in the English press was hostile. Byron, as we have seen, had a few spirited defenders, and the *Times* dared to express the hope that his stay abroad would not be permanent.[73] But Byron was to discover how little such a sentiment accorded with the generality of English opinion. The overwhelming majority of English people seem to have agreed with the poet in the *Morning Chronicle* who bade Byron return forthwith to Turkey

72.   February 22, 1816, *Parliamentary Debates* (London: Hansard, 1816), vol. 32, cols. 804–05. However, it is likely that Heron's remarks were provoked not by the Byron scandal, which had just become a matter of rumor, but by the case of another member of Parliament, General Sir Eyre Coote, which had been publicized several months earlier. Coote, an aristocrat with huge estates, had fought in the West Indies, Belgium, and Egypt. He had been made a general in 1805 and served as lieutenant-governor and commander-in-chief in Jamaica. In November 1815, he was taken before the Lord Mayor for indecent conduct with the boys of Christ's Hospital School. After a military hearing he was stripped of his rank of general and degraded from the Order of the Bath. Coote had paid boys at the school to engage in mutual flogging. His friends argued that his actions were the result of mental derangement and tried unavailingly to mitigate his disgrace.

73.   *Times*, April 24, p. 3, col. 2.

and Athens, an exhortation which no doubt concealed a veiled hint, or with another versifier, quoted by Thomas Moore, who wrote on the occasion:

> From native England, that endured too long
> The ceaseless burden of his impious song;
> His mad career of crimes and follies run,
> And gray in vice, when life was scarce begun;
> He goes, in foreign lands prepared to find
> A life more suited to his guilty mind;
> Where other climes new pleasures may supply
> For that pall'd taste, and that unhallow'd eye.[74]

In the nineteenth century homosexuality was commonly regarded as the resource of jaded appetites; we may recall also Byron's reference to Beckford's "unhallowed thirst."

But English homosexuals were not simply ostracized on their native shores. A generation earlier William Beckford had complained to his daughter of the treatment he encountered abroad:

> I have been hunted down and persecuted these many years. I have been stung and not allowed opportunities of changing the snarling, barking style you complain of, had I ever so great an inclination. No truce, no respite have I experienced since the first licenses was taken out . . . for shooting at me. If I am shy or savage you must consider the baitings and worryings to which I allude—how I was treated in Portugal, in Spain, in France, in Switzerland, at home, abroad, in every region.[75]

In a later section of his defense of 1819, Byron gives a markedly similar picture of English implacability:

> I withdrew: but this was not enough. In other countries, in Switzerland, in the shadow of the Alps, and by the blue depth of the lakes, I was pursued, and breathed upon by the same blight. I crossed the mountains but it was the same—[76]

74. *LJL*, 1:654n. These verses seem deliberately to echo Byron's self-satire, "Damaetas."

75. *The Journal of William Beckford in Portugal and Spain, 1787–1788*, ed. Boyd Alexander (New York: John Day, 1955), p. 13. Alexander thinks this letter to his daughter, Lady Craven, was written about 1790.

76. "Reply to *Blackwood's Edinburgh Magazine*," in *Letters and Journals*, ed. Prothero, 4:479.

until he found refuge in a Venice all but devoid of English residents. When Sir Walter Scott, reviewing *Manfred* in 1817, had dared to echo the *Times*'s hope that Byron "might yet return to England," Byron had a chance to assess the reaction of Englishmen abroad. Scott's wish, he reported, "gave great offence at Rome to the respectable ten or twenty thousand English travellers then and there assembled. . . . I was informed, long afterwards, that the greatest indignation had been manifested in the enlightened Anglo-circle of that year." [77]

As fate would have it, Henry Brougham, whom John Murray was later to identify as Byron's "chief persecutor," arrived at Geneva at the same time Byron did. On July 14, Brougham reported to a friend: "Lord Byron lives on the other side of the lake, shunned by all—both English & Genevese except Mad. Stael—who can't resist a little celebrity—of what kind soever & with whatever vice or meanness allied—." [78] Madame de Staël had indeed pointedly refused to join the English in enforcing the *cordon sanitaire* that was supposed to isolate Byron. One is again reminded of Beckford's difficulties on the same terrain. At that time Gibbon had played Brougham's part in enforcing solidarity in the English ranks in Switzerland. But he had not been totally successful. In the 1790s Beckford had made friends with a young Irishman, Buck Whaley, who then received a public rebuke for daring to associate with the outcast. As Whaley told the story, Gibbon publicly declared "that it was astonishing any Englishman would visit a man who lay under such an imputation as Mr. B—— did: that even supposing him innocent still some regard was due to the opinion of the world; and he would venture to say, that I was the only one among my countrymen who had ever paid that man the smallest attention since his banishment." Whaley, however. was not to be frightened: "The only re-

77.   Ibid., p. 481.
78.   To John Allen, July 14, 1816, *Byron on the Continent: A Memorial Exhibition, 1824–1974* (New York: Carl H. Pforzheimer Library, 1974), p. 20.

ply I made to his impertinent animadversion was, that I
did not look upon this little piece of history as any way deserving the attention of so great a man. The Duchess com-
placently smiled: the rest of the company looked grave; my
pedant was dumb, and I took my leave."[79]

But more often, men inclined to break ranks with British
society on such matters could be terrorized back into line.
When Sir Richard Hoare visited Beckford at Fonthill in
1806, a group of neighbors intimated that he too would be
treated as a pariah unless he could provide them with a
satisfactory "explanation" of his conduct, upon which
Hoare replied abjectly that his meeting with Beckford had
been accidental.[80] A decade later, attitudes toward Byron
became another touchstone in British society. After Lady
Jersey's party, Annabella wrote to her mother that "Mrs.
Ellison . . . says that now one has an opportunity of knowing who are bad & good—that there never was a question
which disclosed morals so decisively."[81] What Bentham
had written of "crimes against nature" in his essay "The Influence of Time and Place in Matters of Legislation" thirty
years earlier was still patently true:

> In England, not only the letter of the law makes them capital,
> as in other parts of Europe, but the law is carried into execu-

79.   *Buck Whaley's Memoirs*, ed. Sir Edward Sullivan (London: Alexander Moring, 1906), p. 298.

80.   See Joseph Farington's diary entry for October 16, 1806 (twenty-
two years after the Powderham scandal):

> Sir Richard Hoare of Stourhead applied to Mr. Beckford to see *the Abbey* which
> Mr. B. granted and attended Sir Richard when He came for that purpose. These
> civilities . . . were reported to the neighbouring gentlemen who took such um-
> brage at it, as conceiving that Sir Richard was giving countenance to Mr. Beck-
> ford that a gentleman wrote to Sir Richard in His own name & that of others to
> demand of Him an explanation of that proceeding as they meant to regulate
> *themselves towards Him accordingly.* Sir Richard applied to His friend the Marquiss
> of Bath upon it, & represented that He had no further desire but to see the Ab-
> bey & the meeting with Mr. Beckford was accidental & to Him unexpected.—
> Such is the determination of the Wiltshire gentlemen with respect to excluding
> Mr. B. from all gentlemanly intercourse. (*The Farington Diary*, ed. James Greig,
> vol. 4 [London: Hutchinson, 1924], 33)

81.   *Lord Byron's Wife*, p. 463.

tion with a degree of zeal which no other species of criminality is sufficient to inspire. [Even] the consequence of being reputed guilty [is] attended with a degree of infamy which can be compared to nothing so properly as that which attends forfeiture of caste among the Hindoos.[82]

Once he had left England, Byron's mood was not one of philosophical reflection but of indignant fury. When Hobhouse chided him for the satire on his wife in *Don Juan*, he replied: "Was it not owing to that 'Porca buzzerena' that they tried to expose me upon Earth to the same stigma —which . . . Jacopo is saddled with in hell?"[83] (Jacopo Rusticucci was confined to the circle of the sodomites in Dante's *Inferno*.) Nor was his later bitterness confined to his feelings toward his wife. As English morality had mobilized a whole society against him, so Byron's hatred extended to his nation generally. Shortly afterward he wrote to Murray: "I am sure my Bones would not rest in an English grave—or my Clay mix with the earth of that Country:—I believe the thought would drive me mad on my death-bed could I suppose that any of my friends would be base enough to convey my carcase back to your soil—I would not even feed your worms—if I could help it."[84]

82.   *The Works of Jeremy Bentham*, ed. John Bowring (1838–1843; rpt. New York: Russell & Russell, 1962), 1:175.
83.   Venice, May 17, 1819, *BLJ*, 6:131. "Porca" means sow; "buzzerena" is a Venetian dialect term derived from "buggerone," a "sodomite."
84.   Bologna, June 7, 1819, *BLJ*, 6:149.

· 6 ·

Perspectives: 1816–1821

In the second epoch of his life, after his rise to fame, Byron had taken his place among the literary, social, and political elite of his native land. At the beginning of 1816 he was a husband, a father, a best-selling author, a sought-after member of society, and a voting member of the House of Lords. Five months later, he was separated from his wife, his daughter, his sister, his male friends, Parliament, and his estate, with only his reputation as a poet untouched. Homosexuality, as we have seen, played a fateful part in this change in fortunes. Ironically, it now ceased (so far as we know) to be an important part of his experience until the final months of his life. At this point, then, it may be appropriate to glance back.

The traditional view of Byron, which held sway for more than a century, was that of a fervent womanizer *tout simple*; more recently this has been superseded by the admission that homosexuality played a minor but hardly significant part in his youthful life. The aim of this study has been to show that it meant more than this. It now seems possible to argue, on the basis of the evidence, that Byron's bisexuality was far more central to his experience and personality than his biographers have so far been willing to grant. Whatever feelings he had about his initiation by Lord Grey, the experience revealed to him a side of his being that left him frightened, excited, perplexed, and, on occasion, exalted. At Harrow, at Cambridge, in Greece, and in the four years after he returned to England this knowledge haunted him. His love for his Harrow friends and for John Edlestone, his anticipations of adventures in Greece, his

236

encounters with Eustathios Georgiou and Nicolo Giraud, his grief for "Thyrza," his revelations to Lady Caroline and Augusta, all formed part of a drama that we can now understand. This, in turn, enables us to perceive more fully the background of Byron's unfortunate marriage. More important, we can now comprehend him as a man who felt himself, by his very nature, an anomaly in his own society. For years he knew he would be rejected with contumely in England if he were known for what he was, and at last his fears proved true.

To a degree, Byron shared a number of important characteristics that have inevitably been part of the life experiences of most gay men and women in Christian societies: hidden desires, alienation, paranoia, and a sense of solidarity with others with similar natures. But though he could not reveal the truth directly in his work, he nevertheless wrote the suppressed lines on Beckford and Ali Pasha, penned the "Greek epistles" to Hobhouse, spoke through the mask of the Thyrza lyrics, and made confessions, veiled or direct, to the women in his life, with what consequences we have seen. Later he was to express himself with painful candor in the Lukas poems, written during his final days in Greece but hidden from public view for some six decades after his death. His fears are shown in his conviction that it was impossible for him to live in England, in his anxiety over the fate of his letters to Hobhouse, in his confession to Lady Caroline, and in his suicidal threats during the separation scandal. His devotion appears in the Thyrza and Lukas poems and in his sense of solidarity with other homosexuals—the weakest side of his "gay sensibility"—in his correspondence with Matthews.

If Lord Grey and Ali Pasha were charmed by Byron's boyish beauty, Byron himself was drawn only to adolescents in the classical Greek fashion. Like many pederasts he was first attracted to boys when he was hardly more than a boy himself. The three boys to whom he was most

strongly attached—John Edlestone, Nicolo Giraud, and
Lukas Chalandrutsanos—were all fifteen when he fell in
love with them. The relation of patron and protégé was
one that Byron's aristocratic and paternal instincts made
particularly congenial to him. Where his relations with
women were often strained or stormy, his love for Edlestone
and Giraud seems to have been unclouded. No difficulties
arose with the boys' families. No doubt they were pleased
that their sons or brothers had won the attention of a
wealthy, influential nobleman. How much they guessed of
the sexual part of Byron's attachment we cannot know.
In our day and age we speak of the sexual exploitation of
the young. This may occur, but in such affairs it is often the
emotional vulnerability of the older male that makes him
most open to exploitation, as Byron's later attachment to
Lukas Chalandrutsanos was to demonstrate. The boys
were all in some sense dependents, but they differed markedly in their degree of femininity. Eustathios Georgiou, according to Byron's own account, was strikingly effeminate.
John Edlestone was shy, passive, and affectionate. Nicolo
Giraud, on the other hand, seems to have been capable
and energetic, and Lukas Chalandrutsanos was what we
would today call a "freedom fighter." Youth and good
looks seem to have attracted Byron whether they took on a
boyish or girlish cast.

How did Byron's feelings for boys relate to his feelings
for women? People unfamiliar with bisexuality are often
baffled by the implied contradiction, assuming that ex-
clusivity is the human norm. But Kinsey's survey of 1948
revealed that almost half of the 5,000 men interviewed admitted to some erotic feeling for both sexes. In other times
and cultures the figures might have been higher. Ancient
Greeks and Romans, medieval Arabs, Persians and Japanese, for instance, all took male bisexuality for granted,
chiefly in its pederastic form. Of course not all bisexuality
falls into a single pattern. Some Casanovas much involved
with women occasionally seek passive men, some domi-

nant male partners. Some androgynous men seem drawn
to men or women more on the basis of personality than of
gender. Among pederasts, some marry and have only
fleeting affairs with boys; others enter into serious emotional involvements and assume educational or parental responsibility for their young lovers.

Homosexuals such as Walt Whitman, John Addington
Symonds, and Edward Carpenter, who have celebrated the
"love of comrades" (i.e., who have been attracted to adult
males), have frequently had strong feminist sympathies,
perceiving in male supremacism a form of oppression
directed against both women and gay men. But writers
whose homosexual feelings have taken a pederastic form,
such as Stefan George and Thomas Mann, have generally
favored the ancient Greeks, preferred aristocracy to democracy and hierarchies to egalitarianism.[1] On the sexual
side, Byron's politics were those of this second group.
Byron had an abiding hatred of political tyranny, but, like
many liberals, he was not wholly consistent: he cham-
pioned oppressed schoolboys, exploited workers, and oppressed minorities such as Irish Catholics and the Greeks
under Turkish rule, and on occasion he chivalrously defended individual women, but not women as a class. The
ingrained sense of superiority that led him to admire
Washington but flinch at the idea of living in the United
States (he preferred semifeudal Venezuela when he considered emigrating) and to ridicule Hobhouse's association
with lower-class radicals carried over to his relations with
the other sex. Intellectual women like Mary Shelley were
not welcome at his literary evenings in Pisa, and Madame
de Staël ceased to be the butt of ridicule only when she
bravely led the pro-Byron faction in Switzerland. He went
so far as to prefer ancient and Eastern to modern Western

1.   But not all pederasts have been antifeminists, e.g., the German
anarchist John Henry Mackay (1866–1933) is strongly feminist in his novels and essays.

manners. His Ravenna journal of January 6, 1821, contains
a sardonic paragraph that strikingly reveals his prejudices:

> Thought of the state of women under the ancient Greeks—
> convenient enough. Present state, a remnant of the barbarism
> of the chivalr[ic] and feudal ages—artificial and unnatural.
> They ought to mind home—and be well fed and clothed—but
> not mixed in society. Well educated, too, in religion—but to
> read neither poetry nor politics—nothing but books of piety
> and cookery. Music—drawing—dancing—also a little garden-
> ing and ploughing now and then. I have seen them mending
> the roads in Epirus with good success. Why not, as well as
> hay-making and milking?[2]

The supercilious tone may tempt the modern reader to
dismiss Byron's jottings as playful exuberance. But Scho-
penhauer quoted the paragraph with approbation in his
notorious essay "On Women," the *locus classicus* of nineteenth-century misogyny. Nietzsche in turn adopted Scho-
penhauer's political view in *Beyond Good and Evil*, and the
Nazis neatly condensed this reactionary program into three
words—*Kinder, Kirche, Küche*. Some of Byron's oft-reiterated
admiration for Catholicism undoubtedly had a cynical side
to it; like Nietzsche, he favored female piety as encouraging female submissiveness.

Byron, for his part, felt he had been much abused by
women. He blamed his club foot (bitterly, if unfairly) on
what he thought was his mother's prudery in rejecting
medical attendance at his birth. At nine, he had been seduced by his nurse. When he was sixteen, Mary Chaworth,
whom he adored, dismissed him from consideration for
his lameness. The first women with whom he had extensive experience were prostitutes whom he paid for sex,
often poor women among whom venality was likely to run
high. His first serious affair was with the eccentric and histrionic Lady Caroline Lamb. We can see why Byron regarded himself as a victim. Yet his antifeminism, like many

2. *BLJ*, 8:15.

prejudices, would probably have existed independently of his unfortunate experiences. It was partly a fashionable posture among cynical radicals of his age, partly an expression of the domineering side of his temperament.[3]

But the political stances of men and women rarely throw light on their personal relationships, especially in matters of sex. There sentiment and desire usually prevail over politics. Byron's movement back and forth between the heterosexual and homosexual poles of his being was sometimes reactive—as when he turned to John Edlestone after his rejection by Mary Chaworth—and sometimes the inexplicable result of mood and fancy—as when he thought the boys at the convent promised "better entertainment" than the Macri sisters. But even when he was most intent on seeking homosexual adventures, he could be deflected, as by Constance Spencer Smith at Malta. The attraction of women was strong even when his interest in boys was paramount.

After Byron left England in 1816, this passion for women seems to have predominated for the next seven years. We hear almost nothing of same-sex liaisons. But he was far from chaste. John Polidori, the young Italian doctor who accompanied him, reported that Byron, on arriving in Belgium, fell upon the chambermaid "like a thunderbolt," as if he were throwing off the constraints of marriage and

3. An adequate treatment of Byron's views on women would require a book or at least a long article. I do not pretend to speak definitively here—only to give a suggestive sketch of the topic in relation to his bisexuality. Critics looking for pro-feminist passages in Byron's writings most often cite Julia's letter in *Don Juan*, Canto I, stanzas 192–97. This letter dramatizes the double standard that shut "fallen" women up in convents but allowed their lovers to travel and enjoy themselves. But I doubt if protest or reform was Byron's purpose, poignantly as he renders Julia's plight. The letter can be read simply as a literary exercise in the tradition of Pope's "Eloisa to Abelard" or Ovid's *Heroides*. Rakes like Ovid could enjoy seducing women and at the same time find pleasure in the aesthetic contemplation of their agonies when they lost their lovers or felt betrayed, situations that underlined their pathetic helplessness. I don't think any feminist sympathy is necessarily implied in such dramatizations.

England. This sexual urgency dominated the first year of his stay in Venice. Byron was to write to John Murray that he had been sexually active there with more than two hundred women of all classes, aristocratic and bourgeois, courtable and purchasable. Yet rumors of his bisexuality persisted in England. On January 20, 1817, two months after his arrival on the shores of the Adriatic, his sister communicated to his wife the startling theory that his affair with Marianna Segati, begun then, was a cover for a homosexual relation. Augusta's speculations have recently been published by Malcolm Elwin:

> It is ye 2nd letter which *suggests* to me to communicate *to you*, I think, *for reasons*—he thinks *me* still in ye dark, but suspects you may not be & wishes to blind you. In short it appears evident that he wishes *such* a communication [i.e., about the Segati affair] to be spread by the whole tenor of both letters. The other day, mon Mari [my husband] told me that he had heard from a person just returned from L[ondon] that there were ye *most horrible reports*. I asked of course *what*, upon which he mention'd the "subject erased," *but* added, qu'on disoit maintenant qu'il y avait *deux* choses [that they now say there were two affairs]—that & the "cover" you allude to. My ignorance is great on such subjects mais je croyais toujours que l'une etoit incompatible avec l'autre [but I believed always that the one was incompatible with the other]. However, it coincided with what I had heard from Mrs. V[illiers] a few days before—of a letter from *M-l-n* mentioning the *atrocious* manner of proceeding *there* being such as to shock even dans ce pays la [in that country]—that the Establishment consisted of two Men & 2 Women.[4]

Unknown to Byron, Augusta regularly sent his letters to his wife for her perusal. Her "reasons" for communicating this rumor—which she more than half-believed—were specific, if unrealistic. Augusta believed the Segati affair would prejudice Lady Byron against any future reconcil-

---

4. Malcolm Elwin, *Lord Byron's Family: Annabella, Ada, and Augusta, 1816–1824*, ed. Peter Thomson (London: John Murray, 1975), p. 130.

iation. By retailing the more lurid version, she was trying to revive the theory that Byron was indeed insane, a
view Augusta clung to long after everyone else had abandoned it:

> My dearest A, do you think it POSSIBLE such a person can be
> free from INSANITY! On the one hand one hears that it is the
> *only* point on which he is afraid—"qui le fait trembler jusqu'au
> au fond de l'ame" ["that makes him tremble to the depths of
> his soul"]. On the other, that it is displayed in this public &
> shameless way, not only *now*, but in a minor degree it must
> have been *before*. Such inconsistency surely can only be at-
> tributed to such a cause.[5]

Perhaps Augusta found balm in ascribing her brother's
bisexuality to mental derangement. There is no other evidence of any homosexual intrigue at this time. The story
seems to be only one of the exaggerated and inaccurate
rumors circulating about Byron, on a par with another to
the effect that Augusta had herself accompanied her
brother to Switzerland disguised as a page.

Byron's own correspondence is now silent on the subject of homosexual involvements. This in itself does not
necessarily mean that there were none. Hobhouse had no
doubt lectured him into epistolary discretion, and he
himself had probably become warier about disclosures as a
result of the separation imbroglio. But one account ema-
nating from Venice deserves some consideration, especially as it comes from an eyewitness. Shelley had met
Byron in Switzerland a year before and formed a warm,
though sometimes troubled, friendship. But on December
22, 1818, he wrote to Thomas Love Peacock, expressing his
dismay at Byron's Italian companions:

> L[ord] B[yron] is familiar with the lowest sort of . . . women
> the people his gondolieri pick up in the streets. . . . He associ-

5. Ibid.

ates with wretches who seem almost to have lost the gait &
physiognomy of man, & who do not scruple to avow practices
which are not only not named but I believe seldom ever
conceived in England. He says he dissapproves [sic], but he
endures.[6]

This letter has caused much speculation. The second sentence appears at first to refer back to the "women," but the
reference to "wretches who seem almost to have lost the
gait & physiognomy of man" suggests a circle of effeminate
males whose mannerisms and make-up mimicked women.
It has usually been taken to refer to a homosexual coterie.
Were these men or transvestite street boys? Did Byron simply find them amusing company, or was he sexually involved? Unfortunately, we have no clues that will allow us
to set Shelley's remarks in an intelligible context.

But though Byron does not tell us anything of a personal nature in his extant letters, he now felt free, for the
first time, to make explicit references to homosexuality in
his satiric poetry. Two years earlier, Coleridge, in the *Biographia Literaria*, had deplored the existence of Greek and
Latin poems on homoerotic themes. "Blest indeed is that
state of society," he wrote sanctimoniously, "in which no
charm of diction or imagery could exempt the Bathyllus
even of an Anacreon, or the Alexis of Virgil, from disgust
and aversion!"[7] A few days after his reunion with Shelley,
Byron began the first canto of *Don Juan*, and in his catalogue
of classical erotic poets, he deliberately mocked Coleridge's
British prudery:

> Ovid's a rake, as half his verses show him,
>   Anacreon's morals are a still worse sample,
> Catullus scarcely has a decent poem,
>   I don't think Sappho's Ode a good example,

6. December 17 or 18, 1818, *The Letters of Percy Bysshe Shelley*, ed.
Frederick L. Jones (Oxford: Clarendon Press, 1964), 2:58.
7. Ed. J. Shawcross (Oxford: Oxford University Press, 1954), chap.
14, 2:9.

Although Longinus tells us there is no hymn
  Where the sublime soars forth on wings more ample;
But Virgil's songs are pure, except that horrid one
Beginning with "*Formosum pastor Corydon.*"[8]

Clearly Byron is here in full reaction against contemporary English literary and social standards. By reiterating Longinus's praise of Sappho's Ode in his essay "On the Sublime," Byron implies that same-sex love might itself aspire to nobility, a position strikingly at odds with the sour treatment of marriage elsewhere in the canto. Obviously, we are invited to take a different view from Coleridge's of the eclogue in which Corydon expresses his love for Alexis. Byron's deliberately provocative approach, of course, was more likely to exacerbate than mollify English prejudice. But it is the closest he comes anywhere in his writings to a public defense of homosexual love.

Though Byron tells us nothing in his Italian letters about his own association with homosexuals, he does comment on the way Italian society viewed such men. Like Hester Thrale half a century earlier, he is fascinated by the contrast between English and Italian mores. Writing to Hobhouse from Ravenna about Tommaso Sgricci, the famous *improvvisatore*, he adopted a mockingly ironic tone quite different from the conventional indignation of English tourists:

> Sgricci is here improvising away with great success—he is also a celebrated Sodomite, a character by no means so much respected in Italy as it should be; but they laugh instead of burning—and the Women talk of it as a pity in a man of talent—but with greater tolerance than could be expected—and only express their hopes that he may yet be converted to Adultery.— He is not known to have b——d anybody here as yet but has paid his addresses "fato la corte" to two or three.[9]

8. *Byron's "Don Juan": A Variorum Edition*, ed. Truman Guy Steffan and Willis W. Pratt, 2nd ed. (Austin: University of Texas Press, 1971), 2:45.
9. Ravenna, March 3, 1820, *BLJ*, 7:51–52.

Sgricci was remarkable for extemporizing entire tragedies before theater audiences on such subjects as Charles I, Samson, and Idomeneo. He had a notable contemporary success, both literary and histrionic, in Rome, Milan, London, and Paris. Byron greatly admired his ability. But in referring to his reputation as a sodomite, Byron characteristically falls once more into the supercilious man-of-the-world tone he adopted in gossiping on such matters with Hobhouse.

The more relaxed atmosphere of Italy made it possible for Byron to look back on his own experiences philosophically. He now set to work on his memoirs, giving installments to Moore in October 1819 and November 1820. It is unlikely that he hinted in these at his bisexual interests: we shall discuss this question later. But, stimulated by this reminiscing, he wrote further comments on his early life in a journal begun at Ravenna in January. There appear his recollections of his friendship with Edward Noel Long and his "violent, though *pure* love" for John Edlestone. Unfortunately, we know this journal only through Moore's transcriptions, which break off at this point in a line of asterisks. We are luckier with respect to the jottings Byron began in October shortly before leaving Ravenna and then continued at Pisa under the heading "Detached Thoughts." This manuscript, which did not pass into Moore's expurgating hands, is the only important biographical fragment to reach us intact and uncensored. As such it is of major significance.

With number 72 of the "Detached Thoughts" there begins a series of notes of extreme interest with respect to Byron's self-analysis, from which we have already quoted but which will bear quoting again, this time in full:

72

When I first went up to College—it was a new and heavy hearted scene for me. Firstly—I so much disliked leaving Harrow that though it was time—(I being seventeen) it broke my very rest for the last quarter—with counting the days that remained.—I always *hated* Harrow till the last year and a half—but then I liked it.—2dly. I wished to go to Oxford and not to Cambridge.—3dly. I was so completely alone in this new world that it half broke my Spirits.—My companions were not unsocial but the contrary—lively—hospitable—of rank—& fortune—& gay far beyond my gaiety—I mingled with—and dined—& supped &c. with them—but I know not how—it was one of the deadliest and heaviest feelings of my life to feel that I was no longer a boy.—From that moment I began to grow old in my own esteem—and in my esteem age is not estimable.—I took my gradations in the vices—with great promptitude—but they were not to my taste—for my early passions though violent in the extreme—were concentrated—and hated division or spreading abroad.—I could have left or lost the world with or for that which I loved—but though my temperament was naturally burning I could not share in the common place libertinism of the place and time—without disgust.—And yet this very disgust and my heart thrown back upon itself—threw me into excesses perhaps more fatal than those from which I shrunk—as fixing upon one (at a time) the passions which if spread amongst many would have hurt only myself.[10]

Byron had sampled the women who entertained undergraduates at Cambridge and found these relations too sordid to attract him. His statement that he could have renounced the world for "that which I loved" reveals, through its telltale neuter pronoun, that he had another boy in mind. There seems to be some hint of blame in the last comment. Who was hurt? Perhaps he felt his affectionate tie with John Edlestone had encouraged the boy in a homosexual direction and led to his later difficulties.

In the next note (73) Byron alludes to the "Melancholy which runs through my writings" and the general wonderment it had aroused. Then he goes on:

74

If I could explain at length the *real* causes which have contributed to this perhaps *natural* temperament of mine—this Melancholy which hath made me a bye-word—nobody would

10. *BLJ*, 9:37–38.

wonder—but this is impossible without doing much mischief.—I do not know what other men's lives have been—but I
cannot conceive of anything more strange than some of the
earlier parts of mine—I have written my memoirs—but omitted *all* the really *consequential & important* parts—from defer-
ence to the dead—to the living—and to those who must be
both. . . .

76
I must not go on with these reflections—or I shall be letting
out some secret or other—to paralyze posterity.[11]

What is most interesting here is Byron's hint that his bisexuality, along with a hereditary predisposition, was the
chief cause of the notorious "Byronic" temperament that so
struck his contemporaries. Some readers, of course, have
discounted Byron's gloomy heroes as merely a fashionable
literary pose, pointing out how common the type was in
fiction *before* Byron gave it his name. But despite the wit
and high spirits of his letters, conversation, and later satirical poetry, Byron's self-communings reveal, I think, that
the gloomy Byron was as real as the sparkling one. If Byron drew on such literary stereotypes as the protagonist of
John Moore's novel *Zeluco* and other *esprits maudits* from
Gothic fiction, he did so because he found in them a significant part of himself. Some sexually active men have
found their erotic vitality a source of joy to themselves and
others. But behind his debonair worldly mask, Byron carried a heavy burden of guilt. There is evidence that he felt
guilty about his harlotry after leaving Cambridge, about
his incest with his sister, and about his subsequent marriage to a "pure" woman of whom he was unworthy. But of
all his occasions of guilt, his homosexual inclinations must
have tortured him most. Given the attitudes of his day, it is
not surprising that he singles out his bisexuality as a significant element in the "Byronic" personality.

In these notes, Byron's sense of detachment from his

11.   Ibid., p. 38.

early life is striking. He seems almost to look at his former self as another person. Yet though he speaks of his school-boy feelings as remote and strange, he was to experience an amazing resurgence of one particular male attachment very shortly after writing these lines. In note 91 he returned to the subject with a new confession:

> My School friendships were to *me passions* (for I was always violent) but I do not know there is one which has endured (to be sure some have been cut short by death) till now—that with Lord Clare began one of the earliest and lasted longest—being only interrupted by distance—that I know of. I never hear the word *"Clare"* without a beating of the heart—even *now*, & I write it with the feelings of 1803–4–5—ad infinitum.[12]

A week or so later, Byron left Ravenna for Pisa where he arrived on November 1. On the road from Bologna to Imola a strange coincidence befell him: he met Clare for the first time in seven or eight years. He recorded the experience in the first note (113) added to his "Thoughts" in the new city:

> This meeting annihilated for a moment all the years between the present time and the days of *Harrow*—It was a new and inexplicable feeling like rising from the grave to me.—Clare too was much agitated—more—in *appearance*—than even my-self—for I could feel his heart beat to the fingers' ends—un-less indeed—it was the pulse of my own which made me think so. . . . We were but five minutes together—and in the public road—but I hardly recollect an hour of my existence which could be weighed against them. . . . Of all I have ever known —he has always been the least altered in every thing from the excellent qualities and kind affections which attracted me to him so strongly at School.—I should hardly have thought it possible for Society—(or the World as it is called) to leave a being with so little of the leaven of bad passions.—I do not speak from personal experience only—but from all I have heard of him from others during absence and distance.[13]

Later Byron told Thomas Moore that Clare visited him briefly at Leghorn in June: "As I have always loved him

---

12. Ibid., p. 44. Byron had, in fact, met Clare in 1801.
13. Ibid., pp. 49–50.

(since I was thirteen, at Harrow) better than any (*male*) thing in the world, I need hardly say what a melancholy pleasure it was to see him for a *day* only." [14] For Byron, boyhood was the age of kindness and affection, unspoiled by selfish interests. The reunion with Clare reawakened this idealism, so at odds with the cynicism of his mature existence. His feeling for the younger peer seems to have been the kind of "romantic friendship" he had earlier mentioned as characterizing his relation with Edward Noel Long, distinct from the love he felt for other young males, like John Edlestone. What startled Byron—and surprises the reader —is the intensity of the emotion he felt himself gripped by, which seems to have existed separately from any homoerotic impulse. Indeed, such impulses now seem to have lain dormant until three years later when he made his second journey to Greece.

14. Montenero, June 8, 1822, *BLJ*, 9:170.

· 7 ·

"Not Paul but Jesus"

In England, the defeat of Napoleon marked the end of a period of extreme reaction in politics and prepared the way for a new era of reform. One of the earliest of these reforms was of significance to homosexuals: the abolition of the pillory. On April 6, 1815, two months before the battle of Waterloo, Michael Angelo Taylor had introduced a bill into the Commons to this effect. Decrying the pillory as "the remnant of a barbarous age and the cruel punishment of Star Chamber authority," Taylor pointed out that it was unpredictable in its consequences: some men condemned to exposure might be applauded and acclaimed by the mob, men accused of less popular crimes might be killed.[1] Taylor deliberately omitted any mention of its common use in homosexual cases on first introducing the measure. But the Earl of Lauderdale, who led the effort for abolition in the Lords three months later, grasped the nettle firmly. After telling of occasions that led to chastisements more lenient than the law intended, he continued:

> In other cases it was more severe; for instance, when the punishment of the pillory was inflicted for offences which had a tendency to exasperate the feelings of the populace, such as the attempting to commit an unnatural and horrible crime. Neither the law nor the judge intended that this crime, abominable as it was, should be punished with death, and yet such was frequently the result. The death, too, which such criminals met with was more severe than the punishment of death when inflicted in the ordinary way. He himself had witnessed

1. *Parliamentary Debates* (London: Hansard, 1815), vol. 30, cols. 354–56.

an instance of this in 1780. A person was pilloried in South-
wark for an unnatural crime, and the criminal was so treated
by the mob that he actually died the moment he was taken
from the machine.[2]

The measure was held back by delaying tactics in the Lords.
When Taylor reintroduced it in the lower house a year later
(February 22, 1816), he candidly admitted that it would end
a punishment often used for homosexuals. His argument
was the familiar one that such exhibitions tended rather
"to increase the vice it was meant to suppress."[3] Taylor's
speech provoked the impassioned plea by Sir Robert Heron
that ostracism now be even more strictly enforced among
the upper classes, to which Taylor made the curious response that "he was sure he could satisfy the hon. baronet
in private, that there was but little hope of reform to be expected from persons addicted to this atrocious offence, under any circumstances of punishment, however severe."[4]

The end of the war and the more promising climate for
change had another effect. It prompted Jeremy Bentham,
after thirty years, to turn once more to the topic of homosexual law reform. On April 18, 1814, just six days after
Napoleon's first abdication, and again on July 27, 1816,
three months to the day following Byron's departure from
England, Bentham resumed writing on the subject, on the
first occasion for a period of three weeks, on the second,
for six. At this time he was a tenant at Ford Abbey in Devonshire, where for most of the year his devoted disciple
James Mill joined him to work on his own *History of India*,
taking with him his numerous brood, including the precocious John Stuart. All in all, during these two sessions of
writing Bentham turned out almost two hundred folio
pages of new notes, which he, or some secretary acting for
him, collated by intermingling into one manuscript.

2. July 5, 1815, ibid., vol. 31, col. 1123.
3. Ibid., vol. 32, col. 804.
4. Ibid., col. 805.

The prospects for reform in other areas of the criminal law were slowly brightening and would become markedly auspicious during the last years of the Regency. But the chance for a change in England's sodomy statute did not look good in 1814. Since 1785, when Bentham had written his ambitious essay, the situation of homosexuals in England had, if anything, worsened. The rate of hangings had actually increased, the pillory had been much in use, and public opinion seemed as obdurately hostile as ever. Worst of all, the taboo against any mention of homosexuality, except in the form of stereotyped expressions of horror following arrests or convictions, still held. Only when the subject "is dragged into notice by the hand of the law," as Bentham put it, could it be mentioned at all. Otherwise, Bentham wrote: "Decency, according to the prevailing notions generally attached to this word, will in general keep it excluded out of the field of conversation."[5] Bentham then gives an interesting survey of national opinion. Prejudice in England, he conjectures, surpasses anything on the Continent. "In Scotland the degree of general exasperation may be stated as standing at much the same pitch as in England. In Ireland as rising if possible still higher and so in the Anglo-American states."[6] If disapprobation reached its zenith in English-speaking lands, "Italy may be stated as the country in which the degree of exasperation produced, if any, stands at the opposite point of the scale. In Italy, or some parts at least of that country, for a demand of this nature a supply may, or at least not long ago might, be obtained from the one sex with little less facility than from

5. "Code Penal," July 1816, box 74a, folio 71.
6. July 28, 1816, box 74a, folio 73. I do not know of any evidence on which to compare Irish attitudes with English. Louis Simond had noted the Scottish judges' disapproval of English pilloryings (*Journal of a Tour and Residence in Great Britain During the Years 1810 and 1811*, 2nd ed. [Edinburgh: Constable, 1817], 1:494). Despite Bentham's remark, no execution in America later than 1780 has as yet come to light; English homophobia seems at all times to have exceeded the American level, high though that has been.

the other."[7] (Bentham had stopped in Italy in 1785 on the way to visit his brother in Russia and may have observed the relative openness of homosexual prostitution and solicitation there at that time.) In France, public feeling was indifferent, and the laws had long gone unenforced. As for Germany and Holland, Bentham, perhaps somewhat naïvely, ascribes their relative lack of prejudice to the frequency with which they had had homosexual rulers. The tastes of Frederick the Great of Prussia and of "a Landgrave of Hesse and other sovereigns" he thinks account for the relatively tolerant attitude toward homosexuality in Germany, while in Holland, "the example however studiously concealed of the King which that country gave to England [William III], added to the recent example of a not very long since departed Prince"—presumably Stadtholder William V, who had died in 1806—had, he thought, produced similar lenience.[8]

Bentham pointed out that English feeling against sexual nonconformity was far more intense than against nonconformity in religion. Though English law excluded non-Anglicans from public office, no one still believed heretics should be put to death or hoped to gain public applause by expressing such a view. With respect to same-sex relations, the matter was different: "Of those in whose eyes, to judge at any rate from their discourse, the utter destruction of a person of the sort in question would be considered as a public good, every idea entertained of mercy a public injury, the number it is believed would upon enquiry be found not inconsiderable."[9] Englishmen had traditionally deplored the intolerance that had lit the fires of the Inquisition but felt no such compunction when they sent men to the gallows for relations with their own sex:

7. July 28, 1816, box 74a, folio 73.
8. Ibid. I have not been able to identify the Landgrave of Hesse to whom Bentham refers here.
9. August 1816, box 74a, folio 186.

The Spanish *auto da fe* in which, under the name of heretics, for a suppo[sed] differing on the subject of religion from the opinion generally professed, men used to be burnt alive, is to every Englishman an object of abhorrence, and though such not many centuries ago was the law in his own country, under laws for such a crime it could never enter into any human heart to exercise any such cruelty. Yet on a subject of infinitely less importance, for a difference not in opinion but merely in taste, with no other difference than that between burning and hanging, will the same man, with indefensible satisfaction behold the same punishment inflicted on his fellow man and fellow countryman in every other respect void of offense. For heresy in religion, no; but for heresy in taste nothing can be more reasonable.[10]

Bentham then tells the anecdote of the exultant judge who so shocked him.

In the face of this intensity of feeling, social reformers might well shrink from voicing opinions at odds with the majority. Bentham still felt the trepidation he had experienced a generation earlier at the thought of speaking out. In July 1816, on taking up his pen again for his second spate of writing, he once more expressed his fears:

In the present has been found one of those unhappy occasions—in which, in his endeavours to render service to his fellow creatures, a man must expose himself to their reproach; and assuredly, of all the occasions which it is possible for reflection or imagination to embrace, not one can be found, in which, whether it be considered in respect of intensity or of extent, the displeasure to which it is necessary he should expose himself is equally great and appalling. . . . Never . . . did work appear . . . from which at the hand of public opinion a man found so much to fear, so little to hope.[11]

Under the circumstances it is perhaps not surprising that Bentham did not dare to make his views public. What is remarkable, however, is the mental energy he brought to the subject and the time he devoted to developing his

10. August 1816, box 74a, folio 187.
11. Box 74a, folio 38.

ideas—within the next five years he was to fill almost five hundred pages with opinions and arguments. More striking still is the way in which his thinking moved ahead from his essay of 1785. While his countrymen became, if anything, more conservative, Bentham's position became more and more radical. Where he had been content to support reform in 1785 with the argument that male homosexuality was no real threat to society, by 1816 he was arguing that homosexuality had positively beneficial effects. He had in one bound overleaped the position of such cautious reformers as the late nineteenth century produced (men like John Addington Symonds, Havelock Ellis, and Edward Carpenter) and anticipated the "Gay is good" stand of liberationists in the 1970s. Using arguments that were strictly in accordance with the utilitarian "greatest happiness" principle, Bentham found himself more than a century and a half in advance of his age.

He was also moved to embark, as we have seen, on a new and more extensive analysis of the roots of homophobia. In hope or fear, he argued, men attempted to propitiate God, not only through the sacrifice of material goods, but by giving up pleasures and especially the most exquisite of pleasures—those of the sexual appetite. So asceticism became an inescapable adjunct of religion. To understand the willingness with which men have made the homosexual a scapegoat, we have only to add antipathy to this cult of sacrifice connected with sexuality. This antipathy begins as antipathy for the physical act (presumably, anal intercourse) and develops into moral antipathy for the agent. "Of this morality a congenial sort of logic is the fruit: this man does what I should not like to do; therefore he deserves hatred and punishment at my hands. The more vehemently I should dislike to do what he does, the greater the punishment he deserves."[12] The cult of self-sacrifice joins with hatred to produce a new kind of propitiation:

12.   August 3, 1816, box 74a, folio 80.

This is a species of sacrifice in the making of which an incom-
parably better bargain is made with the Almighty than by any
other: in the ordinary case, the pleasure sacrificed is a man's
own pleasure: in this case it is another man's pleasure. Giving
meat of one's own to be roasted for a dinner to God and Priest
would cost money: taking a man and roasting him costs
nothing: and moreover it makes a spectacle. On these considerations about the middle of the last century a French Abbé,
the Abbé Des Fontaines, was roasted alive at Paris.[13]

Such asceticism necessarily implied either a vindictive
deity to be appeased or a capricious one to be bribed. To
Bentham the hedonist, a man (or God) who desired another man's pain—or what was the same thing in the
hedonistic calculus, deprived him arbitrarily of pleasure—
is "in so far a malevolent being."[14] Aware that traditional
religionists have always proclaimed the loving kindness of
their deity, Bentham expects them to balk at this epithet:

But in language there is not any imaginable inconsistency of
which fear is not wont to be productive. Upon earth, the most
cruel and unrelenting of tyrants have been, as it is altogether
natural they should be, those on whom the verbal expressions
of love have been with most profusion lavished. In whatsoever
situation he be placed, in the language employed to or in the
hearing of the possessor of power regarded as absolute, the
same cause will of course be productive of the same effect:
the more intensely his malevolence is feared, the more loudly
his benevolence will be proclaimed.[15]

But if religious persons think it is pleasing to God to
abstain from certain pleasures, an inevitable difficulty presents itself. Sexual pleasure cannot be entirely foregone
without endangering the existence of the race. Yet if mar-

13. Ibid. Bentham has apparently confused two episodes here. On
May 25, 1726, Benjamin Deschauffours was burned alive in the Place de
Grève for acts of sodomy; see D. A. Coward, "Attitudes to Homosexuality
in Eighteenth-century France," *Journal of European Studies* 10 (1980):237.
The Abbé Desfontaines had been threatened with the same fate in 1725
but was saved by the intercession of Voltaire.
14. April 22, 1814, box 74a, folio 107.
15. Ibid.

ital sex is grudgingly permitted for the sake of progeny, no such tolerance extends to any nonprocreative act. "This impure and inexcusable pleasure remains a just object of the unbridled and insatiable vengeance of a being in whose composition an infinity of power has for its accompaniment a [supposed] infinity of benevolence."[16] Presumably Bentham has in mind the conclusions derived by the fathers of the church and jurists like Blackstone from the Sodom story. But why should religious fanatics not simply deplore such acts and abstain from them? Why should they persecute the agents in such lively fashion to the point of desiring their deaths? Only if the homosexual is conceived as the special enemy of God does such persecution become intelligible:

> For recommending one's self to any person's favor, no method more effectual can be found than the determination to take and consequent habit of taking for one's enemies all the person's enemies. When the person whose enemies are to be dealt with as our own is no more than a human being such as ourselves, charity may interpose, and to the disposition by which we are led thus to deal with them, apply a sort of bridle: but when the person is the Almighty himself, no such bridle is necessary or so much as proper or admissible. He being infinite, such ought to be our love, such consequently our hatred for his enemies, such consequently the determination and efficiency in the acts in and by which that hatred is avowed, manifested, gratified and demonstrated.[17]

Bentham's account of the way in which piety worked up homophobia to a fever pitch may sound speculative and exaggerated. There is, however, historical evidence to support his view. In the Middle Ages, a tradition, ascribed to St. Jerome, held that all homosexuals had been struck dead at the moment of Christ's birth. Thirteenth-century English treatises on jurisprudence, such as *Fleta*, held that homosexuality was a kind of lese majesty, or high treason,

16.   April 22, 1814, box 74a, folio 109.
17.   April 22, 1814, box 74a, folio 110.

against God. Thomas Aquinas formalized this position in moral theology when he held that sins "against nature" were a direct affront to God himself as the creator of nature and hence worse than such acts as rape and adultery, which immediately affected only other human beings.[18]

In the course of human history, Bentham observes, contrariety of tastes and opinions has frequently led to animosity. If men inspired by ill-will have refrained from vengeance, it has not been for lack of appetite but because the law has restrained them. But sometimes religion itself has given a sanction to such animosities. Among the ancient Greeks, for instance, homosexual acts were not in general punishable.

> It was among the Jews and in the days of Moses that religion, as it should seem, for the first time attached itself to this ground and took it for the theater of its rigours. In the breast of Moses the sentiment of antipathy found an object and an exciting cause in every sort of irregularity belonging to this class. Religion was at his command. Religion in [proscribing] every caprice to which the frolick brain had ever given birth found a ready instrument and that an irresistible one. In English the word impurity, in most other languages some other word or words that correspond to it, has been applied alike to objects offensive to sense and offensive to imagination. In the hand of tyranny, at the nod of caprice, physical impurities were converted into moral ones. Under Moses, as under Bramah, the list of impurities thus created sometimes out of physical impurities, sometimes out of nothing, was a labyrinth without an end.[19]

Bentham was struck, however, by the fact that the founder of Christianity, living as he did in a milieu in which the Jewish code clashed so dramatically with the dominant and all-encompassing Greco-Roman culture, should have shown no symptom of this tribal phobia:

> On this whole field in which Moses legislates with such diversified minuteness and such impassioned asperity, Jesus is alto-

18. *Summa Theologica*, Pt. II–II, Qu. 154, Art. 12.
19. April 20, 1814, box 74a, folio 103.

260 Byron and Greek Love

gether silent,—Jesus from whose lips not a syllable favourable
to ascetic self-denial is by any of his biographers presented as
having ever issued, Jesus who among his disciples had one
to whom he imparted his authority, and another on whose
bosom his head reclined and for whom he avowed his love,—
Jesus, who in the stripling clad in loose attire found a still
faithful adherent after the rest of them had fled,—Jesus, in
whom the woman taken in adultery found a successful advocate, Jesus has on the whole field of sexual irregularity preserved an uninterrupted silence.[20]

But the religion of Paul was another matter. Paul found it
difficult to tolerate even that sexuality "necessary to the existence of the species"; toward the "irregular form" he was
"an implacably condemning Judge."[21] Given these views, it
is not surprising that Bentham should have contemplated
writing a book to be called "Not Paul but Jesus," contrasting the two men's views on asceticism and sex. But he does
not pursue the idea any further in 1814.

Though they were soon to change under the influence
of evangelical reformism, English manners during the Regency were probably the most libertine since the Restoration. The aristocracy still held to the code of the *ancien régime*, which set no premium on marital fidelity. The Regent
himself and his brother dukes balked at domesticity and
kept mistresses, who were many and expensive. Lord
Nelson had lived with Lady Hamilton; the victor of Waterloo and future Tory prime minister found a large number
of fashionable boudoirs open to him. Many leading host-
esses had figured in divorce scandals, reared broods of
miscellaneous paternity, or floated upward from shady origins. At the other end of the social scale prostitution was
extremely widespread and blatant in London. Well might
William Blake declare:

The Harlots cry from Street to Street
Shall weave Old Englands winding Sheet.[22]

20. April 20, 1814, box 74a, folio 104.
21. Ibid.
22. *Complete Poetry and Prose of William Blake*, ed. David V. Erdman,
rev. ed. (Berkeley: University of California Press, 1982), p. 492.

Brutally deprived and victimized themselves, they were not above shouting "sodomite" at an indifferent male or joining in a pillorying.

It was perhaps not paradoxical that this age was also the most homophobic in English history. By seizing on the homosexual issue, the press could, at least in one respect, maintain the cherished national image of a land better than too-tolerant France or decadent Italy. Only one fear must have haunted editors: the concern that someone of their own party would figure in the next sensational scandal. Being the party of prestige and power, the Tories were also the most vulnerable, and, indeed, within little more than a decade they were to be exquisitely embarrassed by scandals, real or imputed, involving a royal duke, a member of the House of Bishops, a lieutenant-governor of Jamaica who was also a Knight Commander of the Bath and a general in the army, and a foreign minister who ranked as one of the architects of the post-Napoleonic world. In the meantime, the age in which cruel sports were for the first time coming to be regarded as disreputable on humanitarian grounds still exposed homosexuals to public wrath. Bentham saw in this practice an example of what sociologists today call scapegoating—and a licence for public brutality. Something more than indignation, a kind of bitter rage seems to have gripped him in commenting on this:

> Among them [i.e., the most ardent denouncers of homosexuality] will naturally be found in an indefinite degree of abundance the most vitious and profligate of mankind: the more incapable of paying for the praise of virtue in the form of self-denial the fair price, the more eager a man will naturally be to obtain it *gratis* in so far as it is to be had upon such terms. Purchasing it at the fair price he would have to keep in a state of subjection every inordinate appetite, every self-regarding and every dissocial affection: obtaining it at no higher price than that of adding his contribution to the torrent of unprovoked invective, he will not have to impose any restraint upon any self-regarding or any dissocial affection. On the contrary to his dissocial appetite he will without the least personal inconvenience afford a feast of gratification not to be derived from any other source. He will obtain for himself the same sort of enjoy-

ment that an ill-taught boy gives himself by tail-piping a dog,
or an ill-taught man by bull-baiting, or an English judge by
condemning a man to the pillory for an offense which affords a
hope of his having a jaw broken or an eye beat out by the surrounding populace.[23]

The style of Bentham's Regency notes contrasts strikingly with what he had written thirty or forty years earlier.
Then he echoed the phraseology of popular rhetoric. Now
he shows a keen awareness of how such terminology
prejudiced moral judgments. Discussing the way descrip-
tive words like *pure* and *impure* had come to take on ethical
meaning, Bentham warns: "It is by the power of names, of
signs originally arbitrary and insignificant, that the course
of imagination has in great measure been guided."[24] In a
disquisition on the use of the word *unnatural* in legal discourse, he admits that

> an epithet which promises to cast on the adversary to whom it
> is applied a torrent of public odium and to produce in all
> breasts that are not already on his side a disposition to join in
> whatever measures may be taken for causing him to suffer for
> everything by which his adverseness has been indicated, is a
> weapon so commodious that it is only by such a regard for jus-
> tice as has seldom indeed, if ever, been exemplified, that a
> man can be restrained from taking it up and using it.[25]

With a growing awareness of the adage "give a dog an ill
name and hang him," Bentham now meticulously avoids
such locutions. He emphatically rejects the use of the adjective *unnatural* in relation to homosexual relations as
senseless:

> The truth is that [when] the epithet *unnatural* [is] applied to
> any human act or thought by man, the only matter of which it
> affords any indication that can be depended upon is the exis-

23.   April 24, 1814, box 74a, folio 117.
24.   April 25, 1814, box 74a, folio 175.
25.   April 1814, box 74a, folio 93. Bentham discusses the use of the
word *unnatural* in relation to several crimes besides sexual ones, e.g., infanticide and rebellion.

tence of a sentiment of disapprobation accompanied with passion in the breast of the person by whom it is employed: a degree of dissocial passion by which without staying to inquire . . . whether the practice . . . be or be not noxious to society, he endeavours by the use thus made of this inflammatory word to kindle towards the object of this ill-will the same dissocial passion in other breasts for the purpose of inducing them to join with him in producing pain.[26]

In these notes Bentham works conscientiously at the task medical men, psychologists, and law reformers in Germany and France were to set themselves during the later decades of the century—the development of a neutral, scientific vocabulary to replace the old abusive terms. The term *Uranianism* came into use in Germany in 1862, *contrary sexual feeling* and *homosexuality* in 1869; in France and Italy, the expression *sexual inversion* appeared in scientific writings in the 1880s, and Havelock Ellis popularized it in England. Bentham begins this reform in his Regency manuscripts. He distinguishes "irregular" from what he calls "regular" modes of sexual intercourse, making it clear that by these expressions he is not rendering judgment but merely differentiating sexual acts conformable to "public opinion" from those which were not.[27] Then he coins such expressions as "the improlific appetite," or the "innoxious" mode, to distinguish homosexual from heterosexual relations that might cause unwanted pregnancies.[28] In the literary proposals he made to Beckford in 1817, homosexuality

26. April 18, 1814, box 94a, folio 90. Two years later, on September 12, 1816, Bentham added another brief note on this subject: "By the use of words which have no precise meaning beyond an expression of the state of the affections of him by whom they are employed towards the object to which they are applied—words such as dissoluteness, profligacy, abomination and so forth—men work themselves up into a state of passion from which all cool and rational consideration is excluded" (box 94a, folio 121).
27. July 28, 1816, box 74a, folio 42.
28. April 27, 1814, box 74a, folio 156; July 28, 1816, box 74a, folio 62. See C. K. Ogden, "Bentham on Sex," in *Theory of Legislation* (London: Kegan Paul, Trench, Trubner, 1931), p. 477.

becomes "the Attic mode" through its association with ancient Athenian culture.[29]

In April 1814, Bentham listed what he calls the "ill-
principled and unostensible causes" for the persecution of
homosexuals. These include, first, the desire for a reputation of virtue and, second, envy, hatred, and the opportunity to exercise "the passion of malevolence without
danger of punishment in any shape."[30] But he also considers those arguments that were not ill-principled, that is, rational utilitarian arguments against homosexuality as an
activity genuinely harmful to society. The alleged harms—
to population, to military defense, to the status of women
—he had of course considered at length in his essay of 1785.
But since that essay had never been published, Bentham returns to them once more, revising or augmenting his case
in the light of changing attitudes and new information.

As to population, public opinion had changed drastically since the appearance of Thomas Malthus's famous
Essay on the Principle of Population in 1798. Bentham still
holds to his earlier theory that the tolerance of male homosexuality does not, in fact, cause a drop in the birth rate.
But now he can argue that, even if it *did*, Malthus has
shown that the real threat is overpopulation, with its attendant overcrowding, poverty, and famine: one bugbear at
least had been laid to rest. As for male "enervation" leading to defeat in battle, Bentham repeats his arguments
from the military triumphs of the classical world. He praises
again the valor of the Theban Band—the association of
men "most celebrated for personal courage" in Greek antiquity—and now adds the examples of Nisus and Euryalus, from Virgil's *Aeneid*.[31] It occurs to him that legends
of mythical heroic lovers, such as Hercules and Hylas, are
even more instructive in reflecting the opinions of the clas-

29. "Sextus," August–September 1817, box 161a, folio 15b.
30. "Code Penal," April 19, 1814, box 74a, folio 97.
31. May 1, 1814, box 74a, folios 144, 143.

sical world than historical examples since they record "the conclusion drawn by opinion from universal and continual experience."[32] In this particular case, poetry was indeed more universal than history.

New anthropological data seemed further to call into question the idea that toleration of male homosexuality leads to the neglect or mistreatment of women. The most brutal abuse of women he has heard of occurs in two diverse tribes, one in New South Wales, the other in eastern Canada: neither culture appeared to practice or condone male homosexuality.[33] Missionary accounts from Polynesia also throw new light on conditions there:

> In the newly-discovered Islands of the Pacific Ocean the prevalence of the improlific appetite, after having been concealed by the prudent delicacy of polished historiographers, has been revealed by the untutored and querulous zeal of pious missionaries. Prostitution by profession and that profession marked by peculiarity of attire has there been observed among the male sex, as in other countries among the female. Yet neither in these any more than in other tropical regions has the treatment bestowed by the stronger to the weaker sex been found to exhibit any indifference.[34]

It is true that Islamic countries generally countenance male relations and oppress their women, but seclusion there arises from the intensity of the Mussulman's jealousy, not from his neglect of women. Turning to Europe, Bentham remarks that England, the most homophobic of nations, was also in his day the one in which women had least influence over men:

> In politics, in literature, in business in general, the influence of the female sex has for a long time been more conspicuous in France than in England. Yet in France, that propensity which in England is matter of ostentatious abhorrence is a source of jest and merriment, to most persons an object of physical dis-

32. May 1, 1814, box 74a, folio 144.
33. April 27, 1814, box 74a, folio 156.
34. Ibid.

gust, to many of religious abhorrence, to some of moral contempt, but scarce to any of moral abhorrence. Neither in Italy nor in Germany have the female sex ever so much as fancied to themselves any cause of complaint or apprehension on the score of indifference on the part of the male. Yet not only in Italy but in Germany the propensity in question is in general regarded with a degree of indifference and even gratified with a degree of notoriety and security the bare mention of which cannot be endured in England with patience.[35]

To indict his countrymen for cruelty and intolerance was a project daring enough, but the inherent logic of Bentham's utilitarian ethic carried him a step further. According to his hedonistic calculus, any pleasure without painful consequences was in itself "pure good." In this category he included most consensual nonprocreative sex acts. In effect, Jeremy Bentham stood Thomas Aquinas on his head. Whereas it was specifically nonprocreative acts—masturbation, contraception, sodomy—against which traditional moral taboos had been strongest, Bentham took the opposite view—that it was the procreative rather than the nonprocreative acts that most often caused real harm. Marital intercourse, though necessary, posed the threat of overpopulation. Fornication produced undesired pregnancies. From these followed abortions (highly dangerous in Bentham's day) and frequent infanticide, which in England was the object of harsh legislation. Seduced women who had lost their reputations and all prospects of a husband were not infrequently forced into prostitution with its attendant horrors of degradation, poverty, disease, and early death. Should not the "irregular modes" of intercourse be encouraged as preferable in their consequences to these?

Bentham developed exactly this line of thought in thirty pages of notes begun in August 1816 under the title, "Beneficial effects of certain of these modes." It was not until 1957 that the Wolfenden Report recommended to the English government that homosexual acts be decriminalized

35.   April 27, 1814, box 74a, folio 157.

on the grounds that prosecutions did more harm than good. But Bentham went beyond this to affirm that homosexuality, as a form of nonprocreative sex, was a positive good to be encouraged. Examining the sources of human happiness with the eye of a moral economist, Bentham saw that material goods were necessarily limited and that each person's portion was constantly threatened by the pressures of population, but these difficulties did not attend sexual pleasure divorced from procreation. Here was a source of enjoyment open to the wealthy and indigent alike, to the "subject many" as well as to the "ruling few." If one were to remove "the cloud of prejudice by which this part of the field of morals has to this time been obscured, what calculation shall compute the aggregate mass of pleasure that might be brought into existence?"[36]

It is not surprising that Bentham left to the end of his notes a consideration of a particularly delicate subject—relations between teachers and their pupils. Would not decriminalization render these more common? Bentham does not think there is much likelihood of their occurring in ordinary schoolroom settings. The jealousy of a class of boys will prevent the master from favoring one, nor is the lack of privacy in the typical boarding school conducive to such relations. But what of private tutors? In such a case he is willing to believe that there may be some advantage in such a relation. The master may teach with greater "zeal" if he is the lover of his pupil. "The pupil on his part, experiencing instead of that moroseness and haughtiness [by] which that commanding situation at present is so frequently exemplified, a degree of attention and kindness so extraordinary, will easily find a pleasure in an occupation which otherwise would have been a painful and laborious one."[37] If, on the other hand, the boy should take advantage of the situation and idle away his time, the affair could be broken

36. July 31(?), 1816, box 74a, folio 219.
37. July 1, 1816, box 74a, folio 208.

off by his parents. Here Bentham approves something like the pedagogic eros of the Greeks.

In all this, Bentham presents a striking contrast with Byron. The philosophical hedonist and moral revolutionary lived the life of an ascetic; the rake who mocked society never seriously challenged its moral premises. Byron is proud of his sexual knowledgeableness in *Don Juan*, but though he portrays an idyllic and innocent love between Juan and Haidée, this does not reflect his usual attitude toward sex. More often his implied stance is, the world has condemned me, but the hypocritical world is as bad as I am. In assuming this posture, he accepts the world's values and "exposes" it as failing to live up to them. Contemporary moralists condemned *Don Juan*. Later ones, such as Paul Elmer More, took a longer view; Byron was less of a moral heretic than, say, Shelley, simply because he did, in fact, have a sense of guilt. But this is to ignore the effect this guilt had on Byron or on the others and, above all, on the women whose lives he touched. Men who hate and despise themselves usually do not treat other people very well either.

Having made a case for the social utility of male homosexual relations and decried the evils of punishment, Bentham, with energy remarkable for a man nearing seventy, took the offensive on another front. Of all the forces making for prejudice, he felt the most formidable was the ascetic morality to which the English gave such fervent lip service. And, behind this, far more significant than philosophical stoicism, was Pauline Christianity. (On this point, Byron would have agreed. In the extensive conversations on religion he engaged in during his second visit to Greece, he remarked that English religion seemed more Christ-than God-centered and even more preoccupied with Paul.) For Bentham, Paul was the antiutilitarian *par excellence*; he came to see in Paul a fear and distrust of pleasure, which, in his view, did not at all accord with Jesus. If the link between the two men's teachings could be weakened,

Bentham thought English Christianity might become less puritanical. With this aim in mind, he began in 1817—the first year of Byron's Italian exile—the lengthy treatise to which he gave the name "Not Paul but Jesus."

The first aim of this magnum opus was to show that Paul's connection with Christ's disciples was tenuous and equivocal: in effect, the authority he presumed to wield was usurped. This was a step toward Bentham's more important goal, which was to question Paul's moral stance, especially his ascetic attitude toward sex in general and homosexuality in particular. Bentham was keenly aware what dangerous ground he was treading. In 1823, under the pseudonym "Gamaliel Smith," he published Parts I and II of his notes in the form of a four-hundred-page book challenging, on historical and scriptural grounds, Paul's right to set himself up as a spokesman for Christ and Christianity. The book bore the title *Not Paul but Jesus*, though in fact it incorporated only the first half of his project and did not touch the more controversial second half. It is not clear to what extent the book was recognized as Bentham's nor to what extent he had collaborators. According to the *Dictionary of National Biography*, Bentham's fellow reformer Francis Place, in a note, claimed the book as his. But the voluminous University College manuscripts leave no doubt that, whatever hand Place had in turning Bentham's fragmentary observations into publishable prose, the fundamental ideas and basic structure of the work were Bentham's.

Inevitably, it caused controversy, as any attack on Paul's apostleship was bound to do. Two books attempted to answer Bentham, and a modest debate ensued. Apparently, the reception was not encouraging enough for Bentham to acknowledge the essay during his lifetime, though it was reprinted after his death with his name on the title page. No doubt a further reason for Bentham's pseudonymity was the explosive nature of the sequel he had planned. After he had fully developed his ideas for the first part of his book and had pretty well determined what he wanted to say in the second, he produced a curious document that clarifies some of these aims. This took the form of a twenty-two-page synopsis or prospectus addressed to William Beckford. In this proposal, he suggests that Beckford might act as a literary collaborator to put his ideas into final shape, supply new materials (especially from classical sources), and provide sympathy, encouragement, and, presumably not least, financial help. We do not know what prompted Bentham to address this précis to his old acquaintance at this particular moment or whether any version of it ever reached him. It is piquant to consider that if Beckford had responded favorably and the book had appeared, the kind of collaboration between Havelock Ellis and John Addington Symonds that led to the publication of Ellis's *Sexual Inversion* in the 1890s might have been anticipated by Bentham and Beckford in the reign of George IV.

Whatever the personal relation between the world-famous philosopher and the ostracized connoisseur-romancer, the document has a unique interest. The characteristically Benthamite title of the summary is "General idea for a work, having for one of its objects the Defense of the principle of *Utility*, so far as it concerns the liberty of Taste, against the conjoint hostility of the principle of asceticism and the principle of *antipathy*." Bentham adds, illuminatingly, that the book will have "for its proposed title, proposed on the ground of expected popularity, or at least protection against popular rage,—'Not Paul but Jesus.'" With magisterial naïveté Bentham states that his object is "the greatest happiness of the greatest number" and his motive "sympathy with the whole human race." Then he adds an intriguing detail. This motive, he claims, is "mixt with as little of personal interest as it is possible for it to be mixt with." Is this a declaration on Bentham's part that he had no interest in homosexual relations himself? It might be construed this way. He wants, he tells Beckford, to reclaim the public mind "from the gloomy and antisocial—and, in proportion as they are gloomy and antisocial, pernicious—notions, involved in the Calvinistic and various other modes of the religion of Jesus, and the antipathies that have sprung out of them." Such terrors derive from Paul as "contradistinguished from the acts and sayings ascribed to Jesus" in whom, he thinks, they find no warrant.[38]

Bentham speculates that English tolerance will allow a book criticizing Paul provided the tone is not bitter or ridiculing. Part I will question his authority, challenge his pretensions "to any connection with Jesus," and expose him as "a mere impostor, erecting an empire to himself on the foundation of that name."[39] Though Part I will touch incidentally on Paul's moral doctrines, to show their incompatability with Jesus, the full critique will be reserved until Bentham can observe the public reception of the "by far least obnoxious" Part I. Bentham is clearsightedly pessimistic about the reaction he expects his revolutionary moral position to provoke—"to the work, and thence to the author, if known, nothing but unpopularity" can accrue "and *that* to a degree beyond all power of measurement."[40] Bentham was fearful what influence he had in the world as a reformer might be forfeited. Then he recalls how exile and ostracism ended the parliamentary career of Sir William Meredith.[41] In mentioning this scandal of 1780, Bentham was delicately reminding Beckford that the proposed book would attack the prejudices that had driven him, too, from society a few years later.

The next ten pages minutely classify, in abstract, scientific language, first sensory pleasures generally and then every kind of sex act, ending with those Bentham now calls relations "in the Attic mode." Then he pauses, no doubt fearing that the wearied Beckford might need some reassurance that this roundabout approach was worthwhile:

38. "Sextus," box 161a, folio 14a.
39. "Not Paul but Jesus," box 161a, folio 14b.
40. Box 161a, folio 14c.
41. See p. 46.

Note here the advantages derived from the comprehensiveness of the plan here pursued: for example, in shewing, that in this last mentioned case, no more ground exists for punishment or disrepute, than in so many other cases, as above, in which no punishment is applied. Among a number of modes of gratification all equally innoxious, *that* indeed would have been *best* worth rescuing from punishment and unmerited reproach, towards which the propensity [i.e., of hate] is most extensive. But any such exclusive plan . . . would have given to prejudice a shock, which by the present course is lessened, if not avoided.[42]

Bentham then rejects the alleged negative social consequences of homosexuality and enumerates its beneficial effects when contrasted with the evils of adultery, rape, and illegitimacy. On one point, however, he is now willing to compromise. Fearing no doubt that so radical a step as complete decriminalization would be impractical, he revives his compromise proposal to make the sanction banishment. He adds a proviso, however, that would have made conviction difficult and the law all but a dead letter: except in cases of violence, two witnesses should be required, neither of them a principal or an accessory.[43]

Bentham also proposes that the projected book devote three chapters to literary and historical topics. One would deal with philosophers and notables of ancient times, another with modern thinkers and jurists such as Hume, Voltaire, Beccaria, Blackstone—and Bentham. His most original idea is to include an analysis of the treatment of homosexuals in contemporary fiction, criticizing homophobic tendencies in Smollett, Fielding, Wieland, Cumberland, and "Madam Graffigny." Bentham has a lively sense of the power of popular fiction to create prejudice: "In passages such as these, in works so extensively diffused, much mischief, viz. by inflaming the antisocial antipathy, can not but be produced. . . . By the thus holding

42. Box 161a, folio 16c.
43. Box 161a, folio 18b.

up to view of these instances of groundless censure . . . the violence of it may, perhaps, be more or less abated."[44] Here we have in embryo an anticipation of the modern idea of "consciousness raising," that is, the bringing to light of prejudicial tendencies in speech or writing which the hearer or reader may be inclined by cultural conditioning to accept uncritically.

Bentham's proposal breaks off abruptly after he has sketched three other chapters, which were to deal, respectively, with Jesus's failure to condemn "divagations of the sexual appetite," with Paul's vehement attack on them, and with the "favorable aspect" shown by some early Christians to matters of sex. Most of Bentham's manuscripts (and indeed all of them dealing with homosexuality, except the essay of 1785) are incomplete. But in this case the abrupt breaking off seems especially odd since this is not a rough draft but a carefully polished essay based on a scribbled first draft, which still survives. Perhaps Bentham felt he needed to develop his ideas on the Bible more fully before attempting to summarize them.

The University College cataloguer has assigned the Beckford prospectus to August and September of 1817. From November 1817 to February 1818, Bentham wrote out

44.   Box 161a, folio 18c. "Madam Graffigny" is a mistake for Thomas Gueulette (see chap. 1, n. 95). Richard Cumberland, in the *Observer*, had, according to Bentham, unjustifiably contradicted Xenophon by denying Socrates's "participation in the propensity in question" (box 161a, folio 18c). Bentham makes the same charge against Bishop Warburton. Cumberland's essay was published in the *Observer* for 1807–1808 and reprinted in *The British Essayists*. The drift of the essay is difficult to make out. Shelley, for his part, read it as an indictment of Socrates (November 3, 1819, *The Letters of Percy Bysshe Shelley*, ed. Frederick L. Jones [Oxford: Clarendon Press, 1964], 2:145). Bentham, on the other hand, may have fixed on the sentence: "Great authorities have ascribed his attachment to Alcibiades to the most virtuous principle; common fame, or perhaps (more properly speaking) common defamation, turned it into a charge of the impurest nature" (*The British Essayists*, ed. A. Chambers, no. 140, vol. 40 [London: Nichols et al., 1817], p. 224). Here Cumberland seems to be discounting the charge. We must remember, of course, that Bentham did not know Plato's treatment of this subject in the *Symposium*.

elaborate notes on the second half of *Not Paul but Jesus*. These three hundred pages seem to have been written helter-skelter and then reorganized under chapter headings for the planned volume. The first six chapters (the notes for which run to over one hundred pages) were to have been a philosophical attack on asceticism in general—which Bentham denounces as absurd, wicked, and mischievous—and the foolishness of its application in particular cases, the chief among these being sexual. Looking at the matter philosophically, Bentham wonders why the "pleasures of the bed," as he now calls them, should be any more restricted than the "pleasures of the table." Why not, he asks, limit sexual pleasures only by the same rules of prudence (avoiding excess) and probity (concern for others) that govern eating and other pleasures?[45] In brief asides, he once again enumerates and dismisses the alleged bad effects of homosexuality and notes the suspect sources of homophobic prejudice.[46]

All this is familiar. In the next three chapters, describing what he interprets as the antiasceticism of Jesus, Bentham contrasts Jesus with a true ascetic like John the Baptist, underscoring his rejection of fasting, his acceptance of wine and feasts, his Sabbath-breaking, and his defense of the woman taken in adultery. What emerges in Bentham's notes of 1818 is not just an antiascetic Christ but an antinomian Christ strikingly similar to the portrait William Blake was elaborating at almost exactly the same time in his unfinished poem "The Everlasting Gospel." In these distichs Blake's Christ (like Nietzsche) rejects Christian humility, gentility, and "Moral Virtue," overrules the law of Moses by pardoning the adulterous woman, is himself the child

45.   January 28, 1818, box 161b, folio 271.
46.   Folios 275–88 of box 161b, written on January 2 and 3, 1818, dismiss the alleged threats to population and the status of women. Folios 303–07, written on January 5, enumerate six "Causes of the vituperation commonly bestowed upon these modes."

of adultery, and sends his seventy disciples "Against Religion & Government."

The remaining six chapters (the last is incomplete) deal with the Bible and homosexuality and are obviously the raison d'être of the book. To begin with, Bentham points out that Jesus nowhere condemns relations between men. He adumbrates modern criticism by dismissing Christ's frequent references to the fate of Sodom and Gomorrah as irrelevant; in none of these gospel passages "is any the slightest allusion made by him to the propensity in question [as] the sin by which the calamity is produced."[47] Jesus seems instead to identify the sin of Sodom with inhospitality and the mistreatment of strangers; repeatedly he compares cities that reject his apostles with the cities of the plain. In doing this, Bentham thinks he is merely following the true emphasis in the original story in Genesis 19. There the relations referred to are not consensual homosexuality but a mass rape whose threatened enormity was compounded by its gross violation of the laws of hospitality so important in primitive societies.[48]

Undoubtedly the Mosaic law prescribes the death penalty for male homosexuality in Leviticus. But should nineteenth-century England hang men on this account? It is a serious error to assume the laws of Moses were meant as "giving direction to practice among nations so far advanced in improvement as even the least advanced of nations of Europe in these our times."[49] Moreover, when we examine the Old Testament critically, we are led, Bentham thinks, to conclude that the Mosaic law (which Bentham, following an earlier scholarly tradition no longer generally accepted, dates about 1500 B.C.) was often in practice disregarded. For instance, in the Book of Judges we find the story of a group of Benjaminites who reenact the Sodom

47. December 1, 1817, box 161b, folio 421.
48. December 20, 1817, box 161b, folio 429.
49. December 23, 1817, box 161b, folio 444.

story: attracted by the beauty of a young Levite, they insist
that his host surrender him; when the shocked host re-
fuses and delivers the Levite's concubine instead, they
rape her so violently that she dies and a retaliatory war en-
sues.[50] Such a tale shows that homosexual passion was well
known in ancient Israel. Moreover, the first and second
books of Kings speak of "sodomites in the land" and do
not always imply intolerance. Indeed, II Kings 23:7 describes "the houses of the sodomites that were by the
house of the Lord." Bentham concludes from this that "so
far from its being punished, we find receptables for this
species of gratification set up and maintained at different
periods in Judah by authority of government."[51]

Bentham's notes include also a full transcription of
the David and Jonathan story from Samuel, ending with
David's famous lament over his dead friend. Bentham argues that we are to take the "love surpassing the love of
women" David felt for Jonathan not only as love of mind
for mind but also as a sexual bond:

> In a country which could give birth on occasion to such a scene
> as that which originated in the beauty of the young Levite, is it
> possible that the nature of that love which had place between
> David and Jonathan would be matter of doubt? or that it could

50. December 28, 1817, box 161b, folios 454–455.
51. November 28, 1817, box 161b, folio 462. The Revised Standard
Version translates II Kings 23:7 as "the houses of the male cult prostitutes that were *in* the house of the Lord" (my italics). There has been
much recent controversy over the King James translation of the Hebrew
word *kedēshīm* (literally, "holy men") as "sodomites." The Revised Standard Version, by rendering the term as "male cult prostitutes," keeps the
homosexual implication. Derrick Sherwin Bailey argues that the sexual
role of these devotees was heterosexual rather than homosexual (*Homosexuality and the Western Christian Tradition* [London: Longmans, Green, &
Co., 1955], pp. 48–53), and John Boswell, in *Christianity, Social Tolerance,
and Homosexuality* (Chicago: University of Chicago Press, 1980, pp. 98–
99), follows Bailey. However, both Bailey and Boswell overlook the evidence of the Talmud (Sanhedrin 54b), which shows that the law banning
the *kedēshīm* was interpreted as a law against homosexuality in Old Testament times.

be more clearly designated by any the grossest than by this sentimental language? . . . From the very outset of the story, the clearest exclusion is put upon any such notion as that the love of mind to mind, or, in one word, *friendship*, was in the case in question clear of all indications of the love of body for body, in a word, of sexual love.—"Love at first sight" in the words of the title to the play.—Yes, nothing can be more natural. But friendship at first sight and friendship equal in ardency to the most ardent sexual love! At the very first interview, scarce had the first words . . . issued from his lips when the soul of Jonathan was knit with the soul of David, and Jonathan loved him as his own soul. In a country in which the concupiscence of a whole male population of a considerable town is kindled to madness by a transient glimpse of a single man, what impartial eye can refuse to see the love by which the young warriors Nisus and Euryalus were bound together in Virgil's fable, and Harmodius with Aristogiton in Grecian History?[52]

But surely, when preachers or rhetoricians have held up the love between these two men and its literary expression for "edification," they have not understood it in this sense. By Old Testament standards, would not "any admixture of sensuality" be enough to make the relation one of the "foulest complexion," meriting severe punishment? Bentham's answer to these difficulties was to introduce a distinction:

But if among the Jews this same propensity which under some circumstances the law . . . made capitally punishable was [sometimes] regarded without disapprobation, this same propensity under other circumstances [was] regarded not merely with indifference but with admiration and spoken of in correspondent terms. In this, whatever inconsistency there were, there would be nothing at all extraordinary. Considered as mere sensuality it would be regarded with disapprobation. Considered as a bond of attachment between two persons jointly engaged in a course of life regarded as meritorious, it might nevertheless be respected and applauded.[53]

52. December 21, 1817, box 161b, folio 458.
53. December 21, 1817, box 161b, folio 459.

Bentham then reviews the references to Sodom and Gomorrah in the prophetic books that conclude the Old Testament. He takes cognizance of the temptation felt by preachers to dwell on natural calamities as indications of divine wrath, noting how frequently the prophets mention the destruction of the cities of the plain. But once again he anticipates modern scholarship in remarking that for all their fondness for the legend, Isaiah, Jeremiah, Ezekiel, Amos, and Zephaniah at no point connect the overthrow of Sodom with the sin of homosexuality.[54]

On this point of interpretation Bentham arrives at the same conclusions reached by Derrick Sherwin Bailey in his *Homosexuality and the Western Christian Tradition* in 1955. His next step, however, was far more daring. Examining the Gospel of St. John with the same attention with which he had analyzed Genesis, Judges, Kings, Samuel, and the prophets, he excerpts all the passages in the story of the Last Supper, the Crucifixion, and the Resurrection in which the "beloved disciple" speaks of the special fondness Jesus bore him. Could John have meant to imply that he and Jesus were lovers? Bentham admits that "good taste and self-regarding prudence would require us to turn aside" from this "topic of extreme delicacy." But "a regard for human happiness and important truth and the sound principles of penal justice compel him to go over it."[55] He speculates on the nature of their love as follows:

If the love which in these passages Jesus was intended to be represented as bearing towards this John was not the same sort of love as that which appears to have had place between David and Jonathan, the son of Saul, it seems not easy to conceive what can have been the object in bringing it to view in so pointed a manner accompanied with such circumstances of fondness. That the sort of love of which in the bosom of Jesus Saint John is here meant to be represented as the object was of a different sort from any of which any of the other of the

54. November 29–30, 1817, box 161b, folios 464–74.
55. November 28, 1817, box 161b, folio 475.

Apostles was the object is altogether out of dispute. For of this
sort of love, whatever sort it was, he and he alone is in these so
frequently recurring terms maintained as being the object.

[As to] any superiority of value in his service in relation to
preaching of the Gospel—no such foundation could the distinction have had: for of this nothing is to be found in Saint
John by which he can stand in comparison with Saint Peter,
and on no occasion is the rough fisherman to be seen "leaning
in the bosom of Jesus" or "lying on his breast." [56]

Bentham thinks Jesus's numerous references to the destruction of Sodom are not germane to the issue since, like
the prophets, he does not seem to have associated the city
with homosexuality. But would he willingly have flown
in the face of the Mosaic dispensation? For Bentham's
antinomian Christ, the answer is an unhesitating yes: "As
to the law of Moses—to him who has resolution enough to
keep his eyes open to it nothing can be more manifest than
that in the eyes of Jesus the law of Moses was but a mere
human law so ill-adapted to the welfare of society that on
no occasion is it ever spoken of as coming under his cognizance without being taken by him more or less expressly
for the declared object of [his] scorn." [57] Bentham was particularly struck by the emphasis on love in the epistles of
John, which contain, apart from a few stereotyped warnings about the world and the flesh, no specific ascetic doctrines. "Of that love which has 'the brethren' for its object
more is to be found in these three short letters than in
all Paul, or even in all Peter: the sexual kind as might well
be supposed is not specially mentioned for the purpose
of commendation, but as little is it for the purpose of
censure." [58]

Perceptions of Christ and the morality he taught or embodied varied remarkably from one nineteenth-century
writer to another. Blake's Christ and Bentham's were icono-
clasts, Tennyson's a blameless moral exemplar who wrought

56. November 28, 1817, box 161b, folios 476–77.
57. November 28, 1817, box 161b, folio 478.
58. December 5, 1817, box 161b, folio 485.

With human hands the creed of creeds
In loveliness of perfect deeds.[59]

Arnold's Victorianization went a stage further. In "He-
braism and Hellenism" he makes Christ an "affecting pattern" of asceticism, whose mission of charity is completed
by his "crucifying" of the flesh. For Arnold, half the meaning of Christianity lay in its opposition to the *alma Venus* of
the pagan world, with what he calls its "vile affections,"
the latter phrase being the one Paul used in Romans to
characterize homosexuality. Later, combining the moral
with the social, Tolstoy would make Christ an anarchist,
and Shaw (following Shelley) would transform him, in
the commentary of the gospels he wrote as a preface to
Androcles and the Lion, into a socialist and egalitarian, critical of the family as an institution and averse to revenge and
punishment.

But Bentham's speculation was, in a sense, more challenging still, given the prejudices of his native land. Where
the Middle Ages had kept alive the legend of a Christ at
whose birth all homosexuals were supposed to have died,
Bentham, less extravagant but more daring, developed a
countermyth whose outlines had only dimly appeared before, a myth that to the typical Englishman would have
seemed a supreme blasphemy, the myth of Christ the lover
of men. Bentham might have written Blake's couplets:

Both read the Bible day & night,
But thou readst black where I read white. . . .
I am sure This Jesus will not do
Either for Englishman or Jew.[60]

Another incident in the gospels, comparatively minor,
also engaged Bentham's imagination and half made a novelist out of him. This was the story of the boy he calls

59. *In Memoriam*, XXXVI, in *The Poems of Tennyson*, ed. Christopher
Ricks (London: Longmans, 1969), p. 894.
60. *Complete Poetry and Prose of William Blake*, p. 524.

the "stripling clad in loose attire" whom Mark alone of the evangelists mentions in his account of Jesus's arrest in Gethsemane. In Chapter 14 of the King James translation the relevant verses are these:

50   And they all forsook him, and fled.
51   And there followed him a certain young man, having a linen cloth cast about his naked body; and the young men laid hold on him:
52   And he left the linen cloth, and fled from them naked.

Six years earlier Bentham had come across a terse paragraph in the *Monthly Magazine*, in which an anonymous writer, commenting on the odd grammar of the King James translation, referred cryptically to the passage as "the episode of the cinaedus" (i.e., boy prostitute).[61] Now Bentham recalls and, in effect, endorses this theory. He prefers the translation "stripling" as closer to the Greek than "young man" and suggests that the boy may have been a "rival or a candidate for the situation of rival to the Apostle" (i.e., to John). Bentham argues that the passage is intelligible only if the boy is indeed a "cinaedus" and the "loose attire" the badge of his profession. Bentham interprets the *sindona* or "linen" that the stripling wore as a "fair and costly" garment and thinks that the men who laid hands on him and it regarded both the boy and the cloth as a "prize," as the men of Sodom regarded the angels.[62] But why should this incident have been recorded in a story "so awful as that of the cruel death of Jesus"? Bentham turns it into a touching romance:

> The answer seems not very difficult to find. The timidity and consequent mendacity of Saint Peter, the earliest chosen and most confidential of Jesus's twelve selected servants, is not only one of the most remarkable features in the history, but

61.   Bentham says he had seen the remark "some 6 or 8 years ago" in a column headed "The Portfolio of a Man of Letters" (November 29, 1817, box 161b, folio 489). The comment had in fact appeared in the *Monthly Magazine* for September 1811.
62.   November 29, 1817, box 161b, folios 491–92.

one the details of which are with every mark of correspondent sense of extraordinariness particularized. With this timidity and backsliding the fond and unexampled attachment of the nameless stripling forms a most striking contrast.

At the conjunction in question, the traitor excepted by whom was let in the multitude by which he was apprehended, Jesus was found accompanied by all the rest of the disciples. At the first onset one of them, according to all the four evangelists, being provided with a sword, stood for a moment on the defensive, and aiming a stroke at the head of an officer of the police, struck off one of his ears: according to Saint John this was Saint Peter. Whoever it was, this boldness neither continued beyond the moment nor found any one to second it. "They all forsook him and fled." Mark XIV:51: this is what is written of the disciples.

Followed him then one only of all his attendants—this loosely attired stripling: like Milton's Abdiel, "Among the faithless, faithful only he." [63]

But what was the young man's relation to Jesus? May he not have been a penitent who had come to present himself? Bentham rules out this possibility. His loyalty to Jesus is not intelligible if we suppose this was their first meeting; somehow Jesus must have won his devotion. Nor, if he was a penitent, would he have presented himself in the questionable clothes of his profession. The presumption is that Jesus did not find his homosexuality offensive. Bentham concludes:

In the acts and sayings of Jesus, had any such mark of reprobation towards the mode of sexuality in question been found as may be seen in such abundance in the epistles of Paul—in a word, had any decided marks of reprobation been found pronounced upon it by Jesus, in the eyes [of a] believer in Jesus could any such body of evidence as here presents itself be considered as worth regarding? But when the utter absence of all such marks of reprobation is considered, coupled with the urgency of the demand for the most pointed and decided marks of reprobation in a new system of religion promulgated by supernatural authority and by supernatural means, the practice in question being universally spread not only over the

63. November 29, 1817, box 161b, folios 493–94.

vast region of the East in which Judaea formed a part, but in the metropolis of the empire and on and about the throne, evidence of this sort thus standing not only [not] opposed but corroborated seems to have that claim to attention which the reader is now in a condition to reject or to confirm, to bestow or withhold, as to him seems reasonable.[64]

A Christian to whom homosexuality is abhorrent will of course reject Bentham's reading of the Gospels out of hand and with vehemence. Certainly the evidence he builds on is fragile and inconclusive, surprisingly so when we remember that Bentham was his age's leading authority on legal evidence. But what people believe, especially in matters of religion and morals, is rarely determined by evidence. Personal or cultural bias is much more important. A Greek ignorant of Paul or Leviticus who read the Gospel of St. John in the first or second century might very well have interpreted it as a homosexual romance, just as, with little more evidence, he interpreted the story of Achilles and Patroclus in the *Iliad* as a homosexual love affair. Bentham's interpretation is neither probable nor impossible. Most responses to Bentham's theory, however, will be less a response to the evidence than an indication of one's feelings about homosexuality or, for that matter, about ascribing sexual feelings of any sort to Christ.

64. November 29, 1817, box 161b, folio 497.

· 8 ·

Shelley—Clogher—Castlereagh

The unpublished portion of *Not Paul but Jesus* was only one manifestation of dissent from traditional sex ethics by an English writer in the last days of the Regency. Bentham broke off his notes on the New Testament in February 1818. This was the year Shelley published *Laon and Cythna*, a poem, which, by making its revolutionary hero and heroine not just lovers but also brother and sister, challenged the taboo against incest. In 1819, the *annus mirabilis* of the younger romantics, Keats attacked sexual asceticism in "The Eve of St. Agnes," and Byron mocked moral hypocrisy in the first canto of *Don Juan*. Their elders, Wordsworth and Coleridge, now turned conservative, had, of course, never expressed radical views on sexual matters. But the contrast was not simply between an older and a younger generation. The seventy-one-year-old Bentham and the sixty-two-year-old Blake were, after all, the seniors of the Lake poets.[1]

Of the poets, Shelley was unique in challenging accepted sex mores in his prose as well as in his verse. Both his Godwinism and his deep immersion in Greek literature

---

1. Benjamin Robert Haydon, a somewhat hostile witness, commenting on Medwin's *Conversations of Lord Byron* (1824), expressed the opinion in his journal that "Byron, Shelley, Hunt were but the fallen Pupils of Godwin—they felt they had incurred the contempt of the world by their attempt to shake the established principles of sexual intercourse." They "would and might have produced a revolution had they not shocked the Country by their opinions on sexual intercourse—This forever bustled up the virtue of the Country" (Duncan Gray and Violet W. Walker, "Benjamin Robert Haydon on Byron and Others," *Keats–Shelley Memorial Bulletin* 7 [1956]: 23–24).

gave him a point of view remote from his countrymen. It was his Platonic studies, in particular, that led him to touch upon the taboo subject of homosexuality. In July 1818, Shelley, then living at the Bagni di Lucca near Pisa, devoted some "ten mornings" to translating the *Symposium*. He was drawn to Plato for several reasons. The philosopher's poetic style attracted him; so did his exalted doctrine of love. But what inspired Shelley to translate the dialogue was its unique significance as a social document throwing light on Greek homosexuality. On July 10, he wrote to John and Maria Gisborne: "I am employed just now . . . in translating into my fainting & inefficient periods the divine eloquence of Plato's Symposium—only as an exercise or perhaps to give Mary some idea of the manners & feelings of the Athenians—so different on many subjects from that of any other community that ever existed." [2]

We may recall how thoroughly the Floyer Sydenham translation of 1761–1767 and the subsequent Thomas Taylor translation of 1804 had been bowderlized. Their distortions and omissions help explain the odd fact that Bentham, though keenly interested in the Greeks, cites Xenophon, Thucydides, and Plutarch (among others) but makes no reference whatever to the *Symposium*, the *Phaedrus*, or any other dialogue by Plato. Even more surprising is the general neglect Plato suffered in the eighteenth and early nineteenth centuries in England. Matthew Arnold was later to single out Bentham's slighting remarks on Plato in the *Deontology* (1834) as a sign of Bentham's limitations as a thinker, but in fact this attitude was characteristic of his age. Scholars writing on the history of Greek studies have noted the almost total disappearance of Plato from the British educational curriculum in this period and have generally ascribed his eclipse to the new philosophical predominance of Locke. His translators fared poorly: Sydenham

2.   *The Letters of Percy Bysshe Shelley*, ed. Frederick L. Jones (Oxford: Clarendon Press, 1964), 2:20.

died in poverty, and Taylor's work was little respected or supported largely because of its scholarly deficiencies.

But Plato's candor with respect to Athenian manners seems also to have influenced his academic banishment. Thomas Love Peacock, in his satirical novel *Crotchet Castle* (1831), has Dr. Folliott complain of the ignorance of Plato in England in these terms:

> I am aware, sir, that Plato, in his Symposium, discourseth very eloquently touching the Uranian and Pandemian Venus: but you must remember that in our Universities, Plato is held to be little better than a *misleader of youth*; and they have shown their contempt for him, not only by never reading him . . . but even by never printing a complete edition of him.[3]
>
> (my emphasis)

Plato had been, of course, a favorite in the Renaissance and had inspired the Cambridge Platonists in the seventeenth century. Given his moral conservatism and his puritanical antipathy to sexuality, to learn that Plato was regarded as a bad influence on youth appears paradoxical. Plato did, however, condone homosexual love if it was given no physical expression. Apparently even this qualified approval exceeded the limits of Georgian tolerance.

But there can be no doubt about the completeness of the obscurity into which he had passed. Three years later, in 1834, the young John Stuart Mill protested in an article in the *Monthly Repository* that despite Plato's "boundless reputation," "of all the great writers of antiquity, there is scarcely one who, in this country at least, is so little understood or so little read":

> Our two great "seats of learning," of which no real lover of learning can ever speak but in terms of indignant disgust, bestow attention upon the various branches of classical acquirement in exactly the reverse order to that which would be observed by persons who valued the ancient authors for what is

---

3. *The Works of Thomas Love Peacock*, ed. H. F. B. Brett-Smith and C. E. Jones, vol. 4 (London: Constable, 1924), 95.

valuable in them: namely, upon the mere niceties of the language *first*; next, upon a few of the poets; next, (but at a great distance,) some of the historians; next, (but at a still greater interval,) the orators; last of all, and just above nothing, the philosophers. An English bookseller, by the aid of a German scholar, recently produced an excellent edition of Plato; the want of sale for which, by the way, is said to have been one of the causes of his insolvency. But, with the exception of the two dialogues edited by Dr. Routh, we are aware of nothing to facilitate the study of the most gifted of Greek writers, which has ever emanated from either of the impostor-universities of England; and of the young men who have obtained university honours during the last ten years, we are much misinformed if there be six who had even looked into his writings. . . . [T]here are, probably, in this kingdom, not so many as a hundred persons who ever *have* read Plato, and not so many as twenty who ever *do*.[4]

Mill tried to compensate in some measure by providing partial translations of the *Protagoras* and the *Phaedrus*. Nevertheless, it is notable how firmly the taboo operated with respect to Plato's forbidden side. Though the theme of homosexuality is woven into the very warp and woof of the *Phaedrus*, Mill managed to excerpt the dialogue in such a way as to leave no hint of its presence. Nor did his introductory discussion make any reference to what had been left out.

It was exactly this kind of obfuscation that Shelley aimed at countering in his translation of 1818. To this end he not only produced a version that was accurate, unbowdlerized, and complete, but he also embarked on a related project. On July 25, he informed Godwin:

The Symposium of Plato, seems to me, one of the most valuable pieces of all antiquity whether we consider the intrinsic

4. "Notes on Some of the More Popular Dialogues of Plato," in *Collected Works of John Stuart Mill*, ed. J. M. Robson, vol. 11 (Toronto: University of Toronto Press, 1978), 39–40. Oddly enough, despite his utilitarian bias, James Mill was an enthusiastic student of Plato. John Stuart Mill records in his autobiography that his father had him read six dialogues of Plato in Greek before he was eight. The Mills admired Plato's logical method but not his political or moral principles.

merit of the composition or the light it throws on the inmost state of manners & opinions among the antient Greeks. I have occupied myself in translating this, & it has excited me to attempt an Essay upon the cause of some differences in sentiment between the antients & moderns with respect to the subject of the dialogue.[5]

The essay he refers to became the second essay in English on the subject of homosexuality presently known to us (after Bentham's unpublished effort of 1785)—Shelley's "Discourse on the Manners of the Antient Greeks Relative to the Subject of Love." Shelley begins by indicting contemporary scholarship for its evasions. He is determined finally to lift the veil:

> The Greeks of the Periclean age were widely different from us. It is to be lamented that no modern writer has hitherto dared to show them precisely as they were. . . . There is no book which [does this]; they seem all written for children, with the caution that no practice or sentiment, highly inconsistent with our present manners, should be mentioned, lest those manners should recieve [sic] outrage and violation. But there are many to whom the Greek language is inaccessible, who ought not to be excluded by this prudery to possess an exact and comprehensive conception of the history of man; for there is no knowledge concerning what man has been and may be, from partaking of which a person can depart, without becoming in some degree more philosophical, tolerant, and just.[6]

Unfortunately, Shelley's good intentions were somewhat marred in the performance. When we set his essay beside Bentham's, it appears distinctly marked by English anti-homosexual bias. Nevertheless, the essay is striking as a conscientious effort to provide a candid, critical, and philosophical discussion of Greek pederasty. Along with John Addington Symonds's *A Problem in Greek Ethics*, first privately printed in a limited edition of ten copies in 1883, it

5. *Letters*, 2:22.
6. "A Discourse on the Manners of the Antient Greeks Relative to the Subject of Love," in *The Platonism of Shelley*, ed. James A. Notopoulos (Durham, N.C.: Duke University Press, 1949), p. 407.

remains a pioneering work in a field not fully and freely explored by an English scholar until Kenneth Dover's authoritative study of 1980.

Its chief limitation is what we may call its "neo-Tyrianism." This interpretation of Greek love, which denied or minimized its physical side, had found eloquent expression in the writings of Archbishop Potter in the seventeenth century. We have seen how his celebrated *Antiquities of Greece* (1697–1699) had included, in its account of the customs of the Greeks, a chapter "On Their Love of Boys," which was glowingly enthusiastic about "this excellent passion." Potter is essentially following the line of Maximus of Tyre, the second-century philosopher who interpreted the loves of Socrates and Sappho as ideally chaste. Potter extends Maximus's views to all Greek love relations with bland assurance, as if the matter were hardly even debatable.[7]

In the eighteenth century Voltaire also followed this "Tyrian" tradition by interpreting the Greek *eros* as friendship, not love. In his essay "Socratic Love" he vehemently opposed those who found a warrant for homosexuality in classical literature:

> I cannot bear to hear people say that the Greeks authorized this license . . . this word *love* has deluded us. Those who were called *the lovers of a young man* were precisely those who are the minions of our princes today, those who were the children of honor, young men assisting in the education of a distinguished child, sharing the same studies, the same military labors: a martial and saintly institution which was wrongly turned into nocturnal feasts and orgies.[8]

But no one who has read the *Symposium* carefully, not to mention the dialogues of Plutarch and Lucian, among a multitude of other documents, can maintain this view of

7. 5th ed. (London: J. Knapton, 1728), 2:242–45.
8. *Philosophical Dictionary*, trans. Peter Gay (New York: Harcourt, Brace & World, 1962), pp. 77–78.

Greek popular tradition. Bentham was keenly aware of the discomfort the historical facts caused his contemporaries: "Another spectacle amusing enough is to observe the distress men are under to keep the peace between 2 favourite prejudices that are apt cruelly to jar: the one in disfavour of this vice, the other in favour of antiquity, especially antient Greece, which itself when close pressed [they] cannot deny to have been so overrun with it as to [have] look[ed] upon it without eyes of blame."[9] In his essay of 1785 he challenged Voltaire sharply:

> The principle by which the union among the members of [the Theban Band] was commonly supposed to be cemented is well known. . . . Many moderns, and among others Mr. Voltaire, dispute the fact, but that intelligent philosopher sufficiently intimates the ground of his incredulity—if he does not believe it, it is because he likes not to believe it. What the antients called love in such a case was Platonic, that is, was not love but friendship. But the Greeks knew the difference between love and friendship as well as we—they had distinct terms to signify them by: it seems reasonable therefore to suppose that when they say love they mean love, and that when they say friendship only they mean friendship only.[10]

With the emergence of Georgian homophobia, such distinctions were discarded by English historians who tended to assume (what they saw as) the worst. Indeed, the standard histories of Greece by John Gillies (1786), William Mitford (1784–1818), and George Grote (1846–1856) avoid discussion completely, limiting themselves to terse asides, as when Mitford calls the love of Aristogiton and Harmodius "utterly abhorrent" to "our manners."[11] What Shelley did was to revive a modified form of Tyrianism while look-

---

9. "Nonconformity," box 73, folio 94.
10. Bentham, "Offences Against One's Self: Paederasty, Part 1," *Journal of Homosexuality* 3 (1978):393.
11. *History of Greece*, ed. William King, 2nd ed. (London: T. Cadell, 1838), chap. 5, 1:406.

ing critically at Greek love from a sophisticated historical-psychological perspective.

Shelley's opening to his "Discourse" parallels the ardent philhellenism of his *Defence of Poetry* in its rhapsodic praise of the literature, philosophy, painting, and sculpture of the Greeks. We need to know all we can, he argues, about the "most perfect specimens of humanity of whom we have authentic record." [12] It was a sign of the height civilization had reached in Greece that they felt the need for personal relations characterized by what we would now call romantic love:

> Man is in his wildest state a social being: a certain degree of civilization and refinement ever produces the want of sympathies still more intimate and complete; and the gratification of the senses is no longer all that is sought in sexual connexion. It soon becomes a very small part of that profound and complicated sentiment, which we call Love, which is rather the universal thirst for a communion not merely of the senses, but of our whole nature, intellectual, imaginative and sensitive; and which, when individualised, becomes an imperious necessity, only to be satisfied by the complete or partial, actual or supposed, fulfillment of its claims. [13]

Unfortunately, Greek women were uneducated and incapable of intellectual sympathies and, if the representations of Greek art are to be trusted, far less beautiful than Greek men. These latter, Shelley thinks, must have

> corresponded in external form to the models which they have left as specimens of what they were. The firm yet flowing proportions of their forms, the winning unreserve and facility of their manners, the eloquence of their speech, in a language which is itself music and persuasion; their gestures animated at once with the delicacy and the boldness which the perpetual habit of persuading and governing themselves and others; and the poetry of their religious rites, inspired into their

12. "Discourse," p. 407.
13. Ibid., p. 408.

whole being, rendered the youth of Greece a race of beings
something widely different from that of modern Europe.[14]

As a result, it is not surprising that "beautiful persons of
the male sex became the object of that sort of feelings,
which are only cultivated at present as towards females."[15]

Thus, two considerations made Shelley sympathetic to
the idea of love between men in Greek times—the high estimate he put on love per se and his sense of the unique
beauty and charm of the young Greek male. This latter
sensitivity comes out not only in the "Discourse" but also,
perhaps even to a greater degree, in his extensive paragraphs on classical sculpture. Nathaniel Brown, in an acute
and scholarly study of Shelley's sexual psychology, notes
how fully Shelley responded to "the aesthetic ideal of Greek
pederasty."[16] Shelley's extensive manuscript descriptions
of classical statues neglect the Venuses and dwell ecstati-
cally on the Apollos, Ganymedes, and Bacchuses—"those
sweet and gentle figures of adolescent youth in which the
Greeks delighted."[17] Brown summarizes:

> Boy-beauty was the principal object of attraction. Most strik-
> ing in its revelation of this attraction is Shelley's impassioned
> description of a youthful Apollo that he examined in Rome, a
> figure whose androgynous grace particularly insinuated itself
> into his imagination. Recalling another statue he had seen ear-
> lier, he observes that it had been "difficult to conceive any-
> thing more delicately beautiful than the Ganymede"—another
> famous boy-beauty, who had inspired a violent pederastic
> passion in no less a luminary than the father of the gods. But
> the Apollo surpassed it, possessing "a womanish vivacity of
> winning yet passive happiness and yet a boyish inexperience

14.   Ibid., p. 409.
15.   Ibid., p. 410.
16.   *Sexuality and Feminism in Shelley* (Cambridge: Harvard University
Press, 1979), p. 21.
17.   *The Complete Works of Percy Bysshe Shelley*, ed. Roger Ingpen and
Walter E. Peck, vol. 6 (New York: Charles Scribner's Sons, 1929), 328. In
his responses to the beauty of Greek males and Greek sculpture Shelley is
strikingly close to Winckelmann whom he read, studied, and imitated in
his own notes.

exceedingly delightful" (VI. 327). This figure was the poet's "favourite," according to Mary, one that he admired far more than the "quantity of female figures in the attitude of the Venus di Medicis" abounding in Rome. He describes the Apollo as "probably the most consummate personification of loveliness . . . with regard to its entire form that remains to us of Greek Antiquity" (VI. 330).[18]

What are we to make of this? Like Winckelmann, Shelley admired especially the androgynous creations of Hellenistic sculpture and was particularly fascinated by the hermaphrodites. (He himself had characteristics of face and voice which struck observers as markedly feminine.) Were these feelings homoerotic? The question may be unanswerable. We simply do not know exactly where the line is to be drawn between the aesthetic and the erotic. Beauty is notoriously enticing. Can aesthetic appreciation of it exist separate from sexual feeling? Kant, who made the aesthetic exactly that which we do appreciate without desire, thought that it could. On the other hand, Thomas Mann, in *Death in Venice*, dramatizes the almost imperceptible stages by which the one can pass over into the other. Things are further complicated in Shelley's case since some of this sculpture obviously evoked feelings connected with the memories of romantic schoolboy friendships of the sort he celebrated elsewhere in his notebooks.[19]

Shelley's appreciation of young male beauty and of love between males suggests that he might have been attracted

18. *Sexuality and Feminism in Shelley*, p. 21. Brown's references are to the *Complete Works*; see n. 17 above.

19. See, e.g., his detailed description of the figures of two males, identified as Bacchus and his youthful lover, Ampelus, whom he compares to an older and younger boy at school. He dwells on the "flowing fulness and roundness" of Bacchus's "breast and belly, whose lines fading into each other, are continued with a gentle motion as it were to the utmost extremity of his limbs. Like some fine strain of harmony which flows round the soul and enfolds it, and leaves it in the soft astonishment of a satisfaction, like the pleasure of love with one whom we most love, which having taken away desire, leaves pleasure, sweet pleasure" (*Complete Works*, 6:319–20).

by Shakespeare's sonnets, and this was indeed the case. Speaking of English homophobia at the end of the "Discourse," he makes this suggestion: "It may blunt the harshness of censure [of the Greeks] also to reflect that in the golden age of our own literature a certain sentimental attachment towards persons of the same sex was not uncommon. Shakespeare has devoted the impassioned and profound poetry of his sonnets to commemorate an attachment of this kind, which we cannot question was wholly divested of any unworthy alloy." [20]

But if Shelley exalted the romance of same-sex love, he still shared many of the prejudices of Regency England with respect to physical relations. At this point, regrettably, the lack of any contemporary scientific vocabulary for discussing the details of sexual behavior makes his essay obscure; as he puts it: "The laws of modern composition scarcely permit a modest writer to investigate the subject with philosophical accuracy." [21] He is persuaded that Greek men must have found sexual release in some mode other than "the ridiculous and disgusting conceptions which the vulgar have formed on the subject." [22] Presumably, what Shelley means is that his beloved and admired Greeks could not have penetrated each other anally. Shelley describes

20. P. 413. This preoccupation with Shakespeare and Greek love left its mark on Shelley's poetry. The unpublished "Fragments Connected with Epipsychidion" deliberately tease readers by leaving the sex of the person to whom the love poem is addressed ambiguous. Perhaps, Shelley playfully suggests, they will think the "friend or mistress" is a hermaphrodite of the sort fashioned by classical sculptors: "that sweet marble monster of both sexes, / Which looks so sweet and gentle that it vexes / The very soul that the soul is gone / Which lifted from her limbs the veil of stone" (Complete Works, 2:378). Shelley invokes Shakespeare's sonnets and the speech of Socrates in the Symposium as precedents. Apparently, however, he regarded this approach as too provocative since he did not publish the lines. His intention seems to have been to resolve the "riddle" in the fashion of Lara; in a canceled headnote he indicates that this "effeminate looking youth" will turn out to be a woman when she dies (ibid., p. 376).
21. "Discourse," p. 411.
22. Ibid.

this undefined and unacceptable act as "detestable," "operose," and "diabolical." (The *Oxford English Dictionary* defines *operose* as "laborious" or "difficult.") The licentious Romans may have indulged in such enormities, but not the Greeks, who would not have subjected their lovers to such "pain and horror." Rather, Shelley imagines them as finding an outlet for their passions in orgasms that were the "almost involuntary consequences of a state of abandonment in the society of a person of surpassing attractions,"[23] a theory that seems at least strained, if not bizarre. In other writings Shelley freely employs the contemporary rhetoric of abuse when speaking of physical relations between men. Of a statue of "a Satyr making love to a Youth" in the Naples Museum, Shelley remarked to Peacock that only "the expressed life of the sculpture & the inconceivable beauty of the form of the youth overcome ones repugnance to the subject."[24] In the preface to his play *The Cenci*, Shelley calls Count Cenci's homosexual acts "capital crimes of the most enormous and unspeakable kind."[25] These sentiments seem to have been typical of his circle. When Shelley visited Germany with Mary Shelley and Claire Clairmont in 1814, the latter noted in her journal: "I find it is the custom for Men to kiss each other at parting—The Canaille take advantage of this & kiss each other all the day which with their horrid leers & shine has a most loathsome effect."[26]

23. Ibid.
24. December 17 or 18, 1818, *Letters*, 2:63.
25. *Complete Works*, 2:69.
26. September 5, 1814, *Journals of Claire Clairmont*, ed. M. K. Stocking (Cambridge: Harvard University Press, 1968), p. 37. English anxieties over homosexuality seem to have had an effect on public manners in the eighteenth century, as Ivan Bloch points out in his *History of English Sexual Morals*, trans. William H. Fostern (London: Francis Aldor, 1936). Speaking of the Restoration, Thackeray had taken note that not only in the works of "Shadwell, Higgons, Congreve and the comic poets of the time," but also in real life, gentlemen embraced and kissed each other (*The English Humorists* [London: Dent, 1968], p. 68). In 1749, the anonymous author of *Satan's Harvest Home* decried public kissing as an effeminate Italian habit leading to sodomy. By the end of the century, manners had changed. A

What lay behind these feelings of revulsion? In matters of sex Shelley's theoretical position largely accorded with Bentham's utilitarianism: "If happiness be the object of morality, of all human unions and disunions; if the worthiness of every action is to be estimated by the quantity of the pleasurable sensation it is calculated to produce, then the connexion of the sexes [i.e., in a marital union] is so long sacred as it contributes to the comfort of the parties." [27] But Shelley, so unconventional and so much the cosmopolitan philosopher in other matters, simply echoed national prejudice when he made an exception of same-sex relations. In the "Discourse" we can find three explicit rationalizations of his aversion. First, he qualifies his utilitarian stand with the condition that the sex act "ought to be indulged *according to nature.*" Bentham, we may recall, had objected strongly to this approach as totally vitiating any real utilitarian ethic. How Shelley reconciled the traditional concept of "natural law" with his own erotic hedonism is not clear. "A volume of definitions and limitations belong to this maxim," he tells us, but, unfortunately, he decides that they "here may be passed over." [28]

The second implicit basis of objections would presumably be the potentially painful nature of anal intercourse, which contravened Shelley's notion that love should promote the sympathetic sharing of pleasures of body and

---

foreign visitor observed: "No embrace is admitted between men, and laughter would be aroused by so doing, as a bow and hand-shaking are the only forms of civility recognised" (Friedrich Wilhelm von Schütz, *Briefe über London* [Hamburg: Bachmann & Gundermann, 1792], p. 122; cited in Bloch, *History of English Sexual Morals,* p. 398). Foreigners attributed this shyness to sexual self-consciousness: "The kiss of friendship between men is strictly avoided as inclining towards the sin regarded in England as more abominable than any other" (Johann W. J. Bornemann, *Einblicke in England und London im Jahre 1818* [Berlin: E. S. Mittler, 1819], p. 179; cited in ibid.). Continental visitors pointedly warned their compatriots not to kiss men when they traveled in England.

27. "Notes to *Queen Mab,*" in *Complete Works,* 1:141.
28. "Discourse," p. 411.

mind. The third objection to male homosexuality sprang from his radical feminism: "Represent this passion as you will, there is something totally irreconcilable in its cultivation to the beautiful order of social life, to an equal participation in which all human beings have an indefeasible claim, and from which half the human race, by the Greek arrangement, were excluded." [29] This was, of course, the ubiquitous eighteenth-century argument that homosexuality threatened the status of women that Bentham had argued against so strenuously in 1785 and 1814. Shelley, having first assumed that the low status of women in Greek society *caused* male homosexuality, now assumes that male homosexuality *caused* this status: but neither proposition is clearly demonstrable. As admirable and sincere as Shelley's concern for women was, one feels that he appeals to it here because he feels the need to find some liberal-sounding principle to justify an emotional bias.

Near the end of his essay Shelley does appear to deprecate the intensity of English homophobia: "Nothing is at the same time more melancholy and ludicrous than to observe that the inhabitants of one epoch or of one nation harden themselves to all amelioration of their own practices and institutions and soothe their conscience by heaping violent invectives upon those of others; while in the eye of sane philosophy their own are no less deserving of censure." [30] Shelley points especially to prostitution in contemporary England as an example. But his intention is to attack prostitution, not to ameliorate the plight of homosexuals: he makes no mention of the hangings and pilloryings common to his age. This silence on the part of a writer who so often went out of his way to protest strenuously against cruelty and intolerance is remarkable. The poor, Irish Catholics, Greeks subject to the Turks, and women generally all roused the sympathies of the man who, like

29. Ibid., p. 412.
30. Ibid.

the madman in his own *Julian and Maddalo,* conceived himself to be

> a nerve o'er which do creep
> The else unfelt oppressions of this earth.[31]

But on the subject of homosexual oppression he has nothing to say. He cannot have been ignorant: we are left with the uncomfortable conclusion that either insensitivity or fear kept him silent.

But in writing his "Discourse," Shelley at least attempted to challenge the taboo of silence on the subject of Greek love. The publication of his essay and of his unbowdlerized translation of the *Symposium* would have been a significant step forward in nineteenth-century England where Greek culture was held in such high esteem. But Shelley was also well aware of how daring even his modest effort was for his times. When he first undertook the task, he told Peacock: "I am proceeding to employ myself on a discourse, upon the subject of which the Symposium treats, considering the subject with reference to the difference of sentiments respecting it, existing between the Greeks and modern nations; a subject to be handled with that delicate caution which either I cannot or will not practise in other matters, but which here I acknowledge to be necessary."[32] Nonetheless, Shelley did not attempt to publish either work during the remaining four years of his short life. After his death, Mary Shelley wanted to include at least the translation of the *Symposium* in the edition of 1840. But when she consulted Leigh Hunt, she ran into difficulties. Hunt was notoriously open about his free love doctrines but decidedly edgy about a candid rendering of Plato. Mary Shelley was perplexed about how to reply to his warnings:

> You have puzzled me much. What you *said* convinced me. You said: "Do as Mills [*sic*], who has just phrased it so that the

31. *Complete Works,* 3:191.
32. Bagni di Lucca, August 16, 1818, *Letters,* 2:29.

common reader will think common love is meant—the learned alone will know what is meant." . . . Thus I was emboldened to leave it so that our sort of civilized love should be understood—Now you change all this back into friendship—which makes the difficulty as great as ever. I wished in every way to preserve as many of Shelley's OWN *words* as possible. . . . I have altered & omitted as you mention—but I could not bring myself to leave the word *love* out entirely from a treatise on Love.[33]

As a result, the printed version of the translation changed unacceptable words like "lover" into "friend," "men" into "human beings," "youths" into "young people," etc., to veil the historical genders. James Notopoulos's edition records dozens of such bowdlerizations.[34] In one respect the 1840 text was more conservative than Thomas Taylor's version of 1804: the speech of Alcibiades was omitted completely. As for Shelley's essay on Greek homosexuality, its publication was unthinkable. The fragment published in 1840 contained only the opening rhapsody on Greek civilization with no hint of what was to follow. Even in 1930 the ambitious and scholarly Julian edition printed only these paragraphs. The complete "Discourse" was first published in a private limited edition a year later and did not become available to the general reader until Notopoulos included it with a full critical apparatus in *The Platonism of Shelley* in 1949, one hundred and thirty-one years after Shelley had written it.

A few days after finishing the "Discourse," Shelley again met Byron (whom he had not seen for two years) in Venice and complained (in December) to Peacock about the company he kept there. Shortly afterward they began work on their contrasting masterpieces, *Don Juan* and *Prometheus Unbound*. Two years later Byron penned the reminiscences of his Cambridge love affair in his Italian journals. Then, in

33.   October (?), 1839, *The Letters of Mary W. Shelley*, ed. Frederick L. Jones (Norman: University of Oklahoma Press, 1944), 2:508–09.
34.   *Platonism of Shelley*, pp. 541–55.

1822, eleven days after Shelley was drowned in the Bay of Spezia, a grotesque scandal erupted in England that was to have curious repercussions in the Byron circle and tragic consequences elsewhere.

This was the notorious case of the Bishop of Clogher. On the night of July 19, Percy Jocelyn, the Irish bishop with whom Hobhouse had dined in 1811, was apprehended with a guardsman of the First Regiment in the White Lion Tavern near the Haymarket, a well-known place of assignation. Newspaper reports indicate once again that both men would have been in danger of their lives if the police had not protected them from a hostile crowd. Charles Fulke Greville recorded with amusement in his *Memoirs* that the bishop "made a desperate resistance when taken, and if his breeches had not been down they think he would have got away." [35] The bishop was heard that night groaning and praying in his cell; next day he appeared in court with the effects of his struggle visible in the form of a black eye. When he was released on bail, he fled the country, no doubt to the relief of the authorities who can scarcely have relished the prospect of a trial. Greville reported, however, that this did not quite solve the problem: "The greatest dissatisfaction would pervade the publick mind at the escape of the Bishop and the punishment of the Soldier." [36] The bishop's nephew, the third Earl of Roden, then provided bail for the other man, who obligingly disappeared.

Public feeling ran high, especially since the coachman whom the bishop had charged with making false accusations in 1810 had been brutally punished. Several weeks after Clogher's arrest the Archbishop of Canterbury wrote that it was still unsafe for a bishop to appear in the streets of London. Jocelyn's palace in Ireland was pillaged by a mob and the authorities actually took the extreme step of

35. July 30, 1822, *The Greville Memoirs, 1814–1860*, ed. Lytton Strachey and Robert Fulford (London: Macmillan, 1938), 1:126.
36. Ibid.

invoking an archaic medieval law, declaring the bishop an outlaw. Needless to say, the established powers of church and state were acutely embarrassed. On July 25, the *Times* felt obliged to take note of the incident:

> An exposure of monstrous depravity has taken place within these few days, all allusion to which we have hitherto suppressed. Mingled feelings of sorrow, humiliation, and disgust, have been in part the causes of our silence; and the respect we owe to public decency might still have induced us to persevere in our reserve, if we could have thereby checked the horrible tale in its progress to notoriety amongst all ages and both sexes, which we fear it has already attained to. The person accused of being the chief criminal—P. Jocelyn, *Bishop of Clogher*—has, it is affirmed, forfeited his bail, and quitted forever the country which his presence had polluted. Bail in such a case! What sum could be named which the wretch would not have sacrificed? We know not whether to rejoice or grieve that he has fled from justice. We know not whether the trial of such a criminal for such a crime, might not have cost more in the way of corruption, than even his death by law, could have paid in the way of satisfaction to good morals. It is dreadful to remember, that a poor and innocent man was sentenced to transportation from his country on the oath of this mitred reprobate, for only threatening to charge him with that which he now stands (by his flight) confessedly convicted. It is more dreadful to think how the church of God has been scandalized and disgraced.[37]

It is also sobering to note that the *Times* thought "good morals" required a hanging for their satisfaction.

On August 12, 1822, just three weeks after the bishop's arrest, came further startling news: Lord Castlereagh, the British foreign minister, had committed suicide. For a generation Castlereagh had been a leading conservative politician, during an era when the Tories held almost uninterrupted power. An Irish peer from Ulster, he had helped suppress the Rebellion of 1798 and been one of the prime movers behind the Act of Union two years later. During

37. *Times*, July 25, 1822, p. 3, col. 3.

the decade before his death he had led the Tories in the House of Commons. Since the titular prime minister, Lord Liverpool, sat in the Lords and was out of favor with George IV, he was in fact the acting prime minister and Britain's most powerful statesman. In his capacity as foreign minister he had represented England at the Congress of Vienna and supported Metternich in redrawing the map of Europe. Among liberals he was much hated, both for his backing of the Holy Alliance on the Continent and for his support of the local authorities whose orders had led to the "Peterloo" massacre at Manchester in 1819. Byron and Shelley both regarded him as the archetype of reaction. In his "Masque of Anarchy," Shelley, shocked by the deaths in the Midlands, had written:

I met Murder on the way—
He had a mask like Castlereagh.[38]

When Byron heard of Castlereagh's death, he penned a bitter epigram:

So *He* has cut his throat at last! He! who?
The man who cut his country's long ago.[39]

How much Byron knew of the inside story of Castlereagh's death is not clear. Some crucial information remained secret until recent years. Hobhouse may have had some inkling of the truth, for he warned Byron to be cautious in his public comments.[40] The official account given out was that overwork from his arduous duties had led to a mental breakdown in the throes of which Castlereagh had opened his carotid artery while unattended. We now know more of the details. Accusations of homosexuality seem to

38. *Complete Works*, 3:235.
39. *The Works of Lord Byron*, ed. E. H. Coleridge, rev. ed. (London: John Murray, 1905), 7:81.
40. When Hobhouse visited Byron in Italy, Byron told him he had written against Castlereagh; Hobhouse then warned Byron to be careful about "how he touched on his death" (H. Montgomery Hyde, *The Strange Death of Lord Castlereagh* [London: Heinemann, 1959], p. 35).

have played a significant part in the events leading to his death. Evidence for this has come to light in the correspondence of his political colleague and friend the Duke of Wellington and in the letters and diaries of two woman friends, Princess Lieven, wife of the Russian ambassador and Metternich's mistress, and Harriet Arbuthnot, wife of the secretary to the Treasury in the Tory government, who were also his political confidantes. From the letters of Princess Lieven, we learn that Castlereagh, highly distraught, had burst in upon George IV on August 9 and informed the astonished king that he was a fugitive from justice. Castlereagh's agitation seemed doubly alarming in a man noted for his courage and the calm, almost inhuman, imperturbability of his public demeanor. When the incredulous king asked why Castlereagh believed he was in jeopardy, he replied, to the king's amazement: "I am accused of the same crime as the Bishop of Clogher"[41] and declared that "a warrant was out against him & that he must fly the country!"[42] This remarkable conversation was reported to Princess Lieven by Lady Conyngham, the king's mistress, who also told her that Castlereagh had shown the king two blackmail letters, one of which threatened to reveal some adulterous intrigues to his wife while the other "concerned a more terrible subject." He also showed the letters to the attorney-general and the solicitor-general. Princess Lieven thought the latter accusation had had a devastating effect on her friend. "This second letter," she wrote to Metternich later, "sent him off his head."[43]

The coroner's inquest found that Castlereagh had committed suicide while insane; such a verdict, supported by testimony from his servants and his physician, allowed the

41. August 12, 1822, *The Private Letters of Princess Lieven to Prince Metternich, 1820–1826*, ed. Peter Quennell, trans. Peter Quennell and Dilys Powell (New York: E. P. Dutton, 1938), p. 189.

42. August 29, 1822, *The Journal of Mrs. Arbuthnot*, ed. Francis Bamford and the Duke of Wellington (London: Macmillan, 1950), 1:183.

43. August 14, 1822, *Private Letters*, p. 194.

government to give him a state funeral in Westminster Abbey, where the corpse was jeered. But what had really happened? Were the blackmail allegations of homosexuality, which undoubtedly existed, based on fact or were they inventions? The one detailed critical examination of the evidence, Montgomery Hyde's *The Strange Death of Lord Castlereagh*, argues for the latter view. Hyde's study is an extremely interesting and carefully written analysis. Like Castlereagh, an Ulster Tory, Hyde took the lead in modern efforts to rehabilitate the reputation of his fellow countryman as a statesman and diplomat by publishing in 1933 a favorable account of his early career. In the course of his research he uncovered evidence about his suicide, which he did not include in this first book. But Hyde, despite his ultraconservative constituency, was also a courageous spokesman for the sodomy law reform proposed by the Wolfenden Committee twenty-four years later. One of the most reiterated arguments for this reform was that the historic British statute gave dangerous power to blackmailers. Publishing *The Strange Death* in 1959, two years after the committee had made its recommendation, Hyde revealed that the most famous suicide in British history had been preceded by just such a blackmail attempt. But he does not take the position that Castlereagh was actually involved in homosexual relations. Rather, he endorses the "explanation" of blackmail set forth by the lawyer-historian John Richardson in his *Recollections* of 1856. In this book Richardson cited an unnamed informant who claimed as his source an unnamed nobleman close to Castlereagh. According to the latter, Castlereagh had been lured to a brothel by a man disguised as a woman and surprised in a private room by blackmailers who demanded money. Later, Richardson tells us, the men conducted a war of nerves against their victim. "Day after day did these miscreants station themselves by the iron railings with which the inclosure of St. James's-square is surrounded, opposite the windows of the Marquis, and take the opportunity, by signs and motions whenever he appeared, to let him know that they had not yet forgotten the scene which they had contrived."[44] Richardson's unidentified nobleman (whom Hyde guesses might have been Lord Clanwilliam, Castlereagh's secretary) told his informant that Castlereagh did not have the resolution to prosecute these extortionists because he feared the effect of the disclosures on his wife. But, more likely, another consideration prevailed: after the Clogher case, charges by men in power that they had been falsely accused of homosexuality were likely to be met with derisive skepticism. The blackmailers, whoever they were, had cleverly chosen a moment when public feeling would stymie any such counterattack.

Hyde regards Richardson's account as the answer to the "mystery" of Castlereagh's death. He quotes another commentator: "It is . . . only fair to adopt the version which receives credence to this day from the great Party to which he belonged, namely, that he had been deliberately entrapped."[45] But why should the general reader accept a statement that gives no explicit sources or authorities and makes its appeal on party grounds? Is there any evidence that Castlereagh may have indeed been, as his contemporaries would have put it, "guilty"? It is interesting that Princess Lieven, who was certainly sympathetic to Castlereagh, thought the unwonted perturbation, acute paranoia, and occasional delusions he suffered from in his last days were the result of guilt. "At times," the princess wrote, "I think he was mad. Terrible remorse was preying on his conscience. But he was not mad when he killed himself"[46]— that is, she rejected the coroner's verdict. Moreover, Castlereagh made explicit confessions to two people. Dr. Bank-

44. *Recollections, Political, Literary, Dramatic, and Miscellaneous of the Last Half-Century* (London: C. Mitchell, 1856), 1:287.
45. *Strange Death of Lord Castlereagh*, p. 184. Hyde is quoting William Toynbee, *Glimpses of the Twenties* (London: Archibald Constable, 1909), p. 128.
46. August 13, 1822, *Private Letters*, p. 192.

head, the physician who had attended him in his last days, told the Duke of Wellington that despite his testimony to that effect at the inquest, Castlereagh was not mad and had confessed to him that he had actually committed the crimes of which he had been accused, that is, that he had indeed been involved in some kind of homosexual activity. At first, the duke told Harriet Arbuthnot, he had believed this version of the case. But he later found it inaccurate as to "two facts" and took the position that Bankhead was simply trying to defend himself against the very harsh criticism he had received for not watching his patient more carefully.[47] Unfortunately, we do not know what the "two facts" were or why Wellington chose to discount them. But it is significant that Castlereagh's wife also received similar confessions, which she discussed with the duke two years after the suicide. Though the duke advised her, "You ought to attribute what he told you to one of the unfortunate delusions of the moment,"[48] we may wonder if this was not a counsel of prudence, aimed at hushing up a scandal that would have reflected on a Tory leader. Certainly, Castlereagh suffered from some delusions at the time—there was, for instance, no warrant for his arrest, but the most reasonable course seems to be to regard the possibility of homosexual involvements on Castlereagh's part as at least an open question. Indeed, the weight of the evidence, when all the details are considered, points, I think, to his actual guilt.[49]

47.   August 15, 1823, *Journal of Mrs. Arbuthnot*, 1:253. There is no indication whether the "two facts" discredited Bankhead's story or Castlereagh's. Possibly Wellington was using the term *fact* in its legal sense to refer to a completed act of sodomy, as opposed to the "attempt."

48.   Letter of March 3, 1824; cited in Hyde, *Strange Death of Lord Castlereagh*, p. 180.

49.   Castlereagh's more recent biographers have followed Hyde. C. J. Bartlett discounts the idea that the blackmail had any basis in fact, citing Wellington's testimony, but leaves the door open. "Even if [it had], it would still not be proven that this was the only cause of the suicide" (*Castlereagh* [New York: Charles Scribner's Sons, 1966], p. 263). John W. Derry, whose study, *Castlereagh* (London: Allen Lane, 1976), is a political defense, accepts the Hyde–Richardson theory (pp. 227–28). Wendy Hinde

As a philosophical radical, Bentham had waged what might be termed a closet war on English homophobia, denouncing the nation's sodomy law as an instrument by which the "ruling few" extended their power over the "subject many." By contrast, popular radicalism, in the wake of the Clogher case, could not resist using the issue of homosexuality to embarrass the church. This neatly reversed the situation in modern America where antihomosexualism is a popular stance on the far right rather than the left. But attitudes toward homosexuality have always been volatile in moments of high political tension. During revolutions antihomosexual laws may be perceived as a form of oppression on the part of the *ancien régime* (as they were in France in 1791, and in the first, pre-Stalinist, stages of the Russian Revolution), or homosexuality may, by contrast, be seen as a decadent vice of the dominant class, aristocratic or bourgeois, and may be vigorously suppressed by the new government, as in Castro's Cuba.[50]

Class antagonism as an occasion for homophobia was one source Bentham failed to analyze in his notes. But there is no question that it stoked the fires of animosity and raised the level of intolerance under George IV. The ruling class, by enforcing the laws with harsh severity, fortified their claim to power by setting themselves up as pil-

---

adopts Wellington's views of Bankhead's revelations but does not mention Castlereagh's confessions to his wife (*Castlereagh* [London: Collins, 1981], p. 280); Hinde thinks his self-accusations were the result of delusions.

50. This paradox can also be seen in Wilhelmine Germany. In 1898 August Bebel, leader of the Social Democratic party, spoke out against Germany's sodomy law in the Reichstag whereas other leftists, as in the Krupp scandal of 1902, used charges of homosexuality to discredit the government. But events contemporaneous with the Cuban antihomosexual campaign of the mid-1960s point up the irony even more sharply; at the same time that large numbers of Cuban homosexuals were being harshly treated in rehabilitation work camps on the grounds that homosexuality was intrinsically counterrevolutionary, a Florida legislator who had instituted a witchhunt against communist teachers in state colleges in Florida turned his campaign into a campaign against homosexual teachers, as a kind of related threat. No communists were found, but many lesbian and male homosexual teachers lost their positions.

lars of morality. But since homosexuality has never been confined to any one class or political faction, they also made themselves vulnerable, and the Clogher affair presented a unique opportunity to the radical press, which, understandably if regrettably, made the most of it. The issue was taken up with greatest vigor by William Benbow. An agitator and minor publisher, the Manchester-born Benbow, a former shoemaker, had been a colleague of William Cobbett in publishing a reforming newspaper, the *Political Register*, until the two men quarreled. He later came into association with Hobhouse and Sir Francis Burdett at radical meetings in connection with Queen Caroline's trial in 1820. Like many radical publishers Benbow had pirated both *Don Juan* and Shelley's *Queen Mab*. He saw Byron as a symbol of radical protest and ironically (in view of the issue he chose to raise) selected as his publishing emblem the sign of the "Byron's Head," presumably a sign with Byron's head painted on it to advertise his printing shop and bookstore. In 1823 he was inspired by the Clogher case to publish a violent diatribe against the church under the title *The Crimes of the Clergy, or the Pillars of Priest-Craft Shaken.*[51]

Though Benbow's book was a compendium of every kind of clerical scandal, it placed a special emphasis on men who had been exposed as homosexuals and forced to flee the country. He took note of the hanging of John Atherton, Bishop of Waterford, in Dublin in 1640 and dwelt at length on the Clogher affair. But the special interest of his book lies in its revelation of how many minor clergy were exiled in Byron's age. He mentions the Reverend John Fenwick of Northumberland, who in 1797 had absconded to Naples, "a country where such monsters are tolerated, and even esteemed"; a Parson Walker of Chichester, a man of "most exemplary character" who was revered as a saint before he was unmasked as an "Unnatural Monster"; the

---

51.   The title-page is dated 1822, but the book contains material from the next year. I am indebted to Professor Hugh Luke for calling my attention to this rare volume and lending me his copy.

Reverend V. P. Littlehales, a learned prebendary of South-well Cathedral and a member of Parliament, who in 1812 had, like Parson Walker, fled to America ("that sanctuary of crime, and hot bed of guilt"); and several contemporary cases, including Richard Milles, who had forfeited bail in 1823, and Thomas Jephson of St. John's College, Cambridge, who had recently been arrested and escaped to the Continent.[52] From Benbow's account it would appear that the clergy were rarely arrested; more often they were simply warned to leave the country. Benbow, who had himself been sent to prison by informers from the Society for the Suppression of Vice for publishing obscene books, took an especially jaundiced view of that organization. When William Wilberforce, the Society's founder, held up Sparta as a puritanical society worthy of emulation, Benbow could not resist the chance for some homophobic spite. In Sparta, he pointed out, Lycurgus's laws "permitted 'the great only' to practice a crime for which we have not a name, and which is with us chiefly confined to the Parsons of the church of England, composing the Members of the Vice Society, of which Mr. W. is a leader."[53] With more wit, Benbow might have noted that the "lurking holes," from which the Society's predecessor, the Society for the Reformation of Manners, had sought to ferret out "miscreants," had often turned out to be pulpits.

One might have wished that Byron had had the decency

---

52. These cases appear in Benbow's *Crimes of the Clergy* as follows: Atherton, pp. 25–26; Clogher, pp. 41–44; Fenwick, pp. 8–14; Walker, pp. 229–30; Littlehales, pp. 238–39; Milles, pp. 138–40; Jephson, pp. 239–40. Benbow also mentions a Reverend Mr. Mills of Bath, who had been arrested but not tried when the book went to press (p. 40). Of Clogher, Benbow remarks: "At the day of judgment there must be more jostling and shoving than Lord Byron describes, if such a fellow slips into heaven and deprives the fire of hell of such a deserving faggot" (p. 44). Benbow's language raises the intriguing question whether or not this is an early use of a contemporary slang term. To date its use has not been authenticated before the twentieth century, despite the much-cited theory (historically impossible) that it derives from the inquisitorial practice of burning homosexuals at the stake.

53. Ibid., p. 137.

not to engage in popular gay-baiting, but Clogher presented too tempting a target for his anti-Tory partisanship. In a letter from Pisa dated August 8, 1822, he asked Thomas Moore impishly: "What do you think of your Irish bishop?"[54] In his highly political preface to Cantos VI–VIII of *Don Juan* Byron not only complained about Castlereagh's state funeral; to embarrass the Tories, he also linked the two scandals in a double reference to "suicide Statesmen" and "heterodox Prelates." In a note, Byron repeats a lame joke defining orthodoxy as *"my doxy"* and heterodoxy as *"another man's doxy."* Then, playing on the innuendo in the word *doxy* (which meant a paramour), he comments slyly: "A Prelate of the present day has discovered, it seems, a *third* kind of doxy, which has not greatly exalted in the eyes of the elect that which Bentham calls 'Church-of-Englandism.'"[55] The editors of the variorum *Don Juan* offer no hint as to the butt of this allusion—the reference is undoubtedly to Clogher. Though the thrust is comparatively mild for Byron, he hardly mends matters by declaring "I have no wish to trample on the dishonoured or the dead" after doing just that.[56]

In stanza 76 of Canto VIII, Byron makes another reference to Clogher in his account of Juan's adventures in eastern Europe. Byron describes a Russian reversal in the war with Turkey as

. . . being taken by the tail—a taking
Fatal to bishops as to soldiers.

Mary Shelley, who had been copying the manuscript, apparently refused to write out these lines; the editors of the

54. *BJL*, 9:191. Judging from the asterisks that follow, Byron seems to have dwelt at length on the bishop's case, presumably in a series of jocularities that Moore excised.

55. Byron's note of 1823, *Notes on the Variorum Edition*, Vol. 4 of *Byron's "Don Juan,"* ed. Willis W. Pratt, 2nd ed. (Austin: University of Texas Press, 1971), p. 143.

56. *Byron's "Don Juan": A Variorum Edition*, ed. Truman Guy Steffan and Willis W. Pratt, 2nd ed. (Austin: University of Texas Press, 1971), 3:5.

variorum *Don Juan* note that they are in Byron's hand.[57] Again, another projected stanza in Canto XI, held up to obloquy "Clogher's bishop" who "sullies / The law, at least until the Bench revert to true / Plain simple fornication." Byron had the grace to cancel this passage.[58] Perhaps Hobhouse's warnings about playing with fire had inspired caution. Conservative journalists would have been glad of any chance, after the government's embarrassment, to expose a "sodomite" in the liberal-radical camp. The exacerbated situation caused by this scandal may well have increased Hobhouse's nervousness about the memoirs he knew Byron had written and entrusted to Thomas Moore. We shall have occasion to return to this question when we consider the fate of this famous manuscript.

57. Ibid., p. 150.
58. Ibid., p. 314. This stanza was originally numbered 76.

· 9 ·

Love and Death in Missolonghi

The composition of *Don Juan*, though the work proceeded apace and grew in length to more than sixteen cantos, did not absorb all of Byron's energies in Italy. Eventually he grew bored and restless. His affair with Countess Teresa Guiccioli, which had begun passionately in the summer of 1819, had now subsided into quasi-domesticity. When it commenced, Byron had been thirty-one, Teresa twenty, and her husband fifty-four. At first Byron fell into the prescribed role of *cavalier servente*, as the public escort and all-but-openly-acknowledged lover of the young wife. Finally, Teresa insisted on a separation, and an agreement was reached with the count. When in the course of time the count sued to force his young wife to return to him, public opinion was on the side of the lovers, and the pope refused to grant his request. This turn of events could only have delighted Byron when he thought of his isolated position in England after his matrimonial troubles.

Nevertheless, the victory had its price, and Byron must have felt even more deeply committed than he would have been by another marriage. It was part of his code that a man could not desert a woman who had left a husband for his sake, her position being a much more anomalous one than an abandoned wife's. Fortunately, Byron and Teresa were temperamentally as well as passionately suited to each other. Her sense of humor and her interest in literature made her a congenial companion. Inevitably, however, there were strains; both were plagued by jealousy, and Teresa, on her part, was discomfited by the mockery and cynicism of *Don Juan*. But after four years of a marriage in all but name, Byron felt dissatisfied with his role as household pet. By that time Teresa's father, Count Ruggero Gamba, and her brother, Pietro, had become deeply involved in the struggle for Italian freedom. Byron in turn was caught up by the cause. When the Gambas were exiled after the failure of the Carbonari revolt of 1821, Byron followed them to Pisa and Genoa where he was briefly reunited with Shelley. After Shelley's drowning, Edward John Trelawny, the Cornish adventurer who had been a member of their circle at Pisa, urged him to help the Greeks in their new war of independence. Byron accepted the challenge as an opportunity to give meaning to a life become dull and empty.

The London Committee for Greek independence had been founded in March 1823. Jeremy Bentham was a founding member and kind of patron of this association of English philhellenes, which included many of his disciples. John Bowring, Bentham's future editor and biographer, was its secretary and in this capacity had extensive dealings with Byron, who began to think seriously about going to Greece in April. He hesitated for two reasons—Teresa and his doubts about whether he could be of use. On his first visit he had been delighted by the climate, the beauty of the people and the landscape, and the freedom from English constraints. But he had formed no very high opinion of the Greek national character and had doubts about the Greeks' ability to wage a successful war against the Turks, desirable as he was convinced their freedom would be. In 1823, the rebellion, only two years old, had not yet fully caught the imagination of Europe. To date, only a few idealists and a motley crew of harum-scarum adventurers, at loose ends after the Napoleonic wars, represented western Europe in the struggle. Rival chieftains on the peninsula showed little inclination to support a central government, and it was not clear whether the country could be united. Byron, on his part, was looked upon as a poet who had helped inspire the new wave of philhellenism; he had, however, no practical experience in military matters, and Teresa strongly opposed his leaving Italy.

But Byron saw a unique chance to do some lasting good and, despite misgivings, decided to commit himself. Since he did not want to become immediately embroiled with the feuding factions in Greece, he sailed first to the island of Cephalonia, off the west coast, in order to familiarize himself with affairs on the mainland. From there he wrote candidly to Charles Barry, his banker in Geneva, about his desire to avoid any amorous intrigue that might have political implications:

> It is not of their ill-usage . . . but of *their good* treatment that I am apprehensive—for it is difficult not to allow our private impressions to predominate—and if these Gentlemen *have* any undue interest and discover my weak side—viz.—a propensity to be governed—and were to set a pretty woman, or a clever woman about me—with a turn for political or any other sort of intrigue—why—they would make a fool of me—no very difficult matter probably even without such an intervention. But if I can keep passion—at least that passion—out of the question—(which may be the more easy, as I left my heart in Italy), they will not weather me with quite so much facility.[1]

Byron's determination to keep clear of feminine influence in Greece was maintained. The last half-year of his life was the only period that seems to have been womanless. But, as we shall see, he did not entirely succeed in keeping "passion out of the question." During his second visit to Greece, as during his first, it was his own sex that engaged his heart and troubled his equanimity. Had Byron foreseen this? Was a revival of the homosexual side of his nature one of the things that contributed to his restlessness in Italy and made a return to Greece seem attractive to him? We have little evidence. There is nothing corresponding to his Falmouth letter to Matthews, and he was no longer writing openly to Hobhouse on erotic subjects.

---

1. October 25, 1823, *BLJ*, 11:54–55; "weather" here means "to get the better of."

But Byron was incapable of living without intimate personal ties of some sort. In earlier days, he had written that his heart always alighted "on the nearest perch." Now he was to repeat the pattern of his boyhood and see patronage blossoming into love—in this case an especially frustrating and unsatisfactory love affair. Once again events cast him in the role of protector, a role which, when young people were concerned, made him peculiarly susceptible. This development came about as a result of a sight-seeing visit to Ithaca. There he took under his protection a formerly well-to-do but now impoverished Greek widow and her family. Madame Chalandrutsanos and her three young daughters had fled from Patras (where Byron's two fevers had raged in 1810) to escape the ravages of the Greek war. When Byron's largesse became known to her fifteen-year-old son, Lukas, he too left the Morea (as southern Greece was then called), where he had been fighting the Turks, to join Byron at Argostoli on the island of Cephalonia. It was Lukas who was to be the center of Byron's emotional life during his last months in Greece.

Apparently Byron found the Chalandrutsanos family somewhat importunate. Like most Greeks of their day, military or civilian, they regarded the English lord who had devoted his life and fortune to their cause as a kind of Midas and all-encompassing providence. Byron's account books of the period, which Doris Langley Moore has excerpted and published, list repeated expenditures on their behalf. By November 2, 1823, Byron's tight-fisted steward, Lega Zambelli, had paid out nearly thirty-three dollars for clothes and goods "for the Moreote family." A few days later Byron complained that Madame Chalandrutsanos was asking too much of him. He wrote in Italian to Zambelli that the "family will not receive from *this* day on more than six dollars a month to maintain the ailing mother."[2] The girls, he suggested, might go into service. He com-

2.   *LBAR*, p. 395.

plained that he had already provided more than one hundred and twenty dollars since he had befriended them in August and that four dollars a month was the standard pay for a Greek soldier, who usually had to provide for a larger family than theirs. It was a week after this that Lukas and a younger brother made their way to the Ionian Islands.

When, after some four months on Cephalonia, Byron at last left for the mainland, Lukas, or Luke, as Byron preferred to call him, accompanied the expedition. Their voyage to Missolonghi past the Turkish fleet proved unexpectedly difficult. The shallow-bottomed "mistico" they sailed in was intercepted by a Turkish vessel and chased back from the approaches to Missolonghi to an inlet at Scrofes. From there, on the last day of 1823, Byron wrote to Colonel Leicester Stanhope, the other representative of the London Committee, who had proceeded him: "I am uneasy at being here; not so much on my own account as on that of a Greek boy with me, for you know what his fate would be; and I would sooner cut him in pieces and myself too than have him taken out by those barbarians."[3] Both Greeks and Turks routinely massacred prisoners, and Byron may also have feared that Lukas would be sexually assaulted because of his youthful good looks. Two days later, Byron wrote from Dragomestri that he had landed the boy at Scrofes "as Luke's life was in most danger," with some money and a letter for Colonel Stanhope.[4] It was Byron's intention that Lukas and a companion would proceed overland to Missolonghi since he feared their boat might yet be captured by the Turks. For whatever reason—the route may have turned out to be more difficult or dangerous than Byron had imagined or he may not have wanted to stay separated from his patron—Lukas did not proceed eastward to Missolonghi as planned but instead made his way

3. *BLJ*, 11:87; see also the letter to Charles Hancock, January 2, 1824, 11:90.
4. To Henry Muir, *BLJ*, 11:88.

north to Dragomestri and rejoined Byron there. For he was once again on the "mistico" when the ship again passed the Scrofes rocks. Bad weather made shipwreck seem imminent. At one point on the voyage Byron assured Lukas "I could save both him and myself—without difficulty (though he can't swim), as the water though deep was not very rough."[5] Though the ship did strike the rocks, it sprang only a small leak, and they got safely to their destination. But Lukas's safety on the trip had caused Byron great anxiety, and these dangers were to remain vivid in his recollection.

Byron's arrival at Missolonghi was his one triumph in the entire Greek campaign. A band played, and the assembled crowd in their colorful costumes must have looked something like an opera chorus. Splendid in his own plumed helmet and red uniform, Byron basked in a brief moment of glory as the Greeks, primed with stories of his wealth and reputation, hailed him as a messiah. But the situation soon revealed its grimmer side. Glowingly idealistic accounts of the Greek struggle in liberal journals had lured scores of young men, first from Germany and Italy, and later from France and England, who later returned in poverty and rags to their own lands to warn others of Greek perfidy and incompetence and to decry their own quixotism. But even for someone steeled like Byron to a more realistic view of the struggle, Missolonghi was a sore trial. The weather was dismally wet and the town a depressing mudhole. The Suliote warriors he hoped to lead against the Turks were an especially galling disappointment. They proved riotous and mutinous and keen only in demanding their pay. When Byron saw a good prospect of capturing the nearby fortress of Lepanto, they balked. He finally dismissed most of them in despair. His position was a lonely one. Prince Mavrocordatos, the titular head of the Greek government, also quartered in the town, was intelli-

5. To Charles Hancock, January 13, 1824, *BLJ*, 11:92.

gent and companionable, but Byron, to avoid identifying himself too closely with any faction, felt it necessary to keep some distance between them.

Byron's one natural ally on the scene was Colonel Stan- hope, the other representative of the London Committee, from whose money-raising efforts the Greeks expected much. Stanhope, like Byron, was an aristocrat; a younger brother of the fourth Earl of Harrington, he succeeded in later years to the title. He was also a Benthamite radical. In the reformist ferment of the post-Napoleonic era, Bentham had been invited to write constitutions and laws for Spain and several new republics in Central and South America. Buoyed by these successes, he and his disciples looked to Greece, rather unrealistically, as fertile soil for the testing of their social theories, which lay great stress on enlight- ened laws, education, and freedom of the press. Byron, more pragmatic, wanted to concentrate on the military struggle, and, always impatient of philosophical theoriz- ing, reacted irritably toward Stanhope's doctrinaire side. There is a story that when the colonel presented the poet with a copy of Bentham's treatise *Springs of Action*, Byron dashed it to the floor with the remark: "What does the old fool know of springs of action—my —— has more spring to it."[6] Byron, not foreseeing Kinsey (or knowing Ben- tham's notes), thought that only a man of the world could appreciate the realities of human sexuality. Another point of contention was Stanhope's energetic campaign to found newspapers in Greece. Byron feared that a press controlled by the radical exiles gathered there would alienate the Eu- ropean powers, whose neutrality he considered essential if the Turks were to be defeated. He suppressed some arti- cles he felt were inflammatory. Stanhope accused him of practicing censorship in the name of freedom.

Amidst these frustrations and discords, Byron's rela- tions with Lukas did not run smoothly. His official status in

6. *BB*, 3:1136, citing Hobhouse's notes of August 1824.

Byron's polyglot household was that of a page. He also held a kind of military rank: Byron had provided him with a handsome Mainote outfit, gilt pistols, and a troop of soldiers to command. Among his prescribed duties was reading modern Greek, or Romaic, with Byron for half an hour every morning. Byron bought Lukas some Greek grammars for this purpose. When we recall the erotic coloring Byron's recollections gave to his Italian lessons with Nicolo Giraud, we may wonder if Byron entertained hopes that his privacy might facilitate a more intimate relation. A contemporary English writer commented on Greek manners of the time:

> The modern Greeks, as living under the government of the Turks, naturally follow their usages. If, therefore, they indulge in antiphysical pleasures, it might be said that they owe it to the example of their masters; however, in a Greek grammar, printed at Vienna some years ago, there are some *Golden Rules for Youth, by Phocylides*, in hexameter verse, in which there is a line shewing that the thing was at least spoken of familiarly to and before young persons, and seems to have been forbidden, in the same strain as we are accustomed to hear fornication forbidden, and probably with the same effect.[7]

Byron's Suliote warriors, who were Albanian Christians, would have looked on an older soldier's partiality for a beautiful young boy with the same sympathy as their predecessors, the Dorian Greeks. One of the members of Byron's entourage, the Dutch physician, Julius Millingen, in his *Memoirs of the Affairs of Greece*, has left a vivid description of Greek chieftains parading with formal pomp in Missolonghi, accompanied by their *psychouioi* (or "soul-sons") and "three or more lads handsomely dressed with their loose tresses floating over the shoulders, bearers of their master's silver-cup, pipe, and tobacco-bag."[8] As for Lukas, he was probably familiar enough with these traditions not

7. *Don Leon*, n. 30, in *A Homosexual Emancipation Miscellany, c. 1835–1952* (1866; rpt. New York: Arno Press, 1975), p. 72.
8. (London: John Rodwell, 1831), pp. 69–70.

to be shocked or surprised by Byron's attentions, however incapable he was of responding emotionally.

Byron continued to make generous gifts. A visitor to his headquarters in January 1824 noticed that "his page was a young Greek, dressed as an Albanian or a Mainote, with very handsomely chased arms in his girdle."[9] On January 18 Zambelli recorded under the heading "Lukas's expenses by order of Milord," the sum of fifty-five dollars and then eleven more dollars for a "fascia" or scarf.[10] On the twenty-first and twenty-fifth there were further substantial outlays. But occasionally Byron felt Lukas's demands were excessive. Byron expressed his irritation in his instructions to Zambelli: "Tea is not a Greek beverage—therefore Master Lukas may drink Coffee instead—or water—or nothing.— The pay of the said Lukas will be five dollars a month paid like the others of the household. He will eat with the Suliots—or where he pleases."[11] By this time the emotional strain of the one-sided affair had begun to tell. Byron had written no poetry since leaving Italy, but the accumulating tension demanded some kind of release. It found expression in the famous lines, "On This Day I Complete My Thirty-Sixth Year." For many decades this poem was believed to be his last. For this reason and because it reads like a testament, it inevitably became one of the best known and most anthologized of Byron's lyrics. But only since the appearance of Marchand's biography and Doris Langley Moore's researches has its context been fully appreciated.

Among the party of philhellenes who followed Byron to Greece was Teresa's brother, Pietro Gamba. It is he who has given us the fullest information about its composition. In his book, *Lord Byron's Last Journey to Greece*, Gamba tells us that on January 22 Byron

9. James Forrester, R.N., quoted in *LLB*, p. 509.
10. *LBAR*, p. 403.
11. Ibid.

came from his bedroom into the apartment where Colonel Stanhope and some other friends were assembled, and said, with a smile, "You were complaining, the other day, that I never write any poetry now:—this is my birthday, and I have just finished something, which, I think, is better than what I usually write." He then produced those noble and affecting verses on his own birthday, which were afterwards found written in his journal.[12]

We may assume that this dramatic announcement prompted those present to ask Byron to recite his poem and that he condescended to do so.

The first stanza must have made his auditors uneasy:

'Tis time this heart should be unmoved
  Since others it hath ceased to move,
Yet though I cannot be beloved
  Still let me love.

Was this a personal confession? If it was—and Byron, who liked sensations, probably projected enough of his considerable histrionic energy into the lines to make it hard for them to regard the poem as anything but personal—who, they must have wondered, was the object of his infatuation? Obviously, he was not referring to Teresa: her unwavering devotion was well known. And there was no other woman on the scene.

My days are in the yellow leaf
  The flowers and fruits of love are gone—
The worm, the canker and the grief
  Are mine alone.

The fire that on my bosom preys
  Is lone as some Volcanic Isle,
No torch is kindled at its blaze
  A funeral pile!

The hope, the fear, the jealous care
  The exalted portion of the pain

12. (London: John Murray, 1825), p. 125.

And power of Love, I cannot share
But wear the chain.

Critics have objected to the strained rhetoric of these lines and to the worn-out Shakespearean metaphors. Byron himself had mocked poets who could not resist "the volcano." But such points of criticism would hardly have concerned his first hearers. The thought uppermost in their minds must have been that Byron was now declaring publicly his love for Lukas, of which they were by this time well aware. We can imagine their reaction. Here was the man on whom they relied to lead them in a difficult and dangerous situation, parading, with typical panache, "the pageant of his bleeding heart" in a way calculated to create the maximum of scandal. James Hamilton Browne tells us that on the ship that took him to Greece Byron had played a cruel joke: he had persuaded the Scottish captain that one of his Greek passengers was, as one of his shipboard companions put it, "addicted to certain horrible propensities, too common in the Levant," in order to enjoy the skipper's consternation and the passenger's puzzled discomfiture.[13] Was Byron now presenting himself as one of these despised wretches? In the Thyrza lyrics Byron had disguised the object of his love by changing his gender. Such a ruse, under the circumstances, would hardly have taken in his Missolonghi associates. It must have been a relief to hear what followed and to realize that Byron, though he had half-lifted the mask, had not irrevocably exposed himself and meant to put this involvement behind him:

But 'tis not *thus*—and 't is not *here*
Such thoughts should shake my soul, nor *now*

13. James Hamilton Browne, "Voyage from Leghorn to Cephalonia with Lord Byron, and a Narrative of a Visit, in 1823, to the Seat of War in Greece," *Blackwood's Edinburgh Magazine* 35 (January 1834):65. Browne treats the episode as an uproarious practical joke that greatly amused Byron.

Where glory decks the hero's bier
Or binds his brow.

The Sword—the Banner—and the Field
Glory and Greece, around us see!
The Spartan borne upon his shield
Was not more free!

Awake! (*not* Greece—She *is* awake!)
Awake my spirit—think through *whom*
Thy Life blood tracks its parent lake
And then strike home!

These lines, it must be admitted, are remarkably forced
and artificial. Their very jerkiness suggests a man desperately calling himself to order, straightening his back, and
thrusting his chin out. So great is his desperation that Byron even goes to the length of invoking his family's tradition of military service as aristocrats. However, this somewhat snobbish gesture must have reassured his listeners
since it directed attention away from the theme of Greek
love to the theme of Greek freedom. But Byron, to complete the poem and resolve the tensions set up by its two
disparate parts, felt bound to return to the amorous theme
he had introduced so alarmingly in the opening lines:

Tread those reviving passions down
Unworthy Manhood;—unto thee
Indifferent should the smile or frown
Of Beauty be.

Obviously the "reviving passions" refer to the love of
boys that had obsessed him in his youth and which he now
deprecates. Though Byron's audience knew there was no
woman in his life, the vagueness of the language would
have pleased them—at least it avoided too open a confession as to where his feelings were involved. And the reference to the "smile or frown / Of beauty," though undoubtedly a reference to Lukas (whom even so down-to-earth an
observer as Byron's munitions expert, William Parry, de-

scribed as "of a most prepossessing appearance")[14] would
have struck them as susceptible to a conventional interpretation by conventional readers.

> If thou regret'st thy youth, why *live*?
>   The Land of honourable Death
> Is here—up to the Field! and give
>   Away thy Breath.
>
> Seek out—less often sought than found,
>   A Soldier's Grave—for thee the best,
> Then look around and choose thy ground
>   And take thy Rest.[15]

Byron's "regret" for his youth might at first appear to refer
to his earlier pederastic love affairs. More likely, however,
Marchand is correct in assuming that what concerned Byron at the time was the effect of age on his own beauty. His
increasing baldness, his tendency to fat, and his decaying
teeth all depressed him. No doubt he felt that they made
him markedly less attractive than he had been to the boys
in the convent fourteen years earlier. These reflections
must have been discouraging to a man who was convinced
that the best of life was over at twenty-three and who had
thought of suicide even at that age. There was a difference,
however: his earlier urge to self-destruction was connected
with satiety, this one with frustration. His decision to make
his death a political gesture inevitably reminds us of another bisexual writer, the Japanese novelist Yukio Mi-
shima, who also subscribed to a warrior's code and disliked the idea of old age and decrepitude. Here Byron
congratulates himself that one act—self-immolation on the
battlefield—will at the same time serve a cause he is committed to and provide a way out of a personal dilemma. As

14. *The Last Days of Lord Byron* (London: Knight & Lacey, 1825), p. 16.
15. I am indebted to Professor Jerome McGann for providing the text
of this poem and the texts of "Last Words on Greece," and "Love and
Death" as they will appear in the last volume of *The Complete Poetical
Works*.

a poem, Byron's oft-reprinted lines are not successful—
they are too theatrical, a kind of literary counterpart to David's painting *The Oath of the Horatii*. But as a personal record of a man under an almost intolerable strain who is trying desperately to pull himself together, they have an
inescapable poignancy.

As if Byron's other troubles were not enough, February
brought with it a variety of illnesses, some alarming. On
the way back from a meeting with Greek leaders at Anato-
lico, Byron's party got thoroughly drenched. Pietro Gamba
developed a fever and colic, and on February 5 Byron
wrote to Charles Hancock, his banker at Zante, that "Luke
(not the Evangelist, but a disciple of mine)" had also fallen
ill.[16] Lukas's illness caused Byron much anxiety, so much,
indeed, that he gave up his bed and undertook to nurse
him personally. Lukas's occupancy of Byron's bed apparently caused some talk in the town where privacy was non-
existent; several months later, Gamba was to comment
nervously about this. But the most alarming development
concerned Byron's own health. On February 15 he suffered
a serious breakdown, the first real indication that he might
not survive the rigors of Missolonghi. The seizure took the
form of a kind of epileptic fit, which frightened both Byron
and his medical attendants, who were inexperienced and
inclined to hysteria. Byron described the attack two days
later in the last journal entry he is known to have written:
"It was very painful and had it lasted a minute longer must
have extinguished my mortality—if I can judge by sensations. I was speechless with the features much distorted."
He ascribed the seizure partly to lack of exercise (because
of the bad weather) and partly to agitation induced by the
tense state of military and political affairs in the town.
Then Byron makes a revealing admission: "I have also been
in an anxious state with regard to things which may be

16.   *BLJ*, 11:106.

only interesting to my own private feelings." [17] This deliberately obscure comment undoubtedly refers to his tormented feelings for Lukas.

One wishes that Lukas had been more sensitive to Byron's feelings instead of causing further pain in an already very trying situation. But Lukas, though handsome and brave, was also vain and greedy. We learn more of their relation in two later poems. For more than half a century, "On This Day I Complete My Thirty-Sixth Year" was supposed to have been Byron's last poetic statement. We now know that this was the first rather than the last of the poems Byron wrote about his love for Lukas. At least two other poems eventually found their way into the hands of John Cam Hobhouse. In 1887, more than half a century after Byron's death and eighteen years after Hobhouse's, another John Murray, the son of Byron's publisher, inaugurated *Murray's Magazine*. In order to add interest to the second number of the enterprise, Murray included some unpublished Byron materials, nothing less in fact than two new Missolonghi poems, written subsequent to "On This Day." The poems were given the place of honor on the opening pages of the February 1887 issue under the heading "Byroniana," but with no clue as to their background except for two comments by Hobhouse, the first of which identified the verses as "the last [Byron] ever wrote; from a rough copy found amongst his papers on the back of the 'Song of Suli.' Copied November, 1824—John C. Hobhouse." [18] For the occasion the editor supplied the somewhat arbitrary titles, "Last Words on Greece" and "Love and Death."

"Last Words on Greece" presumably reflects Byron's mood in February after Lukas fell ill. The contrast with "On This Day" is striking. Where the earlier poem was public and rhetorical, "Last Words" is intimate and down-

17.   February 15, 1824, *BLJ*, 11:113.
18.   *Murray's Magazine* 1 (February 1887):145.

beat. "On This Day" represented Byron's commitment to Greece as triumphing over his love. On this point, "Last Words" negates its predecessor; here, with a vengeance, is "Vénus toute entière à sa proie attachée." Both poems echo Shakespeare. "On This Day" draws its imagery from *Macbeth* and *Twelfth Night*; "Last Words" invites a comparison with the sonnets. Indeed, the brief ten-line poem actually suggests, through its rhyme and movement, a kind of truncated sonnet, the last two lines, though not rhymed, have the summing-up effect of a Shakespearean couplet:

> What are to me those honours or renown
>> Past or to come, a new-born people's cry[?]
> Albeit for such I could despise a crown
>> Of aught save Laurel, or for such could die;
> I am the fool of passion—and a frown
>> Of thine to me is as an Adder's eye
> To the poor bird whose pinion fluttering down
>> Wafts unto death the breast it bore so high—
> Such is this maddening fascination grown,
>> So strong thy Magic—or so weak am I.[19]

It is perhaps worth noting that Byron discussed Shakespeare with the young American historian George Finlay, who visited him at Missolonghi about a week after he had recovered from his fit. In a typically defensive way, Byron had justified his own writings by pointing to the moral disrepute of Shakespeare's most personal poems: "People talk of the tendency of my writings, and yet read the sonnets to Master Hughes."[20] The reference to "William Hughes," on whose name Shakespeare was purportedly punning in his controversial "master–mistress" sonnet, may seem surprising. Most readers associate this theory that Shake-

19. See n. 15. Byron's reference to rejecting a crown was not mere rhetoric. If he had lived, he might well have been offered the throne of Greece.

20. "Extracts of Letters from Mr. George Finlay to Colonel Stanhope," in Leicester Stanhope, *Greece in 1823 and 1824*, 2nd ed. (London: Sherwood, Gilbert & Piper, 1825), p. 524.

speare addressed his sonnets to a young man of this name with Oscar Wilde's "Portrait of Mr. W. H.," but the idea can be traced back to Thomas Tyrwhitt, to whom Edmond Malone ascribed it in his edition of 1780.[21] But if Shakespeare's sonnets express (in the main) Shakespeare's delight in a young man's beauty and friendship, Byron's second Lukas poem is, by contrast, a poem of anguish. The folklore belief that snakes could hypnotize birds was a favorite conceit of the Romantics. Shelley used it and so did Tennyson, but neither to express the force of love: Byron's image is by far the most powerful. Byron's poem also makes us think today of the experience of another writer of European reputation, Thomas Mann, who also fell under the spell of a boy of classical beauty by the shores of the Adriatic and described his humiliation in Death in Venice. Byron and Aschenbach (Mann's alter ego) are equally abject in their surrender to an overpowering erotic obsession, which their age and fame make ridiculous.

It is notable that both "On This Day" and "Last Words" speak of Lukas's "frowns." Lukas gave clear indications of the discomfort he felt at any manifestations of Byron's love. Nevertheless, he continued to be dependent on him and to benefit from his largesse. On March 21, Zambelli recorded another expenditure of forty-five dollars for Lukas and a bill for 1,000 drachmas for gold-laced jackets, rich saddle-cloths, and gilt for his pistols. Byron's infatuation seems to have been fired rather than extinguished by the boy's disdain.

Sometime late in February or during the month of March—we cannot be sure of the exact date—Byron wrote the last of his poems on this unhappy love affair, the last, indeed, of any he is known to have composed. "Love and Death" differs strikingly from the earlier verses inspired by

21. Supplement to the Edition of Shakespeare's Plays . . . to Which Are Subjoined the Genuine Poems of the Same Author (London: Bathurst et al., 1780), p. 579.

Lukas. The poetic language and the elaborate conceits have now vanished; Byron uses the simplest and barest confessional style to convey his feelings so that the stanzas read almost like a versified journal. They enumerate five different episodes in the life of Byron and Lukas after leaving Cephalonia, all well documented: the escape from the Turks during the voyage to Missolonghi, the near-shipwreck at Scrofes, Lukas's illness, an earthquake that struck on February 21, and Byron's fit. Byron observes chronological order in recounting these events, except for reversing the last two:

> I watched thee when the foe was at our side,
>   Ready to strike at him,—or thee and me
> Were safety hopeless—rather than divide
>   Aught with one loved, save love and liberty.
>
> I watched thee in the breakers—when the rock
>   Received our prow, and all was storm and fear,
> And bade thee cling to me through every shock—
>   This arm would be thy bark—or breast thy bier.
>
> I watched thee when the fever glazed thine eyes,
>   Yielding my couch—and stretched me on the ground
> When overworn with watching—ne'er to rise
>   From thence, if thou an early grave hadst found.
>
> The Earthquake came and rocked the quivering wall,
>   And men and Nature reeled as if with wine—
> Whom did I seek around the tottering Hall—?
>   For *thee*—whose safety first provide for—? thine.
>
> And when convulsive throes denied my breath
>   The faintest utterance to my fading thought—
> To thee—to thee—even in the gasp of death
>   My Spirit turned—Ah! oftener than it ought.
>
> Thus much and more—and yet thou lov'st me not,
>   And never wilt—Love dwells not in our will,
> Nor can I blame thee—though it be my lot
>   To strongly—wrongly—vainly—love thee still.[22]

22.   See n. 15.

Perhaps Byron wrote so simply in a final desperate attempt to reach Lukas's heart. It would have been relatively easy to translate these lines into Romaic or Italian.

They are both proud and despairing. We do not know for certain if Byron had anticipated a revival of his earlier pederastic feelings on his return to Greece: he may have. Or he may have been surprised and bewildered by their recurrence and their intensity. In a sense he had come full circle. His letter to Elizabeth Pigot had set his feelings for John Edlestone in the tradition of classical Greek love, the love of Orestes for Pylades, and Nisus for Euryalus. His "Greek epistles," in contrast, have a Petronian playfulness. "On This Day" tries to resume a heroic pose by rejecting love for war. But in "Love and Death" Byron returns to the heroic theme and looks at death not as an escape from love but as an affirmation of it. We are back to the heroic Greek ideal as Phaedrus depicts it in the *Symposium*. An even closer analogy, perhaps, is a speech of Callicratidas in Lucian's *Amores*:

> A lover might well pray that his cherished one should journey to old age without any sorrow through a life free from stumbling or swerving, without having experienced at all any malicious spite of Fortune. But, if in accordance with the law governing the human body, illness should lay its hand on him, I shall ail with him when he is weak, and, when he puts out to sea through stormy waves, I shall sail with him. And, should a violent tyrant put him in chains, I shall put the same fetters around myself. . . . Should I see bandits or foemen rushing upon him, I would arm myself even beyond my strength, and if he dies, I shall not bear to live. I shall give final instructions to those I love next best after him to pile up a common tomb for both of us, to unite my bones with his and not to keep even our dumb ashes apart from each other.[23]

23. *Lucian*, trans. M. D. McLeod, vol. 8 (Cambridge: Harvard University Press, 1967), 221. It is now thought, on the basis of internal evidence, that this dialogue, though Lucianic in style, was in fact written about a hundred years after Lucian's death, i.e., about 300 A.D.

In "Love and Death" Byron complains that he has loved Lukas with this sort of idealism but evoked no response. His abjectness recalls Proust's stricken lovers, the list of benefits unacknowledged parallels Wilde's reproaches in *De Profundis*. Only the brave, if bleak, facing of the truth in the last lines keeps the poem from lapsing into petulance and adds a final touch of dignity to Byron's despair.

No poem of Byron's is more specifically autobiographical or more painful in its revelations than "Love and Death." With our knowledge of how each detail fits Byron's relation with Lukas during the Missolonghi period, we may wonder how the truth went so long unrecognized. Nineteenth-century and early twentieth-century biographers—even Harold Nicolson, who devoted his whole book to this period of Byron's life—failed to connect these lines with Lukas. In part, this was due to the deliberately misleading way in which they were introduced to the public. When the poem first appeared in 1887, a comment by Hobhouse was added, informing the reader that "a note attached to the verses by Lord Byron states they were addressed to no one in particular, and were a mere poetical Scherzo."[24] Thus Byron's readers were invited to interpret some of his most personal and deeply felt verses as a mere literary exercise. Did Byron really write such a note? The effort he took to mislead Dallas about the stanzas on Edlestone in *Childe Harold* suggests that he might have. Yet one wonders why Hobhouse chose to make a copy of the poems rather than preserve the originals. It is possible that Hobhouse himself concocted the sentence to obfuscate evidence that in the eyes of his age would have appeared incriminating.

The interesting question remains as to whether there were once other Lukas poems. Leicester Stanhope was ordered back to England in May 1824. In July he talked at length with Hobhouse and recorded the conversation in

24. *Murray's Magazine* 1 (February 1887):145.

the book he published later the same year on Greece and Byron:

> Mr. John Cam Hobhouse was [Byron's] long-tried, his esteemed, and valued literary and personal friend. . . . Mr. Hobhouse has given many proofs of this, and among others, I saw him, from motives of high honour, destroy a beautiful poem of Lord Byron's, and, perhaps, the last he ever composed. The same reason that induced Mr. H. to tear this fine manuscript will, of course, prevent him or me from ever divulging its contents.[25]

Hobhouse must have gritted his teeth on reading these self-congratulatory lines, which appeared to compliment him while inviting just the kind of speculation he was trying to discourage. Apparently Stanhope and Hobhouse had engaged in some discussion of Byron's pederastic inclinations, for Hobhouse noted in his journal on July 8, 1824: "Stanhope told me one or two truths too true I am sure about Byron's last career in Greece."[26] This exchange of confidences presumably led to Hobhouse's dramatic gesture of tearing up a manuscript.

But what was the poem he destroyed? Doris Langley Moore makes the natural assumption that it was "Love and Death," but there is some mystery here. If Hobhouse did, in fact, tear up the manuscript of the poem before Stanhope's eyes, he was engaging in a disingenuous charade since we know from his own account that he had made a copy of it. But assuming the discussion took place in July as Hobhouse's journal indicates, the poem must have been another one if Hobhouse's statement that he copied the poems in November is correct. So unless there was a subsequent discussion—an unlikely event since Stanhope, rankled by his quarrels with Byron, took a public line critical of him after his return—we are faced with the possibil-

---

25. Stanhope, *Greece in 1823 and 1824*, p. 534.
26. *LLB*, p. 175.

ity that Byron wrote more poems about or to Lukas than
have survived.

Every aspect of Byron's last three months contributed to
making his life miserable. He had returned to Greece with
few illusions. But he was bitterly disappointed at the refusal of the Suliotes to fight and at his inability to unify the
contending Greek factions. Selfishness and calculation predominated over patriotism among the chieftains. Too often
the Greeks rivaled the Turks in cruelty and disregard for
human decencies and were as prone to kill and pillage as
their enemies. Byron's one significant achievement at Missolonghi was to rescue some Turkish prisoners from massacre and to send them home with a plea that the Turkish
commander might consider this a precedent. He befriended
a ten-year-old Turkish girl named Hatagée and dressed her
prettily and extravagantly: this was his one indulgence
apart from his spoiling of Lukas. Finally, the Suliote soldiers became so rapacious and such a threat to civic order
at Missolonghi that Byron paid them off and sent them
away at the cost of several thousand dollars of his own
money. Only this kind of largesse and the hope for a substantial loan from the London Committee he represented
kept the Greeks and foreign philhellenes deferential.

Day by day Byron's health worsened. Fever, dizziness,
weakness, and pain oppressed him. The nervous strain
imposed by recurring political crises in the town kept him
from recovering adequately from his first breakdown. After
April 10 he was continuously ill, barely able to stir or take
exercise. His doctors diagnosed rheumatic fever from chills
and exposure, but modern medical opinion takes the view
that he was suffering from a uremic disorder. Incompetent
to deal with the situation, his medical attendants made
matters worse by extravagant blood-letting, the medical
fad of the age, despite Byron's ever-weakening protests.
His last days were made all the more pitiful by the confusion in his disorganized household. His thoughts naturally

turned to his will and to a realization that his more humble dependents were not provided for in that document. His valet, William Fletcher, later told Hobhouse that Byron had "expressed an anxiety to do something for his favorite *chasseur*, Tita, and his Greek boy Luca, but Fletcher told him to speak of more important concerns."[27] On April 24, 1824, exhausted from fever and repeated bleedings, Byron died.

At least one commemorative statue to Byron in Greece shows him expiring in the arms of his Greek page. Though such a fantasy might have appealed to Byron's poetic sense, Lukas was not present at his death. He had sent him away to spare him the sight of the bloody bandages and any possible death agony. Realizing his death was near, Byron had, however, tried to make some immediate provision for him by giving him the receipt for the several thousand dollars he had loaned the Missolonghi authorities to pay off the Suliotes. When the news of Byron's death was made public, free Greece declared a period of national mourning, and western Europe was shocked and respectful. Lukas, too, must have grieved, if only for the loss of a generous benefactor.

However, this was not quite the end of Lukas's story. As we have seen, Hobhouse and Stanhope were to exchange confidences on the subject in London that July. As a result Hobhouse wrote to Pietro Gamba about Lukas in his capacity as Byron's executor responsible for moneys and as a friend anxious to refute scandal. Gamba replied on August 11 in a lengthy letter. This remarkable document has been deciphered and translated by Doris Langley Moore. In it Gamba confirms that Byron had indeed given the boy the receipt for the Missolonghi debt and reveals a pathetic story before unknown:

> Moreover it was within my knowledge and that of the stewart of the house and Fletcher that more than thirty Spanish dou-

27. *BB*, 3:1227.

bloons and 200 francesconi in silver ought to have been found in possession of Mylord.

After the death of B there was a search for this sum, about 700 [? dollars]—but in vain. It was suspected that Lukas had it. I questioned him skilfully and he insisted that Lord Byron had given him some doubloons to assist his family. We did not wish to press the matter, because to recover the money appeared hopeless, and after all it might have been a cause of gossip damaging to the reputation of our friend. Every friend of Byron must desire that this *mischievous topic* should be buried if possible.

Another matter connected with Lukas also agitated Gamba. This was the rumor that Byron and the boy had shared the same bed. To counteract it, Gamba felt it incumbent to analyze their relation in some detail:

During the voyage and the residence at Missolonghi he watched with [such] particular care over this youth that one might call it a weakness. He gave him splendid clothes, arms, and money; and passed some half-hour every day with him reading Modern Greek. He took him with us in the cavalcade, and in the end gave him the command of 30 irregular soldiers of his own brigade. On one occasion when this boy had a somewhat dangerous illness, Mylord was pleased to give up his own bed and slept in the common room with us on a Turkish divan for 3 or four days. This should not appear so strange, however, when you remember that the illness required a bed, and that no other was to be found in the house—and that on another occasion, when I was ill he made me the same offer; and that in the passage from Cephalonia to Missolonghi, Fletcher having a severe chill, Mylord gave him the only mattress on board and was pleased to sleep, himself, on deck.

Whatever suggestion was made to you that M[ylord] could have slept in the same bed is absolutely false. The donation of 3,000 dollars was given in consideration of his poor family.

If the conduct of Mylord towards that youth might seem to imply weakness, these facts and these few observations will suffice to prove to you that this weakness rose only from a noble source and a generous aim—his pity for the innocent unfortunate.[28]

28.   *LLB*, pp. 179–81.

There is no doubt that Byron was susceptible to pity for unfortunate people of all sorts, conditions, and ages. But Gamba's explanation for Byron's taking Lukas with him to Missolonghi is curious. Since Lukas was of "well-bred manner and person," Pietro told Hobhouse, Byron did not want "to degrade him to the rank of a servant"; we may recall, however, that Byron had no compunction about Lukas's sisters entering service. "Many a time he had said to me that, going to Greece, he would need many young people to serve as pages. We were then on the eve of our departure for Missolonghi, and thus he took Lukas in the quality of page." There may be some naïveté in Gamba's argument here. He seems to be saying that Byron should not be suspected of any erotic interest in Lukas because he had fancied himself as surrounded by "many" young pages in Greece. This is the one suggestion on record that Byron may have had a conscious, or perhaps unconscious, desire to repeat the experiences of his first Greek journey. Byron had told Trelawny, apropos of this visit: "I was happier in Greece than I have ever been before—or since."[29] At least at first, the freer air of Greece seems once again to have exhilarated him. There was some irony here, for Greece under Turkey was, in sexual matters, freer than liberated Greece was to be. After 1829, Turkish tolerance faded out, and the homophobic strain in the Greek Orthodox church, traceable to Chrysostom and Justinian, once again asserted itself in the form of harsh laws. However desirable the fall of the Turkish empire was from the point of view of the peoples enslaved by it, in this one particular it meant the substitution of prejudice and oppression for relative freedom.

It appears that Lukas did not long outlive Byron, but our information on this point is sketchy. In 1832 his young sisters appealed for help to Byron's daughter, Ada. A letter

29.   Elizabeth Longford, *Byron's Greece* (London: Weidenfeld & Nicolson, 1975), p. 125.

addressed to her in Greek speaks of Byron's philhellenism and of his charity to "one of our brothers named Lukas, who was very much loved by the unforgettable Lord Byron, but who died in the midst of the war and in the midst of the happiness which Byron had procured for him." [30] Since the Greek war of independence dragged on for another five years after Byron's death, this would place Lukas's death sometime before 1829. An extract from a journal by Trelawny, published in the *London Literary Gazette* for February 12, 1831, throws some further light on the matter. In the course of his career as an adventurer in Greece, Trelawny had turned violently against Prince Mavrocordatos; the journal accuses the prince (probably unjustly) of appropriating the money Byron had assigned to Lukas from the Missolonghi debt. Trelawny makes the charge that Lukas's "family was left in utter destitution at Byron's death" and that "the young man died six months after, in want of the necessaries of life." [31] Trelawny's contention that Lukas died destitute is contradicted by the sister's declaration that he died "in the midst of the happiness which Byron had procured for him" and may have been made, on the basis of little or no knowledge, to further dramatize the alleged iniquity of Mavrocordatos. His statement that Lukas survived Byron by only a few months is, however, quite compatible with what his sisters say and may well be the truth.

30. *LLB*, p. 182.
31. P. 97.

The Truth Appears

News traveled slowly in a Europe still without railways or telegraphs. Though he must have been the first person in London to be informed, John Cam Hobhouse did not hear of Byron's death until May 14. Then, when the shock of the news passed, his overwhelming concern was with Byron's manuscript memoirs. Byron had begun his autobiography in Venice in 1818 and added to it substantially in 1820 and 1821, entrusting the pages to Thomas Moore to publish after his death. With Byron's permission, Moore had later sold the manuscripts to John Murray. But Hobhouse wanted them destroyed and was now able to bring Augusta and (more surprisingly) Murray himself around to his point of view. Three days later, over Moore's protests, the pages were consigned to the flames in Murray's office in Albemarle Street.

Did the memoirs make any revelations about Byron's bisexuality? Were fears on this score behind Hobhouse's obsessive determination to obliterate Byron's record of his life? Doris Langley Moore has given a full and vivid account of the events preceding the burning and has probed the motives of the participants. In effect, Hobhouse was able to create a mood of hysteria in which "gentlemanly" considerations for the dead man's fame were invoked to override Thomas Moore's scruples. Doris Langley Moore has argued that no explosive secrets were revealed in the memoirs. Though Hobhouse and Murray had not read them, we know that perhaps a score of people had since they circulated widely. William Gifford, who read the manuscript at Murray's request, had pronounced it "fit only for a brothel," but the consensus is that Gifford was overreacting. Byron had told Murray that "the life is *Memoranda*—and not *Confessions*—I have left out all my *loves* (except in a general way)."[1] The first part, dealing with his life up to the point of his exile, was especially discreet. Part two, on his life in Venice, was more candid, but by this time the two most controversial questions—Byron's incest and his bisexuality—were behind him (or so, at least, he presumably thought). Moreover, since the memoirs were intended as an apologia, giving Byron's side of the controversy surrounding his separation from Lady Byron, he was unlikely to afford occasions of scandal. To have written openly would have played directly into the hands of his enemies.

Why then was Hobhouse so frightened? Obviously, he did not trust Byron's discretion. Another possibility is that he feared Moore had read passages the import of which he had failed to grasp. Hobhouse was well aware of Byron's passion for communicativeness and his love of veiled confessions. As we have seen, he had made Byron destroy his Cambridge journal when they were traveling in Albania. It was no doubt Hobhouse's reaction on this occasion that led Byron to give the memoirs not to him but to Moore. Hobhouse must have felt that Byron could not be trusted to eschew innuendoes in what Charles Skinner Matthews had called "the mysterious style." If Moore unwittingly published something of this sort, what was to prevent some enemy of Byron's, or of the liberal-radical wing of English politics with which he was associated, from unraveling the clue and exposing his relations with Augusta or, worse, with Edlestone or Giraud? The Clogher case was not two years old. The radicals Hobhouse worked with had made much of it against the Tories. Defenders of the government would seize with delight a chance to embarrass the opposition in a similar fashion.

1. Venice, October 29, 1819, *BLJ*, 6:236.

Then there was Hobhouse's own vulnerability. No man in England was more closely connected with Byron in the public eye. The unpublished defense of Byron he wrote after the separation from Lady Byron complained that some of the rumors circulating about Byron were damaging to his friends.[2] The common assumption has been that Hobhouse was shocked by Byron's bisexuality and averse to pederasty. Doris Langley Moore thinks that "Hobhouse disapproved severely of sexual deviation," citing as evidence "what is explicit in his *Travels in Albania*" and "implicit in the tenor of his conduct" to Byron.[3] But, as we have seen, Hobhouse's language was merely the required stereotype of the age, and his conduct can be interpreted as resting on fear of exposure rather than moral disapproval. Matthews's Falmouth letter seems to imply that Hobhouse was a fellow "Methodiste." The fullness of detail in Byron's "Greek epistles" is unintelligible unless Hobhouse shared Byron's interests.

But was there any justification in the manuscript itself for Hobhouse's apprehensions? Fortunately, despite the destruction of the memoirs and of the known copies, we do have evidence from readers as to its details, which Doris Langley Moore has painstakingly pieced together. Part one dealt mainly with Byron's life after he became famous in 1812, though there was something about his first journey to Greece. Lord John Russell recalled that Byron's "early youth in Greece, and his sensibility to the scenes around him, when resting on a rock in the swimming excursions he took from the Piraeus, were strikingly described."[4] One wonders if Byron mentioned Giraud's presence on these occasions. The passage that caused the most speculation referred to what Thomas Moore in a letter called "a name-

2.   Hobhouse, *Recollections of a Long Life*, ed. Lady Dorchester (London: John Murray, 1910), 2:350, 352.

3.   *LLB*, p. 90.

4.   *Memoirs, Journal, and Correspondence of Thomas Moore*, ed. Lord John Russell (London: Brown, Green, & Longmans, 1853), 4:192.

less person whom he calls his 'love of loves.'" [5] Byron's friend, the Whig hostess Lady Holland, to whom Moore had lent a copy of the memoirs, thought this was Augusta, but he persuaded her that she was wrong.[6] But who then was this "love of loves"? Doris Langley Moore plausibly suggests it was either Mary Chaworth or "Thyrza," that is, John Edlestone. Probability seems to favor the latter since Byron's love for John seems to have made the more powerful and lasting impression.

But beyond these impenetrabilities it seems unlikely anything more was said in the memoir. Byron had reserved his reflections on this side of his emotional life. Three months after he had finished the first installment of part two in October 1820, he wrote in his Ravenna journal of the "violent, though *pure*, love and passion" he felt for Edlestone. Then, when he had finished his second supplement to the manuscript, he jotted down, in sections 72 to 76 of his "Detached Thoughts," the reflections we have examined in Chapter 6. These were clearly details he dared not put in his formal autobiography. The irony is that Hobhouse in destroying the memoirs and Moore in excising the Ravenna journal left untouched what were probably Byron's most revealing comments on the subject that most frightened them both.

To compensate himself for his loss—he had had to repay Murray the £2000 advance on the memoirs—Moore undertook to write a life of Byron. This venture presented many difficulties. Hobhouse was hostile, Lady Byron cool, and Augusta inevitably uneasy. Obviously Byron's life was full of pitfalls for any biographer who attempted any candor. Even Moore, whose long suits were tact and diplomacy, was taxed. While he was still at work on the biography in 1829, Charles Fulke Greville dined with him in

5.   To Lord Holland, November 5, 1821, in L. A. G. Strong, *The Minstrel Boy: A Portrait of Tom Moore* (New York: Knopf, 1937), p. 305.

6.   *LLB*, p. 49.

London and reported in his journal that Moore, who talked at length about his book, was "nervous about it."[7] It was on this occasion that Moore denied that Byron had any "fancy for Boys" in a way that left Greville suspicious. We do not know if Greville or someone else brought the matter up or whether Moore chose on his own to discount what he understood to be common gossip.

This treacherous topic challenged all Moore's considerable ingenuity. In one way he was daring, for he published Byron's letters to Elizabeth Pigot about Edlestone and the passage about his "violent, though *pure,* love," gave details of the will in favor of Nicolo Giraud, and discoursed at length about his partiality for his Harrow schoolfellows and Robert Rushton. But having made the disclosures, he then tried, as we have seen, to gloss over these affairs as romantic friendships and to obscure the origin of the Thyrza lyrics. On the whole, his ploy succeeded. Whatever questions knowledgeable or suspicious readers (such as Greville) may have had, the reviewers and the press acquiesced to Moore's view of Byron's same-sex attachments, and it remained the publicly accepted one for over a century.

By an irony of fate, it was the nervous Hobhouse whose writings first effectively dissipated the smoke screen Moore had laid down. When Hobhouse read Moore's book in 1830, he peppered the margins with disputatious comments. Among them were those that bore on Byron's homosexuality. They included his comment on Lord Grey, his allegation that Byron wanted no Englishman near him in Greece, and his pointed remark that Moore knew nothing, or would tell nothing, of the real nature of Byron's boyish friendships. Doris Langley Moore thinks he meant to erase his pencilings, but this is not certain. Totally unwilling to trust others—or Byron himself—where Byron's reputation was concerned, insisting that evidence he could not per-

7.   November 29, 1829, *The Greville Memoirs, 1814–1860,* ed. Lytton Strachey and Robert Fulford (London: Macmillan, 1938), 1:325–26.

sonally control be destroyed, he nevertheless carefully preserved the "Greek epistles," which give us an unequivocal
account of Byron's homoerotic adventures and in addition
saved at least two crucial Lukas poems. He was willing that
the truth should see the light of day eventually, provided it
was delayed long enough and ultimately appeared through
his own revelations. No doubt he prided himself, as Doris
Langley Moore suggests, on being in possession of Byron's
most closely kept secrets. If Thomas Moore, of whom he
was always jealous, had got the memoirs, he himself held
one of the most important keys to Byron's character. It was
one thing that proved that Hobhouse and not Moore was
closest to Byron.

Those who were in the dark about Byron remained un-
enlightened after reading Thomas Moore's *Life*. The few in
the know now had more clues to work on. They did not,
however, so far as we are aware, commit their speculations
to paper. There was, nevertheless, one striking exception.
The anomaly was the mysterious and remarkable poem
entitled *Don Leon*, written a few years after Moore's biography, but known to us only in a version printed a generation
later in 1866. This polemical narrative, which purported to
be Byron's own account of his homosexual experiences, is
one of the major puzzles of English literary history. It fills
fifty pages and has fifty pages of notes by some other unknown writer or writers. It does, in fact, set forth something very close to the truth concerning Byron's relations
with Rushton, Edlestone, and Giraud. But who wrote it
and how did it happen that this revealing document was
ignored for more than a century, until G. Wilson Knight
rescued it from obscurity in 1954 and suggested that its
revelations should be taken seriously?

The authorship of *Don Leon* remains a riddle, but it is
possible to understand why the poem was resolutely ignored by nineteenth-century writers on Byron. Part of the
difficulty lay in the form in which the poet chose to convey
his revelations. The obviously fabricated side of the pub-

lication suggested that it belonged to the extensive category of pseudo-Byroniana that appeared after Byron's death with no further aim than to titillate readers and relieve them of their shillings or francs. The title page describes the work as a "Poem by Lord Byron, Author of Childe Harold, Don Juan, &c. &c. and Forming Part of the Private Journal of His Lordship, Supposed to Have Been Entirely Destroyed by Thos. Moore." No knowledgeable contemporary reader would have been taken in by this claim. No one had ever suggested that Byron's memoirs were in rhymed couplets, and the poem makes reference to dozens of events that took place in the decade following Byron's death. This playful pretense that Byron himself is speaking the lines—an obvious impossibility—would in itself have militated against the credibility of these "confessions," though we now know that on many substantial points they come startlingly close to the truth.

The other consideration that led to the general dismissal of the poem as a record of fact stemmed from its shady provenance. Apparently some earlier printed version of these fifty rhymed pages existed, but the only copies known to us come from an edition printed by the London publisher William Dugdale in 1866.[8] Since Dugdale's main line was erotic "curiosa," this led readers to dismiss the lines as a purely fictive concoction prepared for the under-the-counter trade. Even so sophisticated an expert on sexuality as Henry Spencer Ashbee, the one nineteenth-century authority to take any notice of the work, assumed there could be no truth in the poem's implication that Byron was a bisexual.

But who was the poet who knew so much about Byron that he was able to write so revealingly? Knight has sug-

8.   A correspondent signing himself "I. W." in *Notes and Queries* 7 (1853): 66, refers to "a poem (about 1500 lines) which professes to be written by Lord Byron, is addressed to Thomas Moore, and was printed abroad many years since." This is the only evidence we have for the existence of an earlier edition, no copy of which has as yet been identified.

gested that the author was the playwright George Colman the younger whose wit and conviviality Byron enjoyed during their work together at Drury Lane Theater in 1815, the year of his marriage.[9] The parallels between *Don Leon* and some of Colman's satires are striking, but ascriptions of authorship on stylistic grounds are always tenuous. Besides, Colman was old and ill at the time the poem was written—he died in 1836 at seventy-three. On these and other grounds Doris Langley Moore has argued against Colman's authorship and proposed another candidate.[10] At present the authorship must be regarded as an unsolved mystery.

Indeed, all we can say with certainty about the *Leon* poet is that he had a clever wit, a talent for writing forceful couplets, and a remarkable knowledge both of Byron's life (on its homosexual side) and of British parliamentary affairs in the decade following his death. Written with great verve and cleverness, *Don Leon*, though not quite the masterpiece it has been called, is nevertheless a work of real literary significance. The poem itself is full of ideas and information, much of which (especially the detailed parliamentary part) is inevitably obscure to the modern reader. Since the kaleidoscopic turns of thought of *Don Leon* are so many that even someone who has read it two or three times may have only a confused idea of its structure and logic, a fairly extended summary may be useful. It will also communicate, as no other approach can, the concentrated energy of the poem.

But before we look at these details, it is necessary to appreciate another side of the work, a side that was its real

9. G. Wilson Knight, "Who Wrote 'Don Leon'?" *Twentieth Century* 156 (1954):67–79; and G. Wilson Knight, "Colman and 'Don Leon,'" *Twentieth Century* 159 (1956):562–73.

10. In the "Editorial Note" added to the 1977 edition of *The Late Lord Byron*, Moore identifies him (p. viii) as Richard Paternoster, of Madras, who contributed to a Byron monument fund in 1826 and then quarreled with the committee. See also *LLB*, pp. 210–13; and *LBAR*, pp. 449–53.

raison d'être. So far, commentary on *Don Leon*, on the few occasions that it has been noticed, has been concentrated on its Byronic aspects. Nevertheless, what moved the *Leon* poet to write was not, apparently, the revelations he had to make about Byron, sensational as they were, but the problem that had obsessed Jeremy Bentham, the problem of repealing the death penalty for sodomy. Bentham had died in 1832, the year of the Reform Bill. The next year, under the new dispensation, a new parliamentary commission on criminal law reform was set up under Lord John Russell, who had strong Benthamite views. It was this development and two other events of 1833 that seem to have moved the *Leon* poet to write his passionate plea for reform. One of these was the sentence of death pronounced on Captain Henry Nicholas Nicholls on August 12 of that year. Hangings for homosexual relations had continued unabated after Byron's death, despite their rapid decline for other crimes. In the years 1826–1830 there were seven; another took place in 1831, three in 1833 (including Nicholls's), four in 1834, and three in 1835. This was the case in spite of the fact that in this era of rapid reform the status of many minority groups in England had improved. Nonconformists had been relieved of their disabilities by the repeal of the Test Act in 1828, Catholic emancipation had come in 1829, and the reformed House crowned decades of agitation by finally ending black slavery in 1833. The death penalty had already been repealed for dozens of nonviolent crimes, but conviction in sodomy cases had actually been rendered easier by a change of the law in 1828, and the new reform commission seemed unwilling to brave public opinion on this matter.

With more rage and despair than hope, the *Leon* poet makes himself the spokesman for England's gay community by urging the abolition of hanging for sodomy. In the pursuit of this aim, he especially directs his arguments to members of Parliament. In the interval since Byron's death, several members of the House of Commons had joined him in exile, committed suicide, or faced trials. Besides Nicholls's hanging, the other event of 1833 that seems particularly to have spurred him to write was the arrest of Byron's Cambridge friend and fellow parliamentarian William Bankes, which had taken place on June 7. In the notes to the poem, which fill another fifty pages and were apparently written at different times between 1833 and 1859, the last date mentioned in them, legal matters and newspaper reports of scandals bulk far larger than references to Byron.

Thus it is that a poem purporting to be Byron's autobiography opens with a protest against a hanging that took place nine years after his death and against the continuing entrapment of homosexuals by the police:

> Thou ermined judge, pull off that sable cap!
> What! Can'st thou lie, and take thy morning nap?
> Peep thro' the casement; see the gallows there:
> Thy work hangs on it; could not mercy spare?
> What had he done? Ask crippled Talleyrand,
> Ask Beckford, Courtenay, all the motley band
> Of priest and laymen, who have shared his guilt
> (If guilt it be) then slumber if thou wilt;
> What bonds had he of social safety broke?
> Found'st thou the dagger hid beneath his cloak?
> He stopped no lonely traveller on the road;
> He burst no lock, he plundered no abode;
> He never wrong'd the orphan of his own;
> He stifled not the ravish'd maiden's groan.
> His secret haunts were hid from every soul,
> Till thou did'st send thy myrmidons to prowl.[11]

(lines 1–16)

11. My earlier references to *Don Leon* have been to the Arno Press reprint of 1975 (a facsimile of the suppressed 1934 Fortune Press edition), the most readily accessible edition. For quotations from the text of the poem in this chapter, however, I have used the 1866 Dugdale version. The discussion of the poem that follows was published, in a somewhat fuller version, in "*Don Leon*, Byron, and Homosexual Law Reform," *Journal of Homosexuality* 8 (Spring-Summer 1983):53–71. This version has details on the history of law reform, parliamentary scandals, etc., not reprinted here.

The sable cap is, of course, the black cap English judges wore when they were about to pronounce the sentence of death. The annotator of *Don Leon*, in his first footnote, preserves only the thinnest pretense that Byron had written these lines: "In reading the opening of this poem, it would almost seem that the author of it had in his eye Mr. Justice Park [who pronounced death on Nicholls] were it not that the supposed date of the poem would imply an anachronism." Because the *Leon* poet purports to be speaking in the person of Byron, I shall refer to him as "Byron" in the rest of my summary, though in fact the pseudo-Byronic mask is often all but completely dropped in the argumentative sections.

After the opening protest, "Byron" begs Moore to give a sympathetic ear to his "swelling rage" and to print his thoughts unaltered. (This is almost the only reference in the text to the pretense that the poem has some connection with the famous memoir.) England, he complains, tolerates the most open forms of prostitution but condemns "poor misogynists" to the gallows and vilifies them incessantly in the press. The Sodom story is urged against them, though many other ancient cities have vanished without anyone's interpreting their disappearance as instances of divine displeasure. The venal clergy approve only those unions that bring them marriage or baptismal fees and are blind to a love that will "Produce no other blossoms than its own" (line 126).

"Byron" now speaks of his own life and of his hidden affections. During his teens, he tells us, he was aware of an instinct that drew him to other boys. Social custom allowed him to express his love for Mary Chaworth and Margaret Parker, but not these other longings. Now, looking back, he realizes that his feelings for his page Robert Rushton, which once passed for lordly patronage, had a sexual element:

> Full well I knew, though decency forbad
> The same caresses to a rustic lad;

> Love, love it was, that made my eyes delight
> To have his person ever in my sight.
>
> (lines 169–72)

At Cambridge, he feels alienated from the common revels and longs for a kindred soul who might return his affection. He hears John Edlestone singing in the choir, and friendship ripens into love:

> Oh! 'tis hard to trace
> The line where love usurps tame friendship's place.
> Friendship's the chrysalis, which seems to die,
> But throws its coils to give love wing to fly.
>
> (lines 219–22)

(These lines echo Byron's youthful poem "L'Amitié est L'Amour Sans Ailes.") He is tormented by the intensity of his emotions and struggles to understand them. Moral law opposes his desires, but to him they seem natural since they spring from his inner being. He begins to question traditional standards—after all, he is not about to ruin a virgin, betray a husband, or beget a bastard. He seeks to divert himself from these anxieties by losing himself in the pleasures of classical poetry but is inadvertently driven back to the question. Horace, he discovers, loved youths, Virgil sighed for Alexis, Socrates and Plato spoke openly of kissing ephebes, and Plutarch praised the love of Epaminondas for Cephidorus. He rejects these loves as pagan perversions, but when he turns to the history of Christianity, he discovers such attachments again in the lives of popes, devotees, kings, scholars, jurists, and poets:

> Nay, e'en our bard, Dame Nature's darling child,
> Felt the strange impulse, and his hours beguiled
> In penning sonnets to a stripling's praise,
> Such as would damn a poet now-a-days.
>
> (lines 315–18)

(Here the poet seems to draw on the comment on Shakespeare that Byron made to George Finlay, which Leiceister Stanhope had published in 1825.) Obviously, "the great, the wise, the pious, and the good" have had the same susceptibility. In alarm he rejects books and history as morally dangerous guides. But untutored schoolboys take the same path even if they are "in *Justine* unread." This may be better, however, than their risking disease through harlotry. School authorities should quietly ignore such "illicit play": only fools would make a public issue of it.

Edlestone dies (the poem is inaccurate in making this occur before Byron left England for Greece in 1809), and, weary of Cambridge, "Byron" seeks the freedom of the East, with admissions that parallel the real Byron's Falmouth letter to Matthews:

> Love, love, clandestine love, was still my dream.
> Methought there must be yet some people found,
> Where Cupid's wings were free, his hands unbound
> Where law had no erotic statutes framed,
> Nor gibbets stood to fright the unreclaimed.
>
> (lines 423–27)

The account of Byron in Greece is particularly full and striking. In Constantinople he is excited by the traditional tourist visit to taverns with dancing boys but hides his feelings from his friend Hobhouse, affecting to be horrified. (The *Leon* poet was either unaware that Hobhouse shared any knowledge of Byron's tastes or, if he knew, sought to protect him.) He feels alienated from his countrymen and is relieved when he parts from Hobhouse at Zea. "Byron" warmly praises the latter's political work for radical causes in England but himself follows other pursuits: "A demon urged, and with Satanic force / Still goaded on" (lines 494–95). He is enraptured by the historical associations of Athens, moves to the capuchin convent, and then takes up residence in the nearby Lantern of Demosthenes.[12]

While searching through the ruins of the city, "Byron" is invited home by a citizen. There the man's son attends the guest in Oriental fashion. This, it turns out, is the poet's

---

12.   In n. 31, the annotator to *Don Leon* points out that this is a mistake; Byron wrote poems in the Lantern but did not live there.

account of Byron's meeting with Nicolo Giraud, who is identified by name in line 678. (The *Leon* poet follows Moore in mistakenly assuming that Nicolo was Lusieri's son rather than his brother-in-law.) "Byron" is struck by the boy's beauty, courts him, and is urged by the father to take him as his page. He tries to cultivate the boy's mind, gazes on him with affectionate lust while he sleeps, and cares for him with tender solicitude. The dual fires of poetic inspiration and carnal desire rage in him. Though he has met the Macri sisters, they inspire him only poetically; his real passion is for this boy, who finally gratifies him: "So boldly I set calumny at naught, / And fearless utter what I fearless wrought" (lines 690–91). (At this point, the poet comes strikingly close to Byron's "Greek epistles.") There follows a description of how the then Waiwode (or mayor) of Athens was attended by a beautiful catamite on public occasions; such openness, we are told, is common at every level of Turkish society.

The *Leon* poet, dropping any effort to relate his plea to the experience of the historical Byron, now embarks on a frank apology for homosexuality. First, Malthus has dramatically shown the danger of overpopulation, which must breed starvation if not controlled. One must also take into consideration the great diversity of sexual tastes. Some men (such as the English ambassador to Constantinople) are born exhibitionists. Others seek cunnilingus, flagellation, or fellation from women. Incest and lesbianism are not uncommon. Some women have died to preserve their virginity, but others, like the Countess of Blessington, have risen to wealth and social prominence by judiciously losing theirs. When bench and pulpit endlessly maintain that the sexual behavior of the English is morally superior to other nations, they are hypocritical and never more so than when, in the case of homosexuality, they give the impression

That self-condemned, decried, ineffable,
Innominate, this blackest sin of hell,

Had fled dismayed to some Transalpine shore
To sully Albion's pudic cliffs no more.

(lines 854–57)

The press exposes arrested men with cruel glee and enter-
tains its readers with scabrous police reports. The rich and
secure feign horror, never taking into account what may
have led a man into these paths: perhaps he was corrupted
when young, perhaps he shrank from the idea of seducing
a woman, perhaps he was ugly or shy or averse to the
ribaldry or diseases of harlots.

Every rank of English society is involved. The average
British soldier or tar is a priapist prone to take his pleasure
where he finds it. Teachers relish flogging half-naked
schoolboys. Parliament itself is not immune. Looking into
the future, "Byron" prophesies that a member famed for
his learning and book collecting will be forced to flee the
country and later will be cruelly maligned in a libel suit
brought by a father against an editor for having linked his
son's name to the exile's. Another, a young officer who
fought in Sicily, will be tragically drawn into the case. A
third member, a pious advocate of prison reform and the
rights of blacks, will also face the bitterness of exile.[13] The
poet complains indignantly that Peel's revisions of the law
have worsened matters. Liberal legislators such as Richard
Martin, who led the movement to protect animals from
cruelty, and legal reformers such as Sir James Mackintosh,
remain callously indifferent to the plight of homosexuals.

Near the speaker's chair where Charles Manners-Sutton
presides and waits for his peerage sits Sir Stephen Lushington, whom "Byron" curses for having turned Lady
Byron against him. He recalls some of his happy moments
with his wife; in a bedroom colloquy he describes Muslim

13.   The annotator tells us the bibliophile is Hobhouse's friend, Richard Heber, member for Oxford, and conjectures that the officer who committed suicide was James Stanhope. The reformer is identified as Henry
Grey Bennett, the well-known humanitarian (nn. 63, 65, 66).

manners to her and pictures the life of harem women and the Turkish passion for boys. Lady Byron expresses curiosity, and "Byron" enlightens her about Anacreon, Virgil, and Catullus. She is somewhat shocked but allows him to practice anal relations (which he extols) with her because her pregnancy makes ordinary relations awkward. Later, when they are estranged, Lady Byron is pressed to reveal this secret, and friends use it to separate her from her husband.[14]

After a second appeal by "Byron" to Thomas Moore to tell the truth and not bowdlerize his life—if Moore should ever write it—the poem abruptly flashes back to Parliament to cast a spotlight upon another figure, a friend (William Bankes) whom Byron had known since college days. Despite his wealth, the fame of his travels, and his high social standing, Bankes will eventually suffer Byron's fate. Bankes's friend Peel, when he passes Bankes's darkened house and remembers what a staunch supporter he has been in Parliament, may then regret his failure to reform the law.

In conclusion, "Byron" bitterly recalls what abuse he suffered as a man after being praised so highly as a poet. But England is not the universe: its prejudices cannot stand before the light of reason. God's law is higher than Parliament's; it is as outrageous to persecute sexual as religious heresy. Then with a final impish gesture the poet ends with a series of crude and exuberant epigrams on the pleasures of anal intercourse.

Obviously the "Byron" of this poem is something more than the historical Byron. Besides giving a candid account of his own pederastic experiences, Leon-Byron is a spokes-

14. This theme of marital sodomy is central to *Leon to Annabella*, a companion piece to *Don Leon*, published with it in the 1866 edition, which deals entirely with this subject and ignores the question of homosexuality. Some contemporaries, including Hobhouse and Lord Holland, speculated that Byron had attempted anal intercourse with his wife and that this had been one reason for the separation (*BB*, 2:587n.).

man for a persecuted minority, a prophetic voice looking forward to future tragedies, a scandalmonger, and a purveyor of marital secrets. The *Leon* poet exploits Byron's reputation as an opponent of social injustice, plays on curiosity about the burned memoirs, and uses the poem for revelations about the side of Byron that Moore had tried to obscure. The poem's most striking features are, of course, the challenge it posed to contemporary prejudices against homosexuality and the new (and largely true) facts it revealed about Byron's own sexuality. There are, however, material facts the *Leon* poet was not aware of. He did not realize, for example, that the Thyrza lyrics were elegies on the death of Edlestone; and he had no inkling of Byron's love during the final months of his life for Lukas Chalandrutsanos. But whatever its source, the story is worked out with much sensitive detail. The gradations by which ardent friendship melts into erotic awareness are depicted with some subtlety. It is difficult to think of any comparable description of the awakening of homosexual feeling in English literature before the twentieth century. As a portrait of an adolescent struggling toward self-awareness, *Don Leon* adumbrates Forster's *Maurice*, which was not written until eighty years later. This sympathetic dramatization of the stages by which Byron realized his feelings for the male sex works in two ways—as a biographical revelation and as a rhetorical device to moderate homophobic sentiment by showing the anguish of a sensitive boy. The "argument from antiquity" is cleverly handled by having "Byron" discover the truth about Greek and Roman society from his reading.

As for the sociological arguments for tolerance, it is interesting to compare these to Bentham's. There is the same citing of Malthus (who did indeed list "unnatural acts" as a check to population): "Economists, who seek the world to thin, / 'Tis you who teach this so named deadly sin" (lines 775–76). Both protest strongly against the sensationalism and virulence of the British press. Like Bentham, the *Leon* poet also argues that homosexuality is less of a social evil than extramarital pregnancies and adultery. Bentham, in his prospectus addressed to William Beckford, painstakingly enumerated every kind of sexual conduct in order that prejudice might be "perplexed and weakened" by their sheer numbers. The *Leon* poet does something similar, dwelling on a variety of heterosexual techniques with some relish. This is perhaps the least acceptable part of the poem: there is something offensive in his lubricious bandying of names and initials. Where Bentham presents his list in a scientific spirit with dry logic, the *Leon* poet writes with a smirk that is rather reminiscent of Martial; his approach is too much like blackening the kettle to brighten the pot.

Once again, one is brought up short by the language. Like everything else published on homosexuality in its day, this passionately antihomophobic poem uses virulently homophobic expressions. This diction, however, is more difficult to explain than in Byron's Beckford stanza, Hobhouse's paragraph on the Albanians, or Bentham's early manuscript notes and essays. In other contexts such language might be explicable on rhetorical grounds or grounds of prudence. But such considerations would scarcely seem to hold for the *Leon* poet, who frankly celebrates the joys of same-sex intercourse. To find this enthusiasm coupled with references to homosexuality as a "morbid lust," "sport obscene," "rank disease," "impure delinquency," etc., is startling. G. Wilson Knight explains the anomaly as an attempt at "balance," but the effect is more like linguistic schizophrenia.

It is also difficult, given the deadly seriousness of the poem's plea for law reform, to account for the playful eroticism of some of the later pages. Though it is a minor element, there is enough in this vein to have tempted most nineteenth-century readers to dismiss the production as a mere essay in pornography, as the Victorians understood the term. This must have drastically limited its circulation and weakened its impact on all but the least prudish. One possibility is that the more glaring passages—the bedroom scene and the final peroration—were not added until after 1841, by which time all hopes for homosexual law reform, as we shall see, had been finally laid to rest. Perhaps the author felt that, given the circumstances, the only channels of distribution open to him were illicit sales in shops dealing in erotica. This may have prompted him to add these passages. Ironically, this spice, which, under Victorian law, would itself have justified the pamphlet's destruction by the authorities, in fact preserved it since the erotic sections seem to have been what motivated Dugdale to print his 1866 edition.

Some of the contrasts with Bentham, both in tone and argument, reflect the change that had taken place in the political situation between the Regency (when Bentham did most of his writing) and the 1830s. In 1818, when Bentham finished his most extensive notes in favor of the decriminalization of sodomy, criminal law reform in England was still in the future. By 1833, the death penalty had been abolished for many offenses. It was this movement, originating in the House of Commons, that had particularly aroused the hopes of homosexuals. The poem is consequently full of minutiae relating to Parliament and parliamentarians. Though these create many obscurities for the modern reader, they also give it substance and reality. As if specifically addressed to its members, *Don Leon* contains detailed accounts of four men in the House who found themselves threatened by the law in homosexual scandals, and a fifth is mentioned in the notes. Of these, two, Richard Heber and William Bankes, had connections with Hobhouse and Byron.

Writing from Ravenna in 1821, Byron had asked Hobhouse to congratulate Heber on his recent election as a member from Oxford.[15] When Heber, a famous book col-

---

15.   September 12, 1821, *BLJ*, 8:207.

lector, died in exile twelve years later, the English press was full of lengthy obituaries, most of which ignored or made only veiled references to the ostracism he had suffered in his last years. Sir Walter Scott had praised him as "Heber the magnificent" for his library, rendered him thanks in the notes to the Waverley novels, and celebrated their friendship in the sixth canto of *Marmion*. Heber's collection of early English books was the most impressive yet assembled; he left eight houses full of volumes in England and on the Continent. Then in 1826, he was accused of homosexual relations, and he fled to Brussels. Scott noted in his journal that "his life was compromised but for the exertions of Hobhouse under Secy of State who detected a warrant for his trial passing through the office."[16] (This Hobhouse was, in fact, not John Cam but his cousin Henry.) In a long account of Heber's scholarship and politics, the *Annual Register* reported with unusual candor: "In the year 1831, he returned to England, but not into the society which he had left; for rumors had been in circulation degrading to his moral character. With the exception of his visits to the auction-rooms and booksellers' shops, he lived entirely secluded among his books at Pimlico or Hodnet."[17]

During his first year at Trinity College Byron identified William Bankes and Edward Noel Long as his closest student intimates. He called Bankes his "collegiate pastor, and master, and patron" and often joined him and Matthews in Bankes's rooms.[18] Later their paths crossed again under ironic circumstances. Bankes proposed to Annabella Milbanke shortly after Byron had made his first proposal and, like him, was turned down. When Bankes ventured on a long voyage to the East, Byron wrote recommendations for him in Albania and, impressed by his scholarly

16. July 10, 1826, *The Journal of Sir Walter Scott*, ed. W. E. K. Anderson (Oxford: Clarendon Press, 1972), p. 170. Anderson wrongly identifies the undersecretary as John Cam Hobhouse.
17. *Annual Register* (1833), p. 246*.
18. To John Murray, Ravenna, November 19, 1820, *BLJ*, 7:230.

discoveries, took a vicarious pride in his "perilous researches." [19] "Bankes is a wonderful fellow," Byron wrote
Murray in 1820, "I love and esteem him." [20] That same year
Byron wrote an unusually warm invitation to Bankes to
join him in Ravenna to celebrate the carnival. After his return to England, Bankes made his country house in Dorset
a showplace for antiquities and became a close friend of
the Duke of Wellington. From 1822 to 1826 he sat in Parliament as the member from Cambridge; later he represented
Marlborough and Dorset. Then in June 1833, he was arrested and accused of sexual misconduct with a guardsman in a public convenience near the House of Commons.
At his trial in December the duke testified as a character
witness. So did the headmaster of Harrow and a phalanx
of members from both houses. The jury, duly impressed,
found both men not guilty and "without the least stain on
their characters." [21] Eight years later, when Bankes was
again arrested for a similar offense, he followed in Byron's
footsteps by retiring to Venice, where he died in 1855. [22]

Don Leon was written to forward homosexual law reform, but the cause did not prosper. When the Commission on Criminal Law, appointed in 1833, issued their second report in June 1836, they recommended reducing
capital offenses to eight crimes, all of which (except sodomy) involved violence or danger to life. But their only reference to homosexuality was a single sentence: "A nameless offense of great enormity we, at present, exclude from
consideration." [23] A bill to abolish the death penalty for

19.   To William Bankes, November 20, 1819, *BLJ*, 6:243.
20.   August 31 and October 8, 1820, *BLJ*, 7:168, 195.
21.   *Annual Register* (1833), p. 169*.
22.   See n. 88 to *Don Leon*. There is more on Heber and Bankes in
A. L. Rowse, *Homosexuals in History* (London: Weidenfeld & Nicolson,
1977), pp. 120–27; and in my essay, "*Don Leon*, Byron, and Homosexual
Law Reform."
23.   "Punishments, and Particularly That of Death," in *Second Report
from His Majesty's Commissioners on Criminal Laws* (British Sessional Papers,
1836), 36:219.

rape and sodomy passed the Commons in 1841 (where the debate touched only on rape), but the sodomy law reform was killed in the House of Lords. On June 17, the Earl of Wicklow argued that if the Lords passed such a law, "they would lower themselves in public opinion; for as the organ of the public voice, they would sanction what the people of this country would never confirm—that sodomy and rape were not crimes of so heinous a character as to deserve death." Next day, the Earl of Winchelsea proposed an amendment to retain capital punishment for homosexuality alone. "Their Lordships, he was convinced, would do great violence to the moral feelings of a very large class of the community, if they exempted this crime from the penalty of death." [24] Not until 1861, when a comprehensive measure consolidating and revising portions of the English criminal law was passed, was the death penalty for sodomy reduced to life imprisonment, a sanction that remained unchanged for more than a century.

Though it is impossible to speak with real certainty of the author and the date of *Don Leon*, certain considerations do suggest themselves. First, it seems altogether likely that, whatever additions or changes were made later, the poem was completed substantially in its present form sometime in the late summer or early fall of 1833. [25] The two cases that seem to have provoked the work were the arrest of William Bankes in June and the execution of Nicholls in

24. June 17, 1841, *Hansard's Parliamentary Debates* (London: Hansard, 1841), 3rd ser., vol. 58, cols. 1557, 1568.

25. There have been two principal arguments advanced for a date later than 1833. One is that Charles Manners-Sutton, the speaker, did not get the peerage (referred to in line 1041) until March 1835. But as I show in my article, "*Don Leon*, Byron, and Homosexual Law Reform," Manners-Sutton's longed-for peerage was a publicly debated issue in 1833 when the reform Parliament met. The other argument is that line 987 predicts that Henry Grey Bennett will die abroad. Bennett did die in Florence on June 16, 1836. But, as Knight points out, this may simply be a reasonable guess as to what would happen. It is also possible that the poem was revised at a later date.

August. The Bankes episode may have suggested to the poet that members of Parliament would now be ready to listen to reformist arguments since a distinguished Tory member of the lower house had become a victim of the law. Because Bankes's acquittal in December made his case moot, it is likely that the section of the poem devoted to Bankes (which is very near the conclusion) was finished before his trial took place. There is also the curious fact that the substantial list of arrests for 1833, in note 56, includes cases dated February, April, May, June, and early August, but none later. Probably, then, the note was compiled in late August or shortly afterward.

As for the author, one is struck by his minute knowledge of details pertaining to the Commons. He notes, for instance, that Sir Stephen Lushington sat near the speaker and that the "youth with courtly manners" (who may or may not have been James Stanhope) shared the same row with the "elder Bankes," that is, Bankes's father. No one who had not frequented the House often and been closely familiar with its membership would have been aware that these two obscure parliamentarians sat in the same row or could have told the reader that James Brogden spoke in a shy manner at certain moments (as in line 1012). If the author was not an elected representative, he was certainly someone whose duties or interests brought him into close relation with Parliament. His intimate knowledge of Byron's life also suggests that if he had not known Byron, he was at least a confidant of some friend of his. Possibly this friend was William Bankes himself, who, on visiting Byron in Italy on the way home from his Eastern travels in 1821, may have exchanged confidences with him.

But whoever he was, the *Leon* poet has left us a unique document. No further candid discussion of Byron's homosexuality appeared in English until 1935 when Peter Quennell published his *Byron: The Years of Fame*. Not only did the *Leon* poet set forth the main facts about Byron's homosexuality a full century before Byron's more conventional biographers dared to broach the subject; he also wrote, in a form that is telling and powerful, the earliest published protest against homosexual oppression in England that has survived and the first plea for understanding.

Since Hobhouse was still alive in the 1860s, he may have read *Don Leon* in Dugdale's edition. If he did, he must have realized that someone at last knew the truth he had tried so desperately to keep hidden. At his advanced age (he was eighty in 1866) he may not have cared; indeed, he hardly need have—it was almost a century before anyone would pay any serious heed to *Don Leon*. He would probably have been far more concerned had he read the attack on Byron that Harriet Beecher Stowe published three months after his death.

Stowe's "The True Story of Lady Byron's Life" appeared simultaneously as a leading article in *Macmillan's Magazine* and in the *Atlantic Monthly* in September 1869. It caused an international furor by making public for the first time the accusation of incest. Stowe's avowed reason for making her revelations, which were based on conversations she had had with Lady Byron in 1856, four years before her death, was to counteract what she regarded as the pernicious moral influence of the new cheap editions of Byron's poetry. But since it was felt she was recklessly seeking a journalistic sensation, her revelations were coldly received. Her report that Lady Byron believed Augusta and Byron had been lovers was credited, but most Victorians were disposed to believe that Lady Byron was mistaken and that Stowe had injudiciously betrayed her friend's confidences. On balance she received far more blame than praise. But Stowe's essay was by far the most controversial ever published about Byron. Dozens of articles and several books appeared in response, most of them critical. Finally, Stowe herself repeated and defended her charges in *Lady Byron Vindicated* (1870). In the midst of the uproar, it is surprising that no direct hints of Byron's homosexuality surfaced, all the more so since Dugdale's edition of *Don Leon* had been in circulation for several years: the disinclination to credit it or even to acknowledge its existence seems to have been total.

One of the many replies to Stowe's revelations was Alfred Austin's *Vindication of Lord Byron*, which rashly rejected the accusation of incest as absurd. Austin did, however, quote a letter from John Robertson, an acquaintance of Lady Byron, to the effect that during the years he had known Lady Byron at Brighton: "I heard but of one crime of which she accused her dead husband," a crime, he implied, quite different from Stowe's charge.[26] This seems to suggest that Lady Byron made Byron's homosexuality known to her intimates. But nothing more specific than this appears to have found its way into print, and Austin's readers must have been left guessing as to the nature of this crime, which Robertson simply discounted as one of Lady Byron's delusions.

By the seventies, however, at least one homosexual reader of Byron had come close to penetrating to the truth. In an essay on Byron in *St. Paul's Magazine* in 1873, Lord Roden Noel included two paragraphs that hinted at a pederastic strain in the poet's temperament. Noel seems to have been alerted by Shelley's letter to Peacock about Byron's life at Venice, which had been published by Mary Shelley in 1840. He speaks of "some curious references" in this communication without quoting it. By juxtaposing this with Byron's remark about rumors accusing him of the crimes of Tiberius and Heliogabalus, his "passionate" friendships at Harrow, and his predilections for Clare, Edlestone, Rushton and Giraud, Noel succeeds in throwing a very different color over Byron's relations than the romantic friendship theory of Moore, though he does not go beyond veiled suggestions. If the reader had not read Shelley's letter or was hazy about Heliogabalus, he or she remained in the dark. Noel, an admirer of Walt Whitman's

26.   (London: Chapman & Hall, 1869), p. 67.

"Calamus" lyrics, later republished "Lord Byron and His Times" in his *Essays on Poetry and Poets* (1886). This anthology was dedicated "to my friend, John Addington Symonds." In the autobiography that he left in manuscript, Symonds identifies Noel as one of the men who helped initiate him into London's homosexual subculture. A curious thread of relationship also linked Noel and Hobhouse—the latter's son-in-law, the fifth Earl of Roden (a grandnephew of his friend the Bishop of Clogher), was Lord Roden Noel's uncle.

More typical of the age were some diffident speculations on the identity of Thyrza, published in the *Athenaeum* in 1884 by a writer who signed himself "A. B." Reacting to an improbable guess by John Cordy Jeaffreson that Thyrza was Margaret Parker, the writer pointed out that Byron's cousin had died in 1800 when he was only twelve. Since he then quotes Byron's Pigot rhapsody, the relevant letters to Dallas and Hodgson, and the "Cornelian" references, his chain of argument seems to be leading inescapably to Edlestone. But at the last moment, he retreats almost, if not quite all the way, to Moore's position. The idea of Byron's writing a series of love poems about a young man was still not acceptable. "The inference should be," he speculates, "that, as Moore holds, there was strictly speaking, no historical Thyrza; that the poems addressed to her express many blended sorrows; and that among them the sorrow for young Eddlestone [*sic*] was probably the most poignant." But if it was Edlestone he mourned, why did Byron change the gender? The writer suggests that it was less embarrassing to pretend he was writing love poems to a woman than to reveal a personal friendship with a boy of a *lower* class:

> So far as this emotion was in his mind, Byron would feel that he would provoke ridicule (which no one dreaded more in such cases) by uttering in public such a sentiment about his humble friend as he expressed in his letters to Hodgson. He therefore adopted the language of a bereaved lover, and addressed his verses to a feminine name, though . . . the poetry would be equally appropriate in either case. Precedents of the

poetry of friendship resembling the poetry of love will occur to every one.[27]

The writer was, of course, referring to Tennyson's *In Memoriam*, which had now taken its place beside Shakespeare's sonnets as a problematic expression of male affection.

In the meantime, *Don Leon* went unnoticed except by a bibliographer whose speciality was erotica: Henry Spencer Ashbee devoted four short pages to it and quoted a few lines in the first volume of his *Index Librorum Prohibitorum*. This bibliography was printed pseudonymously in 1877, and because of Victorian disapproval of its subject matter, it had only a limited, surreptitious circulation. It is a sign of the times that even Ashbee should have repudiated both its implication of homosexuality and Stowe's charge of incest as equally "heinous and preposterous." But though *Don Leon* was discounted as a salacious squib and remained unknown except to a tiny group of collectors of rare pornography, its existence inevitably posed a threat. Ashbee tells the story of a friend to whom Dugdale had shown a manuscript of the poem about 1860. The friend had warned the publisher "to be very cautious about any application to Lady Byron, as, although they would only laugh at him for being so credulous [Dugdale at that point believed the poem really was by Byron], he might be charged with attempting to extort money if the matter came to the ears of 'The Society.'"[28] Dugdale had apparently intended to use the manuscript for the purpose of blackmail.

Whether or not Lady Byron ever heard of *Don Leon*, there is no doubt that it was known to her daughter Ada's son, Lord Lovelace. Unnamed but unmistakable, it haunts the pages of the curious essay Lovelace had printed pri-

27. "Who Was Thyrza?" *Athenaeum*, no. 2958 (July 5, 1884), pp. 14–15.
28. I.e., the Society for the Suppression of Vice; see *Index Librorum Prohibitorum*, Vol. 1 of *Bibliography of Prohibited Books* (1877; rpt. New York: Jack Brussel, 1962), pp. 192–93.

vately in 1905 under the title *Astarte*. His main purpose
was to defend Lady Byron, who had reared him after the
death of his mother, by showing that there was indeed
substance to the allegation of incest made by Stowe.
Unlike Stowe, who was a crusading moralist, feminist, and popular writer, Lord Lovelace was an erudite and irascible conservative skeptic, who regretted that "Semitic and socialist hordes" were threatening classical education. That so
proud and sensitive an aristocrat should circulate, even
privately, a book convicting his grandfather of incest was
piquant enough. That the book is also concerned to lay to
rest an unspoken accusation of homosexuality adds an ad-
ditional interest to the enterprise.

Lovelace, of course, had access to Lady Byron's voluminous memoranda, which he had typed and then personally classified. From them and Byron's letters he extracts a case for the guilt of Byron and Augusta that most
biographers have regarded as reasonably conclusive. But
he does not think of incest as a particularly horrible sin.
After all, he reminds the reader, it was not unknown
among the great of Byron's day, and Byron and Augusta
were only half-siblings. He even makes the romantic suggestion that they should have defied society by eloping.
Where homosexuality is concerned, however, his insou-
ciance deserts him. Incest, he declares, with characteristic
vehemence, was after all "a sin far less repulsive than some
exaggerations and inventions about [Byron] which human
imbecility and infatuation forged out of infinitely little
knowledge."[29] His strong phobia on the subject is visible in
his comments on Shelley's letter about Byron's sexually
dubious companions in Italy. Though Byron lived a licentious life there, he writes: "Trustworthy contemporary information from Venice, dating from the first half of the
nineteenth century, disposes completely of the most re-

29. Ralph Milbanke, Earl of Lovelace, *Astarte: A Fragment of Truth Concerning George Gordon Byron, Sixth Lord Byron*, ed. Mary, Countess of Lovelace (London: Christophers, 1921), p. 152.

pulsive abominations. There was no foundation for the crass and egregious suggestions of Shelley in a letter to Peacock, which became a favourite quotation for credulous ill-wishers."[30] Lovelace thinks Shelley was imposed upon by rumors promoted by Byron's hostile ex-mistress Claire Clairmont. Obviously, in Lovelace's eyes incest was a family scandal that time might palliate and even glamorize, but not homosexuality.

Lovelace was also hostile to Thomas Moore for including the Pigot letters in his *Life*. Presumably it was the two on Edlestone that especially excited him. "The worst[!] of his letters were included. There were juvenile letters, in which, having nothing to tell, he made up crude realities into idiotic nonsense for idiots to read. Subsequent notoriety could never convert trash written to Pigot into literature or biography. . . . They mean nothing and explain nothing."[31] Lovelace was particularly embarrassed to repudiate the implications of *Don Leon* without directly acknowledging the poem's existence or specifying the nature of its revelations. Speaking of the period immediately after Lady Byron's death in 1860, Lovelace tells the reader:

> Strange invaders reappeared, intent upon campaigns—futile and unprovoked, but sufficient to splash "a noteless blot on a remembered name." Statements and personalities of an unusual description were circulated, which the Byrons must absolutely repudiate and condemn, and that in the most and indeed only effectual manner—by plain truth and tangible evidence—practical exposure of pseudo-Byronese manipulations and fables. . . . The unpopularity of disestablishing favourite delusions [i.e., that Byron did not commit incest] has no terror for those who are already misrepresented.[32]

Lovelace was aware of the rumors in circulation at the time of Byron's separation from his wife. He comments: "It

30. Ibid., p. 124n. It is not clear what "information" Lord Lovelace had seen or what had elicited it.
31. Ibid., p. 129.
32. Ibid., p. 173.

is right to state most distinctly that the separation papers leave no possible place for other charges besides the two commonplace ones of adultery and cruelty, and that connected with Mrs. Leigh." [33] This statement is odd, to say the least, in the light of what we now know, for the Lovelace papers contained Lady Byron's memorandum of her interview with Lady Caroline Lamb. No doubt Lovelace was prepared to discount Caroline's statement as strongly as he had Shelley's.

With his bias it was inevitable that Lovelace should try to discourage the kind of speculations about Thyrza that the *Athenaeum* had published. When E. H. Coleridge undertook to edit Byron's works in 1898—originally with the cooperation of Lord Lovelace—the annotations for "To Thyrza" obviously presented a problem. Coleridge prefaced the footnote on the poem in his editions with the explanation that "the following note on the identity of Thyrza has been communicated to the Editor." We now know that the anonymous annotator was Lord Lovelace and that Coleridge had doubts about his communication, which he nevertheless published. The note reads: "The identity of Thyrza and the question whether the person addressed under this name really existed, or was an imaginary being, have given rise to much speculation and discussion of a more or less futile kind. This difficulty is now incapable of definitive and authoritative solution." Drawing on his knowledge of Lady Byron's papers, Lovelace then declares that "Byron referred to Thyrza in conversation with Lady Byron . . . as a young girl who had existed," thereby giving the impression that whatever else was in doubt about Thyrza, there was no doubt about her gender. [34]

Given the climate of opinion in England, it is not sur-

33. Ibid., p. 182.
34. *The Works of Lord Byron*, ed. E. H. Coleridge, rev. ed. (London: John Murray, 1905), 3:30–31.

prising that the first open surmises about Byron's bisexuality in scholarly contexts appeared in works published in Germany, France, and Italy. In Germany attitudes toward homosexuality were markedly more liberal than elsewhere on the Continent and far freer than in England. Two aspects of German culture contributed especially to this liberalism. One was the exceedingly high prestige of classical studies in intellectual and academic circles: German scholarship on Greek art, history, literature, and philosophy led the world and by implication called into question postclassical prejudices. Substantial learned essays on Greek homosexuality began to appear in German reference works as early as 1830. Candid discussions of this theme in Plato and other Greek writers abounded. The other liberating influence was the respect accorded "science" generally and medical science in particular in Germany. As a result, psychiatrists, jurists, and anthropologists found it possible to discuss the issue in print. Karl Heinrich Ulrichs, a homosexual German legal worker, had opened a debate with a series of studies in the 1860s of what he called "Uranianism." Psychiatrists began to publish case histories, and, though some of these had a negative effect by stereotyping homosexuality as an illness, they at least broke the taboo of silence. Symptomatic of these new developments was the creation of a new scientific nomenclature to replace the old theological language: the word *homosexual* was coined in 1869. Twenty years later, Magnus Hirschfeld, a German physician and sex researcher, organized a group of scientists and intellectuals as the Scientific-Humanitarian Committee to agitate for law reform (a move unthinkable at that time in England) and inaugurated an ambitious scholarly annual, the *Jahrbuch für sexuelle Zwischenstufen*, with lengthy, well-documented articles on scientific and cultural aspects of homosexuality.

These new developments in sexology also aroused interest in France. Volume 15 of the *Bibliothèque de Criminologie*, published in Lyons in 1896, was devoted to *Uranisme et unisexualité*, a title reflecting the German inspiration of its "scientific" categorizing. Its author was André Raffalovitch, a young decadent poet, who had grown up in Paris, settled in London at the age of eighteen, and been associated with the circle of Oscar Wilde. Raffalovitch's study, published the year after Wilde was sent to prison, included biographical entries devoted to a number of famous literary figures, among them Byron, whom he classified as a bisexual. His opening sentence implies that Byron had already been "claimed" by homosexual circles in Europe, though his two pages on the poet's attachments at Harrow and to Edlestone and Giraud do not draw on any information not in Moore's *Life*.[35] This suggests that in some homosexual groups, Moore's "explanations" had already been discounted as veiling the truth.

Inevitably, speculation about Byron appeared in the *Jahrbuch*.[36] But the language barrier, the threat of censorship by customs, and no doubt the high level of paranoia in the still covert gay communities of America and England kept the *Jahrbuch* from circulating in those countries except through medical libraries. Neither the British Museum nor the Library of Congress acquired copies, despite its impressive scholarship and extensive bibliographies, which listed on the average two or three thousand articles published each year in Europe. Some of this research, however, found its way into a six-hundred-page study on homosexuality in English published in Italy. This was *The*

35.   *Uranisme et unisexualité: Etude sur différentes manifestations de l'instinct sexuel* (Lyon: A. Storck, 1896), pp. 308–09.

36.   Review of Hans Rau, "Das Liebesleben Lord Byrons," *Jahrbuch für sexuelle Zwischenstufen* 4 (1902):883–86. The reviewer took notice of some remarks by Rau in the *Neue Heilkunst* for December 1901 and of Richard Ackermann's *Lord Byron*, which had followed Lord Roden Noel in identifying Thyrza with Edlestone. *En passant*, he noted that the editor of the *Neue Heilkunst* claimed to have seen a letter from Lady Byron to Elise Schmitt-Berka, which accused Byron of a propensity for boys. The reviewer called for further research but made no attempt on his own to explicate Byron's poetry except to wonder if the "sin that haunted Manfred in Byron's drama" might have been a "sodomitical offense." *Manfred* is now, of course, taken to reflect Byron's feelings about his incest with his sister.

Intersexes: A History of Similisexualism as a Problem in Social Life, the work of an expatriate American music critic named Edward Irenaeus Prime Stevenson, who used the pseudonym "Xavier Mayne." Though the preface is dated Rome, 1908, it is not clear exactly when it appeared: it draws heavily on the *Jahrbuch* for its scientific framework and for its historical and literary materials but was not reviewed in Hirschfeld's journal until October 1911. Stevenson devotes five pages to Byron, whom, using the scientific jargon of Hirschfeld's circle, he calls a "Dionian-Uranian," that is, a "bisexual." "During all his life," Stevenson wrote, "the great English poet was more or less temperamentally homosexual: an idealistic, hellenic, romantic homosexual." He speaks of Byron's love for Clare, Edlestone, and Giraud and concludes, with significant insight: "In Byron's boyhood and in his university days, his homosexuality was the most really passional emotion of love which he knew." "Greek in his intellectual and sexual nature, he was Athenian at heart."[37] However, like many pioneers Stevenson overstates his case. Having decided that Byron was, indeed, attracted to boys, he errs by concluding that he never was seriously attracted to women. Nevertheless, Stevenson's book is remarkable for providing the first straightforward account of Byron's homosexuality in English. Unfortunately he reached very few readers; he printed only 125 copies, and few found their way into American libraries. The book was all but inaccessible until Arno Press reprinted it in 1975.[38]

---

37. (Privately printed, n.p., n.d.; rpt. New York: Arno Press, 1975), pp. 356, 359.

38. Stevenson has little to say about Byron's poetry with one notable exception. In a section subtitled "Byron's 'Manfred': A Homosexual Allegory?" he tells us he had received "a pertinent comment on *Manfred*" from a correspondent who "claims strong private authority in discussing Byron's homosexualism." According to this account, the writer's grandfather had discussed "Greek love" with Byron and confessed some kind of same-sex liaison:

When my grandfather had finished his account, which you can imagine was done with great embarassment [*sic*], Byron said after a moment—"Pooh, I don't

The difficulty of disseminating scholarly work on the subject of homosexuality was dramatized by the fate of the first English book on the subject, Havelock Ellis's *Sexual Inversion*. In a trial in 1870, the British attorney-general had expressed a sense of gratification that there was "very little learning or knowledge upon this subject in this country," and a defense counselor thanked God that such scientific literature was still foreign to the libraries of British medical men.[39] But the sensation caused by the Wilde case and the intense popular hostility it aroused led Ellis to make an attempt at enlightening the public. This he did, in a book written in collaboration with John Addington Symonds. A German translation appeared without difficulty in 1896, but the opposition he faced in England was formidable. First, Symonds died and his heirs insisted that Ellis destroy the first English edition and remove Symonds's name and contributions. Though Ellis's style was austerely chaste by any standards, the courts found the revised book obscene and issued an order for the destruction of all copies. Later editions were published only in America where legal standards were markedly more tolerant. In 1916, Ellis incorporated some materials on Byron from Raffalovitch and the *Jahrbuch*. He suggested that Byron's feelings for Clare and

---

think any the worse of you for such an affair. . . . Why, let me tell you I expected a while ago to write a drama on Greek Love—not less—modernizing the atmosphere—glooming it over—to throw the whole subject back into nature, where it belongs now as always—to paint the struggle of the finer moral type of mind against it—or rather remorse for it, when it seems to be chastized. . . . But I made up my mind that British philosophy is not far enough on for swallowing such a thing neat. So I turned much of it into 'Manfred.'" . . . Lord Byron then went on to give my grandfather some other observations on the abandoning of his original plan for the poem mentioned.

(pp. 359–60)

If authentic, these remarks are of some interest both as to the genesis of *Manfred* and as to Byron's view of homosexuality. But except for the reference to "British philosophy" the style of the reported conversation does not sound very much like Byron.

39.   Jeffrey Weeks, "Inverts, Perverts, and Mary-Annes: Male Prostitution and the Regulation of Homosexuality in England in the Nineteenth and Early Twentieth Centuries," *Journal of Homosexuality* 6 (1980–1981): 117.

Giraud might have been homosexual and that some of his poems to women were in fact "inspired by men." He concluded, however: "It is probable . . . that here, as well as in the case of Shakespeare, and in that of Tennyson's love for his youthful friend, Arthur Hallam, as well as of Montaigne for Etienne de La Boëtie, although such strong friendships may involve an element of sexual emotion, we have no true and definite homosexual impulse; homosexuality is merely simulated by the ardent and hyperesthetic emotions of the poet." [40] For once, Ellis's scholarly caution served him ill. But even his guarded remarks reached few in England: the British Museum possessed a copy of his banned study but did not list it in the catalogue.

Byron's biographers of this period were not as open-minded as Ellis, whose studies were in sexology. Ethel Colburn Mayne's spirited two-volume life of 1912, which remained the standard scholarly work for more than a generation, was exceptionally naïve, perhaps because Lord Lovelace's fulminations misled her. She fully accepted Lovelace's views on Byron's incest, but she dismissed the *Don Leon* poems (rarely referred to even obliquely in that day) as "little filthy contraband *brochures*" that "told of things unspeakable in villainous alexandrines." [41] Yet the subject of Byron's friendships, which she interpreted idealistically, fascinated and puzzled her. In her very full account of Byron's friendship with Edlestone, she emphatically rejected the theory that he was the object of the Thyrza lyrics on the grounds that Byron told Dallas that the related stanzas in *Childe Harold* did not allude to "any *male* friend." [42] Mayne quotes the passage from the Ravenna journal on the "violent, though *pure*, love and passion" but gives the impression that she does not connect this with Edlestone, though she is puzzled as to why

40. *Sexual Inversion*, Vol. 2 of *Studies in the Psychology of Sex*, 3rd ed. rev. (Philadelphia: F. A. Davis, 1920), p. 48.
41. *Byron* (New York: Charles Scribner's Sons, 1912), 2:1.
42. Ibid., 1:92n.

Byron did not make mention of so important an attachment in these recollections. This puzzlement also comes out in her account of Byron's penchant for Giraud, which she describes as "one of those ambiguous friendships with a youth infinitely below him in rank." She calls Byron's bequest to him a "fantastic feature" of a "fantastic will." [43] One feels that Mayne's upbringing in a society dedicated to silence on the subject of homosexuality made it hard for her to imagine that Byron might have had such interests.

The ultimate in the "blind eye" approach to this matter came in John Drinkwater's popular but well-researched *The Pilgrim of Eternity* (1925). By this time public awareness of male homosexuality had made Thomas Moore's romantic friendship approach obsolete so that Drinkwater simply bypasses the subject. He ignores Byron's boyhood "passions," omits all reference to Edlestone, Thyrza, and Giraud, and refers to Lukas (whom Mayne failed to mention) merely as "a Greek boy whom Byron had taken into his service." It would be impossible from this book, which purports to give a detailed account of Byron's whole life, to derive even the faintest hint of his bisexuality. André Maurois, whose widely read *Byron* appeared in 1930, was more candid but still cautious about offending British sensibilities. He tells of Byron's friendships with Edlestone and Giraud and identifies Thyrza with the former. But we get no clue as to how he interprets these until the "Epilogue," when he sweeps Byron's loves together into one catalogue: "Yes, what Byron was capable of loving in another was a certain kind of innocence and youthfulness—whence Mary Duff and Margaret Parker, whence Edlestone and Nicolo Giraud, or later Teresa Guiccioli and the page Loukas." [44] His including the three fifteen-year-old boys in his list suggests that Maurois perceived Byron as bisexual but was unwilling to say so directly.

43. Ibid., pp. 181, 182.
44. Trans. Hamish Miles (New York: D. Appelton, 1930), p. 555.

But by the end of the 1920s a change had taken place in intellectual circles in the English-speaking world. Though popular feeling and legal opinion remained negative, educated men and women read Mann, Gide, and Proust and found in the writings of Freud an analytical detachment. True, Forster could not conceive of publishing *Maurice* (written in 1912–1913), and D. H. Lawrence's *The Rainbow* was declared obscene in 1915 because it contained a lesbian episode even though Lawrence presented it negatively. But there was now a minority willing to take a stand against censorship. In 1929 James Douglas, a popular London journalist, launched a vitriolic attack on Radclyffe Hall's *Well of Loneliness* in the *Sunday Express*: his argument was that though the fight against novels with explicitly homosexual themes had been lost in France and Germany, English fiction was still uncontaminated and should remain so. Though the judge refused to hear their evidence and ruled that copies of the book should be destroyed, leading literary figures of the day rallied to Radclyffe Hall's defense. The times were undoubtedly ready for a more candid consideration of Byron's sexuality if significant new evidence were to appear. In due course it did—ironically enough from the hand of the man who had tried most energetically in Byron's age to suppress information. The treatment this evidence received, however, was at first far from ingenuous.

Some time about 1920 (he does not give the exact date) Harold Nicolson found Hobhouse's copy of Moore's *Life* offered for sale in a bookseller's catalogue and purchased the volume. Nicolson's *Byron: The Last Journey* (1924) made some use of Hobhouse's marginalia. When he reprinted the book five years later, Nicolson appended a chapter entitled "An Addition to Byron's Biography," in which he claimed to quote "all" of Hobhouse's "perfectly legible" pencil notes. He calls Hobhouse's statement that Byron's connection with Lord Grey "had much effect upon his future morals" a "puzzle" and comments: "We are left guessing" as to what he meant to imply. He adopts the same approach with Hobhouse's remark that Moore had "not the remotest guess at the real reason which induced Lord B. at that time to prefer having no Englishman immediately or constantly near him" in Greece, remarking: "again we are left with a riddle," though his reiteration suggests that he saw some connection between the two notes.[45] One has the impression that Nicolson was deliberately playing dumb. Nicolson, as we know from his son's memoir, was homosexual, but he was exceptionally discreet. Montgomery Hyde has noted that his diaries, full of information about high life in London, are silent on the subject of homosexuality, though it played a part in the lives of many of the men of rank he describes. His training as a diplomat no doubt led him to prefer caution, and his desire for a peerage would have discouraged him from precipitating anything like a new Stowe imbroglio.

Peter Quennell was more daring. Though his *Byron: The Years of Fame* (1935) dealt only with Byron's life in England in 1811–1816, and thus did not cover the period when Byron was directly involved with Edlestone, Giraud, or Lukas, it was the first book on Byron to bring his bisexuality clearly into the open. Nicolson allowed Quennell to examine the Hobhouse pencilings: for the first time these are related meaningfully to Byron's psychology. Quennell connects Hobhouse's remark about Byron's wanting no Englishman near him in Greece with his affair with Giraud. In his chapter on Lady Caroline Lamb, Quennell interpolates an essay "Byron as Amorist," quotes Hobhouse's comment on Grey, and, though not quite explicitly, implies a homosexual interpretation of the incident. He also prints for the first time something Nicolson had omitted— Hobhouse's pregnant remark that "M. knows nothing, or will tell nothing, of the principal cause and motive of these boyish friendships." Having primed his readers with hints,

45. New ed. with a supplementary chapter (London: Constable, 1929), pp. 300, 301.

Quennell finally speaks openly on page 100: "I have suggested that a pronounced strain of homosexual feeling ran
through his life." This is the first time, to my knowledge,
that the word was used in a book on Byron published and
freely circulated in England. At the end, he sums up: "He
wanted love; and it is conceivable that, had he been born
during the fourth or fifth century before Christ, at Athens
or Sparta, his amatory existence might have developed on
happier and more harmonious lines." [46] This was a position
not far from Stevenson's. [47]

It was not until the 1950s, however, that anyone took up
Quennell's theme again. By this time the Kinsey report of
1948 suggested to Americans and English alike that male
homosexuality was not a rare phenomenon but something
involving a significant proportion of the population. Indeed, Kinsey found that some 37 percent of white American men had had such experiences after the age of sixteen
and that fully half of all males were aware of erotic arousal
by other males. But Kinsey's findings did not immediately
usher in an era of official tolerance. In England, arrests for
homosexual offenses, which had averaged about 800 a year
before World War II, rose to 3,000 in 1952. Private homes
were searched, personal papers ransacked for evidence,
and charges brought for acts that had occurred years
before. All this might have gone unnoticed if four well-

46. (New York: Viking Press, 1935), p. 299.
47. There was no repetition of the Stowe scandal. The *Times Literary
Supplement*, the *New York Times Book Review*, and the *London Mercury* (in
which Ethel Colburn Mayne wrote a review) were silent on this aspect of
the book. But Samuel Chew (who knew *Don Leon*) accepted Quennell's
view, and Clive Bell thought it threw meaningful light on the puzzling
reference to passions "unworthy manhood" in "On This Day" (*Saturday
Review of Literature*, November 23, 1935, p. 6; *New Statesman and Nation*,
October 26, 1935, p. 608). John Sparrow even characterized Byron as
"fresher and happier" in his relations with boys than in his involvements
with women (*Spectator*, October 18, 1935, p. 615). Only Frederick Dupee
in *The Nation* adopted a skeptical stance. He described the study as "colored throughout by Mr. Quennell's theory, here and there insinuated,
that Byron was homosexual. . . . This highly unconventional notion is
not impossible but is still far from proved" (January 29, 1936, p. 136).

publicized trials had not taken place. These involved, respectively, a peer, his cousin, and two journalists. The
writers wrote books. The peer was a popular young member of the House of Lords—he was imprisoned, but instead of being ostracized as in Byron's day, he was regarded as the victim of archaic laws and objectionable
police practices. Finally, the British government set up a
Departmental Committee under Lord Wolfenden, which in
1957 recommended decriminalization. Ten years later the
law was changed.

It is at least symbolically significant that two important
books treating of Byron's homosexuality, though in very
different styles, appeared the same year as the Wolfenden
Report. The first was G. Wilson Knight's *Lord Byron's Marriage*. This was Knight's second book on Byron. The first,
Lord Byron: Christian Virtues had appeared five years earlier. Hagiographic in effect, the book cast a halo around Byron. Knight followed Teresa Guiccioli in treating Byron's
patronage of boys as one of his more attractive "virtues."
He writes at length of Byron's youthful friendships with
Clare, Edlestone, Rushton, and Giraud and his relations
with Lukas, but they are considered only as examples of
his "protectiveness, instinctive affection, and consideration for social inferiors." [48] Though Knight links Byron's
patronage to Greek *pederastia*, it is only in the educational
sense and no sexual element is implied. In this respect he
was more conservative than Quennell had been seventeen
years before.

What seems to have moved Knight onward from this
position was his reading of *Don Leon*. The poem had been
reprinted in 1934 by R. A. Caton of the Fortune Press, a
publisher whose list contained a significant number of
erotic titles. [49] A police prosecution led to a court order for

48.   *Lord Byron: Christian Virtues* (London: Routledge & Kegan Paul,
1952), p. 73.
49.   Timothy D'Arch Smith, "R. A. Caton and the Fortune Press,"
Times Literary Supplement, September 12, 1980, pp. 1003–05.

the destruction of three of these, including the new edition
of *Don Leon*. Once again, material that might have alerted
readers to the truth about Byron was suppressed. But in
1954 and 1956, Knight published two essays, "Who Wrote
'Don Leon'?" and "Colman and 'Don Leon,'" which, while
primarily addressed to the question of authorship, nevertheless, made it clear that the controversial poem purported to tell the truth about Byron's homosexuality.

In his next book on Byron, Knight returned to the subject at length, providing by far the fullest analysis to date.
The first chapter of *Lord Byron's Marriage* (1957), "Friends
and Lovers," in effect adopts the point of view of the *Leon*
poet. Knight collects together voluminous details about
Byron's Harrow friendships, speculates that he may well
have been sexually involved with Giraud in Greece, and interprets his feelings for Edlestone as set forth in his letters,
journals, and the Thyrza poems as a love relation. In
Chapter 5 he gives a full account of *Don Leon* as it bears on
Byron's homosexuality, quoting as much as seemed allow-
able under the law of the day. Though Knight's book dealt
at length with the separation controversy and was much
concerned with the questions of incest and marital sodomy, its most significant achievement was to document Byron's bisexuality by a meticulous and exhaustive, if sometimes debatable, marshaling of suggestive circumstantial
evidence.[50]

Despite its focus on hitherto taboo themes, Knight's

---

50. Knight joined the minority of Byron scholars who have been dis-
inclined to accept the incest theory, arguing that it was a "red herring"
used to cloak the more dangerous issue of homosexuality. He introduced
a new "solution" to the separation mystery, based on passages in *Don
Leon* and *Leon to Annabella*, which represent Byron as committing sodomy
with his wife. According to Knight's theory, Lady Byron was unaware of
the seriousness of this offense (which in fact was liable to the death penalty under the same statute that made male homosexuality capital) until
she consulted her lawyer, Sir Stephen Lushington. Hobhouse's remark
(see above, n. 14) adds some plausibility to this view, though conclusive
proof that this was an issue in the separation is still lacking. Doris Langley
Moore argues against Knight's view in her "Appendix 2: Byron's Sexual
Ambivalence," in *LBAR*, pp. 445–49.

book was well received. Critics praised the author's courage and candor. No one protested indignantly that Byron had been slandered, as had been the case with Harriet Beecher Stowe. The vehement Byronic and anti-Byronic partisanship of the nineteenth century was dead. And, of course, Knight was not writing as an accuser but as an admirer of Byron. Popular attitudes toward homosexuality in Britain and America were still strongly negative (as they are today, though to a lesser degree), but among literary critics the influence of Freud had made speculation about the sexual orientation of famous writers almost a fashionable game. Though such hypotheses often lacked biographical evidence and were cavalier in their lack of any sense of social context, they had at least made the unspeakable speakable. But some critics complained of Knight's "license" of interpretation where homosexuality was concerned or noted that *Don Leon*, of which he made so much, had no real authority as evidence.[51] Andrew Rutherford accused Knight of overstressing Byron's bisexuality.[52] Another reservation expressed by reviewers was provoked by Knight's theory that bisexuality was one of the stigmata of genius: this, it was felt, might have unduly influenced his view of Byron's life. But Knight did not lack for defenders. Replying to those who thought his interest in bisexuality "obsessive," the *Times Literary Supplement* argued that "since nineteenth-century morals and decorum forbade discussion or even public admission of a homosexual element in imaginative men, so much the more remains now to be exposed, explored, and weighed up in its larger implications." In the case of Byron, Knight had produced a portrait "truer to the essential genius of the man than all previous efforts."[53]

Though reviewers tended to accept Knight's findings

51.   See the letters on this subject by Alec Craig and Malcolm Elwin, *Times Literary Supplement*, March 1, 1957, p. 129.

52.   "Not as Bisexual as All That," *Essays in Criticism* 8 (January 1958):88–97.

53.   February 8, 1957, p. 82.

generally, one weakness was that his evidence for actual sexual involvement on Byron's part stopped just short of finality. It was Knight's good fortune that Marchand's biography emerged a few months after his own book. Marchand's publication of the Falmouth letter to Matthews showed that Byron had indeed looked forward to affairs in Greece, and his deciphering of the "Greek epistles" provided the proof that had been so long lacking as to the exact nature of Byron's involvement with boys there. His coolly objective recital of the facts of Byron's life, free from any detectable bias or special pleading and uninfluenced by speculative theories, essentially supported Knight on this issue (though not his dubiety as to Byron's incest with Augusta). Especially telling was Marchand's declaration that *Don Leon* had been written by "someone who was no amateur and who knew many of the facts of Byron's life astonishingly well."[54] There was one difficulty: reviewers, faced with the task of responding to so long and detailed a work, generally failed to grasp the real significance of Marchand's subtly worded discoveries or to find space for comment on them. But those whom Knight had alerted to the issue found that Marchand corroborated him at key points. Doris Langley Moore's two substantial studies, which followed in the next decades, provided many more important details about Byron's relations with Edlestone, Giraud, and Lukas; the second, *Accounts Rendered*, appended a balanced and sympathetic essay on the subject.

All of these approaches had their limitations. None of them attempted any exploration of contemporary English attitudes toward homosexuality or tried to place Byron's experiences in the context of his time. As a result, they failed to reveal one important drama of his life. Often this was because the subject was of only incidental concern: much of the new information was scattered piecemeal throughout works where the emphasis lay primarily on

54. *BB*, vol. 2 supplemental notes, p. 61.

other subjects. But the sum of these researches taken as a whole has been impressive, and an essential part of Byron's personality, long denied and obscured, has at last emerged.

The forces that frightened Byron and his friends into so much dissimilation and silenced Bentham, Shelley, the *Leon* poet, and Havelock Ellis (among others) have now waned. Looking back, one is struck by Montesquieu's remark that the three bugbears of his age, judging from its laws, were witchcraft, heresy, and sodomy. Anxieties about witchcraft no longer terrorize us. Religious leaders of all faiths now strongly defend the right of men and women to differ on doctrinal issues, and federal statutes protect the religious heretic's rights to employment and accommodation. But if we tolerate and accept different styles of faith to a degree that even Voltaire could not have imagined, diverse sexual lifestyles still arouse apprehension even when they threaten no direct harm to others. In this particular matter, our culture faces business unfinished by the Enlightenment. By tracing the relevant facts in the life of a famous poet, this study has tried to demonstrate how fiercely the engines of repression have worked in the past through the criminal law and censorship. But it would be naïve to pretend that sexual prejudice, though dramatically attenuated, has disappeared or is not still formidable. Indeed, its persistence through eighteen centuries is a remarkable historical fact, and its continuing strength in present-day America and Europe makes it one of the notable anomalies of our society.

APPENDIX

The Bentham Manuscripts

The manuscript notes and essays on homosexuality by Jeremy Bentham cited in this study are described by A. Taylor Milne in the second edition of his *Catalogue of the Manuscripts of Jeremy Bentham in the Library of University College, London* (London: Athlone Press, 1962) as follows. Roman numerals refer to box numbers, the Arabic numbers to the sheets in each box. (In my notes the box numbers are also given in Arabic numerals.)

LXVIII	10–18. Penal Code—appendix, sexual eccentricities; 1824–1825
LXXII	187–205. [Penal code] Paederasty [ca. 1785]
LXXIII	90–100. [Sexual] Nonconformity [ca. 1774]
LXXIV(a)	1–25. [Sexual] Nonconformity [fragments; ca. 1774] 26–34. Nonconformité [in French, ca. 1785] 35–222. Code penal—sexual; 1814, 1816
CLXI(a)	1–19. Sextus: General idea of a work having for one of its objects the Defence of the Principle of *Utility*, so far as it concerns the liberty of taste, against the conjunct hostility of the principle of asceticism and the principle of *antipathy*; and for its proposed title, proposed on the ground of expected popularity, or at least protection against popular rage—"Not Paul but Jesus." 1817
CLXI(b)	215–523. Not Paul but Jesus—Vol. II or IV forming Part III Doctrine—asceticism; 1816–1818.

The earliest of the manuscripts is the collection of notes most of which Bentham labeled with the heading "Nonconformity." These make up eleven sheets of different sizes in box 73, and twenty-five sheets in box 74a. The large folio sheets numbered 15, 16, and 17 comprise a fantastic *jeu d'esprit* entitled "Castrations to Mr. B by the Daemon of Socrates." Each of these folios is folded to make four large pages, so the essay is twelve pages long. Otherwise, the notes in this collection are fragmentary, brief, and extremely miscellaneous, but all relate directly or indirectly to the subject of homosexuality and law reform.

The essay "Paederasty" in box 72 (dated ca. 1785) is written on folios numbered 191 through 205. Again, each large sheet is folded to make four pages, so there are sixty pages in all. Preceding the essay are three folios (twelve pages) with unconnected paragraphs on various topics relating to homosexual law reform, numbered 187, 188, and 189. This essay, with the accompanying paragraphs, has been transcribed and published by the present author in the *Journal of Homosexuality* 3 (1978): 389–405; and 4 (1978): 91–107.

In April and May 1814, Bentham wrote extensively on this subject on sheets with "Code Penal" written at the top, and again from July to September 1816 on sheets headed "Sex." These make up folios 35 to 222 of box 74a, that is, 188 pages in all. These notes are much more developed than those of 1774, some filling a half-dozen or more consecutive pages. They show signs of being organized into chapters, with subject headings written at the top of many sheets. Most of the pages bear a precise date, but the pages are not presently in chronological order. Pages written in 1814 and 1816 have been interleaved to bring related topics together.

In 1931 C. K. Ogden published significant excerpts from these 1814–1816 notes in an appendix entitled "Bentham on Sex," which comprised pages 476–97 of his edition of *Theory of Legislation* (London: Kegan Paul, Trench, Trubner), without indicating what specific pages he was using or their dates. In this study, I have drawn on some of the passages Ogden has transcribed, but readers who compare the two versions will find frequent differences. There are two main reasons for this. One is the frequent obscurity of Bentham's handwriting. Occasionally, I have corrected words that Ogden seems to have misread. In other cases, there appears to be more room for diversity. Bentham regularly revised his pages by writing alternative expressions over his original words and phrases, only rarely crossing out the first version or indicating whether he really wanted the alternatives to replace it. He seems to be leaving the choice to some future occasion or to an editor. Most often I have used the interlineations as representing his second, if not necessarily his preferred, thoughts. Unfortunately, however, since the interlineations are often written in a hand even more cramped than his usual hasty scrawl, it has not always been possible to decipher these. In such cases I have gone back to the first version. However, since Bentham's interlineations seem nearly always merely to give alternative expressions without any significant change in the sense, this practice has not likely led to any serious misrepresentations. Where it has been necessary to correct the grammar, to abbreviate, or to add words inadvertently omitted by Bentham, I have used square brackets.

The fair copy of Bentham's prospectus to William Beckford, which the cataloguer has entitled "Sextus," fills folios 14 to 18 of box 161a and two pages of folio 19, making twenty-two pages in all. The first thirteen sheets of this box contain a draft of this essay, three sheets of which are dated August 26, 1817, whereas the last sheet is dated September 11, 1817. The fair copy was not dated by Bentham.

Box 161b contains 309 manuscript pages headed "Not Paul but Jesus," which deal with questions of asceticism and sexuality, particularly homosexuality. These pages are individually dated, the earliest on November 19, 1817, and the latest on February 7, 1818, and, in their degree of organization, come close to forming a volume with identifiable chapters.

Finally, Bentham once more returned to the subject of homosexuality and law reform in an "Appendix" to his "Penal Code," written when he was seventy-six. He gives a brief recapitulation of his attack on asceticism and his arguments for a change in the laws on eight pages preserved in box 68. The first four pages are dated December 20, 1824, and the remainder January 13, 1825.

Index

Aberdeen, 67

Achilles, 89, 96, 97

Ackermann, Richard, 369n

Addison, Joseph, 91

Aeneid (Virgil). *See* Euryalus; Nisus and Euryalus

Aeschines, 89n

Aeschylus, 5, 96

Africa, homosexuality in, 25

Agathon (C. Wieland), 43, 43n–44n, 87, 87n, 272

Ageing, Byron's attitudes toward, 324

Albania: and Byron's appreciation of Albanian male beauty, 138; Byron's meeting with the ruler of, 137–38 (*see also* Ali Pasha); Byron's visit to, 121, 124, 132–39 *passim*; compared with Greece, 140, 142; described in *Childe Harold*, 139; Hobhouse's description of homosexuality in, 135–36; homosexuality in, 133–37

Albemarle, Earl of (Arnold van Keppel), 59n

Alcibiades, 90, 91n, 273n

Alexander, Boyd, 66n

Alfred and Westminister Evening Gazette, 163

Ali Pasha, ruler of Albania, 133, 135; Byron described by, 143; and Byron's homosexuality, 237; Byron's meeting with, 137–38, 143; and Byron's relationship with the son of, 148–49; grandsons of, 138; homosexuality of, 139

Anacreon, Bentham's knowledge of, 89n

Anacreon, odes of: Byron's translation of, 95–96; T. Moore's translation of, 93–95

Anal intercourse: and Byron's marital separation, 353n. *See also* Marital sodomy

Annabella. *See* Byron, Anne Isabella

Antinoüs, in Byron's notes to *Childe Harold*, 9, 142

Antipathy, in Bentham's analysis of homophobia, 29, 42, 46, 256, 257, 270

Antiquities of Greece (Archbishop John Potter), 89n, 96, 289

Apollo, and Byron's use of the term "Hyacinth," 128

Apollo Belvedere, Byron's description of, 88

Aquinas, Thomas, and Bentham's views on homosexuality, 259, 266

Arabian Nights, 133; Burton's essay on sodomy appended to, 127; European imitations of, 44n; read by Byron, 111–12

Arbuthnot, Harriet, 303, 306

Arcadia (Philip Sidney), 209

Aristotle, 86

Armstrong, John, *The Oeconomy of Love* by, 54–55

Arnold, Matthew, 187, 188; on Bentham's attitudes toward Plato, 285; Jesus interpreted by, 280

Arran, Earl of (James Hamilton), 54n

Art of Love (Ovid), 24

Asceticism, in Bentham's analysis

Rushton, 131, 199; Byron's fear of her public betrayal of his homosexuality, 195, 200–201, 209; Byron's homosexuality and incest reported to Lady Byron by, 82, 131, 199, 224; Byron's *Vathek* inscribed by, 201; described, 197; husband and marriage of, 197, 201; pageboy disguises of, 197–98, 200; public rumors of Byron's homosexuality and incest initiated by, 221–22, 223, 224, 230; vindictive threats by, 201–2, 222

Lamb, William (later 2nd Viscount Melbourne), 197

Language, homophobic, 9–11, 36; Bentham's attitudes toward, 262, 263n; in Bentham's writings, 121–22; Byron's use of, 9, 120–21; in Christianity, 34–35; in *Don Leon*, 355; "finger twirlers" in, 36; in Gibbon's writings, 23; of Paul the Apostle, 280; implications of "pure" and "impure" in, 262; "miscreant" as, 15, 22, 45, 58; vs. neutral terms created by Bentham, 262–64; in newspapers, 22, 44–45, 63, 301 (*see also* Newspapers); satirized by C. Matthews, 161–62; in Shelley's discussion of Greek love, 294–95; "unnatural" used as, 28, 262–63

Language for homosexuality, 9–11; Biblical terms for male prostitutes, 281; and "buggery," 15, 52, 235n; in classic Greek literature, 89, 128 (*see also* "Hyacinth(s)"); coined by Bentham, 122, 262–64; code derived from the *Satyricon*, 128; development of neutral and scientific words for, 262–64, 368; in English law, 15, 20; among English public schoolboys, 79–80; and gay consciousness, 10–11; in Germany, 368; "Horatian" as a code word

in, 11, 146; "Methodism" and "Methodiste" as code words in, 129, 145, 161, 340; "piece" as, 169, 170; use of the word "philosophy" in, 151, 173

Lansdown, Henry, 118

Lansdowne, Henry Petty-Fitzmaurice, 3rd Marquis of, 230

Laocoon, 88

Laon and Cynthia (Shelley), 223

Larissa, 149

Latin homoerotic literature: Byron's knowledge of, 11, 92–94, 96; Byron's translations of, 94–97

Lauderdale, James Maitland, 8th Earl of, abolition of the pillory advocated by, 251–52

Lawrence, D. H., 374

Lawrence, Gabriel, trial and hanging of, 60n

Lawrence, T. E., 118

Laws on homosexuality: abolition of the death penalty in Europe and the United States, 17; in ancient Rome, 24, 34, 36; Biblical sources of, 13–14, 16, 33–35, 258, 275; and class status, 65; death penalty for, 13–14 (*see also* Death penalty for homosexuality); French reform of, 17, 25, 37–38; in Germany, 368; interaction with religious asceticism, 39–40 (*see also* Asceticism); in Protestant and Catholic countries, 60–61. *See also* English laws on homosexuality

Leicester, 2nd Earl of (George Ferrars Townshend), accused of homosexuality, 125

Leigh, Augusta (Byron's sister), 72; Byron's affair with, 199, 203–5, 215, 217; on Byron's bisexuality and insanity, 243; and Byron's incest, 199, 200, 214, 215, 220–21, 361, 365 (*see also* Incest by Byron); Byron's letter to on his melancholy, 100–101, 124; Byron's letters to about his feelings

Persian literature: bowdlerization of, 116–17; Byron's studies of, 115; homosexuality in, 112, 113–16

Peruvian Tales, 44

Petronius, 11, 35, 93

Phaedrus (Plato), 88, 89, 105; J. S. Mill's partial translation of, 285, 287

Pharisees, 41

Philhellenism, 86; of Bentham, 313, 318; of Byron, 140–41, 157, 194, 313–14, 317–19, 333

Philips, Ambrose, 93

Philosophical Dictionary (Voltaire), 17, 78

"Philosophy," and Byron's homosexual affairs in Greece, 151, 173

Pigot, Elizabeth: Byron's letter to on his feelings for Edlestone, 101–2, 330, 342; Byron's letters to repudiated by Lord Lovelace, 366; and Edlestone's gift of a cornelian to Byron, 179

Pillorying of homosexuals in England, 14; Bentham's attitudes on, 21, 22; crowds and mob violence at, 21, 22, 163–66, 252; death caused by, 31, 251–52; and Dutch refugees, 34n; parliamentary debates on, 230–31, 251–52; protested by Burke, 31–33; of the Vere Street coterie, 164–66; and the zenith of English homophobia, 158–59, 160, 163–71 *passim. See also* Executions of homosexuals in England

Piozzi, Gabriel, 56

Place, Francis, 269

Plato: Bentham's attitudes toward, 285; bowdlerized translations of, 89–91, 115, 285, 287, 299; homosexuality in the writings of, 286–87; J. S. Mill's attitudes toward, 286–87; not read by Byron, 96; minimal role in the British educational curriculum, 285–86; and Shelley's translation of the *Symposium,* 285,

287, 298–99. *See also Phaedrus; Symposium*

Platonism, Byron's ridicule of, 96–97

Pliny, Bentham's studies of, 89n

Police: Edlestone apprehended by, 144; increased surveillance by, 162; methods used by, 163; and pillorying of homosexuals, 21

Polidori, John, 241

Politics of Byron, 226, 308; in *Don Juan,* 310; on Greek independence, 140–41, 157, 194, 313–14, 317–19, 333; and Hobhouse's fears about Byron's memoirs, 339; in Italy, 313; relative to his attitudes on women, 239; role in his death, 324

Polynesia, homosexuality in, 265

Ponsonby, Sarah: relationship to Lady Caroline Lamb, 197; romantic friendship with Lady Eleanor Butler, 102, 103–4

Pope, Alexander, 85, 107

Population growth, effect of homosexuality on: Bentham's analysis of, 48–49, 264; in *Don Leon,* 351; Voltaire's opinion on, 17, 48

Portugal, Byron in, 120, 121

Potter, John (Archbishop): *Antiquities of Greece* by, 89n, 96, 289; on Greek pederasty, 96, 289

Pouqueville, François Charles, 134–35

Powderham scandal, 120n, 234n

Proclamation Society, 61, 62. *See also* Society for the Reformation of Manners

Propertius, 93

Prostitutes, 21; and Byron's heterosexuality, 109, 196, 240, 247; effect of homosexuality on, 49, 50; English tolerance of, 348; prevalent during Regency libertinism, 260; Shelley's commentary on, 297

Protestant Reformation: homophobia in England intensified by, 53–54, 58, 60–61

Compositor: G&S Typesetters, Inc.
Text: Palatino
Display: Palatino
Printer: Vail-Ballou Press
Binder: Vail-Ballou Press